BASEB
CHRONICLES
An Oral History of Baseball
Through the Decades

September 17, 1911 to October 24, 1992

Reflections on baseball
when it was truly Americana —
in the words of the people
who played and lived the game.

MIKE BLAKE

BETTERWAY BOOKS

Cincinnati, Ohio

98 97 96 95 94   5 4 3 2 1

Library of Congress Cataloging in Publication Data

Blake, Mike
    Baseball chronicles, September 17, 1911 to October 24, 1992: an oral history of baseball through the decades / by Mike Blake. — 1st ed.
        p.   cm.
    "Reflections on baseball when it was truly Americana, in the words of the people who played and lived the game." — CIP t.p.
    Includes bibliographical references (p. 315) and index.
    ISBN 1-55870-350-0
    1. Baseball players — United States — Anecdotes. 2. Baseball players — United States — Biography. 3. Baseball — United States — History — 20th century. 4. Baseball — United States — History — Chronology. I. Title
GV865.A1B57   1994
796.357'092'2 — dc20
[B]   93-47539
                                                                                        CIP

Interior design/cover design by Brian Roeth
Cover illustrations courtesy National Baseball Hall of Fame

About the Author

Mike Blake has always been around sports and sports heroes.

He was born in Newark, New Jersey, home of the greatest team in minor league history, the Newark Bears; the Newark Peppers of the Federal League; and the Negro League champion, Newark Eagles.

Blake developed his love for baseball while living in Springfield, New Jersey, in the 1950s. Springfield, a historical Revolutionary War township — George Washington fought there — is home to golfdom's storied Baltusrol Golf Club, and also served as home to Chicago Cubs and Cleveland Indians hurler Joey Schaffernoth. And Blake's fifth-grade teacher, Joan Carroll-Sundstrom, was the daughter of Yankee pitcher Owen "Ownie" Carroll. The entire neighborhood rallied in front of Blake's house on a dead-end street (Becker Road) to while away the springs and summers playing hardball . . . and pity the windows that got in the way.

Moving West, Blake and his family settled in Van Nuys, California, and Blake earned his varsity baseball letter at Van Nuys High School, a mecca for sports standouts and celebrities who attended the school: Don Drysdale (Los Angeles Dodgers), Bob Waterfield (Los Angeles Rams), Rob Scribner (Los Angeles Rams), Anthony Cook (NBA), Gary Sanserino (minor leagues and U.S./Pan-American Games), Robert Redford, Charlton Heston, Stacy Keach, Bruce Dern, Ed Begley Jr., Marilyn Monroe, Natalie Wood and Jane Russell.

Blake attended California State University, Northridge, along with such sports luminaries as Lyman Bostock (Minnesota Twins), Bruce Heinbechner (California Angels), Jason Thompson (Pittsburgh Pirates), Bobby "Schoolboy" Chacon (boxing) and several NFL and NBA players.

From there, it was on to Brea, California, which served as home to Walter Johnson (Washington Senators) and Randy Jones (San Diego Padres), and a barnstorming stop for Babe Ruth in 1924.

Professionally, Blake earned his journalistic spurs as a writer-editor for the late, lamented *Los Angeles Herald Examiner*, leaving the paper for the *Los Angeles Times*'s electronic newspaper, *Times-Mirror Videotex*. He has also been a copyeditor for the *Newport Beach Daily Pilot*, senior editorial consultant for *Orange County Business Journal* and a sports editor for *Orange Coast Magazine*.

Since then he has had more than five hundred newspaper and

magazine articles published in a variety of publications and on myriad topics, most which did not pertain to sports. Most recently, Blake has been a Major League Baseball correspondent for Japan's *Sankei Baseball Monthly*, and managing editor for the NASDAQ small cap stock-discovery magazine, *The Investment Reporter*.

Blake has accomplished all this while putting out four books — two of which were baseball books (*The Incomplete Book of Baseball Superstitions, Rituals and Oddities* and *The Minor Leagues: A Celebration of the Little Show*).

Blake is heard on Dream Weaver's KFXX (1520 AM) Portland, Oregon, show, "Morning Dream Time," every Friday morning at 9 A.M. to deliver topical information, humor and "shtick" with Weaver and his sidekick, "Dan-o."

Blake has appeared on more than seventy TV and radio shows internationally, including the *Larry King Show, Up Close With Roy Firestone, A.M. Buffalo, Tom Snyder Show, Jim Lampley Show*, and multiple appearances on WFAN (New York); OCN (Orange County); XTRA (San Diego); WLAD (Connecticut); and WPTF (North Carolina).

When he's not writing or taking care of his family, Blake takes gigs as a public speaker, and still keeps his hand (and arm, bat and glove) in the game while playing for a Tustin, California, softball league team.

Dedication

As always, first and foremost . . . to Jan, my lover and best friend; my wife, playmate and soulmate, my *raison d'etre*, who makes life fun and worthwhile, who inspires works such as this, and to whom all of my work is dedicated.

To Roxanne Marie, who was taken from us at age 10, much too soon. She gave us joy and love and fun and companionship, and all she asked in return was love. Rest in peace, Roxie.

To Robert F. Hostage, publisher of Betterway Books when this manuscript was signed, who believed in me and in my work, and who made this project happen.

And to all the men who played the game: the twenty-year vets, the one-day wonders and everyone in between — you *are* baseball. From its inception, be it Doubleday's or Cartwright's invention, through the early years, the dark scandal years, the golden years, the war years, the glory years, the Western expansion years, the strike years and the megabuck years . . . you guys have been the game. Without you there would be no works such as this and no game such as the one that has taken America's heart on this exciting, jet-propelled roller coaster ride for the last century-and-a-half. Thanks, guys; I hope this book does you justice.

Acknowledgments

My thanks to Betterway Books/F&W Publications, who have backed me on this project and who have allowed me the figurative space to work and the literal space to thank all those who have made this effort possible. And to Bill Brohaugh, editorial director at F&W, who loves the game and gave me room to develop this concept.

I acknowledge the following individuals, groups and organizations, without whom this book and others on the subject of baseball would be mere dreams, far removed from published realities:

Dave Cunningham (*Long Beach Independent Press-Telegram*), the former president of the Baseball Writers of America (Anaheim chapter), a longtime buddy, whose sage advice on writing style and substance has been taken to heart for all of my books. Dave also was largely responsible for brightening up my days around the batting cage at the "Big A."

Richard Topp (former president of the Society for American Baseball Research), who provided me with friendship, humor, insight and information that spanned the decades. If there was ever a record of any tale ever told, Richard, the consummate researcher, found it for me; and to Barbara Topp for putting up with our "Why did the SABR cross the road?" jokes.

Tim Mead, assistant vice president media relations for the California Angels, the quintessential media director, the best of the best, who allowed me access to the ballpark, the players, photographs and information; I am as lucky to have him as a friend, as the Angels are lucky to have him on their executive staff.

Jeff Idelson, director of media relations and publicity for the New York Yankees, who handles a high-pressure position with aplomb, and who helped me from coast-to-coast and from pinstriped-era to pinstriped-era.

Ben Kaufman (Van Nuys High, '68), my high school pal who envisioned a career such as this for me and who never stopped offering encouragement and humor.

Ed Arnold (KTLA [Channel 5], Los Angeles), who is quick with a helping hand, a kind word, a smile and a wink.

All the Major League beat writers in Anaheim and Los Angeles who make covering this game fun. To Robyn Norwood (*Los Angeles Times*), who takes a sincere interest in her colleagues' work; Bob Keisser (*Long Beach Independent Press-Telegram*), my old friend from the *Los Angeles Herald Examiner*; Mike Terry (*San Bernardino Sun*), who has a real sense of the game's history; Joe Resnick (Associated Press), who gave me a bunch of old Mets stories; Bill Shaikin (*Riverside Press-Enterprise*); Helene Elliot (*Los Angeles Times*); Mike Downey (*Los Angeles Times*), who generously fact-checked for me via his "Friday the 13th" story; Philip Goldberg, a fellow author and baseball fan — he wrote "This Is Next Year," — who also fact-checked for me; and John Hall (*Orange County Register*), who is one of the nice guys.

Dave Barry (*Miami Herald*), hey, he's funny and kind and let *me* sign my books at *his* book signing; Steve "Dream" Weaver of KFXX Radio (1520 AM) in Portland, who's good for a laugh, insight and friendship; Paul White (*Baseball Weekly*); Bob Broeg (*St. Louis Post-Dispatch*); Pat Hartley (*Detroit Free Press*); Al Conin and Bob Jamison (California Angels), who were entertaining and helpful around the clubhouse, and who are class acts wherever they go; and Ken Brett (California Angels), who helped me get to his brother, George.

And these baseball folk who gave me access to their files, players and photos: Linda Stellar and Linda Reiner (New York Yankees); Rich Levin and Jim Small (MLB Commissioner's Office); Chuck Stevens (ABBPA); Leo Sears (MLB Alumni); Jim Schultz (Atlanta Braves); Dick Bresciani (Boston Red Sox); Leigh McDonald and Regina Castellano (Philadelphia Phillies); Tom Skibosh (Milwaukee Brewers); Tom Hawkins, Jay Lucas, Chuck Harris, John Olguin, Michelle Fox and Ruth Ruiz (Los Angeles Dodgers); Duffy Jennings (San Francisco Giants); Jim Ferguson (San Diego Padres); Tom Mee (Minnesota Twins); John Maroon (Cleveland Indians); Jim Trdinich (Pittsburgh Pirates); Jay Alves (Oakland A's); Maribeth Fuqua (Houston Astros); Doug Abel and Barb Kozuk (Chicago White Sox); Patti Kagakis (Chicago Cubs); Dean Vogelaar and Steve Finks (Kansas City Royals); Bill Deane, Tom Heitz and Pat Kelly (National Baseball Hall of Fame); John Chymczuk (Elias Sports Bureau); Wanda Greer (Mantle-Ford Baseball Camp); Greer Johnson (Mickey Mantle Enterprises); Pat Anthony ("Stan the Man" Inc.); Jim Riley (baseball historian/TK Publishing); Phil Dixon (Negro League researcher and author); the Tweed Webb Library of Black Baseball History; the Richard M. Nixon Presidential Library; Jeff Bernstein, the funny SID for Manhattan College; Lou Spadia (San Francisco Chamber of Commerce); Jerry Carriaccioli (Capital Sports); Lawrence Tierney (Sports Marketing Services); Nick Mitrovic (WGN-TV); Marty Adler (Brooklyn Dodgers Hall of Fame); Joe Violone and Ken Brown (*Yankees Magazine*); Bill Beckman and George Pouliot

(Anaheim Stadium); Henry Thomas (Walter Johnson's grandson); Letitia Maitlen (Brea Public Library); the Community Access Library Line (County of Los Angeles) and the Los Angeles Public Library; and the following kind and generous researchers for the Society of American Baseball Research (SABR): Morris Eckhouse; Fred Schuld; A.D. Suehsdorf; Bob Davids; Bob Ruland; Fred Smith; Joe Naiman; Damian Begley; Carl Lundquist; Tom Knight; Steve Nadel; Ed Luteran; R.J. "Jack" Smalling; Jim Ritter; Dick Thompson; Joe Dittmar; and Joe Simenic.

Those who have given me support, love and friendship through the years of struggle in the literary world as well as the real world: Julius Blake; Harriet Blake; Cliff and Merle Travis; Kimberlee Ann Dixon; Greg Dixon; Mark and Sandy Travis; Beverly and Dave Loomis; Lou and Lillian Blum; Irv and Ceil Gordon; Dave and Robin Koerner; Lou and Debbie Ornstein; Howard Blum; Don and Kathy Zody; Chuck and Paula Royal; Bob and Susan Jones; Doug and Melinda Reynolds; Margaret Burk and Marylin Hudson (Round Table West); Rudy Zontini and Bernie Schlameuss (Southern California Sun Hockey Club); Don Powell (Advanx Junior Hockey Team); Peggy Powell, John Robbins and Charlie Ferrazzi (*The Investment Reporter*); T.J. Hutchinson, Bill Lobdell, Steve Marble, Eric Marson and Matt "Mr. Entertainment" Coker (*Newport Beach Daily Pilot*); Muppet Curtis Blake; Mike Kruss (who helped me fix my printer); Jim and Maria Thompson (E-Z Mail, etc.), Mike Jarrard (my Tustin third-baseman); and Larry "Butch" Bellon, an early inspiration and one of the two best darned ballplayers ever to come out of Springfield, New Jersey.

And the most special and heartfelt thanks and acknowledgement to the following players and baseball people who shared their lives, intimate secrets, observations, knowledge of the game, quips and tall tales, and who are the stars of this book, the reason for this book, and the substance of this book. Without you 140 gentlemen and your kindness, there would be no book: Henry Aaron; Ethan Allen; Sandy Amoros; Sparky Anderson; Ernie Banks; Jesse Barfield; Dick Bartell; Bruce Benedict; Johnny Berardino; Yogi Berra; Wade Boggs; Lou Boudreau; Jim Bouton; Bobby Bragan; George Brett; Nelson Briles; Hubie Brooks; Dr. Bobby Brown; Roy Campanella; Rod Carew; Gary Carter; Ben Chapman; Tony Cloninger; Nate Colbert; Jerry Coleman; Harry Craft; Frankie Crosetti; Jimmie Crutchfield; Tony Cuccinello; Babe Dahlgren; Bernie DeViveiros; Johnny Dickshot; Dom DiMaggio; Joe DiMaggio; Larry Doby; Bobby Doerr;

Dutch Dotterer; Don Drysdale; Mike Easler; Harry Eisenstat; Woody English; Carl Erskine; Bob Feller; Rick Ferrell; Rollie Fingers; Whitey Ford; Steve Garvey; Milt Gaston; Charlie Gehringer; Eddie Gill; Joe Ginsberg; Rich "Goose" Gossage; Jim "Mudcat" Grant; Don Gutteridge; Tony Gwynn; Buddy Hancken; Joe Hauser; Von Hayes; Tommy Henrich; Billy Herman; Larry Hisle; Chet Hoff; Tommy Holmes; Frank Howard; Jim "Catfish" Hunter; Monte Irvin; Reggie Jackson; Tommy John; Si Johnson; Jim Kaat; Al Kaline; George Kell; Johnny Kerr; Harmon Killebrew; Clyde King; Darold Knowles; Mark Koenig; Jerry Koosman; Ed Kranepool; Tony Kubek; Clem Labine; Bob Lemon; Walter "Buck" Leonard; Sal Maglie; Mickey Mantle; Marty Marion; Willie Mays; Sam Mele; Al Milnar; Minnie Minoso; Johnny Mize; Paul Molitor; Rick Monday; Terry Moore; Manny Mota; Hughie Mulcahy; Stan Musial; Graig Nettles; Don Newcombe; Phil Niekro; John "Buck" O'Neil; Lance Parrish; Johnny Pesky; Joe Pignatano; Boog Powell; Vic Power; Ted "Double Duty" Radcliffe; Pedro Ramos; Jeff Reardon; Jimmy Reese; Bobby Richardson; Bill Rigney; Cal Ripken Jr.; Phil Rizzuto; Bob "Buck" Rodgers; Johnny Roseboro; Nolan Ryan; Brooks Robinson; Frank Robinson; Joe Schaffernoth; Andy Seminick; Art Shamsky; Roy Sievers; Enos Slaughter; Lonnie Smith; Ozzie Smith; Edwin "Duke" Snider; George Strickland; Ron Swoboda; Marv Throneberry; Bob Turley; "Broadway Charlie" Wagner; Bob Watson; Monte Weaver; Del Wilber; Ted Williams; Dave Winfield; Bob Wright; Jimmy Wynn; and George Zuverink.

Table of Contents

Prologue

"What is past is prologue."
The Tempest, *by William Shakespeare*
Act II, Scene 1

T he above quote is chiseled into and onto the National Archives building in Washington, D.C., and serves to remind us that the wonder of what was (in this case, what was baseball) merely sets the table for what will be (in this case, what will be tomorrow's wonderful world of the diamond).

I didn't set out to write an all-encompassing history book, nor a coffee table book, just a fun-to-read, slice-of-history book, because the stories that follow are America, or at least, Americana. The innocence of the early years gives way to the growth and sophistication of the current era, chronicling, or mirroring, what occurred off the fields in this country.

I hope what follows is an important eclectic collection and recollection of the game. Why do I hope it's important? Easy. This may be the last chance to hear the tales from the guys who lived them. I'm not giving grandiose importance to this work, just to the guys included herein. Some of those men, who are the flesh and blood of this work, performed their athletic acts more than fifty years ago — in several cases, more than seventy years ago and, in one case, more than eighty years in the past — and, quite frankly, if this book, or another one like it, was not produced soon, those first-hand recollections would have been lost forever.

The stories are of various demeanors: some funny; some heartwarming; some observational; some insightful; some trivial. But all are baseball.

This is not a "tell-all" book. It is not for nihilists or iconoclasts. This is a book for traditionalists who love the game for what it is: its indomitable spirit, replete with its beauty and blemishes; grace and clumsiness; love and bigotry; the grand and the grandiose; the good and the bad.

Does this book wax rhapsodic about the game? Though it may be argued that little is more deserving of such visceral treatment than baseball, this tome, while celebrating the diamond, dwells on the players who are the game. The evanescent glory of those who played and the stories they tell become the fabric of the game and the book, because this work will not separate the men from the game . . . they are one and the same.

My parameters (heck, this is a baseball book so let's call them "ground rules"): Only baseball folk still alive at the time I was interviewing, who gave me stories expressly for this book, were included. So, unfortunately, Roger Maris (whom I interviewed in 1980) is not included as a storyteller, though Tony Kubek and Nellie Briles gave me Maris stories for this work; and my 1970s interviews with Thurman Munson have been eliminated, though Larry Hisle has presented a wonderful "baseball etiquette" story about his friend Munson. And my interviews with some of the men who were "done too soon," including Billy Martin, Lefty Gomez, Eddie Solomon and former schoolmates (at California State University, Northridge) Lyman Bostock and Bruce Heinbechner, are outside the forced (by the author) foul lines of this work and so are excluded from the storytelling process, though they may appear in the text of someone else's recollections.

Their names live on by those who told about them. And we've got Babe and Casey and Jackie. And fortunately, I got to interview such gentlemen as Robert Wright, Charlie Gehringer, Roy Campanella, Don Drysdale, Sal Maglie, Sandy Amoros, Jimmie Crutchfield, Ted "Double Duty" Radcliffe, Billy Herman and Mark Koenig for this book; sadly, they passed away before this work was printed.

So these aren't second-hand stories. On the downside, I have eliminated many tales about Babe Ruth, Lou Gehrig, Ty Cobb, Cy Young, Dizzy Dean, Jackie Robinson, Josh Gibson, Roberto Clemente, Casey Stengel and Satchel Paige, to name a very few, but maybe those often-told chestnuts belong in a book that pays second-hand homage to great stars of the past. We do have vignettes about nearly all the men listed just above (nearly one thousand ex-ballplayers are discussed in one manner or other within these covers), but they are through the eyes of living ex-players who were there when the events occurred. I've captured, I hope, the glory, pathos, humor, motivation, struggles, triumph and personal tragedy.

The observations chosen tell a lot about the individual spinning the yarn, as the choices were left up to the player sharing the tale. Some men give their proudest moments in uniform, others their highlights, still others their lowlights or a glimpse of something they witnessed. Some offered picaresque tales of their gloried pasts which have been largely forgotten by the masses but which loom as important vignettes of the evolution of the diamond game. Still others refrained from talking about themselves and devoted the entire process to the exploits of others: Bobby Doerr on Ted Williams; Harry Craft on Mickey Mantle; Jimmy Reese on Babe Ruth; Tony Kubek on Roger Maris; Charlie Gehringer on Hank Greenberg; and Carl Erskine and Mudcat Grant on Jackie Robinson, for example. And some men talked about their mentors rather than themselves . . . take a look at Reggie Jackson and Jesse Barfield. The stories are the players' atticisms and witticisms, and this book is their conduit.

These are not *my* favorite baseball stories; they are the favorite tales of the gentlemen who lived them and chose to remember them here. They are not writers' stories, they are ballplayers' chronicles, by and from and about the guys who've been there and fought the wars of the dream.

If all the stories were my choice, I might have insisted that "The Mick" tell about his 565-foot homer off Chuck Stobbs at Griffith Stadium on April 17, 1953; or that Enos Slaughter give his testimony regarding his intentional spiking of Jackie Robinson in August, 1947; or that Willie Mays recall for us his miraculous over-the-shoulder Polo Grounds catch of Vic Wertz's smash in game one of the World Series, September 29, 1954; or that Reggie Jackson act out a blow-by-blow-by-blow replay of his three-home-run Series performance against the Dodgers, October 18, 1977; or that Joe DiMaggio give us a Lou Gehrig story from the 1930s or a game-by-game account of his fifty-six-game hitting streak in 1941. I'd demand a reenactment from Hank Aaron of his 715th home run, April 8, 1974. I'd have asked "Teddy Ballgame" to reminisce about that final six-for-eight doubleheader, September 28, 1941 to finish the season at .406; or I'd have pleaded with Ernie Banks to come up with a "Let's play two" vignette from Wrigley Field in the 1950s. But I decided against it. This is the ballplayers' book, not mine.

What we have here is not a "Baseball's Greatest Hits" calendar; you can get that anywhere. This isn't a "My Greatest Highlight" book; the players can write those about themselves. This is a book filled with the most important, or most fondly remembered or most "tellable" stories, the favorite stories of the gentlemen who lived them. Remember, these are the stories these players chose to tell, and what's important to them should provide insight into the personalities of the men who shared their lives with us.

This book may not be the literary answer to Brother Jasper, the "Prefect of discipline" at Manhattan College who invented the seventh-inning stretch during a game versus the barnstorming New York Giants in the late 1880s. And this book may not be *Ball Four* or *The Bronx Zoo*, with their tell-all-the-behind-the-scenes dirt. But it stands alone on its own content. It is not *The Glory of Their Times*, nor does it intend to be. *The Glory of Their Times*, a marvelous landmark oral history written by Lawrence S. Ritter, was twenty-six chapters all about the men who embraced the game from 1887 to 1945 — twenty-six players telling their stories about the early days of baseball, with each chapter representing a single player telling his baseball life story. There's no comparison here. My intent is entirely different, with the exception that I, too, pay homage to the game and the glory of its players. The purpose of this book is summum bonum, the highest good; that is, to keep these guys and their stories alive.

What this book is, I hope, is a celebration of the game and those gentlemen who have made the game endure as a linchpin of Americana and the growing up of this great nation. I make no distinction between the early days of the game, the middle age of the game and the current era; they all make my book. And I don't want a player's life story; that's for him to write himself. What I want are nuggets, a quick hit or two, what I hope is the crème de la crème, the best of what each player was or is, as a player, an observer and a man.

Make no mistake about it, while this book in itself may be temporal, baseball is eternal and it is baseball which embodies this work. And the stories within these covers are the skeins from which the fabric of the game is woven.

Once inside the pages of this work, you may notice that some decades are better represented than others. The perfect map of this chronology would be a bell curve, with the 1910s and 1990s rather than in their scope, and an abundance of material from the thirties, forties, fifties and sixties. Why? Only three gentlemen who played in the 1910s were alive at the time I was interviewing for this effort, and I was fortunate enough to get to them all, so I include about a half-dozen stories from those three "earlymen." And as we are less than halfway through the 1990s, with the best stories presumably yet to be acted out and written, we are short on tales from this current stanza. And as I have found that current ballplayers are not great storytellers — that skill, I have determined, is cultivated and bears fruit after one has had an entire career on which to look back — few of today's greats are here; maybe when these men are out of the limelight, their stories take on more importance than while they are actually living them, day in and day out. But I do include some current players, those who have already put in the years and have the glory, and have gained the early knack for adroitly spinning yarns.

Why does this journal run from September 17, 1911, to October 24, 1992? Easy; Chester "Red" Hoff, the oldest living ballplayer at this writing (102 and counting), remembers a great story from his first game — actually it was his second appearance, but eighty-two years later, selective memory moved it up to number one (in his case as with all others, I have related the story as it was told to me, cleaning up the accuracy as I fact-checked along the way). So while Hoff remembers it as his debut, I explain in the text of the tale that he had actually appeared in a game twelve days earlier, and it doesn't hurt the gist, humor and importance of this vignette one iota. And the last story, told and lived by Dave Winfield, who already gave me a good one for the decade of the 1980s, closes out this chronicle with his October stardom, at long last, in the final game of the 1992 World Series.

Ground Rules within the book: (**Author's Note:** This paragraph is fairly technical — sorry about that; the rest of the book is much lighter and strictly for fun, history, nostalgia, glory, insight and information, but this graph is written to placate the lifelong research-types who "need" to know what to expect — so bear with me, bite this small bullet, get through this necessary evil, and enjoy the rest of this work). Each decade is written within the following chronology guidelines; Each decade-chapter begins with news briefs, giving the reader a chronological look at the decade's most important — arbitrarily chosen by the author — events. Then comes the good stuff, the players' vignettes, beginning with the earliest told tale in relation to the decade at hand, under the subcategory bearing the name of the individual who recalled the event and the subhead of the date on which it took place. Following that first story, we continue in that player's subcategory with the player's other recollections from that decade. For the sake of continuity, those remembrances follow, regardless of whether they, too, occurred before or after the next player presented. Whenever possible, I got the exact date of the occurrence. When a story took weeks (or if it was impossible to determine the precise day), I narrowed it down to the month of the year. Now, on first reference, a verbal thumbnail sketch of the player's career and highlights precedes the story. On second or third reference — some players' careers spanned several decades and some have observations from each era — a smaller, different thumbnail precedes the event, so if you want the whole sketch on a player, hit him through each chapter.

Some players fill pages and decades and some players fill only a few lines. Why? Some players are better storytellers than others. But, some players who don't tell 'em well, receive 'em well. Take Mick and Teddy Ballgame, for example. Their personal passages are short, but they are remembered through many observations by their contemporaries.

Let me address the selection process. This is not a book to be outfitted solely with Hall of Famers, though we have thirty-two, and fourteen soon-to-be-inducted heroes; nor by superstars, nor by household names; it is about the baseball Everyman, from those baseball immortals with protracted careers to those largely undiscovered heroes with ephemeral stints. The roster includes one-gamers, one-year men, over-achievers, under-achievers, supernovas, faint glimmers of light and those who fulfilled their goals by just making the Show.

This view of the diamond includes many who may not be headliners but who, perhaps, are the real backbone of the game: Joe Schaffernoth, a young pitcher with a blazing fastball, before he was felled by injuries; Ethan Allen, President George Bush's baseball coach at Yale who was on the field the day Babe Ruth played his final game; Joe Hauser, the minor league home run phenom who was sabotaged by a jealous Ty Cobb; Marv Throneberry, who remembers Ol' Case; Jimmy Reese, who tells of the enigmatic Moe Berg and the larger-than-life Babe Ruth; and such hard-nosed gamers as Dick Bartell, Dom DiMaggio, Johnny Dickshot, Tony Cuccinello, Harry Eisenstat, Babe Dahlgren, Bob Turley, Johnny Berardino and Roy Sievers.

Still, though 140 players are included here, others are not. Why didn't I include everybody? And why 140? I interviewed far more than that number but these, in my opinion, were the cream of the crop stories. If a player was more notable and more famous but just didn't cut it in the story department, I didn't compromise the book to get the bigger name. I included the better stories from other guys who deserve to be remembered just as much as the household namers who failed to come up with an entertaining nugget.

Some guys just can't tell stories, or at least they can't remember any interesting ones. Some guys don't share well with others; they have their own books coming out and don't want to give up any "A" material that might end up in their own book. Some guys were just too tough to get to; some guys don't want to give up private moments of their lives; some wanted money; and some gentlemen were too ill to respond.

This is not a cop-out and not an apology. It's just the way it is. This, and everything in the book is real, it's life. Don't lament who is missing; I don't. Rejoice, instead, for the men who are included.

All of this serves as part of the crazy quilt that is Major League baseball. That is why the Hank Aaron piece is just as important, but not more so, than the George Zuverink tale, and why George Brett's recollection of barely yesterday comingles smoothly with Bob Wright's from three-quarters of a century ago.

Observations: There's more to George Steinbrenner than his much-publicized "My way or the highway" management style; there are several warmhearted kindness and generosity tales as well as the expected "save-face-for-the-club with a harsh move" knee-jerk reaction stories. There are several sides to "The Babe," and "The Mick," and Roger and Reggie. There's a warm side to the usually gruff Thurman Munson. There's the baseball of long ago when money wasn't everything . . . and in some cases, money wasn't anything. There's grit and there's fun, and there are those consumed by the game and those who just enjoyed every moment in "The Show." There's a dark side to the game, an inside to the game and a light side to the game.

For those stat freaks out there who must have their compilations for the perfect order, we have included the original stories from 140 players, thirty-two Hall of Famers, and fourteen sure-to-be Hall members.

To figure the next two statistics, I have arbitrarily made the following decisions: For players by position, I make the assumption that a player's fame, infamy or moment in the sun came while he occupied a certain spot on the field—or my perception that he did so—so even though Babe Ruth played left field nearly as often as he played right field (and was a star hurler as well), I would have included the Bambino as a right fielder because he patrolled right in Yankee Stadium, the home he "built" with his exploits. Following that rationale, I consider Stan Musial an outfielder and not a first baseman; Ernie Banks a first baseman and not a shortstop (though he played nearly the same number of games at each position—1,259 at first and 1,125 at shortstop—he became a beloved elder statesman during his days as a first sacker); I give Bill Rigney his due as an infielder— second baseman—even though he played 654 games in eight years while managing 2,561 games in eighteen years because, hey, he *was* a player; and for me, Roy Sievers was a first baseman (he played 888 games at first and 999 elsewhere); Lou Boudreau was a shortstop (1,539 games in fifteen years) and not a manager for book purposes (2,404 games in sixteen years); and Sparky Anderson qualifies as a manager (based on one season as a second baseman and nearly a quarter-century as a skipper). Hey, someone's got to make these decisions, and since my name's on the book, the choice is mine. Do you understand the process? Author's choice.

When it comes to putting a player in by team, I also make my own arbitrary decisions based on where the individual is most remembered or the team for which he played during the era of his story. Remember, Reggie Jackson was a star for the A's, Orioles, Yankees and Angels and he chose to enter the Hall of Fame as a Yankee. For that reason and for the reason that the story he shared was about his Yankee days, Reggie, too is a Yankee for the purpose of the following compilation. I've made Sal Maglie a New York Giant, and Frank Robinson a Baltimore Oriole. Steve Garvey is a Dodger, Jim Kaat a Cardinal, and Rollie Fingers an Oakland Athletic. Nolan Ryan, for our purposes, is an Angel; Rod Carew is a Twin; Jim "Catfish" Hunter is an Oakland Athletic; Larry Hisle, a Twin; Marv Throneberry, a Met; Lance Parrish, a Tiger; Roy Sievers, a St. Louis Brown (because that's what his stories were about, even though I remember him better as a Senator); but I have Harmon Killebrew as a Senator because he talks of his Washington days, and Bob Watson a Yankee because it was his choice of stories and importance. And some are tough calls: I've labeled Mark Koenig, a member of the 1927 Yankees, a Cub, because his story is about Babe Ruth's "called shot" in the 1932 World Series when Koenig was a Cub. You get the idea ... my book, my rules, with an occasional lift from the individual.

And without being grandiose or self-absorbed, there's so much more in here ... vignettes that tell about the game, the players and the climate of the world at the time the event took place.

Much of what you read here will never appear in "This Day In Sports" or on a baseball calendar. Many of the entries herein are private, inside sharings — the stuff which make up the guts, the arteries, the bones and muscle of the game, as well as some of the fat that makes baseball a well-rounded American creation.

What follows is baseball: the glory and the goats; the humor and the sorrow; the stories of first days and last; of days in the sun with singing birds and freshly cut grass as well as the knife fights in the clubhouse; tales of prejudice and of pride; acts of kindness and those of desperation and ignorance. From the halcyon days of the innocent past — innocence of the game and of this nation — to the sophistication and hype of today, this book contains no parables, allegories, hidden agenda or underlying motives except to honor the game and the men who have made it special for all time.

Yes, what is past is prologue and the wonder of these men and their tales are part and parcel of the foundation for what is yet to come for America and its pastime.

Play ball.

1910s

September 17, 1911 to September 1, 1919

The date, September 17, 1911, refers to the first oral history tale and does not refer to the news briefs that follow. That first tale tells of an unsophisticated and innocent age of baseball, and begins the love affair America has had with the game — the story is from "Red" Hoff. The final date of September 1, 1919, refers to the last vignette from this decade, a story from Eddie Gill of a young man's awe at seeing a baseball legend play like one.

The decade of the 1910s began with innocence and ended with soiled, prostituted disgrace — the "Black Sox scandal" of 1919. It was a decade of fun, frolic, catching balls from monuments, pranks, wildness and poor fielding, but it was fun in the sun for Americans who enjoyed baseball as a picnic before World War I and as a means of getting back to enjoying life after "The War to End All Wars." Baseball was still a closed shop; the Federal League opened and closed as competition, and as black athletes were forbidden from joining in the fun, the Negro Leagues began to take shape. Politics aside, the men who played the game were just there to play hard and have fun — Ty Cobb notwithstanding — and that purity of devotion caught on with America.

As baseball had started to make its way into America's heart with tales of such early day heroes as Cy Young, Napoleon Lajoie, Ty Cobb, Eddie Collins, Walter Johnson, Joe Tinker, Johnny Evers, Frank Chance, "Home Run" Baker, George Sisler, Rogers Hornsby,

Edd Roush, Joe Jackson and Gavvy Cravath, it was nearly destroyed by greed and a "fixed" World Series.

But baseball had a savior who was set to take the game back up where it belonged in the next decade. That savior was Babe Ruth.

Selected decade highlights
(in addition to those told in this chapter)

April 14, 1910 - President William Howard Taft is the first commander-in-chief to throw out the first ball at a baseball opening day game in Washington, D.C. Walter Johnson catches the toss and goes on to pitch a one-hit shutout to beat the A's, 3-0.

July 19, 1910 - Cy Young wins his five hundredth game, at age forty-three, with an eleven-inning, 5-4 victory for the Cleveland Indians over the Senators.

July 25, 1910 - "Shoeless Joe" Jackson is traded by Connie Mack, from the A's to Cleveland for outfielder Bris "The Human Eyeball" Lord.

August 13, 1910 - In a stat-lover's dream, the Brooklyn Dodgers and Pittsburgh Pirates play to an 8-8 tie. Each team had thirty-eight at bats, thirteen hits, three walks, five strikeouts, one hit batsman, two errors, twelve assists and one passed ball.

August 24, 1910 - Spitballing Hall of Famer Ed Walsh throws twenty-three baseballs from the top of the Washington Monument while catcher Billy Sullivan stands on the ground 555 feet below and catches three of the balls traveling 161 feet per second, or 110 miles per hour.

February 14, 1911 - The New York Giants and Philadelphia Phillies introduce new home uniforms, the first pinstripes in Major League baseball history.

May 22, 1911 - Boston Braves pitcher Cliff Curtis sets a dubious Major League mark by losing his twenty-third consecutive decision in a streak that began June 13, 1910.

September 28, 1911 - The New York Highlanders defeat the St. Louis Browns, 18-12, in a comedy of errors and horrible defense: twenty-nine hits, eleven errors, twenty walks and fifteen stolen bases.

October 16-17, 1911 - Frank Baker, third baseman of the Philadelphia A's, earns his nickname, "Homerun" Baker by homering in back-to-back games of the World Series against the New York Giants. On the sixteenth, his two-run homer off Rube Marquard in the sixth inning breaks up a 1-1 pitching duel between Eddie Plank and Marquard. The following day, with Christy Mathewson holding a 1-0 lead

---

over the A's and Jack Coombs, Baker smacks a one-out round-tripper to tie the game, and the nom de guerre is born.

April 20, 1912 - Fenway Park opens; the Red Sox beat the High-landers 7-6 in eleven innings.

August 1, 1912 - New York Giants pitcher Rube Marquard is fined twenty-five dollars for pitching in a semipro game on a day off.

August 6, 1912 - Baseball's first labor strike called by "Players' Fraternity" led by Ty Cobb and Christy Mathewson. The strike is soon rescinded, so no games are lost. Grievance was over Brooklyn's decision to send player Harry Kraft down to the minors.

April 5, 1913 - Ebbets Field opens with the Dodgers beating the Yankees, 3-2, in exhibition game on inside-the-park homer by Casey Stengel, the first round-tripper hit at Ebbets.

April 10, 1913 - In their first official game as Yankees (they had been the New York Highlanders) New York loses to Walter Johnson, 2-1, as President Woodrow Wilson throws out the first ball in Washington.

May 30, 1913 - In this Decoration Day doubleheader, Boston Red Sox outfielder Harry Hooper led off both games of the twin bill versus the Washington Senators with home runs. This was the first time this achievement was ever recorded in the majors and it would not be duplicated for eighty years.

April 13, 1914 - The Federal League opens in Baltimore with the hometown Terrapins defeating Buffalo, 3-2.

July 11, 1914 - Babe Ruth makes his debut for the Boston Red Sox, pitching a 4-3 win over Cleveland. Ruth strikes out in his first at bat and is lifted for a pinch hitter in the seventh.

May 6, 1915 - Babe Ruth smashes his first Major League home run, a blast off Jack Warhop of the Yankees at the Polo Grounds.

June 17, 1915 - In the longest relief stint in Major League history, Chicago Cubs pitcher George "Zip" Zabel comes in from the bullpen with two out in the first inning against Brooklyn and hangs on to win the game, 4-3, in nineteen innings.

June 23, 1915 - Ty Cobb is running loose. He steals home for the fifth time this month. The Tigers beat the Browns, 4-2.

May 9, 1916 - As the A's defeat the Tigers, 16-2, thirty walks are issued—eighteen by the A's.

June 28, 1916 - Rookie Rogers Hornsby picks up his first five-hit game with three singles and two doubles.

June 29, 1916 - In a lesson in frugality, the Chicago Cubs and Cincinnati Reds complete a nine-inning game using only one baseball.

May 2, 1917 - James "Hippo" Vaughn of the Cubs and Fred Toney of the Reds pitch a double no-hitter for nine innings at Weeghman Park, which was later renamed Wrigley Field. Reds win with two hits in the tenth, with the winning run driven in by Jim Thorpe.

May 5-6, 1917 - St. Louis Browns hurler Ernie Koob throws a no-hitter on the fifth and the following day, teammate Bob Groom fires a no-no in the second game of a double header. Both gems were against the White Sox.

June 23, 1917 - Babe Ruth starts on the mound against Washington and after walking the leadoff hitter, Eddie Foster, Ruth argues with umpire Brick Owens, then punches the ump in the jaw. After he's ejected, Ernie Shore relieves, Foster is caught stealing, and Shore retires all twenty-six men he faces. Ruth gets a ten-day suspension.

August 22, 1917 - In a twenty-two-inning game between the Brooklyn Dodgers and Pittsburgh Pirates, the Bucs' Carson Bigbee goes to the plate a then-record eleven times and Pirate reliever Elmer Jacobs pitches a record sixteen and two-thirds innings in relief. The home team Dodgers won it, 6-5.

June 6, 1918 - Casey Stengel, traded by Brooklyn to Pittsburgh before the season, returns to Ebbets Field and, during his first trip to the plate, calls time and doffs his cap; a sparrow he had hidden under the headwear flies out.

February 5, 1919 - To lead off a scandal-ridden year, Cincinnati Reds owner Garry Herrmann and manager Christy Mathewson accuse first baseman Hal Chase of betting against his team and throwing games in partnership with gamblers during the preceding season. National League (NL) president John Heydler dismisses the charges, excusing Chase's poor play as "careless."

August 24, 1919 - Cleveland pitcher Ray Caldwell is struck by a lightning bolt in the middle of a windup. He shakes it off and gets the win over Philadelphia, 2-1.

September 24, 1919 - Babe Ruth sets the Major League mark by blasting his twenty-eighth homer of the year; this one goes over the roof at the Polo Grounds.

September 28, 1919 - Think about today's three-hour ball games. On this date in the Polo Grounds, the fastest nine-inning game in Major League history was played, with the Giants defeating the Phillies, 6-1, in a blazing fifty-one minutes behind the five-hit pitching of twenty-five-game winner Jesse Barnes.

October 1-9, 1919 - Baseball's biggest black eye and near ruination as the heavily favored Chicago White Sox play the World Series against the Cincinnati Reds. The Reds win the Series in eight games as the "Black Sox" are accused of throwing the Fall Classic in a fix masterminded by New York gambler Arnold Rothstein. Indicted in the scandal are White Sox players Eddie Cicotte and Lefty Williams (pitchers); Joe Jackson and Happy Felsch (outfielders); and Chick Gandil, Swede Risberg, Buck Weaver and Fred McMullin (infielders).

December 10, 1919 - Baseball bans the spitball for all new pitchers. Current hurlers who throw the pitch will be allowed to continue wetting the hide throughout the rest of their careers.

The Chronicles

To begin the oral history portion of this book, perhaps it is fitting that the first tale is spun by the oldest living ballplayer, Chester "Red" Hoff, because this is a tale of innocence, of unsophisticated baseball before electronics and replays and tell-all scoreboards. This is baseball of the bygone era when the guys just played and worried little about incidentals like who, what, where, when and how. They just played.

Chester "Red" Hoff
New York Highlanders (Yankees), pitcher
1911-1915

Back in the days when the Yankees were known as the New York Highlanders, and their home field was Hilltop Park at 168th Street and Broadway in Manhattan—a decade before they would move to the Bronx and Yankee Stadium to win their first championship— the club was a scrappy second-division team that recruited many of its players from the New York/New Jersey/Pennsylvania tristate area. One of these athletes was a 5'9", 165-pound lefty pitcher from Ossining, New York, named Chester "Red" Hoff. Hoff, born in 1891, is a perfect example of the ballplayer of that era. His career was short, and while he had a low ERA (2.49) and gave up only sixty-seven hits in eighty-three innings over twenty-three appearances, he appeared mostly as a relief pitcher in the days when relief work went only to those guys who didn't fit in as starters who could go nine innings. Relief was not a specialist's position in those days; it was scutwork. Hoff was in and out of the majors by the time he was twenty-four, thanks in part to the breaking up of the Federal League, which brought several hundred good ballplayers back to the job market. His brief career was also due in part to the fact that Hoff had a family to support, and baseball was not a high-paying job in those days— he found he could earn more money by working full time and playing semipro ball for a few bucks on Sundays. But his contribution to the

Chester "Red" Hoff, pitcher, 1910s
Courtesy: National Baseball Library Hall of Fame, Cooperstown, New York

game is just as important as the contributions of the stars of his time: Ty Cobb, "Shoeless" Joe Jackson, "Smokey Joe" Williams, Tris Speaker, Honus Wagner, Christy Mathewson, Grover Alexander, "Wahoo" Sam Crawford and Ed Walsh, to name a few. Why? Because he was America. He was a young boy who dreamed of playing baseball and made it to the Big Leagues at a time before expanded teams and rosters. His gritty four-year performance is the quintessential Everyman career of the era. Hoff, also known as "Chet" Hoff, finished his career in the minors and in semipro ball, playing against top black teams, professional girls teams and even a few prison teams.

Chet Hoff made his Major League debut September 6, 1911, as a twenty-year-old fresh from semipro ball. That brief performance was largely forgettable (his name didn't even appear in the newspaper box score the next day). His second appearance, however, is another story, and his final appearance is also worth remembering.

September 17, 1911

The Highlanders were losing to Detroit, 9-3, in the sixth inning and ace pitcher Russ Ford was still on the mound for New York. As Hoff remembers, "Manager Hal Chase told me to warm up and after I threw a couple of pitches on the sidelines, as there was no bullpen — I wasn't really loose yet — he comes over and says, 'Go out and tell Russ you're taking over. And go get that lefty.' So here I am at twenty, telling a great pitcher, Russ Ford (who won twenty-six games in 1910 and twenty-two in 1911), I was taking over. I thought Ford would eat me alive, but he took it like a pro and handed me the ball.

"I got my signs together with catcher Jay Sweeney and took the mound. I really didn't know what the score was, how many outs there were, or who I was facing; there were no big scoreboards and I was only twenty with one game's experience. I peered in at Sweeney and the lefty in the Tiger uniform. As I was a lefty, I figured I'd show him a fastball and then set him up for a curve and make him bail out. I gave him two fastballs inside and he fouled them both off — hard. I threw an 0-2 pitchout to see if he'd bite. He didn't and it was 1-2. I then threw him a roundhouse curve that floated across the plate for a called strike three. He didn't even get the bat off his shoulder. He never said a word and he walked back to the bench.

"I wound up finishing the game, going four innings and giving up four hits and a run, and this performance made the team for me. I earned my uniform.

"After the game I showered and went to my hotel.

"The next morning I jumped out of bed and went down to the drugstore to pick up the *New York Journal* so I could read my name in the paper. On the sports page was a huge red headline that said, 'HOFF STRIKES OUT TY COBB.' I had struck out Ty Cobb and I didn't even know it. It was the biggest thrill I ever had, and I was alone, about eighteen hours after the event."

October 2, 1915

"I got to pitch to Cobb several other times and he hit me like he hit everyone else — well. One time he tried to score from third base on an infield fly. He was out by a mile, but knocked the ball loose from catcher Sam Agnew. I treasure the moments I faced the great hitters. I got Rogers Hornsby in an exhibition game when he was a rookie in 1915; I hit him in the shoulder. I struck out Jim Thorpe once and faced Babe Ruth in the minors, but most of all, I remember my last game, against the powerhouse Chicago White Sox.

"I was with the St. Louis Browns and we were losing, 6-1, in the eighth. I faced switch-hitter Buck Weaver and he chased a slow curve and grounded weakly back to me. One out. Then Eddie Collins, a lefty hitting .332, singled to left and then stole second and third. Another lefty, Jack Fournier, hitting .322, took a called third strike on a good curve. Two out. With Collins at third, up came Joe Jackson. I got him to ground to Del Pratt at second, who tossed to George Sisler to end the game and my career. Imagine, my first big out was Ty Cobb and my last, 'Shoeless Joe' Jackson. I'll take that for a career.

"From there I went to the minors and to semipro ball and made more money working during the week and playing semipro on Sundays than I ever would have in the majors."

Bob Wright
Chicago Cubs, pitcher
1915

Robert Cassius Wright, a 6'2", 175-pound fireballer from the farm community of Greensburg, Indiana, was often written about as "the ploughboy with a blazing fastball, a hard curve, and a sweet change of pace." At the age of 101, Wright was still on his farm raising hogs and sheep and still had a deep love for the game he played for a decade — though only one year was in the Majors. Wright made two appearances in relief for the 1915 Cubs, and left because of money; he could make more elsewhere. His career marks: four innings, six hits, three strikeouts and a 2.25 ERA. Then he was gone. Make no apologies for Bob Wright. He left on his own terms and even with only two games in the books, he fulfilled his dream and is an integral cog in this book and in the world of Major League baseball because he played the game. Having played (in the Majors, in exhibitions and in industrial leagues) against such athletes as Ty Cobb, Joe Jackson, Gavvy Cravath and Grover Alexander, Wright is quick to appraise the best: "Buck Weaver (shortstop for the White Sox) is the best ballplayer I ever saw. He was the most graceful man I ever saw and he could do anything he wanted on a ball field."

September 10, 1915

Bob Wright, a twenty-three-year-old right-hander just up from the Northern League, recalls his first game. "We were playing the New York Giants and our season was just about over. We were in fourth place about fifteen games behind Philadelphia and the Giants were in last, about twenty games out. I knew of their pitchers more than their hitters, and I knew Christy Mathewson was having a lousy year (8-14) and so was Rube Marquard (9-8). Their top hitter was a second baseman named 'Laughing Larry' Doyle (.320). I was surprised we were so low in the standings because we had Heinie Zimmerman, a second baseman, a great ballplayer and a very nice man. We also had 'Hippo' Vaughn as our ace pitcher, and he was one of the greats.

"I was in the dugout watching the game and George 'Zip' Zabel was our starting pitcher. He didn't get anyone out; the first six Giants got on, and without any warm-ups, our player-manager, Roger Bresnahan, who was catching, comes to the dugout and says, 'Wright, get us out of this.'

"With no warm-ups, I go out to the mound and Zabel's head is down as he flips me the ball. I didn't have to say a word to him, and Bresnahan didn't say a word. Zabel knew he was gone and I was in. I threw my warm-ups and then I realized there were no outs and the bases were loaded. Fred Snodgrass was up and Bresnahan said, 'Snodgrass is in a slump, throw strikes.'

"I did and it took me five pitches to strike him out. I got the next guy, Chief Meyers, on a double play. He hit the first pitch right back to me. I threw home for one and Bresnahan threw to Vic Saier at first for the double play.

"As I walked back to the dugout, elated, Bresnahan said, 'Good work. You're through for the day,' and he put in a reliever. What a letdown. I was perfect and had a whole game ahead of me and I was done. I was unhappy until I saw Zabel. He looked like a cow kicked him and I figured, *I'm better off than he is.*"

April 1916-1919

"I don't know why I wasn't brought up the next year, but I played in an outlaw league outside of Chicago and did pretty well. In one exhibition game, we played against Ty Cobb, and he got into a fight with three of our guys and licked them all. He took on Boss Schmidt, our catcher and nearly beat the life out of him.

"I made some pretty good money in that league and was approached a few times by Major League clubs, but they never offered any really good money, so I stayed put.

"In 1919 I signed with Nash Motors in an industrial league — five or six manufacturers had teams in the league. They gave me a four-year contract for eight thousand dollars a year. That was two or three times what I'd make in the Majors, and when you added my other jobs, I was making real good cash, so when two or three Big League clubs came to me and said, 'Hey, why are you playing in this bush league when you could be playing serious ball,' I told them to get lost. I couldn't take the pay cut. It was the smartest thing I ever did. The ball was good; we even got a few ex-Major Leaguers like Schmidt and Al Wickland (an outfielder who also played in the Federal League) on our team. It was just as hard to win, and I made enough money to buy my own farm, which I've been working ever since."

Eddie Gill
Washington Senators, pitcher
1919

Eddie Gill, a 5'10", 165-pound righty, played in sixteen games in the 1919 season for the Senators. He finished with a 1-2 record and gave up thirty-eight hits in thirty-seven innings. Still, he did make "the Show," and a vivid recollection of two of the greats: Walter Johnson, with whom he played, and Babe Ruth, against whom he pitched.

The Somerville, Massachusetts, native, who was born in 1895, was twenty-four when he got his only Major League win, an event that remains etched in his memory sixty-four years later, as do his observations of "The Big Train" and "The Bambino."

Gill began, "I faced Joe Jackson and Babe Ruth and Ty Cobb, and I'd like to tell you about Babe — he was the absolute best ballplayer, in every regard, that I ever saw. But first, I must tell you that the man I was most in awe of was Clark Griffith, my manager, who was short and stocky but who carried himself with such power that he could have been ten feet tall. He really never said anything to me other than, 'Go in and throw,' or 'You're through,' or, in my first game, against the Yankees on July 5, when I pitched a perfect inning, 'Nice job.' He probably only said a dozen words to me the entire season I was there, but boy was he something. A real general.

"The other man I must tell you about is Walter Johnson. Walter was another quiet man, and although he was bigger than I was by only a few inches, his stature was also that of a man ten feet tall. He was a silent leader who did little kind things that made me feel at home."

August 21, 1919

"Walter Johnson made it a point to go out of his way to make me feel like I was a part of the team. I was really taken with his kindness. He took me under his wing. He took me to dinner after my first win, to celebrate. Maybe he knew I wasn't very good and I wouldn't be around very long, but he made my stay fun. He didn't really say much, he was kind of quiet, but he always gave me a smile when I needed it, or a word of advice if I needed it, like after I gave up five walks and six hits in four innings against the White Sox — the 1919 Black Sox — on August 21.

"I was really nervous, because these guys were the best — Eddie Collins, Buck Weaver, Joe Jackson, Nemo Leibold — and afterward Walter just patted me on the shoulder and said, 'Son, (and he was only eight years older than me in years, but much wiser and poised), they're just men, just like us and you're just as good as they are. They just win more often than we do but we're all the same . . . all just as good, otherwise we wouldn't be here.' I took it to heart and I pitched better against them the next time I faced them." (**Author's Note:** On September 11, Gill pitched one inning against the ChiSox and gave up one hit and one walk, with a strikeout.)

September 1, 1919

This tale is pure Babe Ruth, from the perspective of one who saw him up close.

Gill painted the picture. "We were playing a doubleheader against the Red Sox in Boston and I marveled at Babe Ruth — he hit with power, ran with speed, pitched with skill and fielded with grace. In the first game, he pitched and held us to one run in beating us, 3-1; he tripled deep to center field and glided around the bases to beat the throw; and he made three acrobatic plays on the mound to get hitters out who should have been safe. I came on in the seventh inning of that one and gave up hits to Everett Scott and Frank Gilhooley. Then I got Harry Hooper, Ossie Vitt and Braggo Roth, all on pops to end the inning. In the eighth, Babe worked me to a 3-2 count and just missed a home run by a foot, foul, before flying deep to Sam Rice in right field. I was lucky and I knew it — he broke his bat on the hit. I then got Wally Schang and Stuffy McInnis to end my stint.

"In the second game, Babe Ruth was unbelievable. He played left field and made several outstanding running, athletic catches; he hit the ball hard all day and in the seventh, after Roth had walked, Babe sent a pitch from Jim Shaw like a rocket into the right field bleachers for the game-winning home run. He received a loud ovation from the crowd of about thirty thousand that lasted for ten minutes. Then the fans threw their straw hats on the field — it looked like a blizzard of straw. And when the inning was over, Babe was cheered from the bench until he arrived in left field. He was totally in control of the game and the fans and I felt like I was really watching a man toying with boys."

1920s

August 11, 1924 to October 28, 1928

The first date above refers to the oral history that follows the news briefs: August 11, 1924, the day that Milt Gaston faced his hero for the first time. The last date above, October 28, 1929, tells the story of Babe Ruth and Lou Gehrig barnstorming the country and the impression it made on a future Major League pitcher.

The Roaring Twenties was the time in which baseball came rebounding back into the hearts of Americans. Babe Ruth was king and the game was still unsophisticated, innocent and fun. The exploits of the larger-than-life "Bambino" served to push the "Black Sox" scandal into the background, and soon, baseball was considered an honorable profession ... for the first time. True, blacks were still barred from the game (a reflection of what went on around the rest of the country), but baseball merely mirrored and mimicked the rest of the nation. Baseball was escapism but it has never been in the forefront of avant-garde thinking, liberalization or progressive thought. It is, instead, a bastion of the status quo, and for the 1920s, that meant Lou Gehrig playing every day, Mel Ott banging out homers, and Carl Hubbell becoming his team's "Meal Ticket." The 1920s marked the beginning of the Yankee dynasty, and stars including Harry Heilmann, Frankie Frisch, Rogers Hornsby, Heinie Manush, Hack Wilson, Al Simmons, Tony Lazzeri, Paul Waner, Bill Terry, Lefty Grove, Dazzy Vance, Chuck Klein and Lefty O'Doul playing hard and honestly, and being the heroes of the morning sports pages. The Golden Age of baseball had begun.

Selected decade highlights
(in addition to those told in this chapter)

January 5, 1920 - In perhaps the biggest trade in baseball history, "The Curse of the Bambino" begins as the New York Yankees announce the purchase from the Boston Red Sox of Babe Ruth. The trade, actually made December 26, 1919, was delayed until Ruth agreed to a two-year contract believed to be worth a total of four thousand dollars. The price of the trade: $125,000 to Red Sox owner Harry Frazee — used to finance the Broadway play "No, No, Nanette" — and guaranteeing a $300,000 loan with Fenway Park as collateral. What curse? The Red Sox haven't won a World Series since the Babe left Boston.

February 9, 1920 - Baseball's rules committee bans all foreign substances and alterations on the ball: saliva, resin, talcum powder, tobacco juice, paraffin, gum, mud, and such scuffed balls as the shine and emery ball. Designated pitchers are allowed one more season; the ban takes effect completely in 1921.

February 1, 1920 - The Negro National League, aka the National Association of Colored Professional Baseball Clubs, is organized in Kansas City, Missouri.

August 16, 1920 - Submarine pitcher Carl Mays fires one inside to Cleveland shortstop Ray Chapman. Chapman, who crowds the plate, doesn't move and the ball strikes him in the skull. Chapman dies of a skull fracture the following day.

September 2, 1920 - A Chicago grand jury indicts the eight White Sox players on charges of fixing the 1919 World Series. The White Sox are only a game behind first-place Cleveland and ChiSox owner Charles Comiskey suspends all indicted players.

September 10, 1920 - In game five of the World Series, Cleveland shortstop Bill Wambsganss completes an unassisted triple play in the fifth inning — with Pete Kilduff at second base and Otto Miller at first, relief pitcher Clarence Mitchell lines to Wambsganss, who steps on second and tags Miller.

June 6, 1921 - Babe Ruth belts his 120th career homer, this one off Cleveland's Jim Bagby, to take over the career leadership in post-1900 four-baggers, supplanting Gavvy Cravath. Five weeks later, on July 6, he'll hit his 137th home run to pass nineteenth-century star Roger Conner for the all-time lead, which he'll hold until Henry Aaron breaks the record in 1974.

June 1, 1921 - Using a special New Jersey mud supplied by A's coach Lena Blackburne from his farm, umpires begin the practice of rubbing dirt on baseballs to cut down on the glare and make them easier to grip.

August 2, 1921 - A Chicago jury brings in a "not guilty" verdict against all Black Sox defendants. Disregarding the verdict, Baseball Commissioner Kenesaw Mountain Landis bans all eight from baseball for life.

September 5, 1921 - Walter Johnson strikes out seven Yankees to break Cy Young's career strikeout mark of 2,796. "The Big Train" will end his career with 3,508 K's and hold the mark until Nolan Ryan breaks Johnson's career mark in 1983.

October 5-6, 1921 - In an all-New York World Series, Frankie Frisch of the Giants puts on a hitting show in defeat. In the Series opener on the fifth, Yankee hurler Carl Mays shuts the Giants out 3-0 on five hits — four by Frisch and one by Johnny Rawlings. The Yanks' Babe Ruth drives in the game-winning run. In game two on the sixth, Waite Hoyt gives up only two hits in another 3-0 Yankee win; again, the hits are garnered by Frisch and Rawlings.

May 30, 1922 - Between the morning and afternoon games of a doubleheader between the Chicago Cubs and St. Louis Cardinals, Cubbie Max Flack is traded for Card Cliff Heathcote. They each played for both teams in the twin bill: Flack went 0-for-4 as a Cub and 1-for-4 as a Card; Heathcote went 0-for-3 as a Card and 2-for-4 in a Chicago uniform; the Cubs swept.

October 1, 1922 - Rogers Hornsby goes 3-for-5 on the final day of the season to push his average to .401, becoming the National League's first .400 hitter since Eddie Delahanty in 1899. Hornsby wins the triple crown, leading the league in batting, home runs (42) and runs batted in (152). His 250 hits break Wee Willie Keeler's league mark of 243, set in 1897.

March 6, 1923 - The St. Louis Cardinals become the first team to wear numerals on their uniforms. The numbers coincide with the players' places in the batting order and change as the lineup changes. The first official season game in which the numbers are worn is April 17 in Cincinnati; the Cards lose in eleven innings, 3-2, to the Redlegs.

April 18, 1923 - Yankee Stadium officially opens with the Yanks defeating the Red Sox, 4-1, on Babe Ruth's three-run home run before a crowd of 74,217.

September 27, 1923 - Lou Gehrig hits his first Major League homer, a blast off Bill Piercy at Fenway Park.

September 16, 1924 - St. Louis Cardinals first baseman "Sunny" Jim Bottomley sets the Major League record for runs batted in (RBIs) in a game. He drives in twelve runs as the Redbirds beat up on Brooklyn, 17-3. Bottomley crushed two homers and knocked out three singles and a double.

April 5, 1925 - Babe Ruth collapses at a railroad station in Asheville, North Carolina. Ruth, suffering from "The Big Bellyache of 1925," will undergo surgery and remain in bed until May 26.

May 5, 1925 - Yankee shortstop Everett Scott is benched by manager Miller Huggins, stopping Scott's Major-League-record of consecutive games played at 1,307. Scott is replaced at short by Pee Wee Wanninger, who is inextricably linked in the passage and birth of two great streaks.

June 1, 1925 - Lou Gehrig begins his record-setting consecutive-games-played streak, which will surpass Scott's mark in 1933. Gehrig will enter the game as a pinch hitter for Pee Wee Wanninger. The next day, first baseman Wally Pipp begs out with a headache and Gehrig plays first base. Also, on this date, Babe Ruth plays his first game of the season.

May 1, 1926 - Leroy "Satchel" Paige, an estimated nineteen years old, makes his debut in the Negro Southern League for Chattanooga, winning a 5-4 decision over the Birmingham Black Barons.

August 15, 1926 - In a play symbolizing the Brooklyn Dodgers of this era, during a game versus the Braves, the Dodgers' Babe Herman doubles—into a double play. With the bases loaded, Herman drives one against the right field wall at Ebbets Field, scoring Hank DeBerry from third; Dazzy Vance rounds third and stops; Chick Fewster goes from first to third and stops; and Herman likewise legs it all the way to third. He slides in, passing Fewster in the process, and leaving three Dodgers at third.

October 10, 1926 - In game seven of the World Series, Grover Alexander, reportedly sleeping off a hangover in the bullpen, is summoned to pitch for the Cards in the seventh against the Yankees. With two out, the bases loaded, and the Cards up 3-2, Alexander whiffs Tony Lazzeri, who missed a grand slam by inches (foul) on the previous pitch. With two out in the ninth, Alexander walks Babe Ruth, who inexplicably attempts to steal second base. Ruth is thrown out with Lou Gehrig at the plate. Gehrig was hitting .348 in the Series.

May 30, 1927 - Jimmy Cooney, Cubs shortstop, makes an unassisted triple play (TP) versus the Pirates. Paul Waner lines one up the middle, Cooney grabs it, steps on second to double Lloyd Waner, and runs down Clyde Barnhart for the TP.

July 27, 1927 - Mel Ott, eighteen-year-old Giant outfielder, hits his first Major League homer, an inside-the-park job. Ott played twenty-two years and blasted 511 four-baggers, but this was his only inside-the-parker.

September 7, 1927 - Babe Ruth belts two homers to go with the three he hit the day before in a doubleheader. He now leads Lou Gehrig in the home run chase, 49-45.

September 30, 1927 - In the eighth inning of a 2-2 tie, Mark Koenig triples and Babe Ruth blasts a low, inside Tom Zachary fastball into the seats for his sixtieth homer and a 4-2 Yankee win.

July 12, 1928 - The heftiest battery in baseball history takes the field as New York Giants hurler Garland "Gob" Buckeye (a 265-pounder) pitches to his catcher, Shanty Hogan (a 250-pounder) in a loss to the Cardinals.

September 3, 1928 - Ty Cobb's last hit, his 4,191st, a double (number 724) is smacked off Washington's Bump Hadley.

October 9, 1928 - Babe Ruth bombs three homers in game four of the World Series. The Yankees sweep the Cards.

December 11, 1928 - The first proposal on the designated hitter reaches the baseball world—forty-five years before it was adopted (first use: April 6, 1973) in the American League (AL)—as National League (NL) President John Heydler asked for the rule to speed up the game, theorizing that fans don't like to see weak-hitting pitchers hit for themselves. The National League backs the plan but the American League votes it down.

April 16, 1929 - Earl Averill, Indians outfielder, becomes the first Major Leaguer to homer in his first at bat when he belts one off Detroit pitcher Earl Whitehill.

April 18, 1929 - The New York Yankees become the first team to put numbers on the backs of their uniforms continuously, to perfect the idea the Cards originated on a haphazard basis in 1923. The Yanks numbered the uniforms based on position in the batting order.

June 18, 1929 - New York Giants first-sacker Bill Terry slams out nine hits in a doubleheader in a losing cause against the Dodgers. Brooklyn won both games, 8-7 and 7-6.

July 31, 1929 - In an unofficial test, Babe Ruth sets a world record by hitting a fungo 447 feet.

October 5, 1929 - Tied for the NL home run lead with forty-two apiece going into the last game, Chuck Klein and Mel Ott square off in a doubleheader between the Phillies and the Giants. In game one, Ott can only connect for a single, but Klein homers off Carl Hubbell to take the lead. In game two, Phillies pitchers walk Ott intentionally five times—the last time with the bases loaded—to keep him from wresting the crown from Klein.

The Chronicles

Milt Gaston
New York Yankees, pitcher
1924-1934

Milt Gaston was a 6'1", 185-pound righty from Ridgefield Park, New Jersey, who went straight to the Majors from the sandlots. His forkball moved so quickly and erratically that catchers feigned illness to keep from catching him. He was traded more than once because of griping by his receivers. He finished with a 97-164 record and twice led the league in losses — for a bad St. Louis Browns club with eighteen in 1926 and for a worse Boston Red Sox team with twenty in 1930. Still, Gaston, born in 1896, is what baseball was in those days, a hard-working hurler who played for poor ball clubs but was happy to compete, which he did with valor and confidence for eleven years.

August 11, 1924

"I really enjoyed my eleven years up there," Gaston reminisces, "and a few games in particular. We were fighting for the pennant with Detroit and Washington and went to Yankee Stadium tied with the Tigers for first. I was a guy plucked right off the sandlots soon after my semipro team, the Paterson (New Jersey) Silk Sox beat the Yankees in an exhibition game thanks to my pitching — no minor league guy could hit me in his dreams — but here I was a rookie in the Majors. With the game on the line, I faced my favorite player, Heinie Manush, with two out in the ninth and the tying and winning runs on base. I struck Manush out. That day, I was king.

"I was with the Yankees, playing alongside Babe Ruth, a big fun-loving guy, and I had met Lou Gehrig, who came to spring camp, and he was a shy, nice guy, and there was nothing more exciting than playing at that big, new ball park, Yankee Stadium. Even brand new, it looked important and some place where history would be written. When I was traded, December 17, 1924, with Joe Bush and Joe Giard to the St. Louis Browns for Urban Shocker, it broke my heart. It had a silver lining, however; I met my wife in St. Louis, so it worked out very well."

Joe Hauser
Philadelphia A's, first base
1922-1929

Joe "Unser Choe" Hauser was a 5'11", 175-pound first baseman with a sweet lefty swing that put him into the minor league record books

Joe Hauser, first base, 1920s
Photo by: George Brace

by blasting sixty-three homers for Baltimore (International League) in 1930 and sixty-nine for Minneapolis (American Association) in 1933, making him the only player to hit sixty or more homers twice in organized baseball. The Milwaukee native's Major League career was cut short when his knee shattered while he was standing at first base on April 7, 1925, following a big twenty-seven-homer season in the dead ball era of 1924. He sat out 1925 in recovery and just started to recapture his home run swing in 1928 when he was thrown into a slump by a teammate (story to follow). In 1929, the Majors dumped him for good when another knee injury limited his range at first base. Still, he had the swing, and he bombed 302 homers in the next seven seasons and 399 in his minor league career. Actually, after his sixty-nine-round-tripper-season in 1933, the thirty-four-year-old was asked by several teams to give the Majors another try; Hauser, happy in Minneapolis with several side businesses and heroic status, declined.

His nickname, "Unser Choe" was bestowed by adoring German-American fans in Wisconsin; it means "Our Joe." Hauser did have his days of glory in "the Bigs." On Aug. 2, 1924, he set the AL record for total bases in a game with fourteen, on three homers and a double; the record was later broken by Ty Cobb with sixteen total bases May 5, 1925. Unser Choe smacked out a few stories dealing with a spitball homer, the pitcher he tagged, and some career-destroying "help" from a very mean superstar.

September 26, 1924

"In 1924, I was with Connie Mack and the Philadelphia A's. I played first base and at the age of twenty-four, was second in the league in homers to Babe Ruth—he hit forty-six, I hit twenty-seven and Baby Doll Jacobson of St. Louis was third with nineteen. We were playing Boston and Jack Quinn, the spitball pitcher, was on the mound. We were losing 2-1 with two out and a runner on. I worked the count to 3-2 and hit a spitball for a home run to win the ball game and finish Quinn's season at 12-13.

"I wouldn't have remembered that game that much except that the next year, Quinn was picked up by the A's on waivers, and two years later, he reminded me of it."

March 5, 1926

"Jack Quinn had been picked up in July, 1925. We were battling for first place with Washington and we thought getting Quinn would help. I was home recovering from my knee injury and wasn't with the team; still, I followed their actions in the newspaper.

"I joined the team in spring training at Fort Myers, Florida, and wasn't thinking of anything other than how nice it was to see some of the guys — Al Simmons, Tilly (Max) Bishop, Jimmy Dykes, Bugger (Frank) Welch and Eddie Rommel — and how great it will be to be back on the field again. I really missed playing.

"I was in the clubhouse getting ready for the game and Quinn came in. He greeted several of the guys on the team — Mickey Cochrane, Simmons and Lefty Grove — and then he came charging toward me, and I didn't even really know the man.

"He lines up eye-to-eye with me, and with a sneer, he growled, 'I remember you, you sonofabitch. You put me under .500 (12-13). How the hell did you hit that spitter?' He remembered the spitball he threw me in 1924, and I was never really sure if he was kidding or not."

May 25, 1928

Hauser begins his next tale matter-of-factly, and not with rancor or anger in his voice, despite the allegations. "Ty Cobb was the meanest bastard who ever lived," he says.

"We had heard the stories about Cobb's meanness and competitiveness. We had heard about the time (September 16, 1909) that he spiked (Frank) Home Run Baker in Philadelphia and was threatened with assassination and that most of his teammates and opponents alike thought the idea was a good one.

"Connie Mack had brought me back to Philadelphia in 1928 after I had a great year in Kansas City (American Association) in 1927 (.353, 20 homers, 134 RBI). I even stole twenty-five bases to show them my knee had healed. The big news was that Ty Cobb and Tris Speaker had also been brought to the team ... in their last years, for some class and talent.

"I noticed in spring training that no one spoke to Cobb. I felt sorry for him. He was forty-one and I figured he'd be gone soon. Then I watched him. He waited until a guy had a few good days, and then he offered to help him with his hitting. Really, it was after the guy was already going well.

"I was hot and he came to me. I didn't need any help, but to be nice, I listened to him. He told me to stand on top of the plate and to hit on my back foot. I tried it but it robbed me of my power and took the strength from my swing, so I abandoned the idea.

"During the season, I was off to a great start—.365 in forty games—and Al Simmons, coming off a .391 season, was at .350 and Jimmie Foxx was starting to come into his own. I noticed that Cobb didn't mess with Simmons, and Foxx just laughed and didn't let Cobb's coaching get to him. Then there was me.

"I had heard that Cobb had bellowed a few days earlier that this kid·Hauser was getting all the press and Cobb was getting none. Then he started hounding me. He'd demand that I listen to his coaching and that I start hitting like he instructed.

"He would yell at me when I was at bat, 'Stand closer to the plate.'

"I was up once with a runner, Al Simmons, at second, two gone in the eighth. We were down 3-2 to the Yankees and George Pipgras had me 1-and-2. Cobb screamed just as Pippy released the pitch, 'Get in on the plate. Hit behind the runner. Hit off your back foot.' I hacked at a ball at my eyes, a pitch I would normally lay off, and I struck out. We lost.

"He'd call me up in the middle of the night when I was trying to sleep, and give me the same instructions.

"I started hearing him and seeing him everywhere and I couldn't block him out. My average dropped a hundred points, and soon I was through. And I really believe it was because he wanted all the spotlight and I was the only one who didn't tell him where to go.

"After Cobb, I didn't look or feel like Joe Hauser at the plate anymore. It took me a full year to get back to my own form, and I was back on track in 1930 and hit sixty-three homers in Baltimore (of the International League) and was really on track in 1933 and hit sixty-nine homers for Minneapolis (of the American Association). I had chances to go back to the Majors but that wasn't for me anymore. I was happy in Minneapolis, and I felt that Major League ball was a different game and I enjoyed it a lot more in the minors."

John Kerr
Chicago White Sox, second base
1934-1924 1929-1934

John Kerr, the stocky, 5'8", 160-pound infielder from San Francisco and Long Beach, California, was a dependable fill-in infielder who rose to starter status in 1929 and 1931 with the ChiSox. He played in 471 games and flirted with .300 in 1930 (in seventy games), settling for a respectable .289. But he may be best known for his stellar and fiery play in the Pacific Coast League, where his career was longer and more stat-packed.

He closed out his career with the Washington Senators and roomed with a baseball enigma, Moe Berg, the catcher, scholar and spy for the U.S. government. Of Berg, Kerr said, "He was really something. The nicest guy around, with a wonderfully dry sense of humor. One game in 1933, Earl Whitehill was on the mound for us. It was in August, a really hot day, and we were playing Philadelphia. The A's hitter was Doc Cramer and every time Cramer would step in, Whitehill would step off the mound. Then Whitehill would get ready to pitch and Cramer would step out of the box. This literally went on for minutes, and Berg was dying back there in all the catcher's gear, so he started a striptease and took off all his gear and dumped it on home plate. He turned to umpire Bill McGowan and said, 'When these guys are ready to play, call me. I'm going to take a shower.'

"Berg was great: a kind man, a good catcher, a lousy hitter — but then, I never hit well either — and the smartest man in baseball. He spoke twelve languages and would read all day long, but you couldn't touch his newspapers because that would "kill them." Berg said, 'Once a newspaper's read, it's dead and you can't read it. You can only read live news.'

Kerr's tale deals with a minor league star who became a Major League star.

October 18, 1925

"The best hitter I ever saw or played with was Tony Lazzeri," said Kerr. "He was my teammate in 1925 for the Salt Lake Bees in the Pacific Coast League. In that year, he became the first professional player to hit sixty home runs in a single season. He also hit .355 and drove in 222 runs that year (**Author's Note:** in 197 games). Tony was about two inches taller than me and about my weight, but he was strong and had a quick, compact swing.

"Late in the season, when Tony already had thirty home runs, he was sold to the Yankees for thirty-five thousand dollars and a couple of players, but he was allowed to finish the season with us.

"He was stuck at fifty-eight homers, one behind Babe Ruth's professional record of fifty-nine, for about a week in October. With one weekend left to play, Ossie Vitt (the Salt Lake manager) moved Tony into the leadoff position to give him a few more swings with fewer distractions. He hit number fifty-nine on Saturday, and that gave him a doubleheader on Sunday (October 18) to set the record. We were all rooting for Tony, one of the nicest guys who ever lived, and I think Sacramento (Salt Lake's opponent) wanted Tony to get the record, too.

"In the first game of the doubleheader, Tony hit the ball hard a few times and popped sky-high twice and finished with a double in five at-bats.

"In the second game, Tony was 0-for-3 when he came up in the seventh and connected for a hard line drive to the gap in left center. Sacramento's left and right fielders were playing Lazzeri right on the foul lines to give him huge gaps in the outfield. The hit, a legitimate double, bounced to the wall, and outfielder Merlin Kopp picked it up and fired a rainbow (a high-arc throw) to the cutoff man and Tony had an inside-the-park homer. Tainted? Yes. But Tony probably hit fifty-seven or fifty-eight legitimate homers that year and how many 'gimmees' did Babe have? Tainted or not, he got the record and I was proud for him."

Dick Bartell
Pittsburgh Pirates, shortstop
1927-1943 1946

Richard Bartell was a scrappy, 5'9", 160-pound shortstop from Chicago, who got the well-deserved nom de guerre "Rowdy Richard" Bartell for his aggressiveness and his fistfights with teammates, opponents and umpires throughout his eighteen-year career. He was well-traveled—six teams—largely due to his demeanor, which wore thin with his employers, but none denied his ability with the glove; he was exceptional. And his intensity was unquestioned as he led three teams to World Series appearances. Rival infielder Tony Cuccinello said of Bartell: "He was the absolute toughest . . . he enjoyed the contact out there. No one ever took me out as hard at second base (on a double play) as Dick Bartell. He almost broke my legs out there and made me feel as if I had all my bones broken. He could play."

Illustrating Bartell's approach to the game, he told of two near-the-bag confrontations. "Dizzy Dean broke me up hard in 1932; he decked me. The next time he slid in, he did so with his hand stretched out, so I stepped on it. He never came close to me again, but he used to throw at me all the time—I led the world in getting hit by the pitcher. And Arky Vaughn used to take four steps to line you up and then knock you down when you pivoted at the bag. In 1942, when I was with the Giants and he was with the Dodgers, he lined me up and I lined him up and threw the ball right between his eyes. He never bothered me again."

Bartell hit better than .300 six times and was a tough out, whiffing only 627 times in 2,016 games, covering 7,629 at-bats. He appeared in baseball's first All-Star game in 1933.

A long-time Bay area resident, he was recently inducted into the San Francisco Hall of Fame.

Bartell could have told the story of his four-double game for the Phillies against the Boston Braves on April 25, 1933, but he preferred to talk about the kindness of a superstar and advice that saved his career.

March 25, 1927

"I signed my contract with the Pirates," Bartell relates, "and as I was still a teenager, I had my Dad with me when I arrived in Paso Robles, California. The first thing I saw when I put on my practice uniform and trotted out to the infield to take a few ground balls was six infielders hanging around second and short. I trotted out there, but it was a veterans' convention, and they wouldn't let me take any practice — the field was theirs. The big six were Glenn Wright, Pie Traynor, Johnny Rawlings, George Grantham and even Joe Cronin and Hal Rhyne, who had paid their dues as rookies in 1926.

"I called my Dad and said, 'Get me outta here.' Pirates executive Joe Devine heard the conversation, called me into his room and chewed me out for being a baby and making waves. Then Donie Bush (Pirates manager) called me into his office, and he chewed me out. So I took the field feeling as low as I could get.

"We were playing a spring training game against the Yankees and I guess Babe Ruth was watching me try to get my grounders at short and second and getting pushed around by the vets. I looked at him; he waved a finger at me and called me over. Here's a nineteen-year-old being called over by the greatest player in baseball.

"I went over to him and stuttered, 'D-d-do you want me, Mr. Ruth?'

"He just smiled and looked at me and said, 'I know you're a rookie and the old guys are giving you a hard time. Put up with it. Work hard and don't worry about other guys. Don't say too much and just let your play do the talking. I've watched you, kid, and I think you're gonna make it big in the Big Leagues. Just be careful and let those old guys do what they want. Soon it'll be your turn.'

"I never forgot the advice and whenever I was down or in a slump or was mistreated by other ballplayers or owners, Babe's advice kept me going and kept me in baseball. I never would have had an eigh-

teen-year career without that advice. When I saw him at the first
All-Star game in 1933 (July 6) in Chicago, even though I was playing
for the National League and he was with the American League, after
the game (which he won with a home run, 4-2), I went over and
congratulated him. He remembered the earlier incident, gave me a
broad laugh and a hearty slap on the back and said, 'See what I told
ya? Ya made me right.' That was the most pleased I have ever been."

Bernie DeViveiros
Detroit Tigers, shortstop
1924 1927

Bernie DeViveiros, a 5'7", 160-pound pepper pot from Oakland only
made it to the Majors for two years and twenty-five games, but he
had a storied career in the minors — seven years with Beaumont of
the Texas League, with whom he invented "the bent-leg slide," a
maneuver he has taught to countless Major Leaguers over the years.
In the Majors he was largely a fill-in, playing behind Charlie Gehringer (second base), Jack Warner (third base), Jackie Tavener
(shortstop) and Marty McManus (utility infielder) for Detroit manager George Moriarty. But the baseball world is braced on the back-
bones of the Bernie DeViveiroses who played out their dream and
got to play in "the Show," regardless of the length of service.

May, 1927

DeViveiros recalls, "I hadn't been in a game because Charlie (Gehringer), Jackie Tavener and (Marty) McManus were playing well and
getting all the playing time. We were in Philadelphia to play the A's
and they had Ty Cobb in center field and Mickey Cochrane catching.
Their pitcher was Lefty Walberg, who had a good curve.

"In the ninth, we were tied at 5-5 with McManus at third base
and one out and Rip Collins, our pitcher, knew he'd be pinch hit
for. Everyone on our bench had been used up but me, and George
(Moriarty) looked up and down our bench three times looking for a
pinch hitter.

"Collins said, 'Hey, George, Bernie can hit this guy.' So Moriarty
walks over to me and softly says, 'OK, go hit.' Then he gave me
advice and the signals.

"Moriarty said, 'Listen. If I rub my left shoulder hard, it's a squeeze
play. Now go grab three bats and look like a hitter.'

"I'm up at the plate and the first pitch curves inside and almost
hits me in the belly. I dart back and take the pitch and the umpire

yells, 'Strike.' I looked at the guy, but I took it silently.

"On the next pitch, I talk to myself to force a swing and I swung at a chin-high fastball and missed it to bring the count to 0-2.

"I look and there's McManus dancing off third. I look over at George and he's really rubbing his shoulder hard. I give him the sign back so he knows I've got it.

"A's catcher, Mickey Cochrane must have known what was up because he called for a pitch-out, high and outside. I jumped a foot in the air with my bat up and bunted down the first base line between first and home. A's first baseman Jimmy Dykes charges in hard and runs past the ball. It won the game as McManus scored.

"When I get back in the dugout, Moriarty said, 'Kid, you sure got the guts.' I looked up at him and said, 'George, it was an order.'

"And, by the way, it was a base hit. The ball just laid on the field after the game; no one picked it up."

Bob Feller
Cleveland Indians, pitcher
1936-1941 1945-1956

First of all, what is a pitcher who began his career in 1936 doing in the 1920s? His story is a Roaring Twenties tale that speaks of kids, baseball, heroes and picking up some spare change.

"Rapid Robert" Feller was arguably the best fastball pitcher of his era. To hear him tell it, he was the best ever, superseding Walter Johnson and certainly Nolan Ryan, of whom Feller says, "We can't be compared; he's walked twice what I walked (1,764 for Feller in 3,827 innings to more than 2,800 for Ryan in more than 5,400 innings) and he gave up more gopher balls (baseball jargon for home runs thrown by a pitcher) than I."

The six-foot, 190-pound fireballer from Van Meter, Iowa, led the AL in wins six times, in ERA once, in innings pitched five times — once he threw 371 innings (1946) — strikeouts seven times and walks four times.

Known for his fastball of nearly 100 mph, he relied on his sharp-breaking slider and soft curve to garner most of his Ks (strikeouts). While also known for his propensity to make a buck doing whatever he could, from barnstorming to endorsing products and memorabilia to charging for his interviews, he was one of the first modern ballplayer-businessmen (he signed his first contract for a bonus of one dollar and a baseball). Feller pitched three no-hitters and set the Major

League record for strikeouts in a season (348 in 1946) before being bested by Sandy Koufax and Nolan Ryan.

He had his uniform number retired by the Indians and was enshrined in the Hall of Fame in 1962.

Feller's story is directly related to his ability to make a buck, particularly during the hard times in the Midwest just prior to the Depression. Feller also appears in the next chapter with a quick pick from the 1930s.

October 28, 1928

Feller paints the nugget: "I was nine years old, and Babe Ruth and Lou Gehrig were playing a barnstorming tour across country—the Larrupin' Lous versus the Bustin' Babes. They came through the Midwest and played a game at Des Moines in West League Park. They were selling balls for five dollars—the money went to Mercy Hospital—that were autographed by Babe and Lou, who would hit for ten minutes off batting practice pitchers, then sign balls. Babe and Lou led off each inning so they could each get nine chances to hit home runs. I still have the ball, written in fountain pen, and can still read their autographs. It was exciting and I knew then that's what I wanted to do. It also taught me how to market myself, years before the players of today sell everything at card shows and on home shopping television. Babe and Lou did it first, and that's what taught me to be a baseball businessman.

"I used to earn money by taking my dad's Dodge truck to the alfalfa fields where I got a bounty of ten cents for gopher claws. I'd trap a gopher in a gunny sack and tie it to the exhaust pipe and gas 'em. One day I caught fifty of them and killed them. I went out and bought a new baseball with the proceeds, and that was my first gopher ball."

1930s

May 21-24, 1930 to August 20, 1939

The first date above deals with the story by Jimmy Reese about his friend and roommate, Babe Ruth, while the last one is a tale about Bob Feller kidding with the umpire.

The 1930s saw the game soar; it was the heart of Baseball's Golden Age. Baseball's first All-Star game was played, and batting averages and home run totals soared. Babe Ruth passed the baton to Lou Gehrig, who passed it to Joe DiMaggio. Bill Dickey and Mickey Cochrane battled as the top catchers. Was Jimmie Foxx or Lou Gehrig supreme at first? Or was Hank Greenberg, Hal Trosky or Zeke Bonura the best first-sacker? Charlie Gehringer, Luke Appling, Ducky Medwick, Rudy York, Johnny Mize, Mel Ott and Enos Slaughter all dominated their positions, and the 1930s saw the beginning of the storied careers of Joe DiMaggio and Ted Williams.

Walter Johnson, Urban Shocker, Dolph Luque and Grover Alexander passed the resin bag to Carl Hubbell, Lefty Grove, Dizzy Dean, Bob Feller, Johnny Vander Meer and Lefty Gomez, and it seemed as though every team, from the haves (Cardinals, Cubs, Giants, Yankees, A's, Senators and Tigers) to the have-nots (Redlegs, Braves, Phillies, Red Sox and Browns) all had their heroes, genuine superstars who brought pride to their communities, their uniforms and the game.

Selected decade highlights
(in addition to those told in this chapter)

May 22, 1930 - As the Yankees bomb Philadelphia, 20-13, Lou Gehrig blasts three homers, and Babe Ruth, who hit three the day before, and one in the first game of this twin-bill day, belted two more in this one. **Note:** If this scenario looks familiar, read back to September 27, 1927.

June 23, 1930 - As the Cubs demolish the Phillies, 21-8, with the wind blowing out at Wrigley Field, Hack Wilson hits for the cycle and gets his fifth hit, a second single along with six "ribbies."

July 23, 1930 - Pittsburgh Pirates third-sacker Pie Traynor hits two game-winning homers as the Bucs sweep the Phils. His ninth-inning homer sinks Philly, 2-1, in the opener and his thirteenth-inning homer wins the finale, 16-15.

July 27, 1930 - Redleg reliever Ken Ash throws one pitch and gets a win. His throw to Cubs hitter Charlie Grimm is bounced into a triple play. Ash is then removed for a pinch hitter and his club wins, 6-5, for Ash's last Major League victory.

August 31, 1930 - Mel Ott bombs three consecutive homers in a 14-10 loss to the Boston Braves at the Polo Grounds.

September 17, 1930 - Cleveland outfielder Earl Averill slugs three consecutive homers and his fourth is ruled foul on a bad call by the umpire. He leads off the second game of this doubleheader with another homer.

April 2, 1931 - In an exhibition game in Chattanooga, Jackie Mitchell, a seventeen-year-old female with a great curve, "strikes out" Babe Ruth and Lou Gehrig (though many say they tanked it for her) and walks Tony Lazzeri before she departs. The Yanks bomb the Lookouts, 14-4, and Mitchell's minor league contract is voided by an all-male hierarchy, though she surfaces two years later, throwing for the House of David barnstorming team.

August 21, 1931 - Babe Ruth poles his six-hundredth homer, this one off St. Louis Browns pitcher George Blaeholder. Lou Gehrig follows with a shot of his own in an 11-7 Yankee victory.

September 1, 1931 - Lou Gehrig hits his third grand slam in four days (his sixth HR in that span) to lead New York to a 5-1 victory over the BoSox.

September 9, 1931 - The Yankees, Giants and Dodgers agree to a fund-raiser to earn money to donate to the unemployed masses of New York during the Depression. A series of exhibition games between the three teams will raise more than one-hundred thousand dollars for the cause. On this day, sixty thousand fans add fifty-nine thousand dollars to charity coffers and see Babe Ruth homer to lead the Bronx Bombers over the Giants 7-2.

September 19, 1931 - Lefty Grove wins his thirtieth game of the year, beating the ChiSox, 2-1.

May 20, 1932 - On the day Amelia Earhart begins her transatlantic solo flight from Newfoundland to Ireland, Pirate Paul Waner steps up his assault on Chuck Klein's season record for doubles (fifty-nine for the Phillies in 1930) by smacking out four two-baggers. Big Poison finished the season with a record sixty-two.

June 2, 1932 - Lou Gehrig becomes the first player in the Majors to hit four consecutive home runs in a game when he blasts four round-trippers in a 20-13 Yankee victory over the A's. Gehrig misses a fifth homer by a foot, and teammate Tony Lazzeri hits for the cycle.

July 10, 1932 - Philadelphia manager-owner Connie Mack brings his A's to Cleveland on a shoestring. To save train fare, he travels with only fifteen players, only two of whom are pitchers. Needing a reliever in the second, Mack calls on his only available hurler, Eddie Rommel, who pitches the rest of the game — seventeen innings to get the win in eighteen, by an 18-17 count. Rommel gives up a record thirty-three hits.

May 27, 1933 - The White Sox score three runs in the top of the eighth to take an 11-3 lead over the Yankees. In the bottom of the inning, sparked by Bill Dickey's grand slam, the Yanks score twelve runs to take a 15-11 victory.

June 7-8-9, 1933 - Philadelphia's Jimmie Foxx homers in his last at bat on June 7 and follows it up with three homers in his first three at-bats against the Yankees on June 8, for four in a row, as the A's outslug the Yanks 14-10. On the ninth, Foxx hits his fifth homer in three games, but the Yankees win this one, 7-6.

June 29, 1933 - On the day Primo Carnera wins the world heavyweight boxing championship on a sixth-round KO of Jack Sharkey, Ethan Allen of the St. Louis Cards hits an inside-the-park home run against the Giants at the Polo Grounds, but is called out for batting out of order.

July 2, 1933 - New York Giant ace Carl Hubbell throws a complete game shutout that goes eighteen innings. He wins 1-0 on a six-hitter with no walks and twelve Ks over the Cards.

August 2, 1933 - A's catcher Mickey Cochrane hits for the cycle against the Yankees in a 16-3 Philadelphia win. It is the second time Cochrane cycles.

August 14, 1933 - Jimmie Foxx hits for the cycle (one of a record eight Major Leaguers to do it this year) and drives in an AL-record nine runs to lead the A's to an 11-5 victory over Cleveland.

October 1, 1933 - In the season finale, thirty-eight-year-old Babe Ruth pitches for the first time in three years and wins the game, 6-5, over the Red Sox. Ruth throws a complete game and homers for the win.

March 20, 1934 - Female track, tennis and golfing great Babe Didrickson pitches an inning for the Philadelphia A's in an exhibition versus the Brooklyn Dodgers. She walks one in her otherwise perfect outing. Like Jackie Mitchell before her, Didrickson joins the barnstorming House of David for several games.

April 21, 1934 - Washington Senator, Moe Berg, a shortstop who taught himself to catch when his team needed a fill-in, sets an AL record by catching in his 117th consecutive errorless game. Berg, a brilliant and enigmatic scholar-athlete who spoke twelve languages, later became an OSS agent (forerunner to the CIA) and was used by the U.S. government during World War II by parachuting him behind enemy lines to kidnap atomic scientists and bring them back to America.

June 6, 1934 - Yankee Myril Hoag goes 6-for-6 with six singles as the Bombers crush the BoSox, 15-3.

July 4, 1934 - Satchel Paige fashions a 4-0 no-hitter versus the Homestead Grays of the Negro National League in Pittsburgh. As soon as the last out is made, he jumps into his jalopy, drives to Chicago, and shuts out the Chicago American Giants, 1-0, in twelve innings.

September 30, 1934 - Dizzy Dean clinches the NL flag for the Cardinals with a 9-0 whitewash of the Cincinnati Reds. The win was Ol' Diz's thirtieth of the year.

April 16, 1935 - In Babe Ruth's National League debut, the forty-year-old slugger singles and homers off Carl Hubbell to lead his Boston Braves to a 4-2 win over the Giants.

May 8, 1935 - Cincy catcher Ernie Lombardi doubles in four consecutive innings — sixth, seventh, eighth and ninth — off four different pitchers. He also hits a single that could have been a double if he had tried to go for two. Reds beat the Phils, 15-4.

May 25, 1935 - Babe Ruth, who will end his career on a groundout six days later, hits three homers and a single against the Pirates in Pittsburgh, as his Braves lose, 11-7. Ruth hits one against Red Lucas and two off Guy Bush. His last one, number 714 of his career, is the first blast to go out of Forbes Field, traveling an estimated six hundred feet.

August 14, 1935 - Detroit ace Schoolboy Rowe beats Washington, 18-2, and goes 5-for-5 at bat with a double, triple and three "ribbies."

May 3, 1936 - Joe DiMaggio makes his debut in pinstripes and gets three hits in the Yankees' 14-5 shellacking of the Browns.

May 24, 1936 - Yankees second baseman Tony "Poosh 'em up" Lazzeri hits three homers—two of them grand slams—and a triple, and drives in an AL-record eleven runs in a 25-2 whipping of the A's at Shibe Park.

September 13, 1936 - Seventeen-year-old Bob Feller of the Indians, sets an AL record with seventeen strikeouts as he bests the A's, 5-2, tossing a two-hitter in the process.

September 29, 1936 - Walter Alston, later a Dodger manager for nearly two decades, plays in his only Major League game as he subs for Cardinal first-sacker Johnny Mize late in the game. Alston makes one error in two chances and is fanned in his only at bat.

May 27, 1937 - "King" Carl Hubbell, "The Meal Ticket," wins his twenty-fourth game in a row, this one in relief, hurling twelve innings to beat Cincinnati, 3-2, on a ninth-inning homer by Mel Ott to extend the streak he began July 17, 1936.

September 19, 1937 - Tiger slugger Hank Greenberg does something Ruth, Gehrig, DiMaggio and Lazzeri were unable to do up to now, as he hits the first home run ever blasted into the center field stands at Yankee Stadium.

June 7, 1938 - Cleveland pitcher Johnny Allen is told by umpire Bill McGowan to cut the tattered sleeves off his undershirt, as he is distracting the hitters. He leaves the mound and doesn't return. He is fined $250, his shirt goes to the Hall of Fame, he gets $2,000 from a tailor to model his shirts and the Red Sox win the game.

June 21, 1938 - Boston third sacker Pinky Higgins goes 8-for-8 in a doubleheader against Detroit to set the Major League mark for consecutive hits with twelve.

June 22, 1938 - On the day heavyweight boxing champion Joe Louis knocks out Max Schmeling in the first round at Yankee Stadium, Chicago White Sox reserve outfielder Hank Steinbacher goes 6-for-6 as the ChiSox romp over the Senators, 16-3. And what Pinky Higgins doesn't do makes history. The Red Sox third baseman strikes out against Detroit's Vern Kennedy to end Higgins's consecutive hit streak at a record twelve hits in a row.

July 27, 1938 - Hank Greenberg, who hit two homers in his last two at-bats yesterday, bombs two more in his first two at-bats for the Tigers in this game for the Tigers, for four in a row.

September 29, 1938 - Gabby Hartnett hits his famous "Homer in the Gloamin" off Mace Brown, Pirates pitcher, to break a 5-5 tie and get the win for the Cubbies en route to their ninth straight win, a key to their pennant.

April 23, 1939 - The Boston Red Sox's rookie outfielder, Ted Williams, goes 4-for-5 and blasts his first home run, but the BoSox lose to the A's at Fenway, 12-8

May 2, 1939 - The news today was what didn't happen; Lou Gehrig doesn't play in a game against the Tigers at Briggs Stadium, ending his consecutive games played streak at 2,130 games. He never played in another game. The Yankees, adrenalin flowing over the importance of the event, destroy the Tigers, 22-2, with Babe Dahlgren at first base.

June 28, 1939 - The Yankees bomb thirteen home runs in a double-header against the A's (eight in the first game) as they sweep, 23-2 and 10-0, with 53 total bases. Joe DiMaggio, Babe Dahlgren and Joe Gordon each belt three homers.

The Chronicles

Jimmy Reese
New York Yankees, second base
1930-1932

Though Jimmy Reese, a 5'11", 160-pound, scrappy second-sacker from New York City only played three years in "the Bigs" — 232 games, .278 average, 8 homers — he was and is an important part of the game, as his career (including a decade in the minors) has spanned nine decades, from his days as a batboy for the Los Angeles Angels of the Pacific Coast League to his current coaching assignment in Anaheim for the California Angels. Backing up such stalwart heroes as Tony Lazzeri, Ben Chapman and Frankie Frisch, Reese has fond memories of those fun days and the sharp wit and honed sense of humor to keep them alive (his favorite Lou Gehrig story: "Lou would come up after a game and say, 'Jimmy, let's get really wild tonight and go crazy . . . let's go to a bar and each have a beer' ").

Well into his nineties, Jimmy Reese is still on the field, for the California Angels, as conditioning coach and fungo hitter, and it has often been said that he has hit more fungoes than any man in history and he can still hit a dime a hundred feet away with a fungoed ball. One of the "nice guys" in the game, what has gotten Reese notoriety is his friendship with his former roommate, Babe Ruth, and his keen eye for baseball talent. Reese cherishes Ruth's memory and says, "He

43

wasn't a choirboy, but he was the nicest man in the world—the fiercest competitor, but the nicest man. And, after seventy-five years in baseball I can say that no one approaches Babe Ruth as the best player, the absolute best I have ever seen." Reese has chosen to share his favorite Babe Ruth story as well as one about an enigmatic opponent.

May 21-24, 1930

"I roomed with Babe Ruth in 1930. Actually, I roomed with his luggage because Babe was hardly ever in the room, unless it was to enjoy a woman or to come in to change his shirt. Babe used to light up a 'victory cigar' after every successful coupling; one time I went down to pick up a paper and have breakfast, and when I came back a few hours later, Babe, with a girl in his bed, was crushing out his seventh stogie. And Babe would do everything to excess—play, laugh, gamble, work, eat. Whenever he and I would go to lunch together, he'd let me order first and then whatever I would order, he'd order and eat twice as much.

"Anyway, we were in the middle of the 1930 season and before the first game of a doubleheader against the first-place A's. I was dressing next to Babe in the locker room and stepped in front of him to get to the field. Babe bellowed mockingly, 'Hey, rook. No one steps in front of me when I go out to the field. That's bad luck. For that, you'll have to go into my locker.' I didn't know what to expect, and Babe picked me up like I was a piece of straw and placed me in his locker. Well, Babe goes out and hits three homers in the first game and another one in the second game.

"The next day, we had another doubleheader against Philadelphia. Before the game, Babe looks at me and says, 'Hey, rook, yesterday was lucky, so I gotta put you in my locker again.' Again Babe hoisted me up like I was a leaf, put me in his locker and we swept both games and Babe hits two homers in each game.

"Now, I'm thinking that I'll be Babe Ruth's locker ornament for the rest of my career, and when Babe puts me in his locker for another doubleheader on May 24 and he hits homers in both games (giving him nine in the few days since he started the practice), I guess I gave him a hangdog look and he waved this big hand at me and says, 'That's all Reese, you're through. I'll get the rest of them (homers) on my own.'"

June, 1930

Though his ballplaying name was Jimmy Reese, and most everyone thought of him as just another "Irish ballplayer," he was born James

Harrison Solomon. Jimmy was brought up Jewish, in a Jewish house-hold, and he understood Yiddish very well. In this game, the Yankees were playing the White Sox, and Moe Berg was behind the plate, catching Dutch Henry. Jimmy remembers: "Moe Berg was really something. He was a great defensive catcher; he was probably the most intelligent guy to play the game. He spoke twelve languages, worked for the OSS in World War II and went behind enemy lines to kidnap Germany's top rocket scientists.

"He also had a great sense of humor. One day I got into a game and he thought I was Irish (and probably knew I only had two home runs and couldn't hit the ball too far). He starts yelling at Dutch Henry in Yiddish, figuring I wouldn't understand him. He tells Henry, in Yiddish, 'Throw this rookie a curve; he won't know what to do with it.' I look down at him and he smiles and then I look at Henry and watch him throw me a curve. I swing hard, hit it, and it barely goes over the fence for a home run. I round the bases and, as I cross homeplate, I look at Berg and tell him in Yiddish, 'Thanks for the curve ball.' He never spoke Yiddish near me again."

Milt Gaston
New York Yankees, pitcher
1924-1934

Milt Gaston was a pitcher with a wicked forkball (see 1920s chapter) who finished his career with the Red Sox and White Sox. He recalls a story from his BoSox days about a good-hit, no-field opponent.

June, 1930

"I was with the Red Sox from 1929 to 1931, and one of my teammates was an outfielder named Russ Scarritt, a good fielder, fair hitter and a great guy. We were playing Chicago one day and there was a great-hitting but lousy-fielding outfielder named Smead Jolley who could hit in his sleep (but looked like he fielded in his sleep, too). After Jolley misplayed a ball at Fenway Park, Scarritt, the opposing out-fielder, came over to Jolley and took the time to show him how to play the unlevel outfield ramp. Scarritt showed Jolley that you don't start straight up the bank—you go up at an angle. During the game, Jolley did what Scarritt showed him. He went up the ramp at an angle, caught a ball, and fell head over heels. Later he scolded Scarritt, 'You showed me how to go up the ramp but not how to come down.'

"There's a story that Jolley once made three errors on a single

Milt Gaston, pitcher, 1930s
Courtesy: National Baseball Library Hall of Fame, Cooperstown, New York

play: The batted ball to the outfield went through his legs (1); rebounded off the wall and as Jolley turned, it went through his legs again (2); and then he picked it up and threw it away (3). I don't know if it's true, but if it could have happened to anyone, Jolley's the guy. But man, could he hit. He'd be today's greatest DH."

Billy Herman
Chicago Cubs, second base
1931-1943 1946-1947

William Jennings Bryan Herman was a 5'11", 180-pound keystone-sacker out of New Albany, Indiana.

Herman was regarded by many as the supreme second baseman in the league from the mid-thirties to the mid-forties; he was a ten-time all-star during that period and led the league in fielding three times.

Herman led the league in hits (with 227) and in doubles (with 57) in 1935. In 1,922 games over fifteen years, Herman hit .304 with 486 two-baggers, and illustrating his skill (as a contact hitter) whiffed only 428 times in 7,707 at-bats. Leo Durocher once said of Herman, a master at the hit-and-run due to his contact hitting, "He's an absolute master at hitting behind the runner."

He was enshrined in the Hall of Fame in 1975.

Herman came from the old school of baseball. He played the game hard and expected it to be played hard against him. He said, "There wasn't much comedy then. We were serious; no wisecracks. We wouldn't look at or talk to anybody on the other team. It was all part of the game—tough. You ran out to center field; you slid in hard. The hardest guy who ever slid into me was Hack Wilson. He wasn't fast; he was a late slider, stocky and heavy and hard. I'm glad he wasn't fast, so I could avoid him."

Herman chose to add a tale about how the game was played, and a pitcher who didn't like rookies.

August, 1931

Herman recalls, "I came up in August for the Cubs, and we were playing in Chicago against Cincinnati. My first time up, I was facing Si Johnson, a tough, hard-thrower who didn't like rookies. My first at-bat I drove a single through the box. My next time up, he came right at me; I mean right at me. He threw a high fastball at my ear. BAM. I went down and they carried me off the field, unconscious. I played the next day, but didn't get any hits.

"Three days later, we were playing the Reds again, in Cincinnati, and I faced Johnson again and went 3-for-3 against him. He came in close on each at-bat but I guess I earned his respect by taking one in the ear, so he didn't hit me ... that day. He hit me later on, though."

Frankie Crosetti
New York Yankees, shortstop
1932-1948

Frank Crosetti, "The Crow," from San Francisco, was a 5'10", 165-pound Yankee shortstop from the Babe Ruth years to the Joe DiMaggio years, and stayed with the Yanks as a third-base coach through the Mickey Mantle years. He was a quick, steady infielder who played in seven World Series and he's seen many greats come and go, but as far as he's concerned, there's only one player deserving of retired number status: Babe Ruth.

"Babe did more for the game than anyone, ever. The game was crooked in 1920 and he single-handedly saved it. Only one number should be retired and no one should ever wear it for any team, Babe's number "3." Babe made people forget about the scandal, and he made us proud to wear the uniform. Man, I was fortunate to be able to put on a uniform every day, and being around Babe and Gehrig and Lazzeri and DiMaggio made a player proud. We didn't make a farce out of the game; we went about our business. We didn't fool around. Manager Joe McCarthy wouldn't stand for it. We played a prank or two, but once the game started, it was all business."

Crosetti kept that as a theme as he offered insights into a prank and into a baseball legend that has become part of baseball folklore.

June, 1932

First, the prank. Crosetti recalled, "In those days we loved pranks, and I remember one that Tony Lazzeri pulled on Babe Ruth. Babe had a superstition; he would always use this eyewash — it was called *Eye-Lo* — before every game. He'd set it on the bench and before his first at-bat, he'd wash his eyes out. Usually, he'd lose track of it and part of his ritual was to say, 'Where's the *Eye-Lo*,' and someone would give it to him. Well, one day, Lazzeri took the bottle, dumped it out, and filled it with water. Babe sees Lazzeri with the bottle and says, 'Gimmee.' Lazzeri says, 'No, gimmee,' and proceeds to drink it. Babe is astonished. He says, 'Don't do that, it'll kill ya. Let me get you to the hospital.' But before he does anything, he goes for the *Eye-Lo*

Frankie Crosetti, shortstop, 1930s
Courtesy: National Baseball Library Hall of Fame, Cooperstown, New York

and washes his eyes out; he'd never vary that routine."

October 1, 1932

Next, the legend and the folklore. The 1932 World Series moved to Chicago, and Babe Ruth and the Yankees had a score to settle with the Cubs, even though the Yanks already had a two-games-to-none lead in the Fall Classic. Crosetti is clear on this historic moment.

"We were glad to be sticking it to the Cubs. We won the first two games in New York and they were easy wins (12-6 and 5-2) and the town of Chicago hated us; after our fourth-game sweep, we went to our hotel on the bus and needed a police escort. We felt we had several scores to settle and we wanted to embarrass them. They had fired Joe McCarthy a year before, even though he was twenty-two games over .500, and we were lucky enough to get him as our manager for 1932. And because of the Mark Koenig thing. Koenig was a good shortstop with the Yanks for six years before I got there and wound up with the Cubs in August of 1932 and was pretty much responsible for them winning the pennant with a great stretch-drive performance. Yet those cheap Cub players only voted him a half-share of World Series bonus money and we Yankees felt a nice guy like Mark deserved better. We called them tightwads and scrooges. We hated that town and the team so much that we decided, as a team, to sing "The Sidewalks of New York," as loud as we could, on our way to the train station. We whipped that town into a frenzy. It was great.

"Well, it was the fifth inning and we're tied at 4-4 and Babe's up. He'd already hit one home run and while he's up, the Cubs in the dugout are really razzing Babe. And in our dugout, we're really giving it back to the Cubs. Babe takes two strikes, both low and on the outside part of the plate and raises one finger—he was sayin' 'I got one strike left' or 'lay one in I can hit.'

"Well, Charlie Root pipes one down the middle, as if to meet Babe's challenge and Babe crushes it into center field for a home run, and that quieted the Cubs' dugout. Never once in the dugout or even after the game until the writers asked him about his 'pointing,' did Babe ever say he pointed. I think he was theatrical and made up the story they wanted to hear, after they had already given him the details, just to have fun with them.

"After being grilled by the writers before game four about his pointing into the stands, Babe sat down next to me and winked. He said, 'You know I didn't point and I know I didn't point, but if those bastards (writers) want to think I pointed to center field, let 'em.' "

Mark Koenig
Chicago Cubs, shortstop
1925-1936

Mark Koenig was a steady, six-foot, 180-pound, shortstop from San Francisco who became part of the 1932 controversy. Coming back from a demotion to the minors, he was acquired by Chicago in August, and hit .353 in thirty-three games for the Cubs in 1932, but was only voted a half-share of the World Series players' receipts by his teammates. Koenig said, "I was disappointed but the Cub players were like that. Hey, they didn't vote Rogers Hornsby (who was fired during the season after going 53-46) any money at all." Keonig was also part of "Murderers' Row," the shortstop of the 1927 Yankees. Of his teammate Babe Ruth, he once commented: "He was just a big kid at heart. I don't think he ever read any books and was not worldly. He didn't know the difference between Cock Robin and Robin Hood. He was just interested in girls, drinking, eating and hitting home runs." Koenig could have told about April 12, 1927, when he went 5-for-5 against Lefty Grove in the season opener before sixty-five thousand fans, but Koenig chose to illuminate us on the "called shot" of the 1932 World Series, giving us perspective by a former teammate from the other dugout.

October 1, 1932

"My heart was still with the Yankees," Koenig said. "Those were my buddies over there, but I was a member of the Cubs and wanted us to win. And the Yanks were embarrassing us in the Series. Still, my Cub teammates were pretty loud, especially in those days, for a team that was down two games to none. The guys were on Babe pretty hard. They were sayin 'oonya oonya.' He had already homered in the first, and Gehrig homered after we got Babe out in the third.

"In the fifth, we're tied 4-4 and Charlie Root is working Babe outside and low. He gets two strikes on Babe, and Babe steps out of the box. He moves back in and the bench jockeying got louder, calling him some names that are unprintable. Babe stood in the batter's box and swept his hand as if to say, 'Lay it in here'—across the center of the plate—or 'it only takes one.' Catcher Gabby Hartnett crouched down and gave the sign, and Babe swept his hand again as Charlie Root delivered. Babe lifted his front leg, stepped into it and swung hard, and pounded it into the center field bleachers for a home run.

"We never thought he pointed; it was more like, 'it only takes one.' But if we ever thought he pointed, he would have been thrown at. Even the pitcher, Charlie Root, told me, 'If that big monkey was pointing into the stands, I would have stuck the next pitch in his ear.' The fact that Root didn't throw at him proves Babe didn't point, but it was still a heck of a shot. And what people forget is that Lou Gehrig followed it up with his second homer of the game, and that one proved to be the game-winner."

Woody English
Chicago Cubs, third base
1927-1938

Woody English, the Fredonia, Ohio native, was a 5'10", 155-pound infielder (more shortstop than third, but he played third base in the game in question) who was a gamer. The Cubs captain, he was regarded as a tough out and a team leader. He was also a clean-cut athlete who didn't drink or stay out past curfew. He was chosen to play in baseball's first All-Star game in 1933. A man respected by his friends and foes alike for being "too nice," he is reported to have said to himself, as he was sent up to pinch hit in the eighth inning of Johnny Vander Meer's second no-hitter June 15, 1938, "I'm not going to go up there and spoil this guy's second no-hitter." He struck out. English wanted to set the record straight on Babe Ruth's "called shot." Here is a third perspective, this one from the opposing third baseman.

October 1, 1932

English begins by giving the inside skinny on the Koenig money vote: "First of all, on the Koenig money issue, it was all fair. He did a great job for us, but only played thirty-three games and joined us August 17 after we had already been playing for four-and-a-half months with only one-and-a-half months to go. On that basis alone, we gave him a half-share. It could have been a quarter-share, but we didn't want to go that low.

"Second, Ruth was up and I peered at him from third base. He was staring right at our guys in the dugout and boy, they were calling him every name in the book. I saw him hold up two fingers, meaning 'That's only two.' He did not call his shot. He was looking at our guys and his hand crossed the plate on his way back to his bat. Then he hit the ball very hard and, although I'm sure he was trying to hit a home run, he never 'called' it."

Ethan Allen
Philadelphia Phillies, outfield
1926-1938

Ethan Allen was a 6'1", 180-pound outfielder from Cincinnati, who began his career for his hometown team. He hit well (.300 career average in 1,281 games) and if he had more power (forty-seven career homers) might have been one of the big stars in the game. He was a good fielder, and his knowledge of the game was second to none.

Perhaps Allen's biggest claims to fame occurred off the Major League diamond. He coached Yale University's baseball team from 1946 to 1968. Among his players was the Yalie captain, first baseman George "Poppy" Bush, who later became President of the United States. Allen says of Bush's skills, "He was an excellent defensive player and he really worked hard at his hitting. In fact, he was nearly signed by scouts one day after he got three hits against North Carolina State, and in the NCAA eastern regional game (June 20, 1947), Bush singled, stole second, and keyed a rally that helped us beat Clemson 7-3."

Another claim to fame is Allen's baseball spinner game, the first of its kind, "All-Star Baseball," which he created and sold in 1941. The game uses scientific stats based on a player's career record and the element of chance — the spinner (one spin for offense and one for defense).

Allen's nuggets are quick hits about some of the game's heavyweights.

March, 1933

"I was playing for St. Louis and during spring training in St. Petersburg I was rooming with Dizzy Dean. He was seldom in the room as he always had a date or a party to go to. We had a big room — because of Diz — and it had a regular bathtub in it so we didn't have to go down the hall and use the public tub.

"After a practice game one day, I was taking a bath and, just as I was finishing up, Diz stuck his head in the room and said, 'Don't pull the plug, I have a date . . . and he jumped right in."

July 4, 1934

"I was playing for the Philadelphia Phillies that year and this hot July day the Phillies were tattooing that old tin wall at the Baker Bowl, which made a '*PING*' sound whenever a ball hit it.

"Walter 'Boom-Boom' Beck was pitching for the Brooklyn Dodgers that day and he didn't have anything. We were all over him. So Casey Stengel walks out to the mound to take Beck out. Meanwhile, Hack Wilson, who was nursing a hangover that day, was standing in the outfield with his hands on his knees, watching the sweat roll off his forehead and onto the ground. He wasn't paying any attention to Casey and Beck.

"Casey asks for the ball, and Beck fumed. He turned and fired the ball at the fence — 250 feet away — right over the head of Wilson.

The ball went 'PING' off the wall. Wilson turned, yelled a cuss word and probably thought someone had hit the ball past him when he wasn't paying attention. He whirled, picked up the ball and fired a perfect strike to second base. When he figured out what happened, he chased Beck out of the ballpark and into the street."

May 30, 1935

"I was playing against Babe Ruth and the Boston Braves at the Baker Bowl. I had played against Babe a few times in exhibitions and saw he was a tremendous hitter and a better all-around athlete than people thought. Five days earlier at Pittsburgh, Babe had hit three homers in a game and we all thought Babe could hit them anytime he wanted.

"I saw him that day and he looked old, and fat, but we still thought he was so great he could still play.

"It was the first game of a doubleheader and when Babe went down in the first inning—Jim Bivin got him on a grounder—he continued walking and went right to the clubhouse, which was in center field. He walked right by me and off the field. He looked dejected, ready to give up. He smiled at me and then tilted his head to one side as if to say, 'that's it.' He retired right then and there."

Monte Weaver
Washington Senators, pitcher
1931-1939

The six-foot, 170-pound lefty from Helton, North Carolina, deserved the nickname "Prof" for his earning of a master's degree in mathematics. He had a great fastball and went 22-10 as a rookie until his education got the better of him and, learning about vegetarian diets, went health-food crazy, lost twenty pounds and his fastball, and struggled until he found beefsteak again.

Weaver, who became a college professor following his playing days, remembered baseball kindness. "On my first day in the Majors (1931), I had been purchased from Baltimore of the International League and joined the Senators. I went to the outfield to shag flies and manager Walter Johnson came up to me and said, 'If you pitch here like you did in Baltimore, you'll do well.' It made me feel good, but the truth was, I pitched lousy in Baltimore. I also lament the fact that we never won the pennant for Walter. We did win for Joe Cronin, who was a good manager and I'm happy we won for him, but Walter was just the most kindhearted man I ever met. He was quiet and not demonstrative, but there was just an honest kindness about the man and a quiet class that trickled down to the entire team. It's sad that that didn't translate into a pennant — though we did win ninety-two games for him in 1931 and ninety-three in 1932."

Who was the best hitter Weaver ever saw? "I got Babe Ruth in 1932, and he hit me pretty good and deep, though he didn't like my curve ball. I did strike him out the first time I faced him. I also played with Joe Hauser in Baltimore the year (1930) Hauser hit sixty-three homers. That man could really swing."

Weaver's story is of a baserunning blunder.

April 29, 1933

Weaver begins, "We were playing at Yankee Stadium and this was the most unusual play I ever saw. We're ahead 6-3 in the bottom of the eighth and Lou Gehrig's up, and he singles. Dixie Walker follows with a single, with Gehrig stopping at second. Next, Tony Lazzeri really rocks one to the gap in right-center field. Gehrig goes back to second to tag up, because he thinks Goose Goslin is going to catch the ball. The ball drops in and Gehrig and Walker, who's right on his tail, are off to the races. Goslin picks up the ball and fires to Joe Cronin, our shortstop, who wheels and fires to the plate. Luke Sewell, our catcher, takes the throw and tags out both Gehrig and Walker, who are sliding in, *bam-bam*, to the plate. A double play on two tags at the plate. I got the Yanks out in the ninth and we won."

Rick Ferrell
Boston Red Sox, catcher
1929-1947

Rick Ferrell was a 5'10", 160-pound catcher from Durham, North Carolina, who (along with his brother, pitcher Wes Ferrell) played for numerous American League teams from the 1920s to 1940s. An iron man behind the plate, Ferrell caught an AL record 1,806 games while hitting a credible .281, striking out only 277 times in eighteen years while accumulating 931 walks. In a baseball oddity, Rick Ferrell had fewer homers than his brother, Wes Ferrell, a pitcher. Wes hit 38 homers in 1,176 at-bats over 548 games, while Rick managed to clout only 28 homers in 6,028 at-bats over 1,884 games. Ferrell was elected to the Hall of Fame in 1984.

Ferrell was a participant in baseball's first All-Star game, which was held in Chicago in 1933. The significance of the event was not lost on Ferrell.

July 6, 1933

"The first All-Star game was important to me for many reasons. First, because it was the very first one. Second, because here were all these great stars that I would play with one day and against the next. There I was, teammates with Babe Ruth, Lou Gehrig, Lefty Gomez, Lefty Grove, Jimmie Foxx, Al Simmons, Charlie Gehringer, Ben Chapman and Bill Dickey. It was experimental, and we never expected it would last—maybe one year or two and then forget it.

"Another thing that was important was that I caught the entire game, all nine innings, and though I went 0-for-3 and bunted a man over once, we won it, 4-2, on Ruth's homer. It was really quite a great ball game.

"Our manager, Connie Mack, and the National League's John McGraw were great rivals and they each wanted to win that game badly. Mack called a team meeting at our South side hotel, the Del Prado, and he told us, 'You're all great ballplayers, otherwise you wouldn't be here, and you're all used to playing every inning, but some of you may not get in. We came here to win and even if we get a lead, I may not make a lot of changes so some of you ballplayers will not play. We must win today. So be happy to be part of a winner even if you don't play.'

Then Mr. Mack came up to me and said, 'You're my catcher today,' which caught me by surprise because Bill Dickey and Mickey Cochrane were there, too. It gave me great pride then—it still does—to know that I started ahead of them and that I played the very first one and they didn't.

"Mack took Ruth out for defensive purposes late in the game and put in Sammy West. He took out Lou Gehrig, Charlie Gehringer, Joe Cronin and Ben Chapman and he kept me in the entire game while he sat Dickey and Cochrane on the bench. I caught Lefty Gomez for three innings, Al Crowder for three and Lefty Grove finished up—the shadows were crossing homeplate, which is tough on the hitters, so I had him stay with his fastball.

"Frankie Frisch homered in the sixth off Crowder to make it close, but Babe Ruth really rocked the place with his homer in the third off Lon Warneke. When that game was over, man, did we have a big party—the biggest, as big as any World Series celebration, and watching Babe Ruth party is a sight to behold."

July 19, 1933

"In a game that was of little importance except to me and my brother, Wes, I was catching for Boston and were playing Cleveland, who had Wes on the mound. In the second inning, I homered off Wes, and in the third inning, he homered off Hank Johnson. It was the first time in history that brothers homered while playing against each other in the same game. We laughed a lot about that, though Wes was upset that I hit mine off him. He didn't like that at all."

Ben Chapman
New York Yankees, outfield
1930-1941 1944-1946

William Benjamin Chapman, a speedy six-foot, 190-pound outfielder from Alabama (by way of Nashville, Tennessee) spent his life in the South and espoused traditional southern viewpoints. The fleet center fielder was known as much for his quick temper as he was for his quick feet, and was sent packing by the Yankees in 1936 (to Washington) upon the arrival of Joe DiMaggio.

Chapman was the speed on Yankee teams known for the power of Babe Ruth and Lou Gehrig. He began his career as an infielder and was moved to the outfield to utilize his speed. Chapman says, "I could catch anything they hit to me at third base, but all my throws sailed into the seats. They used to say, 'Duck, Chapman's got it again.' So Joe McCarthy moved me to the outfield in 1931." Chapman got his arm under control and led the league in outfield assists in 1933 and 1935.

"McCarthy saw my potential as an outfielder and as a base runner. He was the first manager ever to give me the green light to run whenever I felt like it. But you could never steal if you were up by three or down by three, or you'd get the next pitch thrown at your head."

Chapman was regarded as the fastest man in baseball, and in a promotion, he ran a race against Bill "Bojangles" Robinson at the Polo Grounds. Chapman says, "He was fifty-two years old and he let me beat him. He even ran backwards."

Chapman is also known for two of baseball's negative moments. On May 10, 1934, in a game that saw Lou Gehrig hit two homers and two doubles with seven RBI in five innings, Chapman shouted anti-Semitic remarks at a Jewish fan, baiting the fan for a fight. And in 1947, Chapman led a player revolt in an attempt to keep Jackie Robinson (and all blacks) out of the game. He was one of the most outspoken opponents of Major League integration.

Chapman remained controversial—and opinionated—in retirement.

"I'll never make the Hall of Fame," he says. "Look at my statistics;

I belong there — .302, led the league in steals four times, great fielder, played in the first All-Star game. But I'll never make it. No white man from the South makes it. Yeah, they finally gave it to Enos Slaughter, and Catfish Hunter got there, but very few. And because of the Jackie Robinson thing, they'll never let me in. That's why I'm glad I'm in the Alabama Hall of Fame."

Chapman could have bragged about his two inside-the-park homers for a total of three homers in the game, July 9, 1932, or any number of great days, but he chose to supply a quickie anecdote on that first All-Star game.

July 6, 1933

"We all played in lots of all-star games all the time. It was called barnstorming and we made a lot of money doing it. I played for fifty-four hundred dollars, and I doubled that in a month of barnstorming. So to play in the first All-Star game wasn't very important to us at the time. Most of the players didn't want to play in it, especially since we really didn't make any extra money on it. But as time went on, I became proud of the fact that I was the very first hitter ever in the All-Star game.

"I faced Wild Bill Hallahan, and Mr. (Connie) Mack pitched Lefty Gomez. Mr. Mack just looked at me and said, 'Son, you're here because you're a good ballplayer. Just do what you usually do, and if you get on, maybe we'll run.'

"I didn't get on; I grounded to Ducky Medwick. From then on, I wasn't all that excited, and when Babe (Ruth) hit the first homer, it just seemed like playing for the Yankees. No big deal. We just won."

Charlie Gehringer
Detroit Tigers, second base
1924-1942

Charlie Gehringer was a 5'11", 185-pound second baseman from Fowlerville, Michigan, who was called, "The Mechanical Man" for his ability to play the position, day in and day out, gracefully and without fanfare. "You wind him up and forget about him" is an often-told quote about him. He led AL second-sackers in fielding nine times, was an MVP once, a batting leader once and a stolen base leader once. He was a career .320 hitter in 2,323 games, during which time he struck out only 372 times while walking 1,185 times in more than 10,000 trips to the plate. Gehringer was a six-time all-star (he played in the first All-Star game).

Gehringer was voted the game's greatest living second baseman in 1969, had his number retired by the Tigers and was elected to the Hall of Fame in 1949.

He could have recalled "Charlie Gehringer Day" in Detroit (August 14, 1929), when he got four hits, a home run, a stolen base (of home) and made ten plays against the Yankees as the club and town honored him. Instead, Gehringer, a quiet and unassuming man, decided to tell stories about two of his teammates, talking about their deeds rather than his own.

September 10, 1934

"In 1934, we had the best hitting infield in history. I hit .356, Hank Greenberg (first base) hit .339, Marv Owen (third base) hit .317 and Billy Rogell (shortstop) hit .296 and we all drove in a hundred runs and so did Goose Goslin (outfield)." (**Author's Note:** Greenberg drove in 139, Gehringer 127, Rogell 100, Goslin 100 and Marv Owen just missed, with 96.)

"We drove in nearly a thousand runs (958) and had more than a hundred (116) more than the second-best Yankees. This team could really hit. And the team batting average was .300, but to make sure we won, we really needed Greenberg. I think he and (catcher) Mickey Cochrane were the real heart and soul of that team.

"We're in a real tight pennant race with the Yankees in September and we're about to play the Red Sox, who were tough. We needed every win and Hank Greenberg (who was Jewish) wanted to play, but it was an important Jewish holiday, Rosh Hashanah, and he was going to have to sit out and pray that day. The press made a big deal out of it and really put a lot of pressure on him to play. I remember he consulted Detroit's top rabbi (Leo Franklin) who decided Greenberg could play because it says in the Old Testament (the Talmud, actually) that the boys should be playing that day. But now the entire city is watching him, all the local Jews are watching him and the Tigers are counting on him.

"So Hank plays and it's a drizzly overcast day; I remember I had trouble seeing the ball. Hank hits two home runs off Dusty Rhodes and we won, 2-1, with his homer winning it in the tenth. I thought that was really something, and I said to him after the game, 'You should see how I hit on Christmas.' He laughed. I just really think that was an enormous amount of pressure to put on a man and he came through."

October, 1934

This Gehringer tale deals with barnstorming, a means old-time ball-players used to make some money. "We used to go barnstorming after the season and play games all across the country. They were usually all-star teams, so I could play on the same team as Lou Gehrig, Babe Ruth, Jimmie Foxx, Mel Ott, Dizzy Dean, Carl Hubbell, Lefty Gomez and Lefty O'Doul and lots of real nice guys who weren't all-stars, guys who became good friends because of the tours.

"We never lost a game, playing against local teams in small towns, which gave many, many Americans a chance to see their heroes, because there were only sixteen teams in those days, playing in eleven cities.

"Another good thing about barnstorming was the money. I could make more in a month than I could in a whole season in the Majors.

"Well, in 1934, Lefty O'Doul took a team of American all-stars to Japan to play the Japanese all-stars. We arrived by boat in Yokohama and fans covered the docks. And when we got to Tokyo, we could barely get our cars through because the streets were lined with baseball fans and they knew us all, too. And when we played, there were crowds of a hundred thousand in the stands. We won all eighteen games we played, and most of the games weren't close, so sometimes we switched positions — Lou Gehrig and I played in the outfield and Babe Ruth played at first for a few innings. But they really appreciated us and it's hard to remember ever being so appreciated by an entire city that wasn't Detroit.

"And one piece of history: We brought along a very good defensive catcher named Moe Berg, who was with Cleveland at the time. He took his camera wherever we went and snapped thousands of pictures. Occasionally he disappeared for hours at a time; we found out later that he took pictures of Japanese military installations and those pictures were used in America's bombing raids over Tokyo in World War II. And we found out later that Berg was a spy, working for the Army (OSS). We never knew that at the time, but it's interesting to think that we were just there to play ball, and yet we might have won the war because of it."

Si Johnson
Cincinnati Reds, pitcher
1928-1943 1946-1947

Silas Johnson was the last man to strike out Babe Ruth. He also counted Dizzy Dean and Dazzy Vance among his roomates. He likes to talk of Dazzy, who "gave me advice when I was a rookie and he was an opposing pitcher with Brooklyn. He told me to loosen 'em up at the plate when they dug in. He told me never to let them get confident about hitting me. Dust them off. In one game against Brooklyn, Vance came up against me with two on; he shouted to me, 'Listen, kid, you just dug yourself a grave.' Then he went down on a curve/fastball/change-up series—after I had thrown him the duster he advised me to throw earlier."

A 5'11", 185-pounder from Marseilles, Illinois, Johnson pitched for seventeen years and, though he twice led the league in losses, he was a workhorse who pitched 2,281 innings (he pitched over two hundred for four years in a row)—and though he won only 101 games, he had a good excuse—he played for some dreadful teams during his career.

Johnson readily remembers a rookie joke played on him in 1928, typical of the hazing of the day. "Hughie Critz, a second baseman for the Reds came up to me on my first train ride on a night Pullman from Chicago to St. Louis. He whispered in my ear, 'Young fella, you're in the Big Leagues now and I want you to know that someone is stealing all our shoes. You watch out tonight and we'll watch out for you tomorrow night.' I didn't know that the guys all put their shoes out in the aisle to have them shined, so when I saw the porter come by and pick up the shoes at about midnight, I jumped right out of my bed and tackled him. The poor guy was about seventy and I almost killed him. I got him hard, and when I found out I had hurt him, I cried like a baby."

He shares a moment for which he is remembered, but another one of which he is not proud.

May 29, 1935

"I was pitching for the Reds and faced Babe Ruth the day before he retired, and I guess I was the last guy to strike Babe out, but it was nothing to be proud of. I threw him mediocre fastballs right down the middle of the plate. He was behind everything. His reflexes were shot. How he hit three homers in a single game four days earlier is beyond me, because he was through and he knew it. I pitched against Babe in his prime and he would have lost those balls." (**Author's Note:** Johnson whiffed Babe three times in the game, Ruth's last three strikeouts.)

Terry Moore
St. Louis Cardinals, outfield
1935-1942 1946-1948

Terry Moore was the captain of the "Gas House Gang" Cardinals of the 1930s and 1940s. The 5'11", 195-pound center fielder from Vernon, Alabama, was one of the best and most popular outfielders in the game during his career. Though not a powerful hitter or even a big average man (he hit .300 once and .280 for his career), the four-time all-star had the respect of his contemporaries. He was solid and dependable on offense and defense, as well as in the clubhouse.

He chose to give us an anecdote that he feels was part and parcel of the Gas House Gang's approach to the game.

June, 1935

"One funny thing I remember was the year I came up (1935) as a rookie," says Moore. "I roomed with Pepper Martin, the funniest guy in the world, and I played with Dizzy (Dean) and Paul (Dean), who were always being funny. But Pepper was the king.

"We were playing in Philly at the Baker Bowl, and Pepper comes up with a man (Ducky Medwick) on second. Now in those days, we had two umpires for a game — one behind home plate and another on the bases — but in this one, due to an injury, we only had one ump, Bill Klem, behind home plate.

"Ducky leads off second and Pepper hits one to short right field and Philly's right fielder Johnny Moore picks it up and fires home to catcher Al Todd. As Medwick goes into his slide and Klem turns his back on the field to watch the play at the plate, Pepper cuts across the infield, across the pitcher's mound, and slides into third.

"Jimmie Wilson, the Phillies' manager yells at Klem to look at Pepper, and without even turning his back to see Pepper, Klem called him out.

"Pepper is all over Klem, shouting, 'You didn't even see me, how can you call me out?' Klem replied, 'No man in the world could have made it to third. You're out.'"

Johnny Mize
St. Louis Cardinals, first base
1936-1942 1946-1953

Johnny Mize was the "Big Cat." The 6'2", 225-pound slugger from Demorest, Georgia, led the NL in homers twice for the Cards (twenty-eight in 1939 and forty-three in 1940) before he left for military service, and twice for the Giants (fifty-one in 1947 and forty in 1948) after the war, en route to a career total of 359 homers. He hit three homers in a game a record six times, and he struck out only 524 times, remarkable for a man with such pop in his bat.

He appeared big and slow, but he played his position well, and is recognized as a decent fielder, though he said of his range, "I can get to any ball hit within a foot of me in either direction."

He was a ten-time all-star who was enshrined in the Hall of Fame in 1981.

Mize tells of the incident that got him to the Majors—major surgery.

December, 1935

"In the winter of '35, I had both legs operated on. I had an upper leg bone spur removed, and Branch Rickey, who ran the Cardinals, came to see me in the hospital.

"After asking if I was OK, he said, 'You were pretty slow in the outfield before the operation. Now, you can't run, you can't play the outfield, and we can't trade you after this surgery, so we'll play you at first base and keep you in the Majors.'

"That was it. He left and I was with the club the next season and hit .329, and stayed up from then on. Great man, Branch Rickey."

Joe DiMaggio
New York Yankees, outfield
1936-1942 1946-1951

The "Yankee Clipper" was one of the most graceful and classy men to ever play the game. He was the Yankee leader bridging the Babe Ruth-Lou Gehrig era and the Mickey Mantle era during the Yankee dynasty of the 1920s through 1960s. The 6'3", 190-pound center fielder from San Francisco was the toast of New York and the baseball world. He had a song written about him and won two batting crowns, two home run titles, two RBI championships and three MVPs. He hit safely in a record fifty-six straight games in the Majors, after hitting in sixty-one straight one year in the minors. His contemporary, Ted Williams, called DiMaggio "The best pure hitter I ever saw." As talented as he was, he was also a hard worker who typified the pride of the Yankees and of America during three decades. He had his number retired and a plaque dedicated in his honor by the Yankees. He was elected to the Hall of Fame in 1955.

Where does the man who was voted the game's greatest living player begin his recollections? He played with Gehrig and Dickey and Gomez and Reynolds and Berra and Mantle. He was married to Marilyn Monroe. He could have gone with the obvious—his debut May 3, 1936, in which he banged out three hits as the Yanks bested the St. Louis Browns, 14-5; or the day he hit for the cycle, May 21,

Joe DiMaggio, outfield, 1930s
Courtesy: New York Yankees

1948, or two days later when he bombed three homers, two off Bob Feller; or even the day his fifty-six-game hitting streak was stopped — July 17, 1941 — by Cleveland's Al Smith and Jim Bagby (DiMaggio remarked, "Stopping that streak at fifty-six games cost me thousands of dollars. If I had gone to fifty-seven, Heinz and their '57 varieties' would have paid me ten thousand dollars to start an ad campaign and I might have been their spokesman for years"). This private man, who good-naturedly jests that he's more well-known for his Mr. Coffee commercials than for his stellar diamond career, offered a less-than-highlight as his favorite tale, with an observation of his teammate, Lefty "Goofy" Gomez, who apparently deserved his nickname.

July 7, 1936

DiMaggio recalled the fourth All-Star game, at Braves Field in Boston. "In those days, the All-Star games were fiercely competitive. The American League had won the first three games; this was the first All-Star game we had lost . . . and I was responsible for it. My fielding lapses allowed the National League to go up 4-0. Lou Gehrig's homer got us back in it, and I came up with the bases loaded and tried to redeem myself. I hit the first pitch as hard as I could and National League shortstop Leo Durocher leaped at the crack of the bat. The ball dipped and Leo almost broke in half as he bent over while still leaping, and caught the ball at his ankles, though still high in the air. I can't ever remember being so disappointed — even counting the more-publicized catch by Al Gionfriddo (October 5, 1947) with two on in the sixth inning of game five of the World Series when I kicked the dirt — because I was so young, this was my first All-Star game, I was the first rookie to play in the All-Star game and I was the cause for our first loss. Of course, the more important out was that one in the World Series, but I was older and had my success, so this one has never lost its sting."

June, 1937

"Joltin' Joe" tells a story about his roommate, the left-handed pitcher with the nickname "Goofy." DiMaggio recalls, "I remember this game when Lefty Gomez was pitching and there was a man on and two out and the hitter batted one back to the mound. Gomez fielded it cleanly but didn't throw to (shortstop) Frank Crosetti for the force at second or to Lou Gehrig at first. Instead, he tossed the ball to Tony Lazzeri, the second baseman who was standing halfway between first and second. Lazzeri was caught by surprise and asked Gomez how he could do such a thing. Gomez didn't even crack a smile. He said softly, 'I read a newspaper story that said you were the smartest player in baseball and I wanted to find out what such a smart man would do with the ball once he got it.' "

Bobby Doerr
Boston Red Sox, second base
1937-1944 1946-1951

Bobby Doerr, the 5'11", 175-pound second-sacker for the BoSox, came out of Los Angeles and became one of the cogs in the Boston machine for the next decade-and-a-half. He began playing pro ball at sixteen and made "the Bigs" by the time he was nineteen. He acquitted himself with dignity and style at the plate (381 doubles, 223 homers, 1,247 RBI) and in the field (1,507 double plays).

The eight-time all-star was among the best keystone-sackers in the game following the war, and his quiet leadership proved instrumental in the Red Sox's trip to the World Series in 1946.

Bobby Doerr had his number retired by the Boston Red Sox, and he was enshrined in the Hall of Fame in 1986.

Ask Bobby Doerr a question about baseball and he can go on for twenty minutes about the man he feels is the best of all time, Ted Williams. Virtually every highlight and important moment cited by Doerr, a Hall of Famer in his own right, revolves around "Teddy Ballgame." Doerr broke up a no-hitter against Spud Chandler in front of 69,107 fans at Yankee Stadium, July 2, 1946, and he overshadowed his contemporaries at the All-Star game, July 13, 1943, at Shibe Park with a game-winning three-run homer. Nonetheless, Doerr didn't wish to talk about himself; instead he reserved this space for Ted.

July, 1936

"I saw Ted first when I was in the Pacific Coast League (PCL) in San Diego, but I'll never forget how he wowed them. Ted had a tryout with the San Diego Padres; he had just finished school and wanted to play ball.

"Here's this tall, skinny kid leaning against the batting cage as Frank Shellenback was pitching batting practice.

"The old timers started to groan, 'This kid's taking up our time.' Ted stepped in, took seven or eight cuts and lined them all hard — three for homers. He looked good. He was signed before he left the diamond."

May, 1939

"To tell you about Ted's tenacity, well, his work habits were the absolute best. He worked and he studied and he knew more about the games, all aspects of the game, than anyone I've ever seen. And if you challenged him, you'd lose.

"We were in St. Louis (Sportsman's Park) to play the Browns. Their manager was Fred Haney, who I played for in the PCL in 1934, and he was tough, really tough. The Brownies dugout was on the third-base side and you had to walk through their clubhouse to get to ours.

"I saw Fred and came over to talk to him, but he saw Ted, too. Without saying anything to me, he stared Ted in the eye and said, 'I've seen how well you hit. Let's see how you hit sittin' on your ass.'

"When the game started, the first pitch to Ted was right near his ear and knocked the big guy down. Ted got up, didn't even dust off his uniform, took his stance and on the next pitch, drove it against the right field screen for a double.

"The next time up, the first pitch knocked him down and on pitch two, Ted drove it onto Grand Boulevard for a home run. That was that, and it epitomizes Ted's career; he did that countless times. He was the greatest performer in the game and no one ever got the better of him on the ballfield. It was a pleasure to be on his team and to watch him play."

Hugh Mulcahy
Philadelphia Phillies, pitcher
1935-1940 1945-1947

Hugh "Losing Pitcher" Mulcahy was a 6′2″, 190-pound right-hander out of Brighton, Massachusetts, who got his nickname after sports-writers joked that the initials "L.P." (baseball shorthand for "Losing Pitcher") followed his name in the box score so often it looked like part of his name (he led the league in losses in 1938 and 1940 and in a three-year "reign of terrible" from 1938-1940, lost twenty, sixteen and twenty-two games). He was selected for the All-Star team in 1940 anyway (his team lost 103 games, 81 without him) and his 3.60 ERA in 280 innings with three shutouts and twenty-one complete games was much better than his record indicated, or would have been with a better team—any team.

Mulcahy finished with 45 wins and 89 losses in 220 games and 1,161 innings and 144 starts. In relief, he didn't fare much better, going 3-11 with nine saves; but again, in his defense, he played for teams that finished 7th; 8th (100 losses); 7th; 8th (105 losses); 8th (106 losses); 8th (103 losses); 8th (108 losses); 4th and 5th during his career.

As a historical footnote, Mulcahy was the first Major Leaguer drafted (March 8, 1941), and was soon off to fight in World War II.

He recalls an incident prior to the 1937 season, when "The Phillies sent me a contract with a check and small raise. I was elated, so I sent a thank-you note to owner Gerry Nugent. Nugent sent me back a letter that read: 'Thank you very much for your nice letter, but please sign and return the check. It was made out for the wrong amount.'"

Mulcahy remembers a rare win . . . and a loss.

April, 1937

"I may be the only pitcher to win one game on one pitch and lose one game on one pitch," he says.

"I won a ball game on one pitch versus the Boston Bees in 1937 in the old Philly park, the Baker Bowl. I faced Billy Urbanski in his final Major League at-bat and he hit my first pitch to right field. We scored in the bottom of the ninth and got the win. One pitch, one out.

"The next year (May 1938), we were playing in Wrigley Field against the Cubs and I came in with two on, one out and the winning run at the plate. Billy Jurges bunted my first pitch down the third-base line and third baseman Pinky Whitney and I played "Alphonse and Gaston" with the ball and he was safe. Augie Galan came up to bat and manager Jimmie Wilson relieved me with a lefty, Wayne LaMaster, to face Galan, who was a better lefty hitter than righty. Galan hit a triple to score Jurges and I lost it on one pitch.

"All I can say, to paraphrase William Shakespeare, 'Tis better to have pitched and lost, then never to have pitched at all.' "

Don Gutteridge
St. Louis Cardinals, third base
1936-1940 1942-1948

Don Gutteridge was a 5'10", 165-pound second-sacker from Pittsburg, Kansas. He was one of seventy players to wear the uniforms of both the St. Louis Cardinals (1936-1940) and the St. Louis Browns (1942-1945).

He had his days in the sun; his second day as a Big Leaguer, he took part in a doubleheader at Ebbets Field and connected for six hits, a home run and two steals of home. On June 30, 1944, he turned five double plays for the Browns' only pennant-winning club.

He played on some great Cardinal clubs, some poor Browns teams, and took part in the St. Louis-St. Louis Series of 1944, but he chose to talk about his early Cardinal days and the "Gas House Gang."

May 19, 1937

"Dizzy Dean used to pitch all the big games for us," recalls Gutteridge. "And this one was marquee: Dizzy Dean versus Carl Hubbell of the New York Giants.

"Now, a new rule had just been installed that called for the pitcher to come to a stop at the belt to give the runners a chance. Diz just threw and was called for two balks—there was a runner at second and Diz never stopped . . . balk. The runner was awarded third and when the following hitter popped a fly to left field for a sacrifice fly, New York was up 1-0. So Diz was getting madder and started throwing at Giants' heads.

"The Giants got upset. Diz knocked down everyone but Hubbell.

"In the ninth, we're losing, 4-1, and Jimmy Ripple gets knocked down by Diz. On the next pitch, Ripple bunts down the first baseline and it rolls foul. I was at third base and Leo Durocher was at short, and Leo says to me, 'If there's trouble at first, be over there.' We knew Ripple wanted to bunt to first to get Diz covering so he could run over him.

"Diz throws one hard inside but Ripple bunts it fair. Second baseman Jimmy Brown fields it and throws to Johnny Mize at first. Diz started to field the ball but when it got past him, he kept running straight at Ripple and ran him over instead.

"Mize holds them apart, and Leo and I are already over there acting as peacemakers, but we didn't count on twenty-three mad Giants who wanted Diz (Carl Hubbell never left the bench). Leo and I locked arms in front of Diz; we couldn't let him be swarmed over.

"One Giant punched me in the eye. I got knocked down, stepped on and punched and got a black eye. Later I was told I was sucker punched by Dolph Luque, 'The Pride of Havana,' who had first pitched in 1914 and was now a fifty-year-old coach.

"Our rookie catcher, Mickey Owen, hunted for Giants catcher Gus Mancuso. He later told me, 'I thought we were supposed to take care of our own position.'

"Pepper Martin, who was a rough-and-tumble guy, ran in front of me, grabbed a guy from the Giants, pulled him out of the pile and said to him, 'Stay out of there; I'll get to you later.' Then he lined up five guys to fight. Pepper thought this was fun; he was a real whirlwind. He looked at my eye and asked, 'Who hit you?' I said I didn't know, so he wanted to take on the whole team until someone admitted to the deed.

"The umpires and police cleared the field about a half hour later and Hubbell just watched the whole thing. He won his twenty-second straight game and I guess that was more important than getting in a fight. Funny thing was, Ripple was awarded first base after the fight. I guess we forgot to tag him out."

Walter "Buck" Leonard
Homestead Grays (Negro Leagues), first base
1933-1950

Walter Fenner "Buck" Leonard, the 5'10", 200-pound first baseman for the Homestead Grays was nicknamed "the black Lou Gehrig,"

Walter "Buck" Leonard, first base, 1930s
Courtesy: National Baseball Library Hall of Fame, Cooperstown, New York

to complement his teammate Josh Gibson's sobriquet, "the black Babe Ruth."

The left-handed slugger from Rocky Mount, North Carolina, helped lead his two-city club (the Homestead Grays were based in Washington, but when the Senators were in town, they played home games in Pittsburgh) to nine consecutive Negro National League pennants from 1937-1945.

Though not as powerful as his buddy Gibson, Leonard's line drive power served him well enough to reach the walls of the countless parks in which he played, connecting for forty-two blasts in 1942 and winning three home run crowns and three batting titles. As strong a hitter as he was, his defensive play may have been even better. His lifetime Negro Leagues average was around .333 (statistics are sketchy), playing for the Grays, the Baltimore Stars and the Brooklyn Royal Giants.

In his initial season with the Grays, he was indoctrinated into the world of great pitching by Satchel Paige. On July 4, 1934, he says, "I saw Satch pitch a no-hitter against us—and our team could really hit—but it was no contest. Satch just threw his 'Long Tom' fastball and high-kicked us up and out. He gave up a walk and they (the Pittsburgh Crawfords) made an error behind him and that was it. Man, he was something. And later that day, Satch drove to Chicago from Pittsburgh, pitched that night and no-hit the Chicago American Giants—two no-hitters in one day, and with his stuff, I'm surprised he didn't do it more often."

Before Jackie Robinson was a gleam in the eye of Branch Rickey, Washington Senators owner Clark Griffith talked to "the Thunder Twins," Leonard and Gibson, about playing in the majors (1944); Griffith, however, finally bowed to pressure and abandoned his plans. When Bill Veeck asked Leonard to play for his St. Louis Browns in 1949, Leonard said he was too old and didn't want to take the place of a younger player.

After the Negro Leagues disbanded, Leonard played ball in the Mexican League until 1955 and was among the league's leaders in hitting. In 1953, at age forty-six, Leonard made his only appearance in organized baseball, playing ten games for Portsmouth of the Piedmont League, batting .333.

Leonard was enshrined in the Hall of Fame in 1972.

Leonard chose to offer his observations of baseball in the Depression, and some hijinks with a teammate.

June 3, 1937

"Josh (Gibson) really got into one this day. We were playing a doubleheader at Yankee Stadium against the Chicago American Giants and Josh hit one off Ted 'Big Florida' Trent that hit the top of the roof in left field, about 580 feet from home plate. A while later someone calculated that the ball would have gone seven hundred feet if it wasn't stopped. He would have been great in the majors — a better catcher than Campy (Roy Campanella), Yogi (Berra) or (Bill) Dickey. But he died at thirty-five (in 1947), just before he was about to sign a contract.

"Another day, we were in New Orleans for a game, and on our way to a bar we were attacked by pigs, a whole group of them. That was life in the (Negro) Leagues. Pigs one day, broken bottle and knife fights the next, pretty girls and parties the next. Some days in some towns we'd eat real good and be treated like kings and in the next town on the next day, we'd have to hightail it out of town on a bus just to save our skins."

July, 1937

"It was the Depression, and everyone was hurting for money. By this time, I was earning about $375 a month for a five-month season, and fifty cents a day meal money. I eventually made one thousand dollars a month (in 1942), and by 1948 I was paid ten thousand dollars to play both winter and summer; but in 1937 times were still tough. We (the Homestead Grays) played out of both Washington and Pittsburgh and we traveled everywhere in between. We played about two hundred games, and we could make extra money by playing barnstorming games in between our scheduled Negro League games. So if we played a game against Baltimore during the day, we'd then play a semipro team in Rockville, Maryland, that afternoon, and then go to Washington and play at Griffith Stadium (our home field) that night. We could get seventy-five to one hundred dollars a game. And we had 'getting out of the hole days,' when we'd play a big game at Forbes Field, Yankee Stadium, Comiskey Park (that was on weekends) and that was when the team could make its payroll and pay the players what they owed us.

"But being in debt was a way to make more money. We would often borrow from the team, above what they paid us, so if we were in debt at the end of the season, they had to bring us back to play, usually at a higher wage, the next season, just so they would break even. That worked for about four years."

Johnny Dickshot
Pittsburgh Pirates, outfield
1936-1939 1944-1945

John Oscar Dickshot was a scrappy, six-foot, 190-pound outfielder from Waukegan, Illinois who played a part-time role for his first five seasons and was finally given a chance to be the starting left fielder for the White Sox in 1945. He responded by hitting .302, third best in the American League, while stealing eighteen bases, fifth best in the loop.

Jimmy Reese called Dickshot "One of the toughest men I've ever met. He's also one of the nicest, but I would never do anything to make him mad, because he could take you apart. And no matter what kind of injury he had, he played through the pain . . . if he even felt any pain."

Dickshot's favorite remembrance was as a teenager, "driving thirty miles from my Waukegan home to Wrigley Field or White Sox Park to see Guy Bush, Hack Wilson and Gabby Hartnett play."

After graduating from high school in 1928, he kicked around the minors for seven years before getting to "the Show." "I was in the Pacific Coast League in 1932 and 1933. The travel was tough—sixteen guys in a twelve-seat bus; forty-five to eighty-five dollars-a-month salary and driving five hundred miles to play one game and then return—but every day was great for me. I just loved playing the game. Even when I didn't play much for Pittsburgh, and I really thought I could play more, I loved it, and when my manager, Pie Traynor, would play me in Chicago, that was the best."

August, 1937

On a personal level, Dickshot has a game he holds above all others. "We were facing the Giants in a four-game series and Pie Traynor told me I'd be starting all four. That meant I would face Carl Hubbell for the first time, and he had a twenty-four-game winning streak earlier in the season (over two years). My roomie, Pee Gee (Paul Waner), gave me sage advice. He said, 'Just hit what you see. Don't expect anything and don't wait until you're at three balls and two strikes.' I took his advice and went 3-for-4.

"During the series with the Giants, it got exciting. Hal Schumacher was pitching against us, and every time home plate umpire Bill Klem would call a pitch a strike, Woody Jensen (one of our outfielders) would yell from the dugout 'Catfish,' a nickname Klem hated. Klem had big lips and sprayed the air when he talked, so he had this nickname and he hated it. Every time Jensen would yell, 'Catfish,' he would hide, and Klem would look over and throw someone else out of the game. He emptied our bench three times and never did get Woody.

"Moments after the last 'Catfish' outburst, I was up and Schumacher threw one that just missed the outside corner. I took it and Klem yelled, 'Strike.' I turned around and looked at him. Klem barked, 'Turn around, busher, I'll be here long after you're gone.'

"I turned around and said to him, 'What's wrong, Mr. Klem?' He asked, 'Why are you looking at me?' I replied, 'I just turned around to see you, sir.' Klem smiled and said, 'All right, son, get back in there.'

"I was looking for a curve on the next pitch, but Schumacher threw me a fastball. That pitch was right plumb in the middle of the plate and I took it and Klem called, 'Ball.'

"Giants catcher, Harry 'The Horse' Danning, turned around and stared at Klem, who barked to the catcher, 'Turn around, busher, I'll be here long after you're gone, too.' "

Tony Cuccinello
Boston Braves, second base
1930-1945

Tony "Chick" Cuccinello was a sturdy 5'7", 160-pound infielder from Long Island, New York, who played in baseball's first All-Star game in 1933 (he pinch-hit for Carl Hubbell and said, "I'm the most surprised guy in the world."). Cuccinello hit better than .300 five times and, in 1,704 career games, he showed his defensive ability by getting to 6,293 chances and turning 895 double plays.

Cuccinello could have told us about his 6-for-6 performance against the Boston Braves while playing for the Cincinnati Reds August 13, 1931, or the day (July 5, 1935) that he and his brother Al Cuccinello, a catcher for the Giants, homered in the same game. Instead, he turned to two more humorous tales about the elements and, in the 1940s chapter, baseball strategy.

April, 1938

Cuccinello says, "There was a terrific hurricane in Florida, and it tore up the entire East Coast. We were playing a doubleheader in Boston against the St. Louis Cardinals and in the first game we were already feeling the effects of the storm. By the second game, the winds had reached gale force, and Beans Reardon, the home plate umpire, said he'd watch it and call the game if it got worse.

"In the third inning, Enos Slaughter hit a hell of a drive toward right field — with the wind blowing out, it would have been a sure homer. I was playing second base and I knew that with the wind blowing in I had a chance to catch the ball. When I turned my back toward the infield I figured I'd let the ball come back to me, and when I did, the ball started to come back toward the infield as I predicted, but I had to keep backing up as the wind kept carrying it in. The next thing I knew, I was on the pitcher's mound and I had to give up on the ball. Al Lopez, our catcher, ran over to our dugout (which was way over on the left side of the field) and he caught the ball at the dugout steps.

"Beans Reardon called the game right then and there.

"Then we didn't play for four days and we couldn't get to New York for our next series by train because the storm had blocked the tracks, so we had to go by boat from Boston to play our next scheduled game."

Harry Craft
Cincinnati Reds, outfield
1937-1942

Although he only played in "the Show" for six years (566 games), Harry Craft, the mild-mannered outfielder from Houston, Texas (by way of Ellisville, Mississippi), showed the baseball world that he was one of the smoothest, most adroit outfielders in the game. His knowledge of the position — which he later used as a coach and manager (see chapter on 1950s as Craft uses his teaching skills to sculpt a superstar and steer baseball history) — and his ability to make the plays made up for his lack of hitting acumen (good power but poor contact) and put him on the forefront of two NL championship teams.

As a historical sidelight, Craft's curving home run at the Polo Grounds on July 15, 1939, which keyed a donnybrook, was the motivation for the addition of a two-foot screen attached to all foul poles to prevent this type of occurrence. There was already controversy over close calls on homers; this brouhaha was the last straw, prompting baseball authorities to eliminate this flaw in the system.

Craft, who has spent sixty years in baseball as a player, scout, coach and manager, recalls one big night when he was a part of baseball history, "by just being on the field."

June 15, 1938

Craft says, "It was a red-letter day and I had the pleasure of being in on Johnny Vander Meer's two no-hitters.

"On June 11, Johnny beat Boston 3-0 and we made a few good plays behind him. I got a good jump on two balls to help, but it was Johnny's night.

"On June 15, it was the first night game ever at Ebbets Field in Brooklyn. There were forty thousand fans screaming from the first pitch. Babe Ruth was even in the stands.

"The team was aware of what was going on, and into the game, Johnny openly wondered if he could do it (pitch two no-hitters in a row). In the seventh inning, I almost blew it for him. It was the worst play I ever had; Ernie Koy hit a line drive knuckleball at my face and it dropped, making me dive and do a dipsy doodle at my feet.

"In the ninth, Vandy walked three with none out; he was really nervous and so were we. Then he got a strikeout, a ground ball force-out at the plate and then Leo Durocher came up and hit a soft fly to me for the final out. We went wild. It was fun to do it for Vandy, and to be a part of history.

"Later on, Leo always said I caught his diving liner and robbed him of a hit. The truth was, it was like a feather on a feather bed."

Johnny Vander Meer
Cincinnati Reds, pitcher
1937-1943 1946-1951

John "The Dutch Master" Vander Meer was a 6'1", 190-pound lefty from Prospect Park, New Jersey, who is best known for being Johnny "Double No-hit" Vander Meer, the only Major League pitcher to hurl back-to-back no-hit games. He "no-no'd" the Boston Bees June 11, 1938, and four days later repeated the process against the Brooklyn Dodgers (on a night that saw the first night game ever played at Ebbets Field).

A four-time all-star, Vander Meer led the league in strikeouts three straight years (1941-43), whiffing 202 in 1941. Though he struggled with his control and wound up with a mark of 119-121 in a career shortened due to arm trouble, he was recognized as a tough pitcher who wasn't easy to face or beat.

He talks about the proudest moment in his career . . . the second no-hitter.

June 15, 1938

Vander Meer recalls, "All I really wanted to do was just be out there, just like any kid who ever picked up a ball and glove. So throwing one no-hitter, let alone two in a row, was just gravy.

"When I got to Cincinnati in 1937 and got my own locker with my own name on it, it was the happiest moment of my life. Four or five guys came up to me to welcome me: Eddie Joost, Frank (Buck) McCormick, Harry Craft and Willard Hershberger all sat in the same corner as me.

"My first start, in May 1937, was against Carl Hubbell in the Polo Grounds. Peaches Davis was supposed to pitch, but he said, 'Hell, I'm not going against Hubbell' so (Cincinnati manager) Chuck Dressen said, 'OK, let's see what the kid will do.' Now, Hubbell was on his streak and had won about twenty in a row at this point and I almost stopped him. It was 1-1 into the ninth when I was lifted for a pinch hitter. I remember walking down Broadway that night thinking that I had tied my idol.

"So I was always happy with whatever happened and now I'm at Ebbets Field and I've got a shot at a second no-hitter. I didn't really give it any thought until the seventh, because I've seen too many no-hitters broken up in the sixth or seventh on lucky hits. I've also seen too many broken up on a pitch that isn't the pitcher's best, so from the seventh on, I decided that I might have twenty to thirty good pumps left and I went at the hitters as hard as I could.

"The last two innings, the Brooklyn fans rooted for me; for the first seven they had rooted against me and called me every name in the book, but they were with me the rest of the way.

"Somehow I got into the ninth, and that inning went slowly as my heart began to pound and time stood still. I got two guys out and walked the bases loaded. We had a 6-0 lead, so I was in no danger of losing the game, but I really wanted this thing now and I was trying too hard and that's why I walked some.

"I got a count of 1-2 on the last hitter, Leo Durocher. I fired a good fastball that caught the outside part of the plate for a strikeout, but umpire Bill Stewart froze and called it a ball. I threw another pitch just a hair closer to the middle of the plate on the next pitch and Leo popped it to Harry Craft in center for the final out. I can't tell you the emotion I felt. I was exhilarated and drained at the same time and was mobbed by my teammates.

"Just as I was being mobbed, Stewart, the umpire, says to me, 'I'm glad Leo didn't get a hit. I should have had him struck out on the previous pitch. I missed it and I'm glad you didn't make me pay for it.' "

Harry Eisenstat
Detroit Tigers, pitcher
1935-1942

Harry Eisenstat was a 5'11", 185-pound lefty from Brooklyn who lived his dream by breaking into the Majors with his hometown team, the Brooklyn Dodgers. After playing with "the Bums" for three seasons, Eisenstat went on to Detroit, where he lives today.

In a patriotic move typical of the America of that day, following three-and-a-half years in the Army Air Corps, Eisenstat left baseball for good to work in a defense plant. "It seemed more important" says Eisenstat, "to help this country than to play baseball, and Thompson Products in Detroit was manufacturing airplane parts—a defense plant setup—and it seemed to be the right thing to do."

Eisenstat's best season was 1938 with the Tigers, when he went 9-6 with four saves. He won eight games the following season (spent largely with Cleveland), and his shortened eight-year career saw him go 25-27 in 165 games (all but thirty-two in relief), pitching 478 innings.

Eisenstat recalls a game as a starter when he hooked up with Bob Feller.

October 2, 1938

"This game," says Eisenstat, "was great because I did well and still got to marvel at the skill of an opponent. It was a dreary day in Cleveland and Bob Feller was throwing smoke. He struck out six Tigers in a row at one point and struck out a Major League record eighteen men that day. But I threw a four-hitter and beat him, 4-1.

"The excitement of that day was not only Feller's heat, but Hank Greenberg. Hank was going for a record, too, and had fifty-eight home runs going into the game. He delivered a big hit, but was shut down in his homer attempt. It was all very exciting. And, of course, Hank gave me two of my great spectator thrills when he hit four homers in a row over two games (July 26-27, 1938) and when he hit three homers in a doubleheader the next year (of which I was the recipient [as the winning pitcher in both games]).

May, 1939

"I was traded to Cleveland for Earl Averill on June 14, 1939, and I had always had good success against Cleveland, so I was sorry to go to one team I won against.

Harry Eisenstat, pitcher, 1930s
Courtesy: National Baseball Library Hall of Fame, Cooperstown, New York

"Before the trade, I had one last hurrah with the Tigers. I won a doubleheader against Philadelphia. I pitched five innings in relief and got the win in game one, and I pitched four innings of relief in game two and won that game. To make it sweeter, Hank Greenberg hit three home runs in the doubleheader and after the game, (manager) Mickey Cochrane made the remark in the locker room, 'All the Jews of Detroit are going crazy today.'

"Hank and I were very close with the city of Detroit. It was Hank who brought me there after Judge (Kenesaw Mountain) Landis declared me a free agent. I had been the property of the Dodgers, but they sent me out one option too many (to the minors), and since Detroit needed lefty pitching I came here.

"I pitched one day at Yankee Stadium during Rosh Hashanah, the Jewish New Year, and was winning against Red Ruffing in the eighth and he said to me, 'Hey, Jew-man. Good for you, good for you. I don't know what you're doing here today, but you're pitching a great game.' "

Babe Dahlgren
New York Yankees, first base
1935-1946

Ellsworth Tenney Dahlgren, the San Francisco slugger who stood six-feet tall and weighed 190 pounds, was the man who replaced a legend. It was Dahlgren who played first base for the New York Yankees on May 2, 1939, when Lou Gehrig took himself out of the lineup to end his consecutive games streak at 2,130.

Dahlgren played 149 games at first for the Red Sox in 1935 when the BoSox acquired Jimmie Foxx. He was shipped to the minors and played on what may have been the greatest minor league team in history, the 1937 Newark Bears, a Yankee farm club—109 wins and 43 losses, winners of the Little World Series, and stocked with such future Big Leaguers as Charlie "King Kong" Keller, Joe Gordon, Buddy Rosar, Atley Donald and Joe Beggs. Dahlgren was the third baseman on that club, as there was no need of a first baseman in pinstripes with Gehrig playing every game.

Dahlgren, an all-star in 1943, hit twenty-three homers in 1941, dividing the season between the Boston Braves and Chicago Cubs, and hit fifteen and twelve dingers for the Yankees in 1939 and 1940, respectively. He played in 1,139 games in his career and was considered a solid fielder and a steady ballplayer.

He talks of the day he replaced Gehrig.

May 2, 1939

Dahlgren says, "I was surprised I was replacing Gehrig that day and I almost had a day to remember; instead, my performance is largely forgotten. People remember I replaced Lou, but they don't recall that I hit a home run, a double off the top of the fence, and two long outs that could have been homers. I knocked in Joe Gordon and Art Fletcher and showed a great glove throughout the season, but, of course, I was just there and many people still thought of Gehrig.

"I never wanted to go to the Yankees. I signed as a third baseman, but I was a first baseman. But once I signed (after I was dropped by Boston when they got Jimmie Foxx), I was happy in Newark. That was a great club and they taught you the Yankee way of doing things at first base, like tagging runners on wild throws and falling down on top of them, using one hand to get the ball and one hand to trap the runner.

"But, really, I just appreciated playing. I could have had a longer career if I had started elsewhere and just played without having to worry about Foxx or Gehrig, but I'm just glad I played."

Jimmie Crutchfield
Newark Eagles (Negro Leagues), outfield
1930-1945

Jimmie Crutchfield was a 5'7", 145-pound ball of energy and optimism who brought excitement and an upbeat manner wherever he played. Beginning his career for the Birmingham Black Barons in 1930, Crutchfield moved on to the Indianapolis ABC's (for whom he hit .330), Pittsburgh Crawfords, Newark Eagles, Toledo Crawfords, Indianapolis Crawfords, Chicago American Giants and Cleveland Buckeyes. He was a four-time all-star and retired at thirty-five.

Crutchfield played with and against the likes of Satchel Paige and James "Cool Papa" Bell. "Satch," he says, "was class. He could do anything he wanted, both on the field and off, and he was a soft touch for anyone down and out. Cool Papa Bell was really fast; it is true that he could turn off the light switch and be in bed before the room got dark, but there was a defect in the lighting."

Crutchfield remembers the Negro Leagues fondly.

"I had some big games: the 1934 All-Star game in which the score was 1-0 and I threw Mule Suttles out at the plate from the fence, a four-hundred-foot throw on the fly; the 1935 All-Star game at White Sox Park, in which I made a running, bare-handed catch to save the game for Satchel Paige.

"But, really, what I can remember is that every day was sunshine and butterflies and flowers and birds singing, because every day is a sunny day when you're playing baseball. I played with gentlemen who respected each other and who respected the game. Baseball was so much fun, there is nothing ever better, and every day was a story to be shared."

August, 1939

"If I had to pick just one (story)," said Crutchfield, "I'd go to 1939.

"In 1939, Newark was a great baseball town. They had the Newark Bears — who were champions, just one step away from the Yankees — and the Newark Eagles, and some barnstorming teams (The House of David). We had Ray Dandridge at third base, Dick Seay at second, (Willie) Devil Wells at short, Leon Day and Terris McDuffie on the mound, Eddie Stone and Mule Suttles in the outfield (Suttles also played first base), Monte Irvin (he was a rookie at short and in the outfield), Biz Mackey behind the plate and (Lenny) Horse Pearson, a utility player. I believe that team could have played at the Major League level and could have done well.

"Well, we were playing the Homestead Grays and Josh Gibson, a powerhouse right-handed hitter, was up in the ninth with one on and two out and we were up by a run. Gibson was the Babe Ruth of the Negro Leagues and he used to hit sixty homers a year in Negro League and barnstorming games. There was no one who hit them farther. So I was playing him to pull — I was in dead left-center. He hits Leon Day's fastball the opposite way, and I look, and our right fielder had fallen down. I raced from left-center to right field and made a stretched out, full speed catch to save the game.

"After the game, my guys and most of the other team, Josh Gibson included, mobbed me, and they said, nobody has ever made a better catch — not even Joe DiMaggio, who was my favorite player. That was my favorite memory until I made a similar catch the last week of my last season, in 1945 at Cleveland Stadium while playing in the play-offs for Chicago. When I was again compared to DiMaggio, I retired on the spot. I wanted to leave a winner, and I knew I'd never be able to do a third thing that would get me compared to him."

Monte Irvin
Newark Eagles (Negro Leagues), outfield
1939-1948 (Negro Leagues) 1949-1956 (Major Leagues)

Monte Irvin, who also played ball under the name Jimmy Nelson, was a 6'2", 200-pound outfielder/first baseman for the Newark Eagles

Monte Irvin, outfield, 1930s and Larry Doby, outfield, 1930s
Courtesy: National Baseball Library Hall of Fame, Cooperstown, New York

of the Negro Leagues. A seven-time Negro Leagues all-star, he hit as high as .381 one season, and was known for his power. The Columbus, Alabama, native also spent eight years in the Big Leagues, mostly with the New York Giants, and led the senior circuit in RBIs with 121 in 1951. He hit .300 or better three straight years and finished with ninety-nine homers in his big league career. He was elected to the Hall of Fame in 1973.

Irvine disputed Jimmie Crutchfield's "sunshine-and-butterflies" appraisal of the Negro Leagues. Irvin saw a darker side of the game.

August, 1939

"Fred Wilson was a lefty hitter who was in jail in Miami. He was the evilest man I ever saw. One day, his warden told the owner of the Newark Eagles, Abe Manley, to take a look at this guy who was about to be paroled. Manley signed him because he was a great hitter and a fair outfielder.

"When I came to the Eagles, I was a happy-go-lucky guy. My roomie, (Willie) Devil Wells was tough — a real nice guy, but tough. He was also captain of the team and liked to talk to us to pep us up. And one more thing — he carried a knife, which was OK, because many Negro League players carried knives, which was OK because most of the umpires carried guns.

"So Wilson comes to the team and says, 'I don't like that guy (meaning Wells). He talks too much.' I told him to leave Willie alone, and Wilson takes his knife out and says, 'I'll just stick him to see what color his blood is.'

"He was always threatening people with that knife; once, when he got into a disagreement with me, he grabbed his knife and I told him, 'If you draw that knife on me, I'll make you eat it.'

"But he could hit. In Buffalo one day, we were playing Roy Campenella's team and Fred hit third and I hit fourth. First time up, he walked, I doubled and he was out at the plate, second ups, he doubles, I double and he scored. Third ups, he singled, I tripled and he scored. Fourth ups, he doubled, then I doubled and when Fred gets to third, he stops. He yells at Dick Lundy, our manager, 'Hey, Dick Lundy, next time let me bat fourth and him third. He's running me to death and I ain't running no farther.' "

Bob Feller
Cleveland Indians, pitcher
1936-1941 1945-1956

As discussed in the chapter on the 1920s, Bob Feller was one of the greatest fastball pitchers of all time, leading the Cleveland Indians (with help from Mike Garcia, Bob Lemon and Early Wynn), to prominence in the 1940s. Only his losing four seasons to navy service — he earned eight battle stars — kept Feller from three hundred victories (he won 266 and lost only 162 for a .621 winning percentage).

Feller adds one quick tale about his psychology and sense of humor on the field.

August 20, 1939

"Whenever I walked out on the field," Feller says, "I'd make it my business to walk in front of the umpire. I'd look him right in the eyes and say, 'Cal (Hubbard), nice day today, isn't it? If I don't make more than twelve bad pitches today and you don't miss more than twelve calls, I'll have a pretty good ball game.' It sounds frivolous, but it did several things. It broke the ice and let them know I was a friend who could kid with them, and it got them thinking about not missing a corner-painter I was throwing. I know I got some close calls because I could kid with the umps."

1940s

May 14, 1940 to October 2, 1949

The date, May 14, 1940, refers to the first oral history remembrance rather than the news briefs that follow. That first nugget tells about the perfect career of a one-game catcher. The final date (October 2, 1949), is a story about "The Scooter" wanting to dig a hole in a game against Boston.

Baseball managed, in the 1940s, to survive the war, Lou Gehrig's death, and Babe Ruth's death, and finally broke the race barrier with the inclusion of black athletes in America's pastime. Jackie Robinson and Branch Rickey led the way, and Larry Doby soon followed in their footsteps.

It was 1941, the year of Ted Williams's .406 and Joe DiMaggio's fifty-six-game hitting streak. The decade was about Bob Feller and Lefty Gomez and Satchel Paige. It was Johnny Mize and Ralph Kiner and Pete Gray and, of course, Stan "The Man." It was Enos Slaughter's dash from first in the 1946 Series and the All-American Girls Baseball League.

And it was about all the players who lost time to the war . . . and a player who gave up his career for patriotism. It was the end of the Golden Age.

Selected decade highlights
(in addition to those told in this chapter)

April 16, 1940 - The only complete-game opening day no-hitter in MLB history is thrown, and the artist to do it is Cleveland's Bob Feller, who beats the ChiSox at Comiskey Park, 1-0.

May 13, 1940 - In a game in which no umpires showed up and coaches were assigned the task until a real ump, Larry Goetz, finally made it to the ballpark, St. Louis and Cincinnati played to an 8-8, fourteen-inning tie. Card slugger Johnny Mize blasted three homers and Bill Werber pounded four doubles.

July 28, 1940 - Charlie "King Kong" Keller pokes out three homers in the Yankees' 10-9 win over the White Sox.

August 24, 1940 - Boston Red Sox slugging left fielder Ted Williams pitches the last two innings in a 12-1 blowout loss to the Tigers. Teddy Ballgame's highlights include whiffing Tiger star Rudy York on three pitches and being caught by the catcher to receive Babe Ruth's last pitch in 1933, Joe Glenn.

June 29, 1941 - Joe DiMaggio ties George Sisler's consecutive game hitting streak at forty-one with a single off Senator knuckleballer Dutch Leonard in a twin-bill opener. In the nightcap, he sets the record with a seventh-inning safety off Walt Masterson.

July 17, 1941 - As more than sixty-five thousand fans pack Cleveland's Municipal Stadium, Joe DiMaggio's consecutive hitting streak is ended at fifty-six due to pinpoint pitching by Al Smith and Jim Bagby and two spectacular fielding plays by third baseman Ken Keltner. The Yanks win the game, 6-5.

July 25, 1941 - Old Lefty. Lefty Grove wins his three-hundredth (and last) game, as the forty-one-year-old helps the Red Sox beat the Indians, 10-6, at Fenway Park.

August 1, 1941 - Young Lefty. Lefty Gomez of the Yankees walks eleven St. Louis Browns, but shuts them out anyway, 9-0. The Brownies strand fifteen.

September 4, 1941 - The Yankees clinch by Labor Day with a 6-3 win over the Red Sox. They needed only 136 games (91-45) to win the pennant.

September 28, 1941 - Classic Ted Williams. He begins the day—the last day of the season—hitting .3995 (rounded off to .400) and refuses to protect his average. He plays both games of a doubleheader in Philadelphia and goes 4-for-5 in the opener and 2-for-3 against rookie Fred Caligiuri in the nightcap to finish at .406, the last player to finish the season over .400. The second game also marked Lefty

Grove's final appearance, a loss, to finish his career at 300-141.

March 18, 1942 - Two black baseball players, Jackie Robinson and Nate Moreland, work out with the Chicago White Sox in Pasadena, California. Manager Jimmy Dykes watches them work out and sends them home without an offer.

May 28, 1942 - Yankee ace pitcher Lefty Gomez, who calls himself "the worst hitter in baseball," connects for four hits while giving up only four hits in a 16-1 shellacking of Washington.

July 19, 1942 - Brooklyn Dodgers outfielder Pete Reiser crashes headfirst into the wall at Sportsman's Park while attempting to catch a drive in the eleventh inning by St. Louis's Enos Slaughter. Reiser bounces unconscious off the wall and the ball trickles out of his glove as Slaughter races around the bases for a game-winning inside-the-park home run (7-6, Cards).

July 21, 1942 - Classic Satchel Paige. In a Negro League game at Forbes Field between Paige's Kansas City Monarchs and Josh Gibson's Homestead Grays, Paige purposely loads the bases with two outs to face the slugger. Paige tells Gibson where and how fast each pitch will arrive and strikes him out anyway, making good on his boast of the day before. On a historical note, gasoline rationing coupons begin their run on the Atlantic seaboard.

February 20, 1943 - The "league of their own" is born as Phil Wrigley and Branch Rickey begin the All-American Girls Softball League, which eventually switches to hardball. At this point, all games are played in and around Chicago, with teams in Racine and Kenosha, Wisconsin; Rockford, Illinois; and South Bend, Indiana. Pennant winners were Racine, at 20-15 in the first half, and Kenosha, at 33-21 in the second half, with Racine winning the championship of 1943. The league continued in various forms until 1954.

June 1, 1943 - Pirate pitcher Rip Sewell unveils his blooper, or eephus, pitch. Lobbed eighteen to twenty-five feet in the air, crossing home plate at a downward arc in the strike zone, Sewell uses it to win twenty games in 1943.

June 17, 1943 - Joe Cronin, player/manager of the Red Sox, pinch hits three-run homers in each game of a doubleheader against the Browns. It is the third time in three days that Cronin has pinch-hit a three-run homer.

July 12, 1943 - Not a bad line-up: for a fund-raising armed forces effort, an exhibition is played in Boston between the hometown Braves and an armed forces all-star team managed by Babe Ruth, with Joe DiMaggio hitting third and Ted Williams batting cleanup. Ruth is robbed of a homer when he flies to right as a pinch hitter in the eighth, and Williams wins it for the all-stars, 9-8, with a homer.

April 30, 1944 - Phil Weintraub, a slugging first baseman for the New York Giants, belts a homer, triple and two doubles and drives in eleven runs; player/manager Mel Ott reaches base seven times and scores six runs as the Giants whip the Dodgers, 26-8, before fifty-eight thousand at the Polo Grounds.

June 10, 1944 - With a war on and able-bodied baseball players hard to find, the Cincinnati Reds employ Joe Nuxhall (on permission from his high school principal) to throw two-thirds of an inning. Nuxie, at fifteen-years, ten months, eleven days old, is the youngest man ever to play in the Majors. Though Nuxhall gives up five runs on two hits and five walks to the Cardinals, he returns to "the Bigs" eight years later and wins 135 games during his sixteen-year career, with a 3.90 ERA, lowered perceptibly from his 67.50 ERA of 1944.

June 12, 1944 - The Giants again beat up on the Dodgers, this time 15-9, as Mel Ott and Phil Weintraub each rock two homers. Ott has now homered fourteen times in three weeks.

June 26, 1944 - The Polo Grounds was the site of a three-way game between the New York Yankees, Brooklyn Dodgers and host New York Giants to raise money for the war effort. Before fifty-thousand paying fans, Brooklyn wins the contest with the final score: Dodgers 5, Yankees 1, Giants 0.

October 4-9, 1944 - Heaven comes to St. Louis as the hard-luck Browns meet the Cardinals in the Fall Classic. The Cards take the Series in six games in what is dubbed "The Streetcar Series."

April 16, 1945 - Jackie Robinson gets his second Major League tryout, this time for the Boston Red Sox at Fenway Park, along with Negro League stars Sam Jethroe and Marvin Williams, but again, no offers are tendered.

May 20, 1945 - One-armed outfielder Pete Gray leads the St. Louis Browns to a sweep of the Yankees, 10-1 and 5-2. Gray scores the winning run in game two and makes seven exceptional catches in the outfield.

July 1, 1945 - As though he had never left, Tigers star Hank Greenberg returns from four years in the army and homers in his first game.

August 24, 1945 - Bob Feller returns from the navy and wins his first start, a four-hitter in which he strikes out twelve, as his Indians defeat Detroit, 4-2.

September 1, 1945 - Vince DiMaggio, the eldest of the three ball-playing DiMaggios ties an NL record by smacking his fourth grand slam of the year in an 8-3 win for the Phils over the Braves in Boston.

September 30, 1945 - On the last day of the season, Detroit clinches the pennant by beating the St. Louis Browns, 6-3, on a ninth-inning grand slam by Hank Greenberg.

October 6, 1945 - The curse that has endured. "Billy Goat" Sianis buys a box seat for game four of the World Series between the Cubs and Tigers. The Wrigley Field police usher Sianis out and he casts a "goat curse" over the team. They haven't been in a World Series since.

May 6, 1946 - St. Louis Browns hurler Al Milnar induces hot-hitting Johnny Pesky of the Boston Red Sox to ground out, ending Pesky's run of eleven straight hits.

August 11, 1946 - Stan "The Man" Musial goes 8-for-9 as the Cards sweep the Reds in a doubleheader, 15-4 and 7-3.

April 15, 1947 - Jackie Robinson breaks the color barrier and ushers baseball into the twentieth century. He goes 0-for-3 versus the Braves, but flawlessly handled eleven chances at first base in Brooklyn's 5-3 win.

April 24, 1947 - For the fifth time in his career, Johnny Mize hits three homers in a game, but his New York Giants lose to the Boston Braves, 14-5.

May 17, 1947 - At Fenway Park in a game versus the St. Louis Browns, Brownie pitcher Ellis Kinder is about to deliver a pitch when a sea gull flies overhead and drops a three-pound smelt on the mound, interrupting Kinder and the game for several minutes.

June 13, 1947 - As a flying disc (it wasn't called a "flying saucer" at that time) reportedly crash lands on W.W. Brazel's ranch near Roswell, New Mexico—an army/air force press release, July 8, confirmed the extraterrestrial landing but recanted it the following day, calling the device a weather balloon—Fenway Park presents its first night game as 34,510 earthlings watch the BoSox beat the ChiSox, 5-3.

July 5, 1947 - Cleveland's Larry Doby becomes the first black to play in the American League. He strikes out as a pinch hitter versus the White Sox after being plucked from the roster of the Newark Eagles of the Negro American League.

July 13, 1947 - Bobo Newsome joins the Yankees, making this the fourteenth time he has changed teams.

August 16, 1947 - Ralph Kiner is red hot. He hits three consecutive homers for the Pirates in a 12-7 win over the Cardinals. For Kiner, it makes seven homers in his last four games and four consecutive homers (counting one in his last at-bat yesterday). Kiner now edges closer to teammate Johnny Mize in the home run derby; the two finish the season tied with fifty-one apiece.

September 11, 1947 - Ralph Kiner hits three more homers in a row after belting two on September 9.

September 22, 1947 - Stan Musial connects for five hits for the fifth time this year, tying Ty Cobb's record for quintuple-hit games in a season.

October 2, 1947 - Yogi Berra becomes the first player to hit a pinch-hit homer in World Series history when he connects in the seventh inning off Ralph Branca, but the Dodgers prevail, 9-8.

October 3, 1947 - Yankee hurler Bill Bevens is throwing a World Series no-hitter, with two down in the ninth, when pinch hitter Cookie Lavagetto doubles in two runs to lose the no-no and the game, 3-2, in game four of the Fall Classic.

May 21, 1948 - Joe DiMaggio is red hot. He hits for the cycle — two homers, a triple, double and single — as the Yankees thump the ChiSox, 13-2. Two days later, he smacks three consecutive homers against Cleveland — two of those against Bob Feller.

August 16, 1948 - Baseball's most beloved sports figure of the era, Babe Ruth, dies of throat cancer at age fifty-three. Among those who homer on this day are Stan Musial, Del Rice and Erv Dusak of the Cardinals, and Wally Westlake and Hal Gregg of the Pirates.

August 17, 1948 - Yankee Tom Henrich bombs his fourth grand slam of the year, joining Babe Ruth, Lou Gehrig and Rudy York as the only players to this date to accomplish the feat in the American League. Henrich, who began playing for the Yankees in 1937, had never hit a slam until this year.

May 1, 1949 - Elmer Valo, reportedly Major League baseball's first Czechoslovakian-born player, hits two bases-loaded triples, another first, in a 15-9 win for his A's.

May 6, 1949 - Philadelphia A's rookie left-hander Bobby Shantz throws nine hitless innings in relief versus the Tigers. Shantz gives up a run in the top of the thirteenth and A's teammate, fifteen-year veteran Wally Moses, nearing his thirty-ninth birthday, wins the game for Shantz with a two-run homer, his only dinger of the year, in the bottom of the inning, for a 5-4 victory.

July 6, 1949 - Walker Cooper, acquired three weeks earlier by the Cincinnati Reds, pays big dividends in this game as the Redlegs bomb the Cubs at Crosley Field, 23-4. Cooper goes 6-for-7 with three homers, ten RBI and five runs scored.

August 9, 1949 - There's no room for brotherly love in the baseball of this era. The New York Yankees and Boston Red Sox went down to the wire for the AL pennant in 1949, and in this one, Boston center fielder Dom DiMaggio had a thirty-four-game hitting streak on the line when he faced Vic Raschi—the last pitcher to blank him—of the Bronx Bombers. In the eighth inning of a tight game, Dom hits a sinking line drive to center. Yankee center fielder Joe DiMaggio charges hard and makes a shoestring catch of his brother's shot to deny him of a hit. The Yanks win, 6-3.

The Chronicles

Buddy Hancken
Philadelphia A's, catcher
1940

Perhaps the perfect example of the "other side" of this book is Morris Medlock "Buddy" Hancken, the 6'1", 175-pound catcher from Birmingham, Alabama. By the "other side" of the book, it is meant that for every Ted Williams, Joe DiMaggio, Stan "The Man," Hank Aaron, Mickey, Willie, Duke, Whitey or Feller—Hall of Famers all, with long, heroic careers—there are hundreds of Buddy Hanckens whose careers are remarkably short and lacking of newspaper-headlined accolades. Nonetheless, Buddy Hancken is another perfect example of who belongs here because he lived his dream, albeit for one brief moment. One brief moment, indeed; Buddy Hancken's career in the majors lasted one game —one inning—and it is perfect that he remembered everything that occurred during those shining five minutes in the sun that made him forever part of that short-list fraternity of Major League baseball players. He is a member now and forever, thanks to the story that follows.

May 14, 1940

Hancken reports, "We (the Philadelphia A's) were in Cleveland facing Bob Feller. We had a two-run lead in the ninth and with two out, I came in to pinch-run for Frank Hayes (the starting catcher). The inning ended quickly—I was on base for a pitch—and when I got back to the dugout, I picked up my catcher's gear and started putting it on, and since no one said anything, I figured that was OK with everyone and I would catch the last inning. I looked to Mr. (Connie) Mack and he just smiled.

"I caught the last inning for Bill Beckmann, who was closing out the game on the mound for us.

"Hal Trosky was Cleveland's first hitter, and he took three of the damnedest swings — *SWISH* — and wasn't close on any of them. Strike three.

"The umpire, George Pipgras said, 'Damn. No wonder the guy hits so many homers . . . homer or whiff.'

"Next up was Jeff Heath, and he bounced out. Then Ken Keltner came up and blasted a line drive at Bill Lillard, our shortstop. It almost went right through him, but he hung on. Three up, three down.

"When I came into the clubhouse and a few writers asked me my thoughts, I said, 'Hell, I don't remember anything about it.' I did later, and looking back over it, I may be the only catcher in baseball history to have a perfect catching career — no one ever got on against me."

"Broadway" Charlie Wagner
Boston Red Sox, pitcher
1938-1942 1946

Charlie Wagner, the 5'11", 170-pounder from Reading, Pennsylvania, was nicknamed "Broadway" for the well-groomed, dapper and classy appearance he cut as he made the most of his celebrity. Wagner says, "I enjoy dressing up and always bought nice clothes and suits. Johnny Droyne of the Boston Herald called me 'Broadway,' and it stuck. But since I wore mostly gray and brown suits, Fresco Thompson called me 'Two Tone.' That one didn't take."

His two best seasons came right before the war, and a four-year stint in the navy, invaded his career. Wagner went 12-8 in 1941 and 14-11 in 1942, then it was off to join Uncle Sam.

He went 32-23 over his career, appearing in a hundred games, most as a reliever.

Wagner recalls some superstitions among his teammates. "Lefty Grove used to line up his glove in the coaching box between innings — the players left their gloves on the field in foul territory in those days — and one day in 1938, I picked up his glove to help him and he yelled at me, 'Never, ever touch my glove again.' Then he nearly threw me out of the ballpark.

"Also in 1938, no one wanted to interrupt a streak, so you did the same things exactly the same way to keep a streak going. We went on an eight-game winning streak and Red Sox owner Tom Yawkey gave us lamb chops for eight straight days so as not to break the streak; Joe Cronin chewed the same gum for eight days; and I was on prune juice for eight straight days. I'm glad we lost.

"And I was a teammate of Moe Berg. He was super intelligent and had newspapers all over the floor of his room. He would put 'dead' papers on the floor and 'live' newspapers on the seats. Live newspapers hadn't been read yet, and dead ones were read and tossed in heaps. And all the newspapers were in different languages. But he had this thing with his ties. He had ten ties and all of them were the same, exactly the same, and he wore nothing but black, but he was funny. He had a dry sense of humor and, though quirky, was a very nice man."

Wagner's offering is about another quirky man, his roommate, Ted Williams.

June, 1941

"Ted got three bats and brought them up to our room at the Chase Hotel in St. Louis. There was no air conditioning and it was really hot in that room. I get in the room and it's all covered with sand; it turned out to be sawdust and sand. Ted was shaving all the handles of all his bats with sandpaper and a knife, and there were shavings and sawdust all over my bed. Ted kept saying, 'Feel this handle.' I would feel it and swing and couldn't tell the difference and I said, 'Yeah, Ted. Great.' I cleared away the shavings and went to bed.

"Ted said, 'I got the feel now.' Now, we had these four-poster beds with a mirror in between them and Ted lined up between the beds to look at himself in the mirror when he took his cuts. He takes this big home run swing and bangs the poster of my bed and— WHAM—it went down like a ton of bricks. Ted said, 'What a swing. What power. Good bat. Get yourself a new bed.'

"But I'll tell you something about Ted. There never was a nicer guy, he doesn't drink or smoke anymore, and he never talks about himself. There's never an 'I' in a conversation with Ted; he's only concerned with the other guy."

Ted Williams
Boston Red Sox, outfield
1939-1942 1946-1960

No thumbnail paragraph can do justice to a ballplayer who needed four classic nicknames to approximate his value: The Kid, The Splendid Splinter, The Thumper and Teddy Ballgame. Ted Williams, at 6'3", 210 pounds, was controversial, patriotic, competitive, caustic, a perfectionist and self-confident to the point of cockiness; he may have been the best pure hitter the game has ever seen, as well as one of the most dedicated students of the game to ever perform between the white lines. His contemporary, Joe DiMaggio called him "The greatest ballplayer I ever played against." Williams, a San Diego native, ranks high on baseball's career lists for home runs (521), RBIs (1,839), walks (2,019) and batting (.344), and could have gone much higher had he not lost all or part of six prime years to duty in the military service as a fighter pilot. Ted Williams is the last player to hit .400 (.406 in 1941) and he won six batting titles, four home run titles, four RBI crowns and two MVPs. He played hard, seldom got along with the local press and didn't really appreciate the fans. He left the game as he entered it — with a flair, homering in his last at-bat, September 26, 1960, off Jack Fisher — "I had just hit two balls four hundred feet and foul and short (of home run distance) and heard the fans in my corner rooting for me, so I knew I had to hit the next one a little better . . . and I did," said Williams. Williams had his number retired by the Boston Red Sox. He was elected to the Hall of Fame in 1966.

Ted Williams has a ballpark full of great days he could tell us about; he selected his run at .400 in 1941 and an All-Star game in 1946.

September 28, 1941

With one game left in the season, Williams was hitting .3995 (rounded off to .400), making him the first .400 hitter in the American League since Harry Heilmann of Detroit in 1923, and the first .400 hitter in baseball since the NL's Bill Terry for New York (.401) in 1930. Williams's manager, Joe Cronin, went to Williams and said, "Kid, you deserve to be a .400 hitter; you can sit if you want." Williams replied, "I'm playing. I don't want anyone talking about .399. I'm going in with both feet and I'll make it and then some."

Williams picks up the story. "It had rained the night before and the field was a muddy mess. We had a doubleheader to play in Philadelphia and I knew I needed some practice to get my swing sharp, so I got hold of Tom Daley (a coach) and we went to a dry area of the outfield. I told him to keep throwing me pitches until I told him to stop. He must have thrown me 150 pitches and I was banging them off the outfield wall in right. He was tired and he asked me how I was. I told him I was looser than I'd been all season and that the practice would put me over .400. I knew I was going to have a big day and I went 4-for-5 in the first game and 2-for-3 against a rookie (Fred Caligiuri) in the second game to finish at .406. I had the sense of history that day. As that game ended, I knew I'd be remembered as one of the best ever, even though I was only twenty-three."

July 9, 1946

The homer off the eephus. "We were playing the All-Star game at Fenway Park," Williams says. "Now, this was special. First, it was the first time an All-Star game had been played here; second, because it was my home park; third, because it was my first one since 1942 because I had been in the war; fourth, because they didn't play an All-Star game the year before; and fifth, because I was playing with the best — when you play with Joe DiMaggio, Charlie Keller, Hank Greenberg, Vic Raschi, Bob Feller and Hal Newhouser and against Stan Musial, Ralph Kiner and Johnny Mize, you always get the adrenalin up and want to show your stuff.

"We were beating up on the National League 10-0 and I already had a home run off Kirby Higbe, two singles and a walk. I'm up in the ninth with one on and Rip Sewell was on the mound. He threw this lobbed pitch, the eephus, which goes twenty feet in the air and comes across the plate like slow-pitch softball. It's a sissy pitch, and I wanted to kill it. Normally, I would wait on a slow pitch, but I noticed that if you got to it early, you could hit it, so I ran up on it and swung before it crossed the plate, and hit it four hundred feet. That one was really for the fans, but it was for me too, and for baseball . . . to get rid of that sissy pitch."

Tommy Henrich
New York Yankees, outfield
1937-1942 1946-1950

Tommy Henrich was nicknamed "Old Reliable" for hitting and defensive skills that made him a standout in a standout outfield that included Joe DiMaggio and Charlie "King Kong" Keller. While serving his country during the war cut three years out of the heart of his career, the six-foot, 180-pounder from Massillon, Ohio, still managed to belt out 183 homers and drive in 795 runs while leading the league in triples twice (thirteen in 1947, fourteen in 1948) and runs (138 in 1947). He hit better than .300 three times en route to being a four-time all-star.

Henrich says, "My whole career was wrapped up with a great ball club, before and after the war. That club had a lot of love and nobody had more class. They were so professional, it was a joy to join a gang like that, led by the best manager of all time, Joe McCarthy."

Perhaps the one moment in time that will forever link Henrich and Dodger catcher Mickey Owen occurred in the ninth inning of game four of the 1941 World Series.

October 5, 1941

Henrich recalls, "I got a big bang out of the 1941 Series. There was a lot of drama in that baby. Both teams were full of professional talent. Leo Durocher (the Dodger manager) would rip the Yankees in the papers, saying they would run us into the ground. But they won 100 games and we won 101, so the thing was up for grabs and I had a tight feeling all the way through. McCarthy told me he was so nervous he couldn't eat. (Pitcher) Marius Russo was so tense he wobbled. This had to be the emotional high point of my career.

"Now, it wasn't the most important thing in the world to win, but just the same, it would kill me if we didn't beat them. They were a great team, but I knew we were just as good, maybe better.

"We won the first game at Yankee Stadium, 3-2, behind Red Ruffing's great pitching. They tied it up with a 3-2 win in game two and when we took game three at Ebbets Field behind Russo's brilliant pitching (a four-hitter) and his hit off Freddie Fitzsimmons's leg, we were up, 2-1.

"In game four, they were getting the best of us in a tight game. The Dodgers led, 4-3 in the ninth, with Hughie Casey on the mound. Casey had pitched from the fourth inning on and he was sharp. There were two outs in the inning when I came up; we were down to our last out. The count on me was 3-and-2 and Casey threw me the biggest, widest curve he ever threw in his life. I started my swing at the strike zone and the thing just kept breaking. I was protecting the plate, and though you always see Mickey Owen trying to dig it out of the dirt, it was a sharp-breaking curve, a wide, slow-moving ball that suddenly darted through and below the strike zone. It was not a spitter. I started my swing high and the ball broke down low and disappeared and I couldn't hold up.

"I had so much trouble, I knew Mickey would have the same. At that moment I looked around and saw the ball going back to the backstop, and I headed for first.

"Then, of course, we came back. DiMag (Joe DiMaggio) hit the doggonedest line drive, that handcuffed Jimmy Wasdell in left field, for a double that never was more than six feet off the ground, and Charlie Keller hit an 0-2 pitch for an Ebbets Field double (presumably not extra bases in bigger parks); they walked Bill Dickey and then Joe Gordon hit one off the left field wall and Wasdell misplayed that one too, and we had four runs. That broke their backs and they never recovered. When we beat them, 3-1, in game five, we could see that they were emotionally broken.

"Big play ... but to set two things straight: first, it was not a spitball, and two, I had so much trouble with it, that everyone should realize there was no way any catcher was going to make that play. People should stop treating Mickey Owen as if he had misplayed it. He didn't."

Al "Happy" Milnar
Cleveland Indians, pitcher
1936-1943 1946

Al "Happy" Milnar was a 6'2", 200-pound lefty from Cleveland who pitched for his hometown Indians after being plucked from the local sandlots, and was the club's number two starter behind Bob Feller for three years.

His best season was 1940, when he threw four shutouts to lead the league en route to an 18-10 mark.

He finished up with a record of 57-58 in 188 games, 127 as a starter, and a 6-5 record with seven saves in relief.

"He readily admits to giving up Joe DiMaggio's last hit of his fifty-six game hitting streak. "Ken Keltner didn't get any great stops for me. I almost stopped Joe in game twenty-nine. He went 1-for-5 against me, but he was tough any time."

He recalls an obscure rule that deprived him of finishing a game.

August 11, 1942

"We were pitching at Cleveland in the first game of a twi-night doubleheader, and Tommy Bridges of Detroit and I tangled up in a pitcher's duel. I had a no-hitter for eight and two-thirds innings until Roger 'Doc' Cramer singled with two out in the ninth.

"Bridges shut us out for fourteen innings and I shut them out for fourteen innings. Rudy York got a hit off me in the fourteenth, only the second hit off me all day. Nothing-nothing going into the fifteenth. Then the umpires called the game because there was a wartime rule and a Sunday blue law that a game couldn't continue under the lights if it began without lights. So they called our game a scoreless tie, turned on the lights, and a half-hour later began the second game. I took off for home, disgusted because I could have pitched all day."

Buck O'Neil
Kansas City Monarchs (Negro Leagues), first base
1934-1955

John Jordan "Buck" O'Neil was a 6'2", 200-pound first baseman from Carrabelle, Florida, who played in the Negro Leagues for twenty years, spending most of his time with the Kansas City Monarchs (from 1938 to 1955) but also playing for the Memphis Red Sox, Miami Giants and Shreveport Acme Giants. He became the first black coach hired by a Major League team when he was signed by the Cubs in 1962. He led the Negro National League in batting in 1946 (.353) and was generally thought of as an excellent first base-man with a good bat.

One of his favorite stories (dateless and timeless) deals with his best friend, Satchel Paige, who always called O'Neil "Nancy." O'Neil recalls how he got the nickname: "We were playing in North Dakota before the war, at an Indian reservation, and Satch met this very pretty Indian girl named Nancy. When we left town for Chicago, Satch sent for her and asked her to come stay at our hotel. We got her a room next to ours—for appearance sake. Satch didn't know this, but his fiancé, Lahoma, came to the hotel to see Satch. She knocks on the door to Nancy's room, with Satch inside, and wakes Satch up. He yells out, Nancy?' I heard Lahoma coming and I came out and yelled to Satch, 'Yeah, Satch, it's Nancy. Lahoma's here.' I hurriedly told Lahoma that Nancy' was Satch's baseball nickname for me. He made it a point to call me that whenever Lahoma was around, and the name stuck."

The game O'Neil likes to tell about is the second game of the Negro League World Series at Pittsburgh's Forbes Field between the Kansas City Monarchs and the Homestead Grays.

September 10, 1942

O'Neil recalls, "We beat the Homestead Grays in four straight and both teams were great. We opened the series in Washington and Satch threw five shutout innings and we won 8-0—our third base-man, Newt Allen, got three hits for us off their pitcher Roy Wel-maker. We came to Pittsburgh for game two. Now, the best player on our team was Satch and the best player on the Grays was their big slugger Josh Gibson, 'the black Babe Ruth.' Josh and Satch always had a friendly competition going. When they were on the same team (the Pittsburgh Crawfords) Satch once told Josh, 'You never had a chance to hit off me and I never had a chance to pitch to you, but one day, in a big game, with it all on the line, we're gonna see who's better and what you can do against me and what I can do against you.' That day had arrived.

"We're leading the game, 8-4, with two outs in the ninth and Satch is on the mound—Hilton Smith started and pitched well and Satch came in to relieve in the seventh. So Satch gives up a two-out triple past third and down the line to their leadoff hitter, Jerry Benjamin. He calls time and motions for me to come to the mound. He said, 'Hey, Nancy, come here. You know what I'm fixin' to do? We already got two outs and I only need to get one more. So I'm gonna put Vic Harris (the next batter) on base. Then Howard Easterling is up next and he's a pretty good hitter, so I'm gonna put him on base. I want to pitch to Josh with the bases loaded and prove who's the best.'

"By now, manager Frank Duncan has come out to the mound; Satch told him what he was going to do. Frank turns to me and says, 'Buck, you see all these people in the stands? This is what they came to see—Josh and Satch, so whatever Satch wants to do, let him do.'

"So Satch walks Harris, and as he is walking Easterling, he yells to Josh (who is in the on-deck circle), 'Hey, Josh, you remember what we talked about in Pittsburgh about who's the best and what would happen when we faced each other someday?' Josh said, 'Yeah, Satch, I remember.' Satch said, 'Well, Josh, this is the day.'

"Now, the thirty-five thousand people in the stands are all standing and yelling; they *know* what is happening.

"Satch is on the mound and as he lets the resin bag drop to the ground, he says to Josh, 'I'm gonna throw you some fastballs, nothing but fastballs. I'm not gonna trick you. I'll throw you three fastballs. This first one is gonna be letter high. Satch winds up, pivots on one leg, kicks high and fires, but Josh didn't move a muscle. Strike one.

"Satch says, 'Now, Josh, this one is gonna be a little bit faster, but at your belt.' Again, Satch kicks his leg high and fires and again Josh watches. Strike two.

"Now Satch says, 'Don't worry, Josh, I'm not gonna brush you back. I'm not gonna throw smoke at your yolk, I'm gonna throw a pea at your knee, only it's gonna be faster than the last one. Gibson tensed up at the plate and Satch kicked high on the mound as he fired his 'Long Tom' home and Josh started to swing, then couldn't

Stan "The Man" Musial, outfield, 1940s
Courtesy: National Baseball Library Hall of Fame, Cooperstown, New York

pull the trigger. *BOOM*. Strike three. Struck him out.

"Satch strutted off the mound, walked by me and said, 'Nancy, nobody hits Satch's fastball when he don't want him to.' "

Stan Musial
St. Louis Cardinals, outfield
1941-1963

Stan "The Man" Musial certainly was "the Man" for the Cards from the "Gas House Gang" days through the rebuilding days of the early sixties. He was the epitome of quiet class and consistency. It was claimed that the six-foot, 175-pound Musial could see the rotational spin on every ball as it sped toward home plate. He worked hard at the game, and looked graceful and in control at the plate, in the outfield and at first base. It was his mastering of the first sack that enabled him to become the first man to play more than one-thousand games each at two different positions—1,896 in the outfield and 1,016 at first.

From his oft-copied but never mastered (except by Musial) left-handed crouch batting style, Musial won seven batting titles, two RBI crowns, three MVPs, and ranks high on the all-time lists in home runs (475), batting (.331), doubles (725) and RBIs (1,951). At one time, he was the National League career leader in hits, but when apprised of this, the Donora, Pennsylvania, native merely smiled and said, "I also hold the record for making the most outs — more than 7,300 of them." He had his number retired by the Cardinals and a bronze statue was erected in his honor in front of Busch Stadium. Musial was elected to the Hall of Fame in 1969.

Musial could certainly have told us about May 2, 1954, when he slugged five homers in a doubleheader, or his July 12, 1955, All-Star game-winner in the twelfth inning off Frank Sullivan to cap a six-run comeback. He chose, instead, to tell of a brawl from 1943 that showed him the team concept of the sport and an embarrassing moment from 1944; he followed it all up (see 1950s chapter) with a memorable moment later in his career.

August 1, 1943

"We always played it rough with the Dodgers, like we were mortal enemies. They had a reliever named Les Webber who was their closer. One day in St. Louis, we faced him and I really learned what team spirit was all about. Now, I never hit singles against Webber; it was always doubles, triples and homers when I got on. I hit him hard and I guess he was tired of it. In the first game of a doubleheader, he knocked me down three times in a row. Now, it was tough enough to see the ball against the white shirts of the center field crowd — I don't know why, but fans out there always seemed to wear white shirts and it was tough to pick up the ball against that background. Anyway, I barely saw this pitch aimed at my head and I dove to the ground . . . for the third time. Now I had had it and I started to go after him, but I was stopped before a fight started. I get back to the dugout and our pitcher Mort Cooper sat beside me and told me, 'I'll get him for you.'

"Two innings later, Webber came up to bat and on the first pitch, Cooper hit him right in the neck. Both benches cleared and there was a real brawl, with each side out there to protect their own. It was part of the game then and exemplified teamness."

May, 1944

"I was in my third full year and playing center field one day in St. Louis and I was feeling pretty cocky about my ability. There was a very 'high' sky and I had my sunglasses down when Frank McCormick of Cincinnati hit a mile-high fly. I stared up at that expanse for what seemed like five minutes without finding the ball. It finally came down — *THUD* — and hit me on top of the head. Pepper Martin was playing right field and he runs over to me and says, 'Stan, are you all right?' He really looked worried. I shook my head yes, and then, when he knew I was OK, he laughed so hard he almost fell down. See, first he made sure I was OK, then he laughed. There was a teamness to the sport. The event was funny, but health came first, then the laughter."

Tony Cuccinello
Boston Braves, second base
1930-1945

As mentioned in the 1930s chapter, Tony Cuccinello, brother of catcher Al Cuccinello, was a tough, dedicated infielder who played for five teams during his career. He had his moments with his bat and his glove, and he tells of some baseball strategy during the war years.

April 18, 1944

"I was playing third base for the Chicago White Sox and we were opening the season in Cleveland. The night before the opener, the Cleveland Club held a father-and-son dinner and Lou Boudreau, the Indians' player/manager was the guest speaker.

"Lou made a short speech and afterward asked the kids if they had any questions about baseball. One kid asked Lou about the hidden-ball trick and Boudreau said, 'We don't pull that off anymore; it's obsolete.'

"The next day, we were leading Cleveland by one run in the eighth inning and Lou was up at bat. He singled to right field, and that makes him the tying run. The next hitter also got a base hit, sending Lou to third; we made a play on him and he slid in just ahead of my tag. Now he is the tying run at third base, and the winning run is standing at first. It looks like we are in trouble.

"Thornton Lee, our pitcher, walks by me to get the ball and I whispered, 'Stay off the rubber,' and I kept the ball.

"I put the ball in my bare hand and put my glove on over the ball so you couldn't see it. I walked over toward third base so Lou could see my hands (the ball being hidden) and went to my position behind the bag. I kept my eye on Lou and sure enough, he started to take his lead. When I thought I had him, I made a dive for third base. Lou sensed there was something wrong and he slid headfirst right into me. I could hear umpire Cal Hubbard running to call the play, and as he got close, he said to me, 'He's out if you've got the ball.' I took the ball out of my glove and showed it to him and Hubbard hollered, 'Yer out.'

"I saw the pained expression on Lou's face as he got up. It was a long walk back to the dugout and I couldn't help thinking that I never would have pulled the play on him if he hadn't said it was obsolete."

Ted "Double Duty" Radcliffe
Birmingham Black Barons (Negro Leagues),
catcher, pitcher
1928-1950

Double Duty Radcliffe was a 5'10", 210-pound athlete from Mobile, Alabama, who got his nickname handed to him by Damon Runyan, who caught him at the 1932 Negro League World Series played at Yankee Stadium. In the first game of a doubleheader, Radcliffe was the catcher for Satchel Paige, who threw a 5-0 shutout. Radcliffe then put down his catcher's mitt and put on his pitcher's glove, took the hill and threw a shutout of his own in game two.

Radcliffe was known equally for his catching skills and his ability to doctor a baseball on the mound. He threw a spitter, sweatball, mudball, emery ball, tar ball and knife-slice ball. He played thousands of games in his twenty-two-year career in the Negro Leagues and with barnstorming teams and generally hit better than .300 while winning at a .700 clip as a pitcher. He was a member of such Negro League teams as the Detroit Wolves, St. Louis Stars, Homestead Grays, Pittsburgh Crawfords, Cleveland Giants, Columbus Blue Birds, Chicago American Giants, Brooklyn Eagles, New York Black Yankees, Claybrook (Arkansas) Tigers, Memphis Red Sox and Birmingham Black Barons. There is quite a bit of support from the veterans committee to get Radcliffe Hall of Fame status.

His friend Satchel Paige was a boyhood buddy; "Satch and I were raised together in Mobile, and when we played ball together in North Dakota from 1934-36, neither one of us lost a single game, and I caught four of Satch's no-hitters and I got him to catch me one game. He threw a one-hit shutout in the first game and when I gave up a run on a home run—the only hit I gave up—in the seventh inning of the second game, Satch just shook his head and walked off the field and never caught me again."

Radcliffe recalled his greatest memory, from a Negro League All-Star game.

July 17, 1944

Radcliffe says, "In the 1944 East-West All-Star game at Comiskey Park, the East was leading 2-1 in the sixth. I'm up, Ducky Davenport is at third base and my brother (Alec Radcliffe) is on first. I hit a home run into the upper deck, right by the "El" (Elevated Train) off Barney Morris of the New York Cybans and we won, 4-2. As I touched home plate, my mother met me at home. There was fifty-seven thousand in attendance and they cheered and cheered and I was able to say on the loudspeaker, 'God bless you all.'

"You may think it's strange that my mother met me at home plate in the middle of a game, but she was known far and wide for being a great fan—so great, in fact, that she was given a lifetime pass to all games at Comiskey Park."

Marty Marion
St. Louis Cardinals, shortstop
1940-1953

Martin Whitford Marion, a skinny, 6'2", 170-pound skillful shortstop from Richberg, South Carolina, was nicknamed "Slats," due to his thin appearance, and "The Octopus" for his great range in the field.

A member of the Cardinals' "Gas House Gang," Marion helped the Cards get to four World Series in five years in the mid-1940s. He was the National League MVP in 1944 based on all-around leadership and ability and was a seven-time all-star.

Marion, whose greatest thrill was playing in his first World Series in 1942 versus the Yankees ("a country boy to the World Series in seven years," he says), chose to talk about the pranks, superstitions and fun on the field.

June, 1945

"Our club had the craziest people in uniform. 'The Gas House Gang' really liked to get their uniforms dirty. Pepper Martin and Dizzy Dean were a wild breed of ballplayer and they were great enough to back up their eccentricities. As to dirty uniforms, they would work on old jalopies and quit exactly at game time, showing up, in uniform, all greasy and dirty.

"We had some superstitions. Ducky Medwick would search for hairpins and you didn't fool with Ducky when he was looking. He also used to step on third base on his way out to the field. I always threw to Whitey Kurowski at third during throw-arounds; I would never throw it directly to the pitcher.

"I picked up pebbles around the infield before every game. Superstition? Not really. I felt if I stopped I would get a bad back. In fact, I had a bad back all my life and picking up pebbles helped keep me limber; that and Dr. Harrison J. Weaver, the team trainer, who rubbed my back and kept me going. My buddy, pitcher Mort Cooper, was traded by the Cards to the Boston Braves in May 1945 and when our club next went into the Boston park, I got out to shortstop to take infield and I found two-hundred pennies scattered all over shortstop. As I started to pick them up, there was Mort laughing his head off. After he was traded to the Giants in June 1947, the next time we got to the Polo Grounds, Mort and I talked at home plate, and as was our superstitious custom, we raced to the clubhouse; only at the Polo Grounds, the clubhouse was in center field, 490 feet away. We ran and I beat him to the steps, he tripped and cut up his leg and wasn't worth a darn for the rest of the season. I brought him to Dr. Weaver, but Mort was through. But we had to run there; it was our custom."

Roy Campanella
Brooklyn Dodgers, catcher
1948-1957

"Campy," the 5'9", 195-pound solidly built catcher from Philadelphia was the heart and soul of the Brooklyn Dodgers for a dozen years, until one of the real baseball tragedies occurred—Campanella was severely injured in an auto accident on an icy New Jersey street and was paralyzed, cutting short his career and keeping him from joining the Dodgers on their move west in 1958.

He hit better than .300 three times and pounded thirty or more homers four times, and was considered one of the better receivers in baseball.

He played for the Baltimore Elite Giants of the Negro National League in 1936, when he was only fifteen. A three-time MVP, eight-time all-star, he led the Dodgers to five NL pennants and their first World Championship. He had his number retired by the Dodgers and was elected to the Hall of Fame in 1969.

Campanella weaved the story of his entry into the Major Leagues.

October, 1945

"I was catching for a black all-star team in a five-game series against a team of white Major League all-stars managed by Charlie Dressen, the manager of the Dodgers. I never knew the Dodgers scouted me or even heard of me. He came up to me during the series and asked me to come to the Dodger offices the next week.

"I drove over and went into Mr. (Branch) Rickey's office and he had a three-inch thick book on his desk filled with my life. He had all my baseball newspaper clippings in it. Mr. Rickey knew all about me. He said, 'I know your father is Italian and your mother is an American negro. You know, Roy, I was a catcher, too, and I know you are a good signal caller. The most difficult thing for you will be to take an all-white pitching staff and make them take your signals and make them believe you are the *best* signal caller. Can you do that?' 'Yes,' I replied. 'I knew you could,' he said. 'You'll be a great Dodger.'

"By 1947, I was in Montreal (AAA/International League), and by 1948 I was with the Dodgers. Mr. Rickey would call Jackie Robinson and me into his office together. He had us do everything together; he made us roommates so Jackie and I could discuss on-the-field and off-the-field behavior. We were good influences on each other. Mr. Rickey knew that, but where Jackie was boisterous, I was quiet. I always believed I should just let my bat do the talking, so I did."

Lou Boudreau
Cleveland Indians, shortstop
1938-1952

Lou Boudreau, the 5'11", 185-pound shortstop/manager from Harvey, Illinois, was an innovative, talented ballplayer who played with such poise at an early age that he was named playing manager for the Tribe in 1942, at the tender age of twenty-four. As a manager, he invented the shift of infielders designed to stop Ted Williams, transformed infielder Bob Lemon to a (Hall of Fame) pitcher, and out-strategized most managers he faced.

As a ballplayer, Boudreau won a batting title, three doubles leaderships, an MVP award, eight fielding titles and was a six-time all-star.

He had his number retired by the Cleveland Indians and was elected to the Hall of Fame in 1970.

Boudreau certainly could have talked about his inspirational August 8, 1948, performance when he limped off the bench, shrugging off an ankle injury, and delivered a game-tying single before a record crowd of 73,484 at Yankee Stadium to pave the way for an Indian doubleheader sweep of the Yankees. Instead, he chose to set the record straight on his shift strategy.

July 14, 1946

Boudreau sets up his strategy. "When I was first named manager, at twenty-four, I felt every opponent looked at my signs, so I hid my signs with a towel—I even used a towel as a steal sign once, until I had a cold, blew my nose with a hankie and Pat Seerey, a 5'9", 210-pound, very slow-footed outfielder (three stolen bases in seven years) tried to steal second and was thrown out by thirty feet—but this was a strategy that was out in the open for all to see.

"First of all, I'd like to set the record straight. It is the Boudreau shift, not the Williams shift. I invented it, not Ted. I had thought about it for weeks and drew the play on a tablecloth during dinner one night.

"We were playing a doubleheader against the Red Sox, and in the first game I tied a record for extra-base hits in a game with five by hitting four doubles and a homer. Unfortunately, Ted Williams hit three homers and drove in eight runs and beat me, 11-10. I decided to put the shift in for the second game if we got Dom (DiMaggio) out and (Johnny) Pesky out to face Williams with no one on. That way we could experiment with it and see what he'd do. We knew he was the best and he would take the challenge.

"I put every fielder except the third baseman and the left fielder on the second-base side of the field. We knew we could hold him to a single if he bunted and we felt he wouldn't go to left. We pitched him inside and when our catcher, Jim Hegan, hollered 'Yo,' Ted got angry and yelled, 'Get those S.O.B.s back in position.' Umpire Bill Summers said, 'I can't do anything as long as they're between the white lines and in fair play.'

"Ted squeezed the bat and Hegan said later he saw sawdust come out. The key was, we were at League Park at 66th and Lexington, an old park in Cleveland that said 250 (feet) on the wall but was really only 235. Ted could reach that with a stick, but we got him and he grounded out and walked twice.

"We kept charts on it, and we were 35 percent more successful against him with the shift on than without it."

August, 1947

Always thinking strategy, Boudreau came up with this one. "We were playing the Yankees and Billy Johnson comes up for them and he hit the ball deep in the hole. I fielded it, rolled over and flipped the ball to third baseman Ken Keltner, who fired to first to nip Johnson for the out. Bill McKechnie, a coach, had tears in his eyes.

He said, 'I've been in baseball for twenty-five years and I never saw that play worked successfully.'

"I loved doing things like that. I worked a play many times with Joe Gordon as a phantom double play. If Gordon was going to left field and away from the bag, he'd flip to me, coming across the bag, and I'd throw to first. If I'd field a ball up the middle but going away from first, I'd flip to Gordon and he'd throw to first. It worked well."

Johnny Berardino
St. Louis Browns, second base
1939-1942 1946-1952

Johnny Berardino, the 5'11", 175-pound infielder from Los Angeles, may be more well known as John Beradino (without the second "r") and as an actor in TV's long-running soap opera, *General Hospital*, in which he has played "Dr. Steve Hardy" for nearly thirty years.

Berardino was known as "the one-man infield" for his ability to play many positions. A utility starter, he played 453 games at second, 266 at short, 91 at third, 26 at first and a game in the outfield.

Berardino showed quite a bit of pop in 1940 when he connected for sixteen homers, but he never again hit more than five. He was also good for more than thirty doubles twice in his career. A contact hitter, he struck out only 268 times in eleven years.

He had four years cut out of the heart of his career, as so many of his contemporaries did during World War II, but he came back in 1946 to play a career-high 144 games, hitting a solid .265 while playing all but one game at second base and turning ninety-six double plays.

Browns owner Bill Veeck once insured Berardino's face in a publicity promotion.

The "Dr." could have told us about his grand slam home run off Yankee relief ace Johnny Murphy, a blow that took the Yanks out of the pennant race, but he preferred to give us a quick take on the Brownies.

August, 1946

Berardino deadpans, "We were in one of the largest sports towns in America and nobody heard of us. We always had five guys with eighty RBIs but we were always in the cellar because we had no pitching. (**Author's Note:** In 1940, the Browns RBI leaders were Walt Judnich, 89; Harlond Clift, 87; Johnny Berardino, 85; George McQuinn, 84; and Rip Radcliff, 81. In 1941: Roy Cullenbine, 98;

Berardino, 89; Clift, 84; Judnich, 83; and McQuinn, 80.)

"The most amazing thing to me was the absolute lack of press coverage we got. There were times that nobody, but I mean, nobody from the newspapers would show up in the locker room. I was on a twenty-two-game hitting streak in 1946 and the only other guy in town who knew it was my roommate, Johnny Lucadello. That's the kind of PR the Browns had. I guess when you lost as often as we did, it was better if they wrote nothing than something; at least, that's the philosophy the Browns had. And that amazed me, because the team owner, Bill Veeck was the most savvy promotions man in the game."

Dom DiMaggio
Boston Red Sox, outfield
1940-1942 1946-1953

Dominic Paul DiMaggio, one of the three DiMaggio brothers from San Francisco, was nicknamed "The Little Professor," probably because he looked like a teacher when he wore his spectacles. The 6'2", 195-pound outfielder was a slick fielder, as graceful as brother Joe. He could hit too, amassing a thirty-four-game hitting streak in 1949 to challenge Joe's fifty-six-game streak of 1941. He played alongside Joe in three All-Star games, led the league in runs scored twice, triples once and stolen bases once and finished with a .298 career batting average.

DiMaggio recalled, "The greatest satisfaction I have in baseball is that I broke in wearing glasses, and in those days, an athlete wearing glasses was a no-no. You couldn't be an athlete and wear glasses, so when I was successful, I helped open the floodgates and I feel I gave other glass-wearing athletes the courage to stick it out and play.

"As to being part of the DiMaggio family, Joe made it first (1936), and, of course, he was the best there ever was. Vince was older and he made it a year after Joe (1937) and was the best fielder and base runner among us. For me, it was easier to break in in the minors in San Francisco after they had excelled, but once I got to the Majors, their names no longer carried any weight and I was judged on my own abilities.

"I loved every day I ever played, but one day stands out most of all."

October 15, 1946

"It was the seventh game of the World Series and I went from joy to despair in a matter of a moment.

Dom DiMaggio, outfield, 1940s and Joe DiMaggio, outfield, 1930s
Courtesy: New York Yankees

"We were tied with the Cardinals, three games apiece, and had read in the papers that Boston hadn't won a World Series since Babe Ruth left (1918). I was batting against Harry 'The Cat' Brecheen in the eighth inning with the score 3-2, St. Louis. I already had two doubles in the Series when I doubled again to drive in my third run of the Series to tie the game and the Series 3-3. I drove it off the screen and as I rounded first and headed for second, I felt my leg go — a pulled muscle. I was ecstatic that I tied the Series and disappointed that I pulled a muscle and had to come out. That disappointment turned to despair the next inning when, with two out, my replacement in the outfield, Leon Culberson, couldn't get to Harry Walker's bloop double in the bottom of the eighth, and didn't get as much on his throw to Johnny Pesky as I think I could have. That is what allowed Enos Slaughter to score, not Pesky. Johnny got the ball and set up and threw, the play just didn't happen fast enough to get Slaughter. Maybe if I was out there the result could have been different, but that's baseball."

Stan Musial
St. Louis Cardinals, outfield
1941-1963

In addition to the stories offered earlier in this chapter, Stan "The Man" presents one more observation about the Slaughter-Pesky incident.

October 15, 1946

"It all came down to one play. The Series was tied, 3-3, and the game was tied, 3-3. Harry 'The Hat' Walker doubled with Enos Slaughter on first. Leon Culberson fielded it and threw the cutoff to Johnny Pesky, the shortstop. I don't think he really hesitated long enough to make a difference. It's true that Pesky didn't get too much on the throw, but it's little things that win games, and no one helped Pesky, either. If anyone had said to Pesky, "Home, home, home," or if anyone had said anything to Slaughter, there might have been a different result. Blame the team for lack of teamness, not the player."

Of course, the story can best be told by the principals.

Enos Slaughter
St. Louis Cardinals, outfielder
1938-1942 1946-1959

Enos "Country" Slaughter was a 5'9", 180-pound fireball from Roxboro, North Carolina. He was born to hit and finished his nineteen-year career at .300 while leading the league in hits once, doubles once, triples twice and RBIs once. He was a ten-time all-star and only his grizzled looks, which made him appear older than his still-young ability, kept him from being a full-time player—managers insisted on keeping Slaughter around as a role player—into his forties. He claims he could have played into his fifties (he retired at forty-three) if managers would have thought he was younger.

The tobacco farmer hustled on every play as though it were his last and ran to first on every walk and in and out from the field, in the style that would make Pete Rose known as "Charlie Hustle" (only Slaughter did it twenty-five years before Rose, and kept it up over his nineteen-year career). He got his style while playing for Columbus, Georgia, in the Sally League in 1936; while struggling at the plate, he would run to his right field position and then walk back in to the dugout, and his manager, Eddie Dyer, said, "Kid, if you're tired, let me get you some help. If you're gonna play, run." According to Slaughter, "I never walked on a ball field from that day on."

Slaughter is also remembered for leading a player revolt against Jackie Robinson's inclusion into Major League baseball in 1947. Slaughter and teammate Terry Moore attempted to get the Cardinals to strike in protest of Robinson's appearance for the Dodgers. In August, 1947, with Robinson playing first base for Brooklyn, Slaughter grounded one to second, ran hard to first, and was thrown out by three or four steps. However, as Robinson stretched to receive the throw, Slaughter, with apparent deliberateness, spiked Jackie in the leg.

Slaughter played parts of six years for the Yankees late in his career and was one of the top clutch pinch hitters in the game, banging out a league-leading sixteen pinch hits in 1955.

Slaughter was elected to the Hall of Fame in 1985.

October 15, 1946

Slaughter says, "After the war, I was thirty and they already thought of me as old, maybe forty. That may have helped make this play, as I was still pretty fast but opponents thought the old man was running out of gas.

"Now, I set this play up earlier in the game and people forget that. Earlier on, Mike Gonzalez, our third base coach stopped me from scoring. I went to Eddie Dyer (the Cardinals manager) and said, 'Look, if I'm on and running and this comes up again, I think I should gamble and go for home. I'll be responsible. When Harry Walker hit that blooper to left, and I saw Leon Culberson, who had replaced Dom (DiMaggio) go for it, I knew he'd have to turn to come up with it quickly and fire to the cutoff man, Johnny Pesky (the shortstop). The way I saw the play in front of me before I went on to third, I figured that if Pesky turns to his left to receive the throw from the outfield, he could throw me out, but if he turned to his right, I would score. He caught the ball, dropped his glove to his belt and had to spot me to pick me up. He saw me and threw, and I had caught them all napping."

Johnny Pesky
Boston Red Sox, shortstop
1942 1946-1954

John Michael Paveskovich, who played under the name Johnny Pesky, came out of Portland, Oregon, as a 5'9", 165-pound shortstop who could hit with alacrity—he led the league in hits his first three seasons—and perform solidly at shortstop.

Pesky is known best, or perhaps worst, for two plays that didn't end well: the 1946 World Series play discussed above and covered again from Pesky's perspective; and a play on August 25, 1952, when Virgil Trucks got credit for throwing a no-hitter over the Yankees when Yankee shortstop Phil Rizzuto hit a hard grounder to short in the third inning. Pesky gloved it, but couldn't extract the ball from his glove in time to make the play. The official scorer ruled it a hit until he called Pesky in the dugout in the seventh inning and Pesky said he should be charged with an error, making the one-hitter a no-hitter.

Pesky related his version of the "hesitation."

October 15, 1946

Pesky says, "This is all people want to talk about and they all saw it, but all I can say is, Harry Walker hit it to left and Leon Culberson picked it up and didn't drill it but threw it to me. I had my back to the plate and turned to pick up Slaughter to see if he was going and if I had a shot at him either at third or at home. As I wheeled, I dropped my hands to get ready to throw and I picked him up and threw—too late to get him. He hustled all the way. Good play. But I didn't hesitate. I dropped my hands and to some it looked like I cradled the ball and held it. Really, I was just trying to get ready to throw as I tried to see where the hell he (Slaughter) was. If anything, I might have saved motion, but I'll never convince the baseball world of that."

Tommy Holmes
Boston Braves, outfield
1942-1952

Tommy Holmes, known as "Kelly" to his friends, was a Brooklyn-born outfielder who knew how to hit. The 5'10", 180-pound Brave led the league in hits twice, doubles once, homers once and struck out only 122 times in eleven years.

Undoubtedly, Holmes's biggest claim to baseball fame was his NL-record 37-game hitting streak from June 6 through July 8, 1945, a mark that stood for 32 years, until Pete Rose broke it.

While Holmes's story in the 1950s chapter deals with the one that got away, his nugget here covers a day he played against a retired legend.

March, 1947

Holmes remembers, "I've always liked heroes. In 1945, Paul Waner, one of my heroes, taught me how to pull the ball and I led the league in homers. That same year, I played in barnstorming games against Negro League players for five to eight dollars a game. I played Satchel Paige and the Kansas City Monarchs. I played for Bay Parkway, and I saw Josh Gibson, who had arms like hamhocks, hit one two hundred feet past me in left field . . . and I was at the fence, 415 feet from home plate. Two weeks later, the Yankees almost offered him a contract. He would have been the best.

"I loved Ernie Lombardi, another hero of mine. In 1942, Lom led the league in batting at .330—he *had* to hit, any little league kid could outrun him. In one game he caught, much against his wishes, knuckleball ace Jim Tobin, who hit Lom in the mask, the shin, the chest, the shin and the shin on five of six consecutive pitches; Lom finally took his gear off and yelled, 'Get yourself another catcher.' But he was a great catcher and a great man.

"So I love legends, and when I played for the Boston Braves in an exhibition game against Babe Ruth, it was very special to me. Babe had been retired for a dozen years and he already had cancer and was near death even though he hung on for another year. He could barely carry the bat up to home plate, but since I never saw him play when he was young, this day will always be special to me.

"Babe hit a pop fly between me and Tony Cuccinello. Tony looked at me to see if I could make the play and I said, 'Let it fall; Babe can go out with a base hit.' It made me feel like a king.

"Mickey Mantle was the most powerful hitter who ever lived—I came to the ballpark just to see him play—but Babe Ruth was the greatest player who ever lived, and that one swing was still sweet, all those years later."

Bobby Brown
New York Yankees, third base
1946-1952 1954

Dr. Bobby Brown was a 6'1", 180-pounder out of Seattle who was a dependable hitter, a first-rate pinch hitter and a weak fielder, forcing the Yankees to platoon him.

Studying medicine while he was playing ball—he retired in 1954 to pursue a medical career—he became an odd-couple roommate with Yogi Berra, in a room filled with medical texts (his) and comic books (Yogi's).

Brown hit .439 in four World Series, and knocked out a record three pinch hits in three at-bats in the 1947 Fall Classic (see story below).

Following a successful career as a surgeon, he returned to baseball and became the president of the American League.

September 30 - October 6, 1947

"The most exciting part of my career, if you're talking about sheer thrills, was the 1947 Series," says Brown.

"The entire Series was exciting. We pulled out the first game; after Ralph Branca retired the first twelve hitters, we unloaded and I got a pinch hit in the fifth as we scored five runs and won the game when Joe Page pitched four innings in relief.

"Game two was a rout. We won, 10-3, as Tom Henrich homered and Allie Reynolds was tough all day.

"Game three: Brooklyn won, 9-8, and it was a tough loss.

"Game four: Brooklyn won, 3-2, in one of the best games ever. Bill Bevens was one out away from a no-hitter, the first in the World Series, when Cookie Lavagetto doubled home two runs and won the game.

"Game five saw us win in Brooklyn, 2-1, on Joe DiMaggio's homer and Spec Shea's pitching.

"Game six was the one in which we lost, 8-6, and virtually everyone on both sides got to play (**Author's Note:** thirty-eight players were used) in a chess game between Bucky Harris (the Yankee manager) and Burt Shotten (the Dodger skipper). In this one, in the sixth, with two on and two out, DiMaggio hits one 415 feet away and Al Gionfriddo makes a sensational catch to rob Joe of extra bases—that's the only time on a ball field Joe ever showed emotion; he kicked the dirt. That hit could have won it for us.

"Game seven was my final contribution. I already had come up twice in pinch-hitting situations and delivered two hits, a double and a single. I certainly wasn't going to crack that starting lineup, with George McQuinn (first base), Snuffy Stirnweiss (second base), Phil Rizzuto (shortstop), Billy Johnson (third base), Yogi (Berra) behind the plate and an outfield of Joe DiMaggio, Tom Henrich and

Johnny Lindell. So I was just happy to be there and happier still to contribute.

"In game seven, we were obviously tied at three games apiece and the Dodgers had a 2-1 lead on us in the fourth. All our pitchers were hurt and I came up to pinch hit for Bill Bevens against Hal Gregg. I doubled (my third straight pinch hit and third RBI), to tie the score and Henrich followed with an RBI single, the second time in the series he had driven me home and the third clutch RBI he delivered, and suddenly we were up, 3-2.

"We scored two more later and Joe Page shut 'em out the rest of the way (five innings) and we won, 5-2, for the championship."

Bob Lemon
Cleveland Indians, pitcher
1946-1958

Bob Lemon, the six-foot, 190-pound pitcher who found his niche on the mound after a lackluster career as an infielder, learned his craft as he went and credits teammate and coach Mel Harder with teaching him everything he used on the mound.

Lem, the long-time Long Beach, California, resident who was born in San Bernardino, California, won twenty games or more seven times over a nine-year period from 1948 to 1956 as part of one of baseball's best starting rotations: Lemon, Bob Feller, Early Wynn, Mike Garcia and Herb Score. Using a sinker and sinking fastball, Lem led the AL in strike outs in 1950 (170) and was a workhorse on the hill, leading the loop in innings pitched four times.

A great hitting pitcher, with thirty-seven home runs and 274 career hits, Lemon says, "I really wasn't much of a hitter, otherwise I'd have stayed in the infield. They stuck me on the mound to survive."

Lemon was enshrined in the Hall of Fame in 1976.

Lemon, a low-key, self-effacing man, did dredge up a favorite memory and credits his team with making it special.

July 30, 1948

Lemon says, "I was lucky my entire career. I was lucky to play in the days when we took train rides everywhere and seven or eight guys would go to dinner together and we'd play day games and have a lot of time together and develop a lot of camaraderie. Your teammates become family and it's a closeness they just don't have today.

"And I was lucky to room with Jim Hegan for sixteen years, a wonderful friend.

"And I was lucky to have Mel Harder with me. I wouldn't have had a career without pitching and Mel was instrumental in 80 percent of my career. I inherited his work habits and his book on the hitters; I threw like him and I listened to him. He never told you, he would only suggest why you might want to try a new approach.

"And I was lucky July 30, 1948, when I threw my no-hitter against Detroit. There were fifty-thousand fans in Briggs Stadium and they were hollering from the seventh inning on as we won, 2-0. You know, I never really thought much about a no-hitter; my feeling is that the only legitimate no-hitter a pitcher deserves is when he strikes out all twenty-seven batters. Otherwise, it's a team no-hitter. And in this one, it definitely was a team no-hitter.

"Left fielder Dale Mitchell made a hell of a catch on George Kell in the fourth, with his glove on his right hand, smack dab down the left-field foul line; if his glove was on his left hand that play doesn't get made. And Ken Keltner backhanded one behind third base in the fifth that saved me, and from then on, the team just did what they had to behind me. So, I get credit for it, but it was a Cleveland no-hitter all the way."

Jerry Coleman
New York Yankees, second base
1949-1957

Jerry Coleman, a six-foot, 165-pounder from San Jose, California, was a graceful and deft-fielding second baseman for the dynasty Yankees of the 1950s. A highly decorated World War II and Korean War hero as a marine pilot, he was once thought to be Hall of Fame material — Frankie Frisch predicted as much — until several injuries diminished his abilities. He led the AL in fielding as a rookie, and prior to his retirement in the broadcast booth where he became the master of the malaprop, Coleman played in 723 games during the regular season and had a strong seven games in the 1957 World Series, in which he hit .364 and turned three double plays.

Coleman talked of his first year as a Yankee, 1948, which doesn't show up on his official record because he was called up from the minors and sat for six games without getting into the lineup. Still, he saw a legend get his due.

October 3, 1948

"We had gone down to the last weekend in a battle with Cleveland and Boston, and were eliminated the day before by the Red Sox. I was picked up for the last six games of the season and I just sat on the bench and shook with awe.

"It was the last day of the season and we're in Fenway Park, Yankee-haters' territory. Joe DiMaggio is having his last big season as a superstar. He's got a bad leg, a charley horse, but (Yankee manager) Bucky Harris kept DiMag in center field even though he knew he was hurting.

"Boston was killing us, 10-2 (they eventually won 10-5), but Joe had four hits. Harris finally took him out in the seventh and the fans — the Boston, Yankee-hating fans — stood and cheered him for ten minutes. The applause was so loud, it stopped the game cold. It gave me chills; here was a rivalry where the two teams wanted to kill each other and it stopped them dead. When the game resumed, the pitcher had to take eight warm-ups.

"Even forty-five years later, it remains the most awesome display I've ever seen in baseball . . . it was a lesson in respect."

Larry Doby
Cleveland Indians, outfield
1947-1959

Larry Doby, the 6′1″, 190-pounder from New Jersey (by way of Camden, South Carolina), may be best known for being the first black athlete to play in the American League, signed by the Indians' Bill Veeck in August 1947, after playing four years for the Newark Eagles of the Negro National League for whom he hit .414, .397 and .392 in his best years.

Commenting on his breaking of the AL barrier, Doby says, "Jackie (Robinson) got all the publicity and I got very little because the press didn't want to go through the same story all over again. But nonetheless, I thank Jackie for his contribution because he, along with athletes such as Jack Johnson, Paul Robeson and Jesse Owens made it possible for me to get as far as I got in baseball.

"In 1947, I knew the race relationship was supposed to be tough, but I never saw it. You must understand, I was part of the team concept and so were my teammates. But once I left the field, I was not part of the team. I was a pal on the field but seldom off, until the 1948 Series."

Doby twice led the league in homers, once in RBIs and was a seven-time all-star. A powerful swinger from the left side, Doby bombed 253 home runs in thirteen years and drove in 969 runs.

His contribution to this journal is from the 1948 World Series when, he says, the tide changed.

October 9, 1948

"It was game four of the World Series and Steve Gromek pitched a whale of a game for us, holding the Boston Braves to one run, and they had a good ball club.

"We were up, 1-0, when I got up in the third and hit a home run off Johnny Sain—it was the first time a black man had homered in the World Series—and it put us up, 2-0. That's all we got, and when we hung on to win, 2-1, to take a 3-1 lead in the Series.

"We were all so excited that I ran over and hugged Gromek and he wrapped me up in a big bear hug of his own. We were teammates. I'm wrapped up in the togetherness thing and Steve and I embraced each other from a teammate standpoint. That gave me total acceptance.

"I grew up in a mixed neighborhood and never looked at color, but it must have been tough for other Major Leaguers who had never been around blacks.

"The ball is white, but baseball should be color blind. We are Americans all and it was always my hope to see a total team concept with mixed races where it didn't make any difference because it's one for all and all for one. The team is first and foremost and on that standpoint, all is equal.

"When the photograph of me hugging Gromek made the papers the next day and that is all anyone saw, I knew we were on the right track. I had been accepted and soon, I hoped, people would stop being referred to as black ballplayers or Jewish or Irish ballplayers or Latin ballplayers, but ballplayers. And that hug may have started it all."

(**Author's Note:** The photograph appeared in the papers the next day, white pitcher Gromek hugging black teammate Doby, and it represented to America that blacks had been accepted into the team sport, perhaps even more so than Jackie Robinson's breaking of the color barrier. This one picture served as a banner that the game had become integrated.

One aside ... Gromek later said that while he was excited and happy and liked Doby, Doby initated the hug and Gromek was so scared that he might get hugged to death by his enthusiastic teammate that he "hung on for dear life and hugged him harder than he hugged me out of self-preservation."

Later, when he received some flak from white players for hugging Doby, Gromek said, "Hey, the man is a teammate and he won the game for me with a homer. If you want a kiss from me, hit me a homer and I'll do the same for you.")

Don Newcombe
Brooklyn Dodgers, pitcher
1949-1951 1954-1960

Don Newcombe, affectionately called "Newk" by the Brooklyn faithful, was a 6'4", 230-pound fireballer from Madison, New Jersey, who pitched for the Newark Eagles in the Negro Leagues before moving on to play for "the Bums." Newk started his career in style, throwing a 3-0 shutout over Cincinnati in his May 22, 1949, debut. Over ten seasons, Newcomb had three twenty-win seasons and led the NL in Ks in 1951 (164).

Newcombe was a four-time all-star, a rookie of the year, an MVP, and the initial Cy Young award winner in 1956—27-7, 3.06 ERA, 268 innings, 46 walks and 139 strikeouts. And Newk could hit; he knocked seven homers in 1955 and fifteen in his career.

In the shortest story in this book, Newk tells a quick one on himself and his favorite battery mate, Roy Campanella.

June, 1949

"I had never seen the St. Louis Cardinals up close, and they had a great lineup: Stan Musial, Enos Slaughter, Marty Marion, Red Schoendienst, Eddie Kazak and the rest. And I started off and gave up four hits to the first four guys I faced. I said to Campy, 'I don't know; do I have good stuff or bad stuff or are they just good hitters?' Campy didn't miss a beat; he cackled, 'I don't know. I haven't caught any of your pitches yet.' "

George Kell
Detroit Tigers, third base
1942-1957

George Kell could hit, and though the Swifton, Arkansas, native was also a deft fielder, his bat is what made him a ten-time all-star. The 5'9", 175-pound third baseman won one batting title, twice led the league in doubles, and finished his career with a .306 mark. He led the league in fielding seven times and in chances four times. Kell has been in the game for more than fifty years as a player, coach and broadcaster. He was elected to the Hall of Fame in 1983.

Kell could certainly share many insights gained from his half-century in the game, but he chose to set the record straight on an accomplishment that has been misreported, misremembered and misrepresented.

October 2, 1949

"This was the day I won the AL batting championship over Ted Williams in the closest race ever — Williams hit .3427 and I hit .3429, winning it by .0002.

"Many people tell the story that I sat out the last game to protect my average. That is not true. Others say that I took myself out of the ball game when I had the lead over Williams — Williams let that story go in one of his books — but that is not true.

"In those days, it would be considered unmanly to sit out, and I felt if I won it, I'd earn it, which I did.

"Williams went 0-for-2 in his game against the Yankees (with Vic Raschi on the mound) and I was going against Bob Lemon and Bob Feller of Cleveland. I got a double and a single against Lemon and then Feller came in to relieve and I walked and struck out. With the game on the line (we were down 5-3), there were two outs in the ninth and I was in the on-deck circle waiting to hit when the game ended. I was told Red Rolfe, our manager, was going to pinch hit for me. I was yelled at later on that 'Kell, you shoulda batted one more time,' but I was there ready to bat and I wanted to so I could try to win the game and the title. I was there at the end and won it in sporting fashion."

Phil "Scooter" Rizzuto
New York Yankees, shortstop
1941-1942 1946-1956

Philip Francis Rizzuto, the New York-born fielding whiz, played far larger than his 5'6", 150-pound body would have appeared to let him. Phil was a giant and a team leader in every sense of the word. His plaque in Monument Park at Yankee Stadium is enscribed: "Philip Francis Rizzuto — A man's size is measured by his heart. Scooter sparked the Yankees to ten pennants and eight World Championships. 1950 Major League Player of the Year, MVP in the World Series of 1951. Has enjoyed two outstanding careers. All-time great Yankee shortstop, one of the great Yankee Broadcasters; 'Holy Cow.' Erected by New York Yankees, August 4, 1985."

He was one of the spiritual leaders during the Yankee dynasty

Phil Rizzuto, shortstop, 1940s
Courtesy: New York Yankees

years of the 1940s and 1950s and played in nine World Series (fifty-two Series games played).

Rizzuto finished his career with 1,661 games played. He was a tough out—only 397 strikeouts, 651 walks in 5,816 at-bats. He had decent speed, stealing 149 bases (for a non-running team) and turning 1,217 double plays during his tenure on the field. Just as New York City had the who's-the-better-center-fielder controversy (Willie Mays/Mickey Mantle/Duke Snider), so did it have the who's-the-better-shortstop controversy (between Rizzuto and Dodger shortstop Pee Wee Reese). Rizzuto has gotten support from the veterans committee for inclusion to the Hall of Fame, and it is thought by many that someday he will be enshrined. His number was retired by the Yankees.

Rizzuto, one of those rare "nice guys," about whom no one has a bad thing to say (except in jest) is a man who pokes fun at himself and laughs heartiest at his own foibles. It is not surprising that his offering here is about one of his errors, with a similarly oriented tale in the 1950s chapter.

October 2, 1949

"The Boston Red Sox came to Yankee Stadium to close the season. They were one game ahead with two to play and needed to beat us just once to win the pennant. On October 1, Boston took a 4-0 lead, but Joe Page came in to pitch five innings of shutout ball in relief, and we came on to win, 5-4, on Johnny Lindell's homer.

"In the season finale, with the pennant on the line and seventy thousand fans in the stands, Vic Raschi is pitching a whale of a game against Ellis Kinder and we lead, 1-0, in the eighth. Boston loads the bases with no outs—Johnny Pesky leads off first, Dom DiMaggio leads off second and Vern Stephens leads off third, with Ted Williams up.

"Ted is going for the batting title and he's gonna be tough, so Casey Stengel has us put on a 'Williams Shift.' I'm on the first base side of second base and Vic Raschi, who's throwing a good fastball, fires one to Ted. Ted hits a screaming line drive right at me—a base hit if I'm playing a normal shortstop—with a lot of overspin. I leaped up, felt the ball in my glove and start running to second base for a double play, and then on to tag Pesky for an unassisted triple play. Then I see what happened; the ball ripped the webbing right out of my glove, for an error, and two runs scored. What a shot that was, but it was my error, and I was so embarrassed in front of those seventy thousand fans, I wanted to dig a hole and never come out of it. We won the game, 5-3, and the championship, but all I wanted to do was hide my face."

1950s

June 2, 1950 to September 27, 1959

The date of June 2, 1950, begins the oral history section of this chapter with a story about George Kell and his cycle and does not refer to the news briefs that follow. The final date of September 27, 1959, refers to a story of Bobby Richardson's quest to hit .300 and all the help he got that didn't help a bit.

The 1950s may have been the unofficial end to baseball's era of innocence. Why? By the decade's end, Brooklyn was no longer in the National League, and with Western expansion came a sophistication that a younger, more naive baseball didn't have.

Nonetheless, the Yankees and Dodgers' competition of the decade epitomized World Series rivalries. We had Don Larsen's perfect game. We had the arguments about who was better, Stan Musial or Ted Williams? Mickey? Willie? The Duke? Whitey Ford was the money lefty in the AL while Warren Spahn was his counterpart in the NL. Aaron and Mathews were every bit as powerful as Mantle and Berra. The Indians won ... for the last time. The St. Louis Browns moved to Baltimore and started winning.

New faces included Clemente, Kluszewski, Skowron, and "Mr. Cub" (Ernie Banks). Koufax and Drysdale came in and Joe DiMaggio went out. And black ballplayers finally made their appearances on every Major League team.

Selected decade highlights
(in addition to those told in this chapter)

April 18, 1950 - Sam Jethroe, Negro Leagues star, en route to becoming the AL Rookie of the Year after seven years with the Cleveland Buckeyes, is the first black to play for the Boston Braves. He goes 2-for-4 with a homer in his debut. In another debut, Billy Martin, the fiery second baseman for the New York Yankees, doubles early in the eighth inning of a 15-10 Yankee win over the Red Sox. Later in the inning, Martin singles to become the first Major Leaguer to get two hits in one inning in his first game.

May 9, 1950 - Ralph Kiner, the streak-hitter's streak hitter, knocks his second grand slam in three days and accounts for seven "ribbies" in the Pirates' 10-5 humbling of the Dodgers.

May 30, 1950 - The Duke of Flatbush bombs out three dingers at Ebbets Field. Duke Snider's homers sink the Phillies, 6-4.

June 1, 1950 - Slam, slam, slam! Three National Leaguers connect for grand slams. Marty Marion leads the Cards over Brooklyn, 5-2; Sid Gordon powers the Braves past the Pirates, 14-2, and Hank Thompson propels the Giants to an 8-7 win over Cincy.

June 3, 1950 - Sid Gordon of the Braves blasts his third grand slam of the season (he also nailed one at the Polo Grounds on April 19), one of two homers he hits in this one as he drives in seven runs to give Boston a 10-6 win over the Pirates.

June 8, 1950 - In a game that seemed to exemplify the St. Louis Browns' futile existence, the Boston Red Sox annihilate the Brownies, 29-4, at Fenway Park. The BoSox set six records in the process: most runs; most extra-base hits (17, including 9 doubles, one triple and 7 homers); most total bases, 60; most extra bases on long hits, 32; most runs for two games, 49 (thanks to scoring 20 the day before, on 23 hits); and most hits in two games (51, including 28 in this game).

June 25, 1950 - Ralph Kiner hits for the cycle and poles two homers. His eight "ribbies" trip Brooklyn, 16-11.

June 30, 1950 - The DiMaggio brothers both homer in the same game. Joe hits one for the Yanks, and Dom belts one for the BoSox for a 10-2 victory.

July 3, 1950 - Although he hates it, Joe DiMaggio plays first base for the only time in his career. Subbing for Tom Henrich and Joe Collins, The Yankee Clipper fields thirteen chances flawlessly in the Yanks' 7-2 loss to the A's.

July 4, 1950 - It's Sid Gordon again ... his fourth grand slam of the year dumps the Phillies, 12-9.

August 2, 1950 - A big hitters' day. Andy Pafko bombs three homers, but his Cubs lose to the Giants, 8-6; Larry Doby blasts three dingers in Cleveland's 11-0 win over Washington; and as the A's crush the Chi-Sox, 10-3, Czechoslovakian-born Elmer Valo hits for the cycle.

August 31, 1950 - Gil Hodges of Brooklyn ties a Major League record by blasting four home runs in a single game as the Dodgers rout the Boston Braves, 19-3. Hodges also singles, for a seventeen-total-base game.

September 10, 1950 - Joe DiMaggio becomes the first player to belt three taters out of Griffith Stadium in a game, leading the Yanks past the Senators, 8-1.

September 15, 1950 - Johnny Mize, recalled earlier this season from the minors, clouts three homers for the sixth time in his career, but the Yanks lose to the Tigers, 9-7.

May 3, 1951 - Yankees rookie Gil McDougald hits a two-run triple and a grand slam home run in an eleven-run ninth inning as the Yanks beat the St. Louis Browns at Sportsman's Park, 17-3. Mac's six RBIs in one inning tie a Major League mark.

May 16, 1951 - A's slugger Gus Zernial pokes his seventh homer in four games to help beat the Browns, 7-6.

September 13, 1951 - The St. Louis Cards participate in a baseball oddity by beating the New York Giants, 6-4, in a day game resched-uled from a rainout the day before. Then, in the regularly scheduled night game, the Giants lose to the Boston Braves, 2-0. It is the first time since 1883 that a team meets two different teams in a non-exhibition on the same day.

August 15, 1951 - In a scene that would be replayed in the World Series of 1954 (see September 29, 1954), Willie Mays makes a spec-tacular over-the-shoulder full-speed catch in deep right-center on Carl Furillo's drive, whirls 180 degrees and throws out base runner Billy Cox before Cox can tag up at third, to preserve a 1-1 tie. Mays's Giants outlasted the Dodgers, 3-1.

August 19, 1951 - Bill Veeck's greatest stunt. He signs 3'7" Eddie Gaedel to pinch hit for the Browns. Gaedel, wearing number "⅛" walks on four pitches from Tiger lefty Bob Cain. Jim Delsing goes in to pinch run for Gaedel.

August 24, 1951 - OK, this is Bill Veeck's greatest stunt. On "Fans Managers' Night," his Browns beat the visiting A's, 5-3, as fans vote by applause on what the team's strategy should be. The coaches hold up signs bearing such maneuvers as "bunt," "steal," "hit and run," "remove pitcher," "take two" and "swing away."

September 14, 1951 - Browns' rookie Bob Nieman sets a Big League mark in his first game as he homers in his first two at-bats (the first

Major Leaguer to accomplish this) off Boston's Mickey McDermott, but the BoSox win, 9-6.

September 28, 1951 - Allie Reynolds, the Yankees "Super Chief," throws his second no-hitter of the season as the Yanks dispatch the Red Sox, 8-0. And to do it, he had to get Ted Williams twice in the ninth. With two out, Teddy Ballgame pops one foul that Yankee catcher Yogi Berra had, then dropped, in foul territory. Given another chance, Williams hits another foul that Berra corrals for the final out.

September 30, 1951 - Jackie Robinson homers in the fourteenth inning to power the Brooklyn Dodgers to a 9-8 win over the Phillies. The win enables the Brooks to tie the Giants for the NL flag, forcing a play-off.

October 3, 1951 - Bobby Thomson's dramatic "Giants win the pennant" three-run homer with one out in the bottom of the ninth, off Ralph Branca, gives the Giants a 5-4 play-off victory over the Dodgers and brings them into a crosstown Series against the Yankees.

April 23, 1952 - New York Giants knuckleballer Hoyt Wilhelm wins his first Major League game in relief and hits a home run at the Polo Grounds in his first MLB at-bat. It was the only four-bagger Wilhelm ever hit in his 1,070-game career.

April 29, 1952 - Al Rosen explodes for three homers with seven "ribbies" and is only the second-best hitter on the field, as teammate Jim Fridley goes 6-for-6 and Cleveland bags the A's, 21-9.

April 30, 1952 - Ted Williams is off to war, but before leaving to join the U.S. Marines in Korea as a fighter pilot, "The Thumper" connects for a two-run homer in his last at-bat, against Tiger hurler Dizzy Trout, to give Boston a 5-3 victory.

May 4, 1952 - "Fabulous" Faye Throneberry of the Red Sox belts his second grand slam of the season, to beat Early Wynn and the Indians.

May 21, 1952 - The Brooklyn Dodgers explode for fifteen runs in the first inning to pave the way for a 19-1 shellacking of the Cincy Reds at Ebbets Field. Duke Snider homers and goes to the plate three times in the inning—as do Pee Wee Reese and Billy Cox.

July 14-15, 1952 - Detroit power hitter Walt Dropo goes 5-for-5 against New York on the fourteenth and follows it up with a 4-for-4 performance versus the Senators in the first game of a twin bill on the fifteenth. In the second game, Dropo hits safely his first three at-bats to run his mark to 12-for-12. He finishes the game at 4-for-5 (13-for-14 over two days).

June 19, 1952 - Carl Erskine of the Brooklyn Dodgers no-hits the Chicago Cubs, 5-0, to stop the Brooks' four-game losing skein to the

Cubbies. The no-no was accomplished as "Oisk's" teammate Dick Williams did a "play-by-play" in the dugout, mentioning the no-hitter with every out beginning in the third inning. As the gem continued, Williams's teammates made the "broadcaster" continue with his report, and he did so through the final out in the ninth.

September 29, 1952 - Stan "The Man" Musial, a prolific hitter and a successful pitcher during his minor league career, takes the mound for his only Big League appearance. He faces the number-two hitter in the league, Frankie Baumholtz of the Cubs. Musial (who leads the NL at .336), faces Baumholtz (who will finish at .325) and induces him to ground to short, though he reaches first on an error. Musial is lifted for Harvey Haddix, and the Cubs win, 3-0.

April 16, 1953 - Phillies infielder Connie Ryan gets six straight hits against Pittsburgh in a 14-12 loss.

April 26, 1953 - The Connie Ryan Show again blasts the Pirates. Ryan goes 5-for-5 as the Phils win, 7-5.

May 6, 1953 - St. Louis Browns pitcher Bobo Holloman pitches a no-hitter in his first MLB start, a 6-0 win over the A's. It was the only complete game he ever threw; he won only three games in his career and was out of the Majors within three months.

May 18, 1953 - Cincy pitcher Bud Podbeilan beats the Dodgers, 2-1, in ten innings, despite walking thirteen Brooklyn batters. Ted Kluszewski wins it in the tenth with a home run.

June 10, 1953 - Red Sox outfielder Jimmy Piersall goes 6-for-6 in an 11-2 win over the St. Louis Browns.

June 15, 1953 - The St. Louis Browns end their losing streak at fourteen games by beating the Yankees, 3-1, at Yankee Stadium to halt the Bronx Bombers' eighteen-game winning streak. The loss allowed Yankee shortstop Phil Rizzuto to throw out the gum he'd been chewing for nearly a month. "Scooter" popped in the spearmint before the Yanks' first victory, May 23, and teammates talked the superstitious infielder into keeping the stale rubber in his mouth every game so as not to jinx the streak.

June 18, 1953 - Boston Red Sox rookie outfielder Gene Stephens knocks out three hits in one inning as the BoSox send twenty-three men to the plate in a seventeen-run barrage in the seventh to paste Detroit, 23-3.

August 4, 1953 - Pitcher Vic Raschi helps his own cause in a big way. The Yankee hurler shuts out Detroit, 15-0, and bangs out three hits to drive in seven runs. After the game, Yankee teammates fill "The Springfield Rifle's" locker with bats.

April 13, 1954 - Willie Mays returns from two years in the army and belts a two-run homer to beat Brooklyn, 4-3.

May 2, 1954 - Stan Musial crashes five home runs in a double-header versus the Giants. Nate Colbert, an eight-year-old who would later become the second player to hit five dingers in a twin bill, was at the game watching his hero, Stan "The Man."

May 16, 1954 - In Memorial Stadium's first season as the home of the Baltimore Orioles, center field was bordered by a six-foot-high wire fence which stood in front of a row of high hedges. But that fence was not erected until June, so in this game, the hedges were the home run barrier. Mickey Mantle blasts one into and over the hedges and O's center fielder Chuck Diering leaps above and into the vegetation to rob Mick of a homer. Had he hit the same shot a couple of weeks later, Mantle would've had another four-bagger for the season.

May 24, 1954 - In an unusual defensive shift to thwart Stan Musial, Redlegs manager Birdie Tebbets moves shortstop Roy McMillan to the outfield to create a four-man outfield, with outfielder Nino Escalera playing the gap between left and center (he is listed in the official score book as the "shortstop" for that at-bat). Musial, who hit .330 with thirty-five homers for the season, is struck out by pitcher Art Fowler as the Redlegs beat the Cards, 4-2.

June 3, 1954 - Two Giants win this game against the Cardinals. In New York's 13-8 triumph, Hank Thompson hits three homers and drives in eight runs, and Willie Mays bombs two round-trippers to knock in the other five scores.

June 7, 1954 - Not normally a speedster, Dodger catcher Roy Campanella beats St. Louis, 7-5, with his legs as well as his bat. His home run gets the Dodgers close and his stolen base of home in the twelfth inning ensures the win.

June 14, 1954 - On the day the phrase, "one nation, under God" is added to America's pledge of allegiance to the flag, the Giants take over first place with a win over the Redlegs on Hank Thompson's two-out, ninth inning, three-run homer.

July 22, 1954 - The master lineup juggler, Casey Stengel, switches Phil Rizzuto to second base and puts center fielder Mickey Mantle at shortstop against the White Sox. Mantle hits the game-winning homer in the Yankee tenth for a 3-2 victory.

July 24, 1954 - Well, it doesn't always work. In this one against Cleveland, Yankee manager Casey Stengel lifts shortstop Phil Rizzuto for a pinch hitter in the eighth and moves Mickey Mantle in to play short. Not satisfied with the maneuver, he moves Mantle to second, switching spots with second-sacker Willie Miranda against right-handed hitters, switching back against lefties. The Indians win anyway, 5-4.

July 31, 1954 - Milwaukee first baseman Joe Adcock breaks his favorite bat and has to borrow a teammate's. He copes and belts four homers and a double (for an MLB mark of eighteen total bases) as the Braves beat the Dodgers at Ebbets Field, 15-7.

September 10, 1954 - Joe Adcock loves Ebbets Field. He hits his ninth homer of the year against "the Bums" at Ebbets to get the only hit off Brooklyn's Billy Loes in a rain-shortened 2-1 Dodger win.

September 29, 1954 - "The catch." In game one of the World Series between the Giants and Indians (and the score tied, 2-2, in the eighth inning at the Polo Grounds), Tribe slugger Vic Wertz, who already had hit a two-run triple earlier, bombs one to dead center field, some 460 feet from home plate, with two men on. Willie Mays sprints back and makes an over-the-shoulder catch, whirls, and fires the ball back to the infield to keep the runners from advancing. Proving that shorter is sometimes better, Giant pinch hitter Dusty Rhodes dinks a 260-foot three-run homer down the line in the tenth inning to give New York a 5-2 win.

April 13, 1955 - While America's youth are bedecked in coonskin caps and fringed leather jackets while carrying "old Betsy" Daisy air rifles (the nation's first TV craze, Davy Crockett-mania), the Yankees begin their march toward recapturing the American League pennant with a 19-1 shellacking of the Washington Senators. Whitey Ford gives up only two hits to get the win and bangs out three hits himself.

April 17, 1955 - Tiger right fielder Al Kaline blasts two homers in the sixth inning and three homers in the game to lead Detroit to a 16-0 victory over the Kansas City A's. Steve Gromek hurls a shutout for Detroit.

April 23, 1955 - White Sox catcher Sherm Lollar doubles his pleasure twice in this 29-6 rout of Kansas City. As the Sox pound out twenty-nine hits, Lollar becomes the only player to get two hits in an inning twice in the same game (the second and sixth). Bob Nieman drives in seven runs and Chico Carrasquel finishes 5-for-6.

May 5, 1955 - This is not Tommy Lasorda's greatest day. In his first Big League start, the Dodgers' lefty pitcher throws three wild pitches in the same inning, gets spiked by Cardinal outfielder Wally Moon on a play at the plate, and shouts at Roy Campanella for calling poor pitches and setting up a bad target.

May 13, 1955 - Mickey Mantle serves notice on the American League. He drives in all five runs in a 5-2 Yankee win over Detroit, blasts switch-hit homers for the first time in his career (he'll do this ten times before he's through) and winds up with three homers and a single.

May 27, 1955 - Norm Zauchin drives in ten runs for the Boston Red Sox with three homers and a double (all within the first five innings) en route to a 16-0 romp over the Senators.

May 30, 1955 - Showing prowess with his bat as well as his arm, Dodger hurler Don Newcombe hits two homers in the same game for the second time this season (he'll finish the season with seven homers) as "the Bums" beat the crosstown Giants, 10-8.

July 8, 1955 - Joe DeMaestri (who hits .249 this year), goes 6-for-6 for the A's in their 11-8 loss to Detroit.

August 4, 1955 - Chicago's "Mr. Cub," Ernie Banks, crashes out three homers at Wrigley to beat the Pirates, 11-10.

August 27, 1955 - Showing what was ahead for opposing hitters, Dodger rookie southpaw Sandy Koufax K's fourteen Cincy batters for a 7-0 victory.

September 7, 1955 - Whitey Ford throws his second consecutive one-hitter in a 2-1 win versus the A's. Jim Finigan gets Kansas City's only safety with a single in the seventh. Five days earlier, Ford's only mistake against the Washington Senators was a seventh-inning single by Carlos Paula.

September 18, 1955 - Willie Mays loves Ebbets Field. The "Say Hey Kid" ties Joe Adcock's record by blasting his ninth homer at a road park, but "the Bums" beat the Giants, 7-5.

September 25, 1955 - A tale of three champions. As heavyweight boxing champion Rocky Marciano KOs Archie Moore in the ninth round in "the Rock's" last fight, twenty-year-old Detroit Tiger outfielder Al Kaline becomes the youngest AL batting champ, finishing at .340, and Willie Mays wins the NL home run crown by belting his fifty-first homer in victory over the Phils.

October 3, 1955 - Brooklyn's wait is over. They capture their first World Championship with a seventh-game 2-0 win over the Yankees behind Johnny Podres. Sandy Amoros's running grab of Yogi Berra's smash to left saves the game (read Amoros's story in this chapter).

April 17, 1956 - Mickey Mantle's favorite spectator, President Dwight Eisenhower, who reportedly played minor league ball in Kansas under an assumed name in 1909-1910, threw out the first ball and Mantle bombed two homers off Washington pitcher Camilo Pascual—both measured at more than five hundred feet—in the Yankees' 10-4 win. Mantle hit some ten homers in games attended by the president.

April 19, 1956 - In the first Major League game ever played in New Jersey, the Brooklyn Dodgers beat the Philadelphia Phillies,

5-4, in ten innings at Roosevelt Stadium.

May 16, 1956 - Wally Moon hits the first MLB homer in New Jersey, but his Cards lose to the "home team" Dodgers, 5-3.

May 18, 1956 - Mickey Mantle sets a new standard by hitting switch-hit homers in the same game for the third time in his career—he was tied with Jim Russell (Pirates/Braves/Dodgers outfielder from 1942-51)—to beat the ChiSox, 8-7, in ten innings.

May 24, 1956 - En route to a Triple Crown, Mickey Mantle goes 5-for-5 with a walk to raise his average to .421 in an 11-4 thumping of the Tigers.

May 28, 1956 - With Carl Erskine as his latest victim, Pirates slugging first baseman Dale Long homers in his eighth consecutive game to set a Major League mark as the Bucs whip the Dodgers at Forbes Field. He'll finish the year with twenty-seven four-baggers and his record will go unchallenged for thirty-one years.

May 30, 1956 - Mickey Mantle loves May, 1956. He hits his twentieth homer of the year—the quickest anyone had gotten to twenty in "the Bigs"—as he rockets a Pedro Ramos fastball to within eighteen inches of clearing Yankee Stadium's 108-and-a-half-foot-high facade, as the Yankees beat Washington. As the ball was still rising when it hit the roof some 396 feet from home plate, it has been estimated that it could have traveled nearly 650 feet if unimpeded.

June 17, 1956 - Joe Adcock really loves Ebbets Field. He hits three homers against the Dodgers in this doubleheader, and one of them, off Ed Roebuck, clears the eighty-seven-foot-high wall in left, at the 350-foot mark. Adcock obliterated the road-park mark he shared with Willie Mays by finishing the 1956 campaign with thirteen round trippers in Brooklyn.

July 25, 1956 - On the day the Italian liner *Andrea Doria* collided with the Swedish liner *Stockholm* off Nantucket Island, Massachusetts, Brooklyn Dodger right fielder Carl Furillo becomes the first Dodger to hit a home run in Jersey City as "Skoonj" belts one at Roosevelt Stadium to give "the Bums" a 2-1 win over the Cincinnati Reds.

August 23, 1956 - Chicago White Sox second baseman Nellie Fox chokes up and smacks out seven consecutive hits in this doubleheader against the Yankees. Mickey Mantle shows he can get on with power, speed and finesse, as he homers, triples and bunts for a single in the second game, which the ChiSox win, 6-4.

August 31, 1956 - This time Jim Lemon loves President Eisenhower. With the commander in chief in attendance, the Senators' slugger booms three homers, though the Yankees prevail, 6-4.

September 25, 1956 - As the first transatlantic telephone cable goes into operation, Sal "The Barber" Maglie no-hits the Philadelphia Phillies as the Dodgers win, 5-0.

October 8, 1956 - The perfecto. Don Larsen achieves baseball immortality by throwing the only perfect game in World Series history. The Yankee right-hander uses ninety-seven pitches to blank the Dodgers, 2-0, in game five to best Sal Maglie, who only gives up five hits (including Mickey Mantle's two-run homer in the fourth). Maglie tells his observations of the game in this chapter.

October 17, 1956 - The "What if?" game. Washington Senators owner Clark Griffith, who will eventually move his team out of the nation's capital and relocate to Minnesota, is rebuffed in his attempt to move the club to Los Angeles, and announces his plan to study bids from Louisville and San Francisco. Baseball keeps Griffith under its thumb and the move is never allowed to become a reality.

December 13, 1956 - The trade that made them cry. Jackie Robinson is dealt by the Dodgers to their hated crosstown rivals, the Giants, for pitcher Dick Littlefield. Robinson retires to avoid playing for the enemy.

August 1, 1957 - Dodger first baseman Gil Hodges hits his NL-record thirteenth career grand slam. It is the last slam in the history of the franchise located in Brooklyn.

August 17, 1957 - Ouch! Ouch! Philadelphia's Richie Ashburn, who has fouled off as many as seventeen pitches in an at-bat, hits the same spectator twice in the same trip to the plate. Ashburn fouls one off Alice Roth and breaks her nose. Moments later, as she is being removed from her seat for medical attention, Ashburn plugs her again as she lies down on a stretcher. The Phils win the game, 3-1.

September 22, 1957 - Red Sox slugger Ted Williams hits his fourth consecutive homer . . . sort of. He is walked eleven times over four games and only gets four official at-bats, all of them round-trippers. A single later in the game gives "The Kid" sixteen consecutive times reaching base safely.

October 24, 1957 - The "What if?" game, part two. The Cincinnati Reds waver, but at the last moment decline to move their franchise to Jersey City's Roosevelt Stadium.

April 15, 1958 - Baseball goes west. In the first game in San Francisco, the Giants beat the Los Angeles Dodgers, 8-0, at Seals Stadium. Ruben Gomez hurls a shutout and Daryl Spencer hits the first homer.

April 18, 1958 - Now it's the Dodgers' turn. In their home opener at the Los Angeles Coliseum, the Dodgers whip the Giants, 6-5. Hank Sauer hits two homers for the Giants and would have tied the score in the ninth, except that teammate Jim Davenport is called out for failing to touch third base.

May 13, 1958 - Willie Mays goes 5-for-5 with two homers, two triples and four "ribbies" in a 16-9 shellacking of the Dodgers. Teammate Daryl Spencer bombs two homers and drives in six.

May 18, 1958 - In the American League, Cleveland's Carroll Hardy, who will become a historical footnote by pinch hitting for Ted Williams on September 20, 1960, pinch hits for Roger Maris and smashes a three-run homer off Chicago's Billy Pierce for a 7-4 Indian victory.

June 26, 1958 - Kansas City A's outfielder Hector Lopez belts three homers in an 8-6 win over Washington.

September 29, 1958 - Phillie pinch hitter Dave Philley safely bangs out his eighth consecutive pinch hit, an MLB record, as the Phils beat the Pirates, 6-4, in ten innings.

April 22, 1959 - Wild thing. Kansas City A's reliever George Brunet (who holds the career record for most strikeouts in the minor leagues with more than 3,300), can't find the strike zone in this one. With the bases loaded, he walks five Chicago White Sox hitters and hits one batter to force in six runs without giving up a hit. The Sox score eleven runs in the seventh on one hit. Chicago wins, 20-6.

May 3, 1959 - Charlie Maxwell, the Tigers' "Sunday Player" (named for his hot performances on that day of the week), hits four consecutive homers in a Sunday doubleheader sweep of the Yankees, 4-2 and 8-2, at Briggs Stadium.

May 26, 1959 - Nearly perfect, or when one is better than twelve. Pirate pitcher Harvey Haddix pitches perfect ball for twelve innings against Milwaukee. In the thirteenth, Felix Mantilla gets on via an error, Hank Aaron is intentionally walked, and Joe Adcock homers for a 3-0 win. Aaron leaves the field before touching all the bases and Adcock passes him. Both are called out and the official score is 1-0. Lew Burdette goes thirteen innings and gives up twelve hits for the win.

June 2, 1959 - The game at Comiskey Park between the ChiSox and the Orioles is delayed for twenty-eight minutes as a blinding swarm of gnats invade the field. After numerous attempts by fire, smoke and water to terminate the swarm, a smoke bomb is attached to a center field fireworks display and ignited. The gnats depart and the O's beat the Sox, 3-2.

June 10, 1959 - Cleveland Indians outfielder Rocky Colavito hits four consecutive homers to lead the Tribe to an 11-8 win at Baltimore.

July 4, 1959 - On the day the United States officially adds Alaska's forty-ninth star to the American flag, Yankee starter Bob Turley tosses a one-hitter against the Senators and wins, 7-0. The only hit off Turley is Julio Becquer's soft fly that drops in front of lackadaisical left fielder, Norm Sieburn. The Yanks sweep the Nats in a double-header as shortstop Tony Kubek goes 8-for-10.

July 21, 1959 - The Boston Red Sox become the last Major League team to employ their first black player as Pumpsie Green pinch runs against the White Sox.

July 30, 1959 - Willie McCovey makes his Major League debut for the Giants and goes 4-for-4 with two triples off Robin Roberts of the Phillies as San Francisco wins, 7-2. Though he stayed up with the Giants all season, and won the Rookie of the Year award in only two months of play (.354 and thirteen homers in fifty-two games), he also won the Pacific Coast League home run title, where he had smacked twenty-nine for Phoenix before his call-up.

August 14, 1959 - Cincy teammates Vada Pinson and Frank Robinson each go 5-for-6 as the Redlegs beat the Phillies, 15-13.

August 31, 1959 - Sandy Koufax ties Bob Feller's record of eighteen strikeouts in a game, as he fans eighteen Giants before 82,074 spectators at the Coliseum. Dodgers win, 5-2, on Wally Moon's three-run homer in the ninth inning.

September 5, 1959 - Washington's Jim Lemon hits two homers in the third inning and drives in six as the Senators beat Cleveland, 14-2.

The Chronicles

Harry Craft
Cincinnati Reds, outfield
1937-1942

As mentioned in the 1930s chapter, Harry Craft was a knowledgeable ballplayer who played the outfield as deftly as any during his time. He used that knowledge of the pasture to mold a superstar, as he shared a story that had a profound effect on Major League baseball history.

June-September, 1950

"Lee MacPhail, director of player personnel for the Yankees, called me to manage his minor league club in Independence in 1949 in the K-O-M League. We had nothing but high school kids—seventeen to nineteen years old, who never played pro. And we had this young shortstop named Mickey Mantle. He looked good, good range, a real strong arm, but he wasn't smooth at short.

"In 1950, I moved up to Joplin, Missouri, in Class C ball and I took seven kids with me, including Mantle. I called MacPhail and asked him to let me move Mantle to third base or the outfield to give him a chance, but MacPhail said, 'Absolutely not.' He said, 'Phil Rizzuto's getting old and I want Mickey Mantle to be the next Yankee shortstop.'

"But I looked at the Yankee organizational depth chart and I knew that besides Rizzuto, who I thought still had four or five good years left in him, the Yankees also had Woodie Held, Clete Boyer, Gil McDougald and Jerry Lumpe waiting in the wings, and all were much smoother at short than Mantle. And then I looked at the outfield and saw that other than Jackie Jensen, I didn't know who else the Yankees might have to take Joe DiMaggio's place. So I went to Mickey and told him what I thought.

"I told Mickey, 'You play shortstop in 1950, but before every game and during all of our practices, I'm going to hit you flies and teach you all about the outfield. He worked so hard. He took all my advice to heart and he was so conscientious that I had a great deal of faith in him. We would talk baseball on all of our moments off together and I am so proud that he used the information.

"I certainly hoped I had helped him. When I got him in 1949, the Yankees sent me a report that said, 'Can't miss. If he doesn't get hurt, he has the arm, power from both sides of the plate, and can outrun the wind.' Still, as early as 1949, I told Yankee GM George Weiss, 'Mantle can not play shortstop. He can cover the ground easy but he fights it and ties himself up in knots. He's a Class B shortstop and nothing more. But with just a shred of coaching, he'll be a Triple-A outfielder in a few weeks, and a Major League outfielder in a month.'

"They fought me in 1949 and 1950, but when they called me before 1951 and asked if I thought Mickey could play the outfield, I said, 'You just watch him. Now . . . he can't miss.' And he certainly didn't. He made me proud every day he put on a uniform."

(**Author's Note:** One of Harry Craft's big days was June 8, 1940, when he slashed out a homer, triple, double and two singles for a rare cycle, in a 23-2 Cincinnati Reds shellacking of the Brooklyn Dodgers. Twenty-nine years later to the day, June 8, 1969, the Yankees retired his number-one pupil's famous number "7," before 60,096 fans.)

Jim "Mudcat" Grant
Cleveland Indians, pitcher
1958-1971

Jim Grant, the 6'1", 185-pound pitcher who toiled mostly for the Indians and Twins over his fourteen-year career, led the AL in wins in 1965 with twenty-one, becoming the first black to win twenty games in the junior circuit in the process. The "Mudcat" finished with a 145-119 record—including 25-15 in relief—and was successful both as a starter and as a relief man (he made eighty relief appearances covering 135 innings for Oakland and Pittsburgh in 1970, fashioning a 1.87 ERA and twenty-four saves, making him one of the few pitchers ever to win twenty in one season and save twenty in another). He might have recalled October 13, 1965, when he hit a three-run homer and pitched a complete game six-hitter for a 5-1 win for the Twins over the Dodgers in game six of the World Series. Instead, he reflects on the impact Jackie Robinson made in his life and relates a story about the man who broke baseball's race barrier.

October 20, 1950

"I remember meeting Jackie Robinson on a barnstorming tour in Tampa, Florida when I was fifteen. I was chosen to play in this all-star sandlot game against the Florida State Negro League. The organizers picked the best players in the state, most from around St. Petersburg and Bradenton and most played in the Negro Leagues.

"Roy Campanella, Don Newcombe, Larry Doby and Jackie were there collecting receipts and I wanted to talk to them. I didn't want an autograph; I just wanted to talk baseball. I was hurt when Jackie turned me down, but Doby explained that he was too busy. Larry Doby was my hero.

"I did get to talk to Jackie later and through conversation I understood what he went through . . . the hard knocks and the downside of baseball life. He suggested that I don't horse around, always perform to my full capacity regardless of the humiliation or situation, and carry myself with respect. I took it to heart on the field and whenever I thought I had it bad, I'd think what he went through. I never mentioned it when I was in Cleveland or when I was in Minnesota, but I did make a comment once in 1965.

"I was in Baltimore and became the first black to win twenty games in the American League. I thought about Jackie and Larry all game and was aware I'd be embarking on a 'first.' The game was a breeze and when it was over, I barely had time to savor the moment when Howard Cosell shoved a microphone in my face and asked, 'How does it feel to be the first black pitcher to win twenty games in the American League? Are you concerned that people will be upset?' I then sounded off, for me, and said, 'I don't want to hurt anyone's feelings, but I just want to be regarded as a pitcher. I am so proud of the achievement, but Jackie Robinson and Larry Doby made it possible for me, so the honor should go to those guys. Me, I'm just a pitcher.' "

Minnie Minoso
Chicago White Sox, outfield
1949 1951-1964 1976 1980

Saturnino Orestes Armas "Minnie" Minoso was a 5'10", 180-pound outfielder from Havana, Cuba, who had left his mark on the game.

Minoso led the league in stolen bases three times, triples twice, doubles and hits once (in different seasons), and nearly every year, he led the loop in getting hit by pitched balls — 189 times in his career.

A quick and fearless fielder, Minoso would often crash into unpadded fences to rob opponents of hits (he was a four-time gold glove recipient), and as an eight-time .300 hitter, he was dependable at the plate.

One of baseball's nice guys, Minoso, a six-time all-star, is also superstitious, and once, after going 0-for-4 against the Red Sox in Boston, Minoso showered with his uniform on to "rid himself of the evil spirits" that made him hitless. When he went 4-for-4 the following game, eight of his ChiSox teammates jumped into the shower with their uniforms on to work the same magic.

Minoso is also an ageless wonder. He appeared in three games in 1976 at age fifty-four for a White Sox promotion (and banged out a hit), and appeared in two games in 1980 to become a five-decade player. Plans to allow him to play in 1991 and become a six-decade player failed when the commissioner put thumbs down on the idea. Minoso played in the Minors two years later, instead.

Minoso lists Hank Greenberg and Martin Dihigo as his favorite ballplayers and another of his favorites gets most of the remembrance on the day Minnie shares here.

May 1, 1951

Following a brief career with the New York Cubans in the Negro Leagues, Minoso was signed by the Cleveland Indians. When he was traded to the Chicago White Sox on April 30, 1951, in a three-way trade between the Indians, ChiSox and Phillies, he became the first black player to wear a White Sox uniform.

Minoso tells what happened the next day, his first game.

"I was in Comiskey Park and the crowd was huge. They (the fans) didn't know me. I was just over from Cleveland and the big deal that I was the first black was just another reason I wanted to give them reason to be proud of me. (Chicago manager) Paul Richards put me at third base and I hadn't gotten anything there when I came to bat in the first inning.

"My first at-bat in a White Sox uniform, against the champion Yankees, I faced Vic Raschi, and I hit a home run over the center field wall. That was the most exciting moment of my baseball career, and many people remember that game, but not because of my homer, or my appearance in a White Sox uniform or because we lost, 8-3. What they remember is that in the sixth inning of the game, our pitcher, Randy Gumpert, gave up a home run to Yankee outfielder Mickey Mantle for his first Major League home run.

"Some company, huh?"

Andy Seminick
Philadelphia Phillies, catcher
1943-1957

Andrew Wasil Seminick was a steady, solid catcher (all-star in 1949) for the Phillies and Reds for fifteen years, during which time he played 1,304 games and hit 164 homers. A good handler of pitchers, Seminick may not have gotten the media attention that Yogi Berra or Roy Campanella got, but the 5'11", 190-pounder from Pierce, West Virginia, was well-respected among his peers.

He remembers being in awe about nearly everything. "When Willie Mays first came up in May, 1951, he joined the Giants in Philadelphia and I saw him in batting practice — his first day up — and I had never seen anyone hit them so far, so often. He ran the bases so gracefully, so swiftly. I just wondered how one man could have so much talent.

"And when I came up, I was awed by everything. Seeing Johnny Mize, Walker Cooper, Ernie Lombardi . . . I was so nervous, I didn't even touch the ball the first five times I was up at bat. But the sixth time up, I homered and I felt then that at least I didn't have to go back down (to the minors) empty.

"But I enjoyed every moment up there. Playing against Musial

139

and Ott was fantastic, and watching Jackie Robinson come up was historic and great to be a part of. With Musial, he would talk Polish to me and say 'How ya doin'?' and I'd answer in Russian, 'Fine, Stash, how about you?'

"My highlight would be June 2, 1949, when I hit two homers in one inning against Cincinnati — off Ken Raffensberger and Kent Peterson — and I wound up with three homers in the game. We hit five home runs in that eighth inning to tie a Major League record, and having my name on two records (two homers by one man and five by a team in an inning) was just wonderful."

Seminick talks of competition, a fight and a fine.

August 11-12, 1951

"We were playing the Giants and the dirtiest player in baseball (but a great, great ballplayer), Eddie Stanky. Stanky would wave and flap his arms from second base whenever I would go to bat. He was told by the umps to cut it out. He did for a while. The next game (August 12), I slid in to third and came in high on Hank Thompson to jar the ball loose, and on my next at-bat, Stanky was flapping and waving again and (umpire) Lon Warneke tossed Stanky out of the game. Still, we had bad blood with the Giants and on a double play after my at-bat, I took out Stanky's replacement, Bill Rigney, with a clean but hard slide. Before I knew it, both benches emptied and there was a brawl like I had never seen before. Rig and I were fined twenty-five dollars and a few days later, the commissioner (Ford Frick) ruled that you couldn't wave and flap like Stanky did, or you would automatically be tossed and the batter awarded first base."

Roy Sievers
St. Louis Browns, first base
1949-1965

Roy "Squirrel" Sievers, a 6'1", 195-pound slugger from St. Louis, was a solid hitter on some of the worst teams in baseball. Sievers toiled for the St. Louis Browns from 1949-1953, and just when they moved to Baltimore and began to achieve respectability, he was sent to Washington to play for the Senators through 1959 and some more bad teams.

Through it all, Sievers managed to win the Rookie of the Year award in 1949, a home run title (with forty-two) in 1957, an RBI crown the same year (114) and four all-star selections.

He was solid at the plate and in the field and was a silent-but-

Roy Sievers, first base, 1950s
Courtesy: National Baseball Library Hall of Fame, Cooperstown, New York

strong presence in the clubhouse. Washington's highest-paid player, he got his nickname for his basketball skills . . . hanging around the "cage" all day long.

Sievers talked of life with the Brownies.

August 19, 1951

"With the Browns from 1949-53, we didn't win many games but we had a lot of fun.

"I roomed with Satchel Paige for a week, but he had the room filled with so many ointments, snake oils, and stuff for his hair and his arm that I couldn't get in the room. You couldn't tell his age, but he looked like he was in his late fifties and he once said smilingly that 'fifty was too early,' meaning, I think, that he was over fifty.

"Max Patkin was one of our coaches and in one of his funny bits, he'd take an empty bucket and throw it in the stands — the fans thought there was water in it — and he hit the bat boy in the head with it . . . fifteen stitches.

"But the biggest kick was the Eddie Gaedel deal. Using a midget to play in a Major League game was a secret, but earlier that day, we had a party and (team owner) Bill Veeck had this big cardboard cake and Gaedel pops out of the cake. We talked about it in the dugout all day. Then at game time, Gaedel pops up to bat wearing uniform number '⅛' and Veeck tells him not to swing or he'll shoot him. Gaedel is only 3'7" and Bob Cain of the Tigers threw him four high pitches. We all cracked up. Jim Delsing pinch ran for him and that's the last time a midget was allowed in the Majors — they changed the rules on us, but it was typical of Veeck and the Browns. Every day was a party and losing wasn't so bad when you're having so much fun."

Del Wilber
Philadelphia Phillies, catcher
1946-1954

Del "Babe" Wilber was a 6'3", 200-pound receiver from Lincoln Park, Michigan, who is the lesser known of three Cardinal catchers of his era (the two more well-known backstops being Del Rice and Joe Garagiola). Wilber insists that it was New York columnist Eddie Dyer who first came up with the quote on St. Louis's three catchers: "One can't hit, one can't throw and one can't catch." Wilber also tells this one on his teammate Garagiola and his buddy Yogi Berra: "I took Joe to his first banquet; it was in St. Louis to honor Yogi.

After a big warm-up speech to give Yogi an award, Yogi stood up, said, 'Thanks,' sat down, and Joe hasn't stopped talking since."

Wilber went on to Philadelphia as a back-up for Phillies catcher Andy Seminick and later to the Red Sox as "number two" behind Sammy White. Wilber played 299 games in his career, made only seventeen errors and hit a career-high eight home runs in only eighty-four games in 1951.

The Cardinals were a "fine bunch of guys," Wilber recalls. "Stan Musial made me proud to be on the same ball field, but when I was traded to the Boston Red Sox in 1953, that was the best team I ever played for — Ted Williams, Dom DiMaggio, George Kell, Mel Parnell and Lou Boudreau, one of the game's real gentlemen was the manager. Boudreau would always play me when we traveled to Detroit, because that was my home and he knew I'd have family and friends at the game."

Wilber's nugget, however, comes from his year with the Phillies.

August 27, 1951

It was a dream game for a ballplayer, a perfect day. Wilber recalls, "I was really sick that day. I had chills and it was ninety degrees out. I put on a jacket between innings. It was the second game of a doubleheader against Cincinnati — Andy Seminick caught the opener — and we had a wild left-hander named Ken Johnson pitching for us. He was really throwing well that night and shut out the Reds, 3-0. Our three runs . . . I got them all.

"I was up three times and took three swings and hit three home runs, all against Ken Raffensberger who gave up only three hits all night — mine. My illness made me so loose I just swung hard at the first pitch and hit them all out.

"I saw a headline that read: 'Wilber 3, Cincinnati 0.'

"I get to the ballpark the next day and Eddie Sawyer, our manager, had me on the bench. Three homers and I wasn't in the lineup. Unbeknownst to me, Andy Seminick, the starting catcher, went to Sawyer and told him he was sick so I could start. I was told just before game time, 'Hey, Wilber, you're catching, Seminick is sick.' I felt good on that day and in a game against St. Louis, Gerry Staley, the guy who was renting my house in St. Louis, was the starter. He threw me a curve and I swung hard, trying for my fourth homer in a row, but the fly ball I hit was caught near the fence by Erv Dusak. I came back to the bench, and there's a suddenly healthy Seminick smiling at me, saying, 'Well, I got you up to bat, anyway.' "

143

Clyde King
Brooklyn Dodgers, pitcher
1944-1945 1947-1948 1951-1953

Clyde King was a 6'1", 175-pounder from Goldsboro, North Carolina. His playing career began during the war and he was still in baseball, managing for George Steinbrenner's Yankees, in 1982.

A reliable relief pitcher, King won thirteen games in relief in 1951, and made 179 relief appearances in his seven years (along with twenty-one starts), quite a few stints in the days when relievers were not used as often as they are now. King finished 35-25 (19-14 as a reliever and 13-11 as a starter).

King likes ball the old-fashioned way, the way it was when he was pitching in 1945. In the days when players lined up their gloves in foul territory between innings, Brooklyn manager Leo Durocher called upon King to pitch. "I had relieved three days in a row and my arm was dead, but Leo was such a wonderful guy, I gave it all for him. Except that he hadn't wanted me to pitch and wanted to rest me, so he told me before the game, 'Don't take your glove onto the field today.' When I had to go pitch, I had no glove. When he asked me in the ninth, 'Can you do it?' I grabbed Ralph Branca's glove and pitched with it and got the save. I came back and said to Ralph, 'Here, your glove got the save.'

"The next day, the clubhouse guy, Danny Commerford, came to me and said, 'Leo wants to see you.' I was scared. I thought I was going to be sent to Montreal (the minors). Leo was in his office wearing this Carolina blue plaid coat. He said, 'Look at this coat. Do you like it? I had one made for you.' He gave me the coat. That was Leo's way of thanking me without saying thanks."

King managed for the Giants, Braves and Yankees, and he used the style of the old-time manager, like that taught to him by Durocher and by Chuck Dressen.

August, 1951

"Chuck Dressen was one of my favorite managers. He taught me the stall. I was pitching for the Dodgers and the starter ran into some quick trouble so I was called in without enough time to get warm.

"As I hit the mound and told him I wasn't warm, Dressen told Pee Wee Reese to pretend he had something in his eye, after I had completed my eight warm-ups. While Pee Wee tried to get his eye clear, I warmed up with Jackie Robinson until I was warm.

"There were two out and runners at first and third and I got the third out on a pop-up. Good tactics by Chuck."

Clem Labine
Brooklyn Dodgers, pitcher
1950-1962

Clement Walter Labine was a six-foot, 180-pounder from Lincoln, Rhode Island, who was one of the 'Boys of Summer' in Brooklyn in the 1950s.

Labine made his mark in relief, throwing his sinker and leading the NL in saves before it became fashionable to do so, with nineteen in 1956 and seventeen in 1957. Overall, Labine saved ninety-six games in an era when saves were rare. He appeared in 513 games (thirty-eight as a starter), pitched 1,079 innings, finished with a career mark of 77-56, and was named to two all-star squads. Labine's unique claim to fame is the fact that he retired Stan Musial in forty-nine consecutive at-bats.

Labine pitched in five World Series, including the Dodgers' first championship team (1955) and Pittsburgh's 1960 championship team.

He ended his stint with the 1962 Mets.

September, 1951

"In April 1950, Carl Erskine and I had made the Brooklyn Dodgers — Carl was coming off an 8-1 record in 1949 — but in those days, clubs used the option rule based on the number of times you could be sent down. It was a ploy to keep salaries down, and Carl and I each had one option left. Branch Rickey, the team's owner and general manager, was a man who could mesmerize you with his oratory; he called Carl and me in to his office and told us Carl was being sent to Montreal and I to St. Paul. We questioned the move and he said, 'Let me explain; you two cannot hold men at first base well and you need experience.' I said, 'You've got Rex Barney, Ralph Branca, Bud Podbielan and Jack Banta and none of them went 8-1 like Carl and none of them can hold a guy on first.' And Rickey said, 'But they have experience.'

"So in April 1951, I came up from St. Paul at the same time Mickey (Mantle) came to the Yanks from Kansas City and Willie (Mays) to the Giants from Minneapolis, but I was to play one last minor league game before going to Brooklyn. Late in that game, I slid in at home and twisted my ankle against Clint Courtney's shin guards.

"I arrived in Brooklyn on crutches. The Dodgers didn't want to waste an option so they kept me. And since we had a thirteen-and-a-half-game lead, I wasn't needed.

"Well, I got better and our starting staff was getting tired and since I was throwing batting practice, Dressen (Dodger manager Charlie Dressen) decided to start me and give the staff a shot in the arm. I responded with four straight complete games and was scheduled to start the first game of a home stand in September following a long road trip.

"A train foul-up and delay got us home at four A.M. and none of us slept, so I went into this game versus Philadelphia already tired. I couldn't get the curve over and loaded the bases in the first. Normally, I'd go to a full windup but I decided to pitch from the stretch because of my tiredness. I went to the stretch and Dressen called time, came out to the mound and said, 'Take a full windup.' I told him I couldn't get the curve over. He said, 'Take a full windup.'

"As soon as he turned his back, I went into the stretch, fired a curve to 'Puddin' Head' Jones, and he blasted a grand slam into the upper deck at Ebbets Field.

"Dressen kept me on the bench for three weeks as Preacher Roe, Newk (Don Newcombe), Ersk (Carl Erskine) and Branca grew wearier. Dressen wouldn't even let me go to the bullpen. I was to sit and watch. Finally, in the second game of our play-off with the New York Giants, I pitched and tied the play-off with a 10-0 win.

"Actually, I pitched two great games that no one remembers. I won the game before Bobby Thomson hit his home run heard 'round the world' off Branca, and I beat Bob Turley, 1-0, in ten innings in the 1956 Series, the day after Don Larsen's perfect game. And that (Larsen's perfect game) is the greatest thrill I've ever had on a baseball field . . . and I was on the wrong side."

Phil "Scooter" Rizzuto
New York Yankees, shortstop
1941-1942 1946-1956

As discussed in the 1940s chapter, Phil Rizzuto, the pint-sized shortstop who scooted all over the field to take every ground ball in his domain, played much larger than his size. He also had a great deal of heart and a great deal of laughter, especially about his own abilities. He chose to tell a story that has gotten him the most ridicule, dealing with the 1951 World Series.

October 6, 1951

If 1946 is the "Johnny Pesky hesitation" Series and 1941 is the "Mickey Owen dropped third strike" Series, then to many, the 1951 Series is the "Stanky kicked the ball out of Rizzuto's glove" Series.

The Yankees were expected to sweep the Giants in 1951, and when the two crosstown rivals were even at a game apiece, there were some worries of a letdown in the Yankee clubhouse.

In the fifth inning of game three, with the Giants up, 1-0, Giant second baseman Eddie Stanky was on first via a hit. Rizzuto picks up the action: "The infield was in shadow and (Vic) Raschi was on the mound. Yogi (Berra) picked up the hit-and-run sign and called for a pitchout. Raschi fired a fastball outside and Yogi had Stanky out by twenty feet. Stanky came in high and kicked some kind of weird soccer kick. I had the bag blocked and as I made a phantom tag, Stanky kicked my glove out to DiMaggio in center field. This all opened the floodgates, and the Giants won the game, 6-2.

"Now here's the skinny. Stanky never touched the bag. I had it blocked. He went to third and I called for the appeal but the umpires didn't see it. So he got the best of me. He and I played against each other in the minors and he was the dirtiest player in that league. One time I slid in and he grabbed my uniform and swung me around and off the bag. The next day, I was on second and he yelled at me, calling me a 'dumb Dago.' His pitcher tried to pick me off as I turned to see him, so I started for third and Stanky hit me in the head with the ball. So he got me, but we had the last laugh because we won the Series, winning the next three games, and we may have won because of Stanky. Here's what happened.

"We Yankees had a lot of pride in those days, but we also had a lot of individuality. When we hit the field, we always sauntered out as we felt like it, usually in groups of two or three but never as a team. Before game four, which was at the Polo Grounds, Frankie Crosetti (third base coach) called a team meeting—and we never had team meetings in those days. The team showed me a lot of support and said we had to go get 'em (the Giants) for making me look bad. DiMaggio even said, 'Let's show 'em we're Yankees.' At that moment we really became a team. We decided to all hit the field together—twenty-five guys and coaches all at once.

"The clubhouse at the Polo Grounds is about five-hundred feet from home plate, so when twenty-five Yankees in pinstripes walked boldly from the outfield to the dugout, and the fans, many of whom were Yankee fans, gave us a standing ovation, we knew we wouldn't lose again . . . and we didn't. DiMaggio got red hot and got six hits and a homer the rest of the way, Gil McDougald hit a grand slam, Hank Bauer hit a bases-loaded triple, and Allie Reynolds, Eddie Lopat and Vic Raschi pitched gems. We got the last laugh indeed . . . and the World Championship."

(**Author's Note:** Although Scooter would never brag about this, Rizzuto fielded flawlessly the rest of the way, and for the Series hit .320 (8-for-25) scored five runs, drove in three and belted a homer, and was named MVP of the World Series.)

Tommy Holmes
Boston Braves, outfield
1942-1952

As discussed in the 1940s chapter, Tommy Holmes could hit. He was the first player ever to lead the league in homers (twenty-eight) and have the fewest strikeouts in the league (nine) in the same season (1945). He could also recognize hitting; when he managed the Boston Braves in 1952, he tried to acquire a friend, one he knew could hit. The trade might have saved him his job.

April, 1952

It has become baseball lore that the best trades have never been made. And it is baseball legend that some of the biggest trades would have been made — or were made — only to be pulled back because one of the trading parties couldn't pull the trigger. Joe DiMaggio was traded by the Yankees to Boston for Ted Williams in 1946, only to have Larry MacPhail of the Yankees and Tom Yawkey of the Red Sox think better of it before the press conference was called and once they had sobered up, cancel the deal. Whitey Ford and Mickey Mantle nearly went to Milwaukee for Warren Spahn and Hank Aaron in 1960, and the Yankees nearly made a five-for-one swap with Washington for Camilo Pascual in 1959. Tom Seaver nearly went to the Dodgers for Don Sutton in 1976; the Yankees turned down a deal that would have sent Wade Boggs to New York in March, 1989, for Al Leiter and Mike Pagliarulo (the Yanks said no to the Leiter inclusion, only to ship him to Toronto a month later in the Jesse Barfield deal). But the deal Tommy Holmes relates here would have sent Brooklyn fans in lynch mobs to the offices of Walter O'Malley, had Holmes completed the deal he had made and was ready to announce.

Holmes recalls, "The Dodgers had lost the play-off to the Giants in 1951 and wanted a change, and I wanted to acquire my best friend, so in April 1952, I negotiated a deal with Walter O'Malley of the Brooklyn Dodgers in which I would send them my first baseman, Earl Torgeson, coming off a .263, twenty-four-homer, ninety-two-RBI year, and trade him for Gil Hodges, coming off a .268, forty-homer, 103-RBI year.

"The trade was made and Walter O'Malley had set up a joint press conference for the next day where we could announce the trade together. But first we had to play one more game, my Braves against his Dodgers — and Hodges.

"We're up, 3-2, in the ninth and Warren Spahn is on the mound. Hodges comes up in the potential game-winning spot, with one on. I walked out to the mound and told Spahn to walk Hodges. He said, 'No.' I said, 'Walk him, goddamnit. Put him on.' Spahn said, 'I don't want a walk on my record.' I said, 'Goddamnit, I'll put in a reliever to walk him. He's coming to us tomorrow and I don't want to hurt him and don't want him to hurt us. I don't want to make him look good or bad, so walk him.'

Spahn looked over at the runner at first and says, 'That will put the tying run in scoring position at second.' I said, 'Walk him and get the next guy.'

"I turned and walked to the dugout. I hadn't even gotten to the top step when Spahn brushed Hodges back with an inside pitch. But Hodges stood his ground, swung, and smashed it for a game-winning home run.

"Walter O'Malley called me the next morning and I said, 'I've got four media members here to announce the trade, what's up?' O'Malley said, 'I can't. They'll hang me. After that homer, we're in first place and he's a hero so I just can't trade him. I'm sorry.'

"So Gil Hodges was my best friend and I couldn't get him. I tried, but I couldn't get it done. Almost, though, and since Gil hit .254 with thirty-two homers and 102 RBIs, while Torgeson hit .230 with five homers and thirty-four RBIs, Hodges would have been great for Boston. And after that trade failed, so did the Braves. I was fired in two weeks."

Al Kaline
Detroit Tigers, outfield
1953-1974

While Mickey Mantle, Willie Mays, Hank Aaron and Duke Snider garnered more attention and headlines, Al Kaline, the 6'2", 175-

pound outfielder for the Tigers, toiled in relative anonymity (except around the Motor City, where he became a god) and merely put up Hall of Fame numbers in a twenty-two-year career during which time he was the epitome of class in uniform, a latter-day Joe DiMaggio.

The Baltimore-raised Kaline, known as "Mr. Tiger," was a fifteen-time all-star, hit 399 career homers, 498 doubles and connected for 3,007 hits and won ten gold gloves. When he won the batting title (.340) in 1955, he was, at twenty, the youngest player ever to win the AL crown. Kaline had his number retired by the Tigers and was elected to the Hall of Fame in 1980.

When the Tigers moved the left-field fences in at Briggs Stadium (later Tiger Stadium) to accommodate Kaline's right-handed power, he mused, "Yankee Stadium was 'The House that Ruth Built,' and Tiger Stadium is 'The House They Tore Down For Kaline.' " In his typical self-deprecating style, Kaline confirms the story of a fan in New York coming up to him in the early sixties, after Kaline had robbed Mickey Mantle of an extra-base hit with an outstanding play in the outfield. The fan barked, "Kaline, you ain't half the player Mickey Mantle is." Not missing a beat, Kaline smiled at the young man and said, "Son, nobody is half the player Mickey Mantle is." That statement would find some argument in Detroit.

Signed off the Baltimore sandlots, Kaline never played a single inning in the minors, and his first day is the day he remembers best.

June 25, 1953

Kaline recalls, "I was in a high school gym one day and a Major League clubhouse the next. I joined the Tigers in Philadelphia just as the team bus was pulling away from the hotel; I never even had a chance to check in. I was skinny and scared and small.

"I got to the field, and when I put on my first uniform — with number '25' on it — it was and is the greatest moment I ever had in baseball. My first uniform was so big on me, I had to wear the batboy's uniform pants.

"In those days, the rookie got the shortest end of the stick. In most clubhouses, I had a locker right next to the john. In Chicago, my locker was a nail on the wall. But I also noticed even the older guys didn't pick on me; they really made me feel at ease and at home. Veterans such as Johnny Pesky and Steve Souchock showed me the ropes and taught me game strategy. When I've read or heard stories about Mickey Mantle being ignored by Joe DiMaggio, or some old vet making it tough on a rookie, I really appreciate what the Tigers' vets did for me all the more, and I always tried to do the same for Tigers' rookies when they came up."

George Strickland
Cleveland Indians, shortstop
1950-1960

George Strickland was a 6'1", 180-pounder from New Orleans, Louisiana, and was the shortstop on Cleveland's last championship team (1954). A steady fielder, he led the AL in double plays once and fielding once, and turned five double plays on May 27, 1952.

Strick hit a career-high .284 for the 1953 Tribe and in 971 career games connected for thirty-six homers.

He speaks reverently of his Indian teammates: "I admired the Cleveland pitching staff. When they got jocked in a game, their only answer was, 'I got jocked.' No excuses, none of this 'I didn't have rhythm' or 'didn't have velocity.' The great ones — Wynn, Lemon, Mossi — would say 'I didn't have it.' That's all. Honest admission.

"It's true we used to celebrate off days like they were wins, but we were a good group of ballplayers. And we all had our quirks. One of my favorite teammates was Minnie Minoso. Minnie didn't trust banks so he'd cash his paycheck and carry his money in a cigar box. During the game, he put his money in a white sannie (baseball sanitary stocking) and wear it. When he was running, you could hear the change jingle, but he said it padded his legs when he slid."

His recollections are of typical Indian luck.

September, 1953

"We were playing at Yankee Stadium and the hot summer sun had baked the ground rock hard. Al 'Flip' Rosen was playing third base and late in the game, Yankee pitcher Allie Reynolds was up with a man at first. We were thinking bunt. Reynolds instead took a full swing and hit an infield pop-up. Rosen says to me while the ball is in the air, 'I'm gonna trap it and get a double play.' But the Yankee infield was like concrete and the ball bounced and took a high bad hop and Rosen couldn't get anyone. The Yankees scored a run that inning.

"Next inning, with runners at first and second and no one out for us, Bobby Avila is up and grounds into a third-to-second-to-first triple play and we lose. I told Rosey, 'No wonder the Indians never beat the Yankees. They must have known the outcome all along.' "

Henry "Dutch" Dotterer
Cincinnati Reds, catcher
1957-1961

Dutch Dotterer was a six-foot, 210-pound catcher from Syracuse, New York. He was a backup backstop who managed to get into 107 games while hitting .247. He was a good defensive player, committing only six errors in his career.

While his career stats in the Majors begin in 1957, Dotterer was a nonplaying member of the Cincy club in 1954 when it embarked on a bizarre promotion.

Dotterer could have blown his own horn with the story of his grand slam off Sandy Koufax for a 4-3 victory on June 10, 1960, but he decided to stick with the promotion that made him a record-holder.

June, 1954

"I had just gotten out of the army and had been with the club for a month but hadn't played; I wasn't officially on the roster. We were playing the (New York) Giants and somebody on the Reds decided to go after Gabby Hartnett's record of catching a ball from the Washington Monument, 555 feet high. So Cincinnati decided to have a helicopter hover at 575 feet high and someone would drop balls and see if the catchers could set a new record.

"Giants manager Leo Durocher didn't want to injure his catchers because they were in the pennant race, but (Cincy manager) Birdie Tebbetts said it was OK so Andy Seminick, Hobie Landrith, Eddie Bailey and I got set for the contest — at night with two spotlights shined on the falling ball.

"They dropped one ball first so you could track it, and then drop one for you to catch. Seminick, our starting catcher, put on full catcher's gear after he saw a ball sink about six inches into the ground upon impact.

"I stuck out my glove and the ball just happened to land right in it for the record. I got five hundred dollars for the catch."

Edwin "Duke" Snider
Brooklyn Dodgers, outfield
1947-1964

Edwin Snider was "The Silver Fox," "The Duke of Flatbush," or merely "The Duke" to throngs of Brooklyn Dodger fans in the 1940s and 1950s. He is the third of the great center fielders of New York—

Willie, Mickey and The Duke—to be thought of as the best in the city . . . and in baseball. It was Snider—not Mickey Mantle or Willie Mays, his metropolitan area counterparts—who led the Majors in homers for the decade of the 1950s by connecting for 326, many in cozy Ebbets Field.

Although immortalized for his bat—407 homers, 1,333 RBIs, seven years better than .300, one home run title, one RBI crown— the six-foot, 200-pound, prematurely gray outfielder from Los Angeles was also considered a quick and graceful center fielder with a rocket-like throwing arm.

Snider was loved, and hated, by fans who wanted the best from him and all "The Boys of Summer" at all times, and he was thrilled with the Dodgers' move from Brooklyn to his hometown of Los Angeles in 1958. He fittingly knocked out the first hit to open Dodger Stadium. His number was retired by the Dodgers and he was elected to the Hall of Fame in 1980.

Snider reflects on the special closeness that Brooklyn had with its team in the early fifties and the estrangement that followed.

August, 1955

"I lived in the Bay Bridge area of Brooklyn during the season, within walking distance of my teammates Preacher Roe, Pee Wee Reese, Carl Erskine and Clem Labine. We, and all Brooklynites, were family. The residents threw block parties and easily talked and joked and played in the streets with us. Then came 1955.

"We had a big lead and by August it was slipping away. I was cold; I couldn't buy a hit (he dropped his average from .331 to .298). First, they (the fans in attendance at Ebbets Field) booed the team and then me. And then really me. They booed me from the rafters from the time my name was announced until the time I reached center field to the time I reached the batter's box. It was thunderous and I blame the media for making a big deal out of it when I said, after a tough loss, 'They are the worst fans in baseball; they don't deserve us. Let 'em boo. They don't deserve to win. That's why we're going to Jersey City next year.'

"Then I read in the headlines, 'Snider blasts fans,' and the booing got even worse. It was loud and constant.

"So I yelled at a couple of writers before our next game, 'You writers want to give them something to boo about? Give them this game.' I went out and got a single, a double and two homers; 4-for-4 with four RBIs and the fans came alive and cheered like I was their

Whitey Ford, pitcher, 1950s
Courtesy: New York Yankees

prodigal son, and it filled the papers and drove the stories about President Eisenhower off the front page."

Whitey Ford
New York Yankees, pitcher
1950-1967

Eddie "Whitey" Ford was the Yankee stopper, "the Chairman of the Board." His office was the pitcher's mound, and the Yankee lefty was as cool and poised as any man who ever toed the rubber. Ford, a New York City native, was born to play for the Yankees and was destined for the Hall of Fame on looks and poise alone. His inside-the-locker-room nickname says it all; he was "Slick." The 5'10", 175-pound Ford won 236 games in sixteen years while losing only 106, for the second-best winning percentage of all time at .690. He won two ERA titles and wound up with a sharp 2.75 career ERA. He set the World Series mark for consecutive scoreless innings — breaking Babe Ruth's string of twenty-nine and two-thirds innings — at thirty-two shutout frames. He is the World Series leader in wins, starts, innings pitched and strikeouts. Ford won a Cy Young award and is generally considered as having one of the best pickoff moves to first in the history of the game. He had his number retired and a plaque dedicated in his honor by the Yankees. He was elected to the Hall of Fame in 1974.

Whitey could have talked about his 1961 season in which he went 25-4 and led the Yanks to one of the top records in baseball history at 109-53, but as Whitey says, "I won twenty-five games that year, but with Mantle and Maris going after Babe Ruth's record and the team hitting 240 homers, no one remembers it.

"There's so much I could talk about, like my friendships with Billy Martin and Mickey Mantle, or the sage advice I got from Eddie Lopat to keep a 'book' on every hitter and change what they saw every time I faced them. He made me think like a Major Leaguer. And he and Jim Turner watched my motion and found I was telegraphing my pitches, tipping off the hitter. They straightened me out and if they hadn't, it would have been a short career."

September 23, 1955

"Nearing the end of the season, we were locked in a battle with the Red Sox for the pennant and, man, we had a fierce rivalry with them in those days. Well, we needed to win this one to clinch the pennant and Don Larsen was pitching a helluva game at Fenway Park. He gave us a 4-1 lead into the eighth. With one out, Boston had runners at second and third with Billy Goodman up and Ted Williams on deck, both lefties. Casey Stengel came out to the mound, took out Larsen, and called me in from the bullpen. Casey told me 'We'll get this fella (Goodman), then walk Williams, and pitch to the next guy.'

"Well, I had nothing that day and couldn't get loose. I walked Goodman and had to pitch to Williams. I was careful because he could put them in front with one swing, so I fell behind 3-and-1. I wasn't going to walk Williams and I hoped he didn't know how bad I was that day, so I threw him a fastball — a mediocre fastball at best — right down the middle. On any other day, Williams would have belted that thing out of the park, but on this day, I think he was surprised by how slow this fat fastball was and he bounced a two-hopper to Billy Martin, who started a double play to get us out of the inning. Ex-Yankee Jackie Jensen homered off me in the ninth and we won, 4-2. We had won the pennant and I did it with 'no' stuff. I walked off the field and headed straight to the clubhouse, which was the classy way we handled things in those days ... no high fives or hand slaps."

Sandy Amoros
Brooklyn Dodgers, outfield
1952-1960

Edmundo "Sandy" Amoros was a 5'7", 170-pound reserve outfielder for the Dodgers during the 1950s. He is remembered largely for one catch that propelled Brooklyn to its only World Championship, in 1955.

Amoros, born in Havana, Cuba, played 517 games and twelve World Series games—in three different Series—and was employed by the Dodgers as a pinch hitter in 150 games. He was an integral part of the metropolitan rivalry of the fifties between the Dodgers, Giants and Yankees, but his celebrity was assured with one play ... the catch.

October 4, 1955

Amoros was reticent to talk about his catch, saying it was "just one play that other people made a big deal out of."

Game seven was at hand at Yankee Stadium in the classic World Series duel between the New York Yankees and their crosstown rivals, the "Wait 'till next year" Brooklyn Dodgers. The "Bums" had never won the big one, but they were close this time. Amoros was not a starter for the Dodgers that day, as manager Walt Alston platooned Amoros against lefties, and the Yankees starter that day was lefty Tommy Byrne. Amoros picks up the story: "I came in in the sixth inning and we were ahead, 2-0. Johnny Podres was pitching a great game for us. I was in left field and was playing (the Yankee hitter) Yogi Berra to pull in left-center. Berra sliced a shot into the left field corner, right near the line and heading for the foul pole. I ran as fast as I could and stretched as far as my arm would go and made the catch with the tip of my glove. Another two inches and that ball was gone. Then I turned nearly a full circle and threw to (shortstop) Pee Wee Reese, who was behind third base. He then made a rope of a throw to (first baseman) Gil Hodges to double Gil McDougald off first for a double play (McDougald had rounded second base in an attempt to circle the bases in the likelihood that Berra's drive fell in). Podres shut the Yankees out the rest of the way and we won the game, 2-0, and the Series.

"People still tell me they saw that catch, almost forty years ago, and how that won the Series. I'm amazed they still remember."

Carl Erskine
Brooklyn Dodgers, pitcher
1948-1959

Carl Erskine, known affectionately as "Oisk" by the Brooklyn faithful, was a 5'10", 165-pound pitcher from Anderson, Indiana, known for his ability to change speeds on his curve and change-up.

Erskine's best years were 1953, when he went 20-6 for a league-leading winning percentage of .769 in 246 innings, and 1954 with his 18-15 mark in a career-best 260 innings pitched. Erskine finished his career with a 122-78 record, good for a .610 percentage in 335 games and 1,718 innings. He pitched in five World Series for the Dodgers and went 2-2.

He remained with the Dodgers his entire career, joining them for two years following the move west, but he relished the closeness of the game in Brooklyn.

Erskine says, "Ebbets Field fans were so close they were truly a part of the game; the opponents were intimidated and the umpires felt the crowd was down their necks and they truly feared reprisals. One day, Beans Reardon was umpiring at second base in a game against the Giants, and the rafters were packed. You couldn't move. You couldn't see the aisles; it was solid people. The fire marshalls looked the other way because it was a red-hot battle with the Giants. So on this play, Alvin Dark was leading off first and tried to steal second. Campy (Roy Campanella) took my pitch and fired to (Pee Wee) Reese at second and in a bang-bang play, Reese, Dark and the ball all arrived at the same time. Reardon's right arm shot up in the air, thumb sticking straight up and he yells, 'You're safe.' Dark looks up, Reese looks up, and Reese has the ball on his foot. They both asked Reardon, 'Beans — out or safe? Out or safe?' Reardon says, 'The three of us here know you're safe, but forty thousand fans saw me call you out. You're out.' "

Erskine threw two no-hitters, and talks about one of them here.

May 12, 1956

Erskine begins, "Jackie Robinson was so dominant a player and individual for years. He was a classic. We were close friends ever since he saw me pitch at Fort Worth in 1948 against the Dodgers in an exhibition game. He didn't know me (I was only 22) but he sought me out and said, 'Don't worry, you'll be with us soon.' Two-and-a-half months later I was up with Brooklyn.

me out and said, 'Don't worry, you'll be with us soon.' Two-and-a-half months later I was up with Brooklyn.

"Jackie went through his struggles and saw me go through many shoulder problems and ups and downs. We helped each other as teammates and friends through those struggles.

"I was pitching Saturday afternoon, May 12, 1956, against the Giants. Dizzy Dean and Buddy Blattner were there to cover it for the *Game of the Week*.

"I had an injection in my shoulder the day before. I had a very bad shoulder and didn't think I could pitch at all.

"I read that Tom Sheehan, chief scout for the Giants, had indicted the Dodgers in an article, saying we were no competition for the Giants in 1956. The article said that Campy was over the hill, Jackie had slowed down and was well past his prime and Erskine can't win with the garbage he throws. And this article will come into play later.

"I was just about to go tell (Dodger manager) Walt Alston that I couldn't go, but before I could say anything, he handed me a new ball . . . the game ball. I couldn't tell him. I'd never asked out of a start and I wasn't going to now. I felt down, but as I got to the dugout and heard those forty thousand fans in the stands, I felt these people paid to see me do my best against the Giants.

"It was a tough game against Al Worthington of the Giants, but we scored three runs in the seventh and we had the lead. I was mixing up my pitches, a fastball here and there, a lot of change-ups and curves, and I had a no-hitter through seven. By the eighth, the crowd was screaming, 'Oiskin-oiskin, we're wit yuz . . . ya got a no-hitter.' At times it was all I could hear, the din was so deafening.

"Al Dark hit a two-hopper back to me for the final out and it was the most gratifying win and no-hitter of my career. But that's not what makes it so memorable.

"During the game, Jackie made a fantastic stop at third on a smash by Willie Mays to preserve the no-hitter, and I learned later that Jackie had that damning article in his hip pocket. He had torn it out of the paper, and as soon as the game was over and I had my no-hitter, he walked over by the Giant dugout, found Tom Sheehan, and handed him the article and said, 'How do you like that garbage?'

"Jackie read all the New York papers. All of them. He never missed a thing. And contrary to popular belief, he was not adversarial. He was high-spirited, fiery, strongly competitive, never satisfied, never happy, but he just demonstrated what more needed to be done, both on the field and in life for equal rights and equal treatment. He was sensitive and intelligent, and he knew he had to exert self-control as part of Branch Rickey's experiment. It took, not *a* Jackie Robinson, but *the* Jackie Robinson to make that experiment work."

Sal Maglie
Brooklyn Dodgers, pitcher
1945 1950-1958

Sal "The Barber" Maglie was a feared, 6'2", 190-pound pitcher for the Giants and Dodgers. He owned the inside of the plate; his penchant for shaving the batters with inside brushback pitches earned him his "Barber" sobriquet. The Niagara Falls, New York, native was barred from Major League baseball by Commissioner "Happy" Chandler in 1946 after Maglie jumped to the Mexican League, but upon reinstatement, Maglie took his place as one of the most menacing pitchers National League hitters ever had to face. With his omnipresent "five o'clock shadow," his sneer and determination to own the plate (and three different types of curveballs to complement a good fastball), he made life miserable for hitters.

Maglie had his biggest seasons for the Giants—he went 18-4 in 1950 and 23-6 in 1951—and finished his career with a respectable 119-62 record for an exceptional winning percentage of .657, with twenty-five shutouts.

Maglie was "the other pitcher" the day Don Larsen made baseball history by throwing a perfect game in the 1956 World Series.

October 8, 1956

Maglie said, "I was thirty-nine and knew I didn't have too much life left in me. I had a bad back but I pitched well for the Dodgers (13-5) since they bought me from the Indians (May 15, 1956). On September 25, I threw a no-hitter against the Phillies at Ebbets Field to keep us a half-game behind Milwaukee.

"I knew I was throwing well, but I never dreamed I'd be in another no-hitter in two weeks.

"We got to the World Series against the Yankees and we had quite a rivalry—especially with me since I was with the Giants first—and in those days everybody hated the Yankees. I started the Series opener and they were real tough—Mickey Mantle and Billy Martin homered off me—but Jackie Robinson and Gil Hodges homered for us to win, 6-3. By the time it was my turn again, the Series was tied at two games apiece and we were playing in Yankee Stadium. We were facing big Don Larsen, a big thrower with a no-windup delivery. He was no problem for us in game two and we beat him, 13-2. I really figured that while the Yankees were tough hitters, I would probably win the game because we could score all day against Larsen.

"For the first three innings, there was nothing going on. We both had no-hitters but you don't think about it that early. In the fourth, I made a good pitch but Mickey Mantle just blasted it for a home run. By the seventh, I was still pitching a great game and we were down, 2-0, and it dawned on us that Larsen was pitching a smooth game and we didn't have a hit. Then we realized he hadn't given up a walk. It kind of snuck up on us.

"When I came out of the game for a pinch hitter in the ninth, I had given up only two runs and five hits, and still felt I could win it; when Dale Mitchell checked his swing for a called strike three to end the game and Yogi Berra jumped into Larsen's arms and the perfect game was history, we didn't have a sense of how important it was. It didn't seem like he threw a no-hitter or a perfect game and the fact that no one else has done it in nearly a hundred World Series makes me proud I was a part of it. I just wish I had thrown it and not Larsen."

Brooks Robinson
Baltimore Orioles, third base
1955-1977

Brooks Robinson, the human vacuum at the hot corner, was a 6'1", 180-pounder from Little Rock, Arkansas, who made fielding excellence a sure-fire trip to the Hall of Fame. He was such an acrobatic fielder that any time a youth in America made a great play, he was undoubtedly met with shouts of "Nice play, Brooks."

For twenty-three years he patrolled third base for the O's. While not known as a hitter, he did have his moments, and did manage 268 homers, hit better than .300 twice and drove in 1,357 runs. Still, his glove was his meal ticket, earning sixteen consecutive gold gloves and sixteen trips to the All-Star game. He was an MVP once and Series MVP once.

Robinson was a quiet team leader who was one of those rare gentlemen about whom none said a disparaging word.

Robinson had his number retired by the Orioles, and was elected to the Hall of Fame in 1983.

He certainly had twenty-three years of diving stops to recall, or his first World Series at-bat home run, October 5, 1966, but typically,

Robinson chose praise for someone else, in quick fashion and one quick stab and throw to get the out.

April, 1957

"Baseball to me is a passion to the point of obsession," Robinson said.

"And in twenty-three years of it, I've seen a lot of very nice things and outstanding things, but nothing is as important to me as my first full year.

"I was just out of Arkansas and shy and not confident enough to know if I'd make it. I didn't play ball in high school and was playing in a church league when I was signed.

"I get to Baltimore and one of the greats was already playing third base, George Kell, who hails from Arkansas like me and was a hero of mine.

"You hear of vets who give rookies a hard time, and treatment like that might have really hurt my career, but George Kell and his wife took me under their wing and allowed me to grow, both in the big city and in baseball. He worked with me as a player and as an individual and he allowed me to mature into both worlds. If not for him, I might still be the unfinished boy he first saw, and one without the savvy to play this game."

Joe Ginsberg
Baltimore Orioles, catcher
1948-1954 1956-1962

Myron Nathan "Joe" Ginsberg was a 5'11", 180-pound catcher from New York. He toiled for Detroit, Cleveland, Kansas City, Baltimore, Chicago and Boston, all in the American League, before coming home, just in time to land on the 1962 Mets as their opening day catcher.

Considered a funny man in the clubhouse, Ginsberg was all business on the field . . . and he had to be to try to handle Hoyt Wilhelm's flutterball. He was one of the first catchers to wear the big glove in an effort to corral Wilhelm's darting knuckler.

As a hitter, Ginsberg only connected for twenty homers in 695 games but one of them, on June 13, 1952, ended Yankee hurler Vic Raschi's no-hitter in the ninth. Ginsberg hit .290 dividing time between the Tigers and Indians in 1953. A contact hitter with a good eye for the strike zone, he struck out only 125 times in 1,716 at-bats over his career while walking 226 times and delivering 414 hits.

He recalls a manager's defensive strategy.

April, 1957

"We were in New York to play the Yankees and Paul Richards, one of the great baseball theorists and managers, was our skipper.

"Connie Johnson was on the hill and Mickey Mantle was on second base when Bill Skowron lashed a single to left center. Jim Busby fielded it and fired home. I was wearing a 'two-handed' glove, which was tough to field with and even tougher to tag with. Mantle slid in home, I tagged him but he almost kicked it out; it juggled but I held the ball in my glove and Mick was out.

"After the game, Paul said, 'You know, Joe, you almost lost that ball.' 'Yeah, Paul, but I was able to hold it,' I said.

"Paul said, 'But let's think. When a runner's at second base and a batter singles to center field, where does the pitcher go?' I answered, 'To back up home plate in case of an overthrow.'

"'Right,' Paul said. 'So what's to prevent the catcher from swapping gloves and using the pitcher's glove to make the play . . . thus using a better glove for tagging?'

"'Nothing.' I said.

"So we worked the play in practice and Gus Triandos and I played glove relay with the pitchers and waited for our chance.

"Well, one day in mid-season, we were in Chicago and Larry Doby was at second base for the Sox, Walt Dropo was at first, and Minnie Minoso was at the plate. Minoso lines a single to center field and as the pitcher ran to back me up, I yelled, 'Give me your glove.'

"The pitcher, Bill Wight, threw me his glove and I realized he was a lefty. So there I was, in front of thirty thousand people with a lefty glove on the wrong hand, to make a play on a speeding, sliding base runner. *Safe.*"

George Zuverink
Baltimore Orioles, pitcher
1951-1959

George Zuverink, alphabetically the last pitcher in baseball history, was a 6'4", 200-pound righty from Holland, Michigan. Zuverink had a good season as a starter in 1954 with Cincinnati and Detroit, going 9-13 in 209 innings, but was converted into a reliever by the Baltimore Orioles the next season.

His best season in relief was 1956, when he appeared in a league-leading sixty-two games and saved a loop high of sixteen.

He finished at 32-36 in 265 games with forty saves covering 642 innings.

Zuverink remembers a colorful character and a power hitter.

May, 1957

"We (the Orioles) had gotten Billy Loes from the Brooklyn Dodgers and he was always funny. He told his Dad he'd never work a day in his life, and he was proud to say he never did, especially on the ball field.

"This one game, Gus Triandos was catching and (home plate umpire) Jim Honochick kept calling pitches that looked like dead strikes, balls, and Billy was just fuming. After one more ball call, Billy started walking toward Honochick and Jim walks out to meet him halfway. Bill walks right by him and talks to Triandos instead. Honochick threw him out anyway and Billy was fined fifty dollars for not talking to the umpire."

Bob Turley
New York Yankees, pitcher
1951 1953-1963

"Bullet" Bob Turley was a 6'2", 215-pound no-windup fireballer from Troy, Illinois.

Turley was fast, but wild. He led the league in strikeouts in 1954 with Baltimore (185). He also led the loop in walks that year (181) and the next year (177) with New York, as well as in 1958 (128), the year he went 21-7 with a 2.97 ERA and six shutouts on his way to picking up the Cy Young award.

Turley finished his career with a 101-85 record, gave up only 1,366 hits in 1,712 innings and was 4-3 in five World Series.

He was one of the center points in one of the biggest trades (in sheer numbers) of all time, an eighteen-player swap between the Yankees and the Orioles on November 18, 1954. The trade (part one): The Yankees got Turley, Don Larsen and Billy Hunter and gave up Harry Byrd, Jim McDonald, Hal Smith, Gus Triandos, Gene Woodling and Willie Miranda; (part two): The Yankees got Dick Kryhoski, Mike Blyzka, Darrell Johnson and Jim Fridley, and Baltimore got Bill Miller, Kal Segrist, Don Leppert, Ted Del Guercio, and a player to be named later.

Turley, a sheriff in Florida, was a master at stealing other teams' signs and pitches. To tip off his teammates, he would whistle different frequencies, and Mickey Mantle and Bill Skowron feasted.

Turley began his career with the St. Louis Browns; when the club became the Baltimore Orioles, he won the first game back in Baltimore (April 15, 1954), a 3-1 win over the White Sox.

Turley offered a laugh at teammate Mickey Mantle's expense and another on a name mix-up.

August, 1957

Turley recalls, "Casey Stengel was the manager and we were playing in New York. Mickey Mantle was in a slump and struck out and angrily threw his bat. It slid down the dugout and narrowly missed Casey. Then Mickey threw his batting helmet and it bounced wildly. He kicked the water fountain and slammed down right near me on the bench.

"Casey walked over to him and said, 'If you quit losing your temper, you'll do better. Lay your bat down, it costs money. Put your helmet in the helmet case; treat it well. Think about why and how you struck out and how to do better next time. Be happy.'

"Mickey looked at him and we all looked on.

"Two innings later, Mickey struck out again. We all looked at Mickey, then Casey, then Mickey, then Casey.

"Mick took his bat and gently laid it down. He smoothly placed his helmet in the helmet case. He walked up face-to-face with Casey and said sweetly, 'Ha-ha, I struck out . . . mmmmm . . . ha-ha.' Casey fell on the floor laughing and the whole dugout cracked up.

"On the other hand, Bobby Richardson would never swear. He and Stengel got into an argument and when Casey used a four-letter word, Richardson said, 'Go wash your mouth out with soap.' I think that cracked us up even more."

July 1958

"We had just gotten Virgil Trucks from Kansas City, and we had Johnny Kucks on the pitching staff, too. We were playing Chicago and Casey called pitching coach Jim Turner and said, 'Get Kucks up.' Jim misunderstood and thought he said, 'Get Trucks up.' Virgil had just thrown batting practice and was dead, but he got up anyway.

"In the top of the ninth, we were up by a run. Casey went out to the mound and waved his hand toward the bullpen, meaning he wanted Kucks. Trucks jumped out of the pen and Casey has his hands over his head and sighs, 'It's the wrong guy.'

"As Casey's shaking his head in resignation, Trucks strikes out the first hitter, Sherm Lollar. Then he gets Billy Goodman to ground into a double play. Wrong guy, right move."

Yogi Berra
New York Yankees, catcher
1946-1965

Perhaps the most quoted and (misquoted player) in baseball history was St. Louis-born Lawrence Peter "Yogi" Berra. The 5'8", 185-pound catcher was Casey Stengel's "coach-on-the-field" for fourteen pennant-winning teams and was well-known for being one of the best pitch callers and handlers of pitchers during his era. Yogi set fielding records in his early years and was one of the top clutch hitters in the game. A contact hitter, he only struck out twelve times in 151 games in 1950, while slugging twenty-eight home runs in 597 at-bats. When he retired, he was the top home-run-hitting catcher (since surpassed by Johnny Bench and Carlton Fisk). Berra still remains first in World Series games played, hits and doubles. He won three MVP awards. Berra's versatility is often overlooked; he came to the Yankee organization as an outfielder and was converted to catcher to fill a need, but still played the outfield 260 times in his career, including eighty-seven times in 1961. One of the most popular, endearing and enduring baseball figures around, Berra also had a successful managerial career following his playing days. He had his number (an honor shared with Bill Dickey, who wore the number before Berra) retired and a plaque dedicated in his honor by the Yankees. He was elected to the Hall of Fame in 1972.

Berra certainly had his choice of stories. He played with some wild and hard-playing teammates, such as Mickey Mantle, Moose Skowron, Hank Bauer and Whitey Ford. He crouched behind the plate and jabbered with such opponents as Ted Williams, Al Kaline, Duke Snider and Willie Mays. He hit the first pinch-hit homer in World Series history against Brooklyn on October 2, 1947, and, of course, he caught the World Series perfect game of Don Larsen, October 8, 1956. But Yogi chose a quick anecdote about a rival he seldom saw, but one destined for immortality.

October 5, 1957

In the third game of the World Series between the Yankees and the Milwaukee Braves, the Yanks were in the midst of clobbering the Braves thanks to a pair of homers by Tony Kubek and one by Mickey

Yogi Berra, catcher, 1950s
Courtesy: New York Yankees
Photo by: Merion Bluegrass Assoc.

Mantle, when a slumping Milwaukee power hitter came up in the fifth with New York ahead, 5-1. Yogi takes it: "Hank Aaron came up to the plate and I noticed the label on his bat pointing to the ground. We were always taught that the label should be up so you could see it, and that would give you a sweet spot to hit on and keep the bat from breaking. Don Larsen was working him away and I kept trying to get Aaron's attention, but he didn't hear me and kept saying, 'What?' The count worked to 3-1 and finally I said, 'Hey, Aaron.' He turned around and said, 'What do you want?' I said, 'Your label is down, you've gotta be able to read your label.' He turned away and looked at Larsen and said, 'I'm here to hit, not read.' Well, he hits the next pitch for a two-run homer and hit two more homers in the Series and they beat us. I think I woke him up and he beat us."

Stan Musial
St. Louis Cardinals, outfield
1941-1963

Stan "The Man" Musial was a talented, Hall-of-Fame-destined Everyman from the steel-mill town of Donora, Pennsylvania (see 1940s chapter). He left many marks on the game and one mark has remained in his mind as a memorable moment he chose to share here.

May 13, 1958

"My three-thousandth hit was a memorable occurrence because, at the time, not too many players had reached that figure (Musial was the eighth). We were in Chicago at Wrigley Field and our manager, Fred Hutchinson, wanted to rest me that day to save me and the record for the St. Louis fans—we were going home to St. Louis the next day. It was late in the game and we needed a rally so I was sent up to pinch hit against Moe Drabowsky; I got a double off him and scored to key the rally that won the game, 5-3. We left Chicago by train and when we pulled in to the St. Louis train station it was just loaded with people who were there to congratulate me. There were hundreds of kids there who had taken the day off of school to come down and see me. It was so nice, such a warm tribute. I could really feel that St. Louis loved and respected me and I was so proud that I could accomplish this for them."

Pedro Ramos
Washington Senators, pitcher
1955-1970

Pedro Ramos, the six-foot, 175-pound pitcher from Pinar del Rio, Cuba, was a very good pitcher with some very poor Washington

Senator teams in the late 1950s, and that alone may have kept "Pete" from being considered one of the greats of his era. He led the AL in losses four straight years (eighteen in 1958; nineteen in 1959; eighteen in 1960 and twenty in 1961). Following a trade to the Yankees in 1964, he became one of the best relievers in the game and in 1964, he struck out 119 and walked only twenty-six in 154 innings.

He was a good hitter (fifteen career homers) and a quick runner — he repeatedly tried to get Mickey Mantle to race him for paychecks, but Mick declined because he was making five times what Pete was.

Ramos, famous for his sense of humor, offered a few humorous tidbits from his files.

May, 1958

"I had just eaten a big meal before this game against Cleveland. Eating was important, especially since I didn't speak English when I first came up, so I always pointed to pork chops in restaurants and that's all I ate for three months in 1955.

"So I was belching on the mound and it sounded like music, and Jimmy Piersall comes up and starts singing, 'I've got the whole world, in my hands.' I whiffed him, and Clint Courtney (the Washington catcher) sings to Piersall, 'I've got the whole world, in my glove.'

"By 1958, the funniest thing was playing for Washington; it was a joke playing for them, they were so bad every year. And the team looked like the Cuban National team; we had (at one time or another) me, Camilo Pascual, Julio Becquer, Jose Valdivielso, Zoilo Versalles, Juan Delis, Ossie Alvarez and Carlos Paula. It didn't help. We didn't want Castro over here — we were glad to get away from him — but the Senators could have used Fidel's curveball. It couldn't have hurt."

Vic Power
Cleveland Indians, first base
1954-1965

Victor Pellot y Power, the six-foot, 190-pound first baseman from Arecibo, Puerto Rico, had style. He was one of the first first basemen to make all of his catches one-handed, and as he often led the league in fielding, it made old-timers shudder. His pendulum swing before each bat — he was right-handed and before each pitch he would swing the bat outward with his left hand and touch his right hand with it as that hand swung out to meet it and then continue the process out-and-in-and-out-and in, touching the free hand five or six times before gripping the bat just prior to release of the pitch — also made batting instructors wince, but Power came through often with his hits. Of that pendulum warm-up, Powers recalls, "The worst ball for a hitter to hit is a low ball, so I used the pendulum and crouched low to psych the pitchers into thinking I wanted it low. They threw me high and probably added twenty points to my batting average."

Power's hitting ability made him revered in baseball circles, and many players — Jose Oquendo, Ruben Sierra and Ivan Calderon among them — travel to Power's hitting clinic in Puerto Rico to receive instruction.

Power's sweet swing enabled him to hit better than .300 three times and reach double figures in homers ten times, and limited his strikeouts to only 247 times in 1,627 games covering 6,036 at-bats. He was a four-time all-star and a seven-time gold glove.

Power's style, and also his unabashed love for his fellow man and belief in equality, kept him from being the first black member of the New York Yankees. Power and Elston Howard became Yankee property in 1953 and it was generally assumed that Power would be brought in to play first base in pinstripes. Power, however, had some run-ins with the white establishment: He attempted to eat in an all-white restaurant in the South and ordered rice and beans. When they told him they didn't serve negroes, Power said, "I don't eat negroes, I want rice and beans." And when Power asked out an attractive waitress who happened to be white, the Yankees decided to trade him to Kansas City and wait for a more "proper" black man to assume the role in New York. As Power says, "In Puerto Rico, we are all Puerto Ricans. There is no black or white, we're all Puerto Ricans. I thought it would be the same in America, but I was wrong." Power got the last laugh, however, "When President Kennedy's civil rights law passed, I went back to several of the restaurants that wouldn't serve me before, and ate there."

Power did, indeed, return to those restaurants and he recalls several incidents from his career — including the restaurant situation — in which his Puerto Rican accent got him into trouble.

"America wasn't used to hearing that accent and my mispronunciation caused trouble. One of those restaurants that wouldn't serve me was in West Palm Beach, Florida, and when I went back I ordered a steak. They gave me my steak but no eating utensils, so I said to the waitress, 'I wanna fork,' and I guess the word 'fork' sounded like a dirty word for sex. She asked me what I said, and I repeated in my accent, 'I wanna fork,' again sounding like I was asking for sex. Two big guys threw me out of the restaurant and I almost got thrown in jail. I'm glad I learned how to speak the language better, but not until after I made some enemies on the Cleveland staff when I was still with Kansas City.

"I was asked about facing Bob Lemon, Bob Feller, Early Wynn and Mike Garcia, the Cleveland aces, and I said, 'Those aces' (which sounded like I said, 'Those asses') were really something. I then said, 'Some of their pitchers are really tough,' and that sounded like 'Son of bitches were really tough.' I didn't know why all those guys kept trying to hit me with their fastball until I joined them later on and they told me. Man, I was glad I lost my accent."

Power tells of a great game in which he did the unexpected . . . twice.

August 14, 1958

"I was with the Indians and we were playing Detroit against Frank Lary. In the eighth inning, we were down by a run and I was at third base; suddenly I broke for home and stole home to tie the game. Then in the tenth inning, I was at third again, with Rocky Colavito at the plate, and suddenly I broke for home and stole home again and we won the game, 10-9.

"After the game, a Detroit sportswriter came up and asked me how I could try to steal home with Rocky Colavito on deck — Rocky was on his way to forty-two homers that year. I told him, 'Rocky will hit forty homers this year in six hundred at-bats. That means fourteen times out of fifteen he isn't going to hit one. The odds were better with me and the law of averages told me he wouldn't hit one this time.' He wasn't amused and said I was too fat and too big and not recognized for being fast. I told him, 'I'm black and it's a night game; no one saw me.' "

(**Author's Note:** Power was the first AL player since 1927 to steal home twice in the same game . . . and he stole only three bases all season long.)

Roy Campanella
Booklyn Dodgers, catcher
1948-1957

As mentioned in the 1940s chapter, the Hall of Fame catcher from Philadelphia was the Brooklyn Dodger team leader for twelve years and was one of the most popular players in the game during the 1950s. His career was cut short by an unfortunate accident, but that

Roy Campanella, catcher, 1950s
Courtesy: Los Angeles Dodgers

never cut short his positive attitude, his kindness, his sense of humor, or his love for the game.

Campanella recalled "his night" as his most memorable moment.

May 7, 1959

Before a record crowd of 93,103 on "Roy Campanella Night" at the Los Angeles Coliseum, the Yankees beat the Dodgers in an exhibition game, 6-2. The game meant very little by comparison as the occasion was called to pay tribute and raise money for one of its own,

171

Roy Campanella, who was permanently disabled in an automobile accident in January 1958.

Campanella says, "I was so honored by just the thought of the Dodgers having this night for me, and that our arch rivals the Yankees would come all the way across the country to be here for me was such a tribute, that would have been enough to make me cry. But when I saw the seats just packed with more than ninety-three thousand people and the thunderous ovation they gave me, there has never ever been anything like it my life to compare with it.

"First I saw all of my old teammates from Brooklyn (now Los Angeles), and it was just like old times. At times I really forgot that I was in a wheelchair. Pee Wee Reese rushed me to the mound—I think he was afraid he'd tip the wheelchair over—and Vin Scully announced that there would be a candlelight tribute, and everyone lit candles and matches and cigarette lighters, and the whole place went dark except for the flickering lights in my honor; it was the warmest feeling a human being could ever get. I felt as if all the love in the world was right there inside the Coliseum and was being directed at me. I was so thankful for my life at that moment that anything I'd ever have to endure after that was already paid for with that moment. I felt, like Lou Gehrig said, that I was the luckiest man on the face of the earth."

Harmon Killebrew
Washington Senators, third base
1954-1975

Harmon Clayton Killebrew, the six-foot, 210-pound gentle giant from Payette, Idaho, struck fear into the hearts of opposing pitchers for three decades and was the linchpin of Minnesota's three pennant-winning teams (1965, 1969 and 1970). Though usually remembered as a first baseman (he played 969 games there), he was versatile and played 792 games at third, 470 games in the outfield, and eleven games at second during his career of 2,435 games in twenty-two years.

The "Killer" lived up to his name by bombing 573 homers, driving in 1,584 runs and, with his big swing, struck out 1,699 times.

The eleven-time all-star was an MVP in 1969 and won six home run titles and three RBI crowns. His power was legendary; on June 3, 1967, he hit a 530-foot shot against the Angels in Minnesota that shattered two seats—the seats were painted orange and have never been sold since.

Considered one of baseball's nice guys, Killebrew didn't drink, didn't argue with umpires, and was a gentle man who befriended young players who came into the league. Graig Nettles said of Kille-brew, "Harmon and his wife took care of me and took me in — they let me stay at their house and fed me and counseled me — when I broke in in 1968. If not for them, I may never have made it in this league." Killebrew just says, "As a seventeen-year-old kid when I came up, a lot of the older guys helped me out. My first day at the park (1954) they threw me equipment I could use since I didn't have any, and Johnny Pesky, my first roommate, was so kind and helpful. He was a good guy who found me a place to stay and (taught me) how to act. It's only right that I pass that on to the next generation of ballplayer and hope they pass it on and so on."

Killebrew was enshrined in the Hall of Fame in 1984 and had his number retired by the Minnesota Twins (the relocated Washington Senators).

He likes to talk about his relationship with the President of the United States.

May 29, 1959

"As a young kid playing in Washington, DC, I was starstruck. Some amazing things happen in the nation's capital that you can see no-where else. On any given day, you could see the president, the vice president, senators, congressmen, cabinet members, celebrities or foreign ministers, diplomats or heads of countries sitting right up there next to the dugout. You got a real sense of excitement and history.

"On this day, President Eisenhower was at the park with his entire staff. He called me over to his box seat and said, 'Please give me an autographed ball for my grandson David.' I said I would if he would give me an autographed ball in return. I still have that ball, and after meeting David Eisenhower a few years ago, we talked and he still has the ball I gave him.

"And I hit a home run that day to beat the Red Sox, 7-6. Having him there really keyed us up and I think many of us played well when he was there. I must have hit twenty homers when he was there and Jim Lemon hit three off Whitey Ford when Ike was there. Of course, I think Mickey Mantle also hit ten homers against us when Ike watched, but I loved playing in front of the president."

Bobby Richardson
New York Yankees, second base
1955-1966

Bobby Richardson was the 5'9", 170-pound fielding whiz (973 double plays in his ten years as a starter) from Sumter, South Carolina, who was the clean-cut antithesis to the hard-partying Yankees of Hank Bauer, Mickey Mantle, Moose Skowron, Whitey Ford and Billy Martin of the fifties. In 1960 when the Yanks had the pennant clinched, private detectives were hired to follow the high-living Bombers in tow. Says Richardson, "They were like real-life 'Keystone Cops.' They followed Tony Kubek and me and all we did was go to the YMCA and play Ping-Pong, followed by some popcorn and a movie. They followed the wrong guys; Tony and I became known as 'the milk shake twins,' though I don't think either one of us drank a milk shake all season."

"I wasn't so clean-cut," Richardson adds. "I didn't drink or smoke, but once when I was 0-for-27, I tried chewing tobacco . . . it didn't help."

Richardson was a deft fielder and a good contact hitter who struck out only 243 times in 1,412 games covering 5,386 at-bats. He twice hit .300 and once led the league in hits (209 in 1961).

Richardson broke in as a shortstop, but Casey Stengel told him, "We have Phil (Rizzuto) and Mac (Gil McDougald), so you'd better find yourself another position." Richardson says, "I love shortstop, but I found peace at second. Mac hated third but Casey stuck him there except for one game when Mac just said to Casey 'I can't go there today, put Bobby there.' So on October 5, 1958, in the fourth game of the World Series (against Milwaukee), I played third and we lost to Warren Spahn, 3-0. I played third base and it was the only game my father ever saw me play. Like Mac, I hated third." (**Author's Note:** The author was in attendance that day at Yankee Stadium and was surpised to see Richardson at the hot corner in place of Andy Carey.)

Recognized by many as the premier second baseman in the league from the mid-fifties to mid-sixties (Nellie Fox of Chicago has his backing too), Richardson won five gold gloves, was a seven-time all-star and led the Yanks into seven World Series — he was World Series MVP in 1960 when he set a Fall Classic record by driving in twelve RBIs, hitting .367, and belting a grand slam. In the 1962 Series, his great reaction grab of Willie McCovey's screeching liner ended the Series. Richardson was stellar in the Series, hitting .305 in thirty-six games.

Richardson tells of an act of kindness and baseball camaraderie, tempered by competitiveness.

September 27, 1959

"For the first time in many years," begins Richardson, "the Yankees had a terrible year. We were in third place with few highlights and going into the last game of the season, I was leading the team in hitting at .299.

"Casey (Stengel) came up to me and said, 'Bobby, we'd all very much like to have a .300 hitter. So get a hit and I'll sit you down.'

"We were playing Baltimore and Billy O'Dell, one of my best friends, must have heard about the .300 situation so he comes up to me before the game and says, 'I'm starting today. I'll lay one in to you and you can give it all you got to get that hit.'

"Brooks Robinson, the Orioles' third baseman says, 'Lay down a bunt. I'll play deep and you'll beat it out.'

"Joe Ginsberg, the Orioles catcher says, 'I'll let you know what's coming.'

"Umpire Ed Hurley was umping first base and he says, 'You make it close and I'll give it to you.'

"With the entire ballpark pulling for me and playing for me, I hit a hard, sinking liner into the gap in right-center and Albie Pearson, the center fielder for the Orioles (and my best friend in the world), makes a full-out diving catch to rob me of a hit.

"I then got two legitimate hits to bring my average to .301 and Casey pulled me. That last day was tougher with help than the entire season was on my own."

1960s

May 27, 1960 to September 18, 1969

The date, May 27, 1960, opens the first oral history tale and does not refer to the news briefs that follow. That 1960s story is about the "Elephant Glove," designed by Baltimore Orioles manager Paul Richards in an attempt to block Hoyt Wilhelm's dancing butterfly. The final date of September 18, 1969, gives us a nugget about Fenway Park fans and a less-than-deserved standing ovation.

The 1960s began a loss of innocence in this nation and in baseball. Flower children were not allowed in the grand old game; even Dock Ellis's hair curlers were a decade away, and Joe Pepitone's hair dryers nearly brought on heart attacks in the old guard.

Mickey came and went, Willie kept on charging, the 1961 Yankees gave way to the 1969 Yankees, and expansion had its upside (the 1962 Angels) and its downside (the 1962 Mets).

Selected decade highlights
(in addition to those told in this chapter)

January 21, 1960 - Stan Musial, unhappy with his own play over the past two years, demands that the Cardinals cut his pay the maximum allowable, 20 percent. The Cards accede to his wishes and slice his wages from $100,000 to $80,000.

April 17, 1960 - On Easter Sunday, one of baseball's biggest deals is completed, sending home run champion Rocky Colavito from Cleveland to Detroit for batting champion Harvey Kuenn.

April 19, 1960 - Minnie Minoso hits a grand slam for the ChiSox against Kansas City in the fourth, singles in a run in the sixth, and wins the game with a leadoff homer in the ninth to win the game, 10-9.

April 24, 1960 - In a Yankee Stadium game witnessed by the author (who was ten at the time), the Yankees score eight runs before the first out is made in the first inning against Baltimore. The Yanks hold on to win, 15-9, despite Oriole grand slams by Albie Pearson and Billy Klaus.

May 10, 1960 - In Rip Repulski's first AL at-bat, he slugs a grand slam to give Boston a 9-7 victory over Chicago at Fenway Park. Teammate Vic Wertz also hits a slam.

May 27, 1960 - The big mitt. As there is no rule governing the size of a catcher's mitt, and since Oriole catchers Clint Courtney, Joe Ginsberg and Gus Triandos have botched eleven of Hoyt Wilhelm's fluttering knucklers for passed balls this year (thirty-eight a year ago), Baltimore manager Paul Richards designs a mitt that is fifty percent larger than normal equipment. Courtney is the guinea pig and is perfect as Wilhelm leads the Birds past the Yankees, 3-2.

June 24, 1960 - The quintessential Willie Mays. The Giant center fielder hits two homers, singles, steals home, and runs down ten drives to the outfield for ten putouts, scores three and drives in three to lead San Francisco to a 5-3 victory over the Reds.

June 30, 1960 - Dick Stuart bombs the Giants by knocking three homers and driving in seven runs for the Pirates in an 11-6 win at Forbes Field.

July 4, 1960 - As Hawaii's fiftieth star is officially added to the American flag, Mickey Mantle connects for his three hundredth career homer, this one off Washington's Hal Woodeshick, but the Senators prevail, 9-8.

July 19, 1960 - High-kicking Giant right-hander Juan Marichal makes his debut and throws no-hit ball until two are out in the seventh and Clay Dalrymple singles for the Phillies. Marichal whiffs twelve and fashions a 2-0 one-hitter.

August 3, 1960 - The manager trade. Tiger manager Jimmy Dykes (44-52) is dealt to Cleveland for Tribe skipper Joe Gordon (49-46). Dykes goes 26-32 with Cleveland and Gordon is 26-31 for Detroit.

August 30, 1960 - Boston keystone-sacker Pete Runnels goes 6-for-7 in a fifteen-inning win over the Tigers, and his double in the final frame drives in Frank Malzone to win the game. In the second game of this twin bill, Runnels knocks out three more hits for nine on the day.

September 15, 1960 - Willie Mays's day at the office consists of five hits, of which three are triples, one a double and one a single. His eleventh-inning triple wins the game for San Francisco over the Phils, 8-6.

September 20, 1960 - After fouling a ball off his ankle, Ted Williams is forced to leave the game, and for the only time in his career, surrenders to a pinch hitter, Carroll Hardy.

September 26, 1960 - Teddy Ballgame goes out in style. In his final at-bat, Ted Williams jumps on a Jack Fisher offering and blasts it 450 feet into the seats for his 521st career homer to give the BoSox a 5-4 win over Baltimore.

October 14, 1960 - Though the Yankees demolish the Pirates by scores of 16-3, 10-0 and 12-0, and use spectacular performances by Whitey Ford (two shutout wins), Bobby Richardson (.367, eleven hits, one homer, twelve RBIs), Mickey Mantle (.400, three homers, eleven RBIs), Bill Skowron (.375, twelve hits, two homers), Hector Lopez (.429) and John Blanchard (.455), while outscoring the Bucs 55-27, out-homering them 10-4, and out-hitting them .338-.256, the Pirates take the World Series in seven games on a ninth-inning home run by Bill Mazeroski off Ralph Terry for a 10-9 Pittsburgh victory.

April 11, 1961 - The Los Angeles Angels win their first game as Eli Grba bests Baltimore, 7-2, behind two homers by Angel slugger Ted Kluszewski.

April 17, 1961 - The Cuban "Bay of Pigs" invasion is defeated and Dodger hero Duke Snider has some good news and bad news. The good news: he hits his 370th home run, moving him ahead of Ralph Kiner into seventh place on the all-time list. The bad news: St. Louis beats the Dodgers, 7-5, behind the pitching of Bob Gibson, who breaks Snider's elbow with an errant fastball.

April 26, 1961 - Roger Maris hits his first homer of the year and Mickey Mantle bombs switch-hit homers for the eighth time in his career as the Bronx Bombers humble Paul Foytack and the Tigers, 13-10.

April 28, 1961 - Forty-year-old Warren Spahn throws a no-hitter versus the San Francisco Giants at Milwaukee.

April 30, 1961 - After breaking his favorite bat, Willie Mays borrows teammate Joey Amalfitano's lumber and blasts four homers and drives in eight "ribbies" to lead Giants to a 14-4 drubbing of Milwaukee.

May 9, 1961 - Jim Gentile bombs grand slam homers in consecutive innings to join Tony Lazzeri (1936), Jim Tabor (1939) and Rudy York (1946). He gets Pedro Ramos in the first and Paul Giel in the second. Gentile finishes with nine RBIs as the O's club the Twins, 13-5.

May 30, 1961 - In the year of the homer, the Yankees get two homers apiece from Roger Maris, Mickey Mantle and Bill "Moose" Skowron, as well as one from Yogi Berra at Fenway Park in a 12-3 rout of the Red Sox.

June 29, 1961 - Willie Mays puts on another show with three homers at Philadelphia. His third four-bagger wins it in the tenth inning, 8-7.

July 11, 1961 - All-Star defense hardly reigns supreme at windy Candlestick Park in the first of two Mid-season Classics played this year. The whirling gusts blow NL pitcher Stu Miller off the mound and All-Star gloves are nicked for seven errors as the Nationals beat the American League, 5-4.

July 17-18, 1961 - St. Louis Cardinal first baseman Bill White goes 8-for-10 in a doubleheader sweep of the Cubs on the 17th and follows it up with a 6-for-8 in another doubleheader sweep of the Cubs the next day. White's fourteen hits in two days ties a mark set by Ty Cobb in 1912.

July 25, 1961 - Yankee right fielder Roger Maris clubs four homers in a doubleheader sweep of the White Sox at Yankee Stadium. Mickey Mantle hits one and trails Maris, 40-38, in the home run race.

July 26, 1961 - Yankee pinch hitter and backup catcher John Blanchard hits his fourth consecutive homer over three games and drives in four runs in a 5-2 decision over the White Sox.

August 6, 1961 - Hey, he's no Maris or Mantle, but . . . It took Maury Wills 1,167 at-bats, but he finally hits his first home run in an 11-4 Dodger win over the Cubs.

September 5, 1961 - Los Angeles Angel outfielder Lee Thomas cranks out nine hits in a doubleheader, five in the first and four in the second, including three homers, but the Halos lose both games to Kansas City, 7-3 and 13-12.

October 1, 1961 - Roger's moment. Roger Maris belts historic home run number sixty-one off Boston's Tracy Stallard in the final game of the season at Yankee Stadium to break Babe Ruth's hallowed single-season home run mark set in 1927. The Yankees win, 1-0.

October 8, 1961 - It's a bad month for the Babe. Yankee ace lefty Whitey Ford follows up a World Series opening game shutout over Cincinnati with five more scoreless frames to erase Babe Ruth's Fall Classic record of twenty-nine and two-thirds shutout innings. Ford stretches his skein to thirty-two innings as the Yanks take Cincy,

6-0. They go on to win the Series in five games.

April 10, 1962 - The Houston Colt .45s begin play at Colt Stadium. Bobby Shantz pitches Houston to an 11-2 win over the Cubs as Roman Mejias hits two three-run homers.

April 24, 1962 - Sandy Koufax ties his own record by whiffing eighteen Cubs in a 10-2 Dodger win.

May 5, 1962 - Los Angeles Angels rookie sensation Bo Belinsky fires a no-hitter to beat Steve Barber and the Orioles, 2-0.

May 22, 1962 - With Mickey Mantle out of the lineup due to injury, Roger Maris (who hit ahead of the Mick in the lineup and didn't receive a single intentional walk during all of 1961 and all of this season until Mantle's injury), is intentionally passed four times and receives a fifth walk as well, but the Yankees outlast the Angels, 2-1, in twelve innings. Four Pinstripe pitchers (Whitey Ford, Jim Coates, Bud Daley and Bob Turley) limit the Halos to a single hit, by Bob "Buck" Rodgers with one out in the ninth. Ford leaves with back spasms after seven no-hit innings.

May 23, 1962 - Yankee rookie Joe Pepitone hits two homers in a nine-run New York eighth inning to defeat Kansas City, 13-7.

June 17, 1962 - Marvelous Marv. As the Cubs sweep a doubleheader at the Polo Grounds from the Mets, and Lou Brock smashes a 460-foot homer into the center field bleachers, Mets first baseman Marv Throneberry hits an apparent triple that would have put the tying run at third in the opener. Throneberry is called out on appeal, however, for failing to touch second. When Mets manager Casey Stengel comes out to argue, he is told by umpires that Throneberry had also failed to touch first.

June 24, 1962 - In a twenty-two-inning marathon, Jack Reed, often called "Mickey Mantle's Legs" for his late-inning substitutions for the Mick in center field and on the bases, hits the only homer of his career to give the Yanks a 9-7 win over the Tigers in an MLB record seven hours. Rocky Colavito bangs out seven hits for Detroit.

July 7-8, 1962 - Forty-one year-old Stan Musial becomes the oldest player to hit three homers in a game, and four in a row. On the 7th, Musial's homer beats the Mets, 3-2, and he follows it up by crashing out three in his first three at-bats on the 8th in a 15-1 win.

August 7, 1962 - Tony Kubek has just returned from a stint in the military and the Yankee shortstop homers in his first at-bat to spark the Yankees to a 14-1 rout of the Twins.

August 19, 1962 - Mickey Mantle belts a grand slam home run, steals two bases and gets seven RBIs but takes a back seat to teammate Elston Howard, who hits two homers and eight RBIs. The Yankees bomb Kansas City, by a 21-7 score.

October 16, 1962 - On the day the Cuban missile crisis begins as President Kennedy is informed that reconnaissance photos reveal the presence of Soviet missile bases on Cuba, the Yankees pull off the play that breaks San Francisco's heart. In the seventh game of the World Series, with the Yankees up, 1-0, in the bottom of the ninth, the home team Giants have the tying and winning runs in scoring position with two outs when Willie McCovey hits a lightning line drive that second baseman Bobby Richardson snares for the final out.

April 12, 1963 - Pete Rose connects for his first Major League hit, a triple off Pittsburgh's Bob Friend.

May 4, 1963 - The senior circuit's umpires are calling the balk rule closely this season and Braves hurler Bob Shaw gets nailed five times in a 7-5 loss to the Cubbies. Shaw is called for a record three balks in the third inning.

June 6, 1963 - A game for Lindy McDaniel to remember and one for Willie Mays to forget. In a battle for first place between the Cubs and Giants, the score is tied at 2-2 in the twelfth when reliever McDaniel comes in with the bases loaded with Giants and one out. McDaniel picks Mays off second base and strikes out Ed Bailey, then wins the game by belting a homer in the bottom of the inning for a 3-2 win. It would take the Oklahoma righty nine years to hit another four-bagger.

June 19, 1963 - Tiger pinch hitter Gates Brown homers in his first Major League at-bat, but the Bengals lose at Fenway to the BoSox, 9-2.

June 23, 1963 - After making a bet with teammate Duke Snider, Jimmy Piersall runs the bases backward after hitting his one hundredth career homer. Snider had hit his four hundredth career blast nine days earlier (June 14) and only received a few paragraphs of coverage from the local press. Piersall boasted he'd get more "ink" for his one hundredth . . . and he did, getting several pages worth of articles. Dallas Green, Phillies pitcher off of whom Piersall hit the shot, fumed on the mound and swore he'd get Jimmy for showing him up.

September 6, 1963 - Major League baseball's 100,000th game is played and in it, the Washington Senators beat the Cleveland Indians, 7-2.

September 17, 1963 - Capping a 25-5 Cy Young award season in which he fashioned a 1.88 ERA, Dodger lefty Sandy Koufax fires his eleventh shutout and Los Angeles beats St. Louis, 4-0.

September 29, 1963 - Stan "The Man" Musial calls it a career by going 2-for-3 at Busch Stadium as the Cards defeat the Reds, 3-2.

April 17, 1964 - The New York Mets christen Shea Stadium with a 4-3 loss to Pittsburgh. Willie Stargell hits Shea's first homer.

May 31, 1964 - In a long day at the ballpark, the New York Mets and San Francisco Giants play a doubleheader that takes nine hours, fifty-two minutes to complete. The nightcap is a twenty-three-inning affair that lasts seven hours, twenty-three minutes. Juan Marichal wins the opener, 5-3, and Del Crandall's single makes a loser of Galen Cisco in the finale, 8-6.

June 21, 1964 - On Father's Day, Philadelphia's Jim Bunning pitches a perfect game, 6-0, against the Mets. His catcher, Gus Triandos, becomes the first receiver to call no-hitters in each league.

July 10, 1964 - Jesus Alou of the Giants clubs out six hits against six different pitchers to help San Francisco beat Chicago, 10-3.

August 12, 1964 - Mickey Mantle hits switch-hit homers in the same game for a record tenth time (later tied by Eddie Murray), as the Yankees beat the White Sox at Yankee Stadium, 7-3.

August 20, 1964 - The harmonica incident. Following a 5-0 loss to the White Sox, the bus taking the Yankees to the airport found manager Yogi Berra in a foul mood and he demanded silence. Egged on by teammate Mickey Mantle, Yank utility infielder Phil Linz raises his harmonica to his lips and toots out "Mary Had A Little Lamb." Berra slaps the mouth organ out of Linz's hands and fines him two hundred dollars.

September 1, 1964 - San Francisco relief pitcher Masanori Murakami becomes the first Big Leaguer to make the jump from the Japan League. He shuts out the Mets in his first inning, but the Giants lose, 4-1.

April 9, 1965 - Harris County Domed Stadium (aka the Astrodome) opens as President Lyndon B. Johnson throws out the first ball. Mickey Mantle christens the ballpark by belting out the first indoor homer, but the Astros beat the Yanks, 2-1, in this twelve-inning exhibition.

June 14, 1965 - It doesn't show up as a no-hitter, but Jim Maloney pitches a whale of a game. He fans eighteen Mets and pitches ten innings of no-hit ball, only to have Johnny Lewis hit an eleventh-inning homer to give New York a 1-0 win over Maloney's Reds.

July 20, 1965 - Yankee ace Mel Stottlemyre becomes the first pitcher in fifty-five years to hit an inside-the-park grand slam as he beats the Red Sox, 6-3.

August 19, 1965 - This one counts. Jim Maloney pitches another ten-inning no-hitter, but this one ends with a 1-0 decision in favor of the Reds over the Cubs at Wrigley on a round-tripper by shortstop Leo Cardenas. Maloney walks ten and Ks twelve in the days before pitch counts.

September 9, 1965 - Sandy is perfect. Sandy Koufax tosses his fourth no-hitter, a perfect game, and he needed it to win. His Dodgers beat the Cubs, 1-0, and manage only one hit off losing pitcher Bob Hendley, who gives up an unearned run in defeat.

September 25, 1965 - Satchel Paige makes a publicity-stunt appearance. The fifty-nine-year-old hurler starts for Kansas City and pitches three shutout innings against Boston, yielding only a single to Carl Yastrzemski. Reliever Don Mossi gets the loss, 5-2, as Boston rallies after Paige's departure.

April 11, 1966 - In baseball's opener in Washington, Emmet Ashford becomes Major League baseball's first black umpire. Cleveland wins the game, 5-2, over the Senators.

April 19, 1966 - Anaheim Stadium opens the regular season for the California Angels who lose to Chicago, 3-1, despite a home run christening by bonus baby Rick Reichardt.

May 28-29, 1966 - Ron Santo wins back-to-back games with extra-inning homers. On the 28th, his three-run blast in the twelfth propels the Cubs to an 8-5 decision over the Braves. On the 29th, his tenth-inning shot beats Atlanta, 3-2.

September 22, 1966 - Truth in journalism. A record-low crowd of 413 fans at Yankee Stadium watch the Yanks play out the season in a 4-1 loss to the White Sox. Yankee broadcaster Red Barber supervises a camera shot that shows 66,587 empty seats. Barber loses his job for the act.

April 14, 1967 - Red Sox rookie pitcher Bill Rohr makes his debut at Yankee Stadium and takes a no-hitter into the ninth inning. Leading off the inning, Tom Tresh blasts an apparent extra-base hit but is robbed on a circus catch by left fielder Carl Yastrzemski. With two out, Elston Howard ruins the no-no with a single to center. The Red Sox win, 3-0, and after one more start, Rohr is dropped to the minors.

May 14, 1967 - He promised his wife. On Mother's Day, after promising his wife he would hit one, Mickey Mantle bombs his five hundredth career homer, this one off Baltimore's Stu Miller to give New York a 6-5 win.

August 6, 1967 - Orioles third baseman Brooks Robinson hits into a triple play for the fourth time in his career—a Major League record.

August 29, 1967 - While a record number of Americans are glued to their TV sets to watch the final episode of "The Fugitive," the Red Sox and Yankees play twenty-nine innings in a doubleheader.

Boston wins the opener, 2-1, and the Yankees take the twenty-inning second game, 4-3.

October 5, 1967 - Boston Red Sox hurler Jim Lonborg tosses a one-hitter to beat the Cardinals, 5-0, in the World Series. Julian Javier's two-out eighth-inning double is the only safety off Lonborg.

May 9, 1968 - Jim "Catfish" Hunter does it all. He throws the first AL perfect game in forty-six years to defeat the Twins, 3-0, and drives in all the runs himself.

May 11-18, 1968 - Big Frank Howard homers in his sixth consecutive game — a record ten homers in that span — and sets the mark for most four-baggers in a week (Sunday through Saturday) with ten.

June 8, 1968 - All things must come to an end, and Don Drysdale's fifty-eight and two-thirds-inning shutout streak falls to Howie Bedell's sacrifice fly in the fifth. LA beats Philadelphia, 5-3. It is the only run Bedell would drive in this year.

June 25, 1968 - Giants rookie Bobby Bonds debuts and hits a grand slam, the first player since 1898 to break in with a slam.

June 29, 1968 - Detroit's Jim Northrup belts his third grand slam in a week in a 5-2 win over the ChiSox.

July 3, 1968 - Luis Tiant, pitching for Cleveland, fans nineteen Twins, scatters six hits, and doesn't walk a batter in a ten-inning 1-0 victory.

September 10, 1968 - Cubs outfielder Billy Williams hits three homers to single-handedly beat the Mets, 3-1.

September 19, 1968 - Detroit's Denny McLain wins his thirty-first game of the year in a win over the Yankees, and he gives up a tainted home run to Mickey Mantle; McLain purposely grooved a pitch (and catcher Bill Freehan told Mantle what was coming) that the Mick hit out because McLain wanted to give Mantle a shot at passing Jimmie Foxx. The two had been tied at 534 homers. Mantle hit one more homer off Earl Wilson to finish his career with 536.

April 14, 1969 - Montreal's Jarry Park is the scene of the first Major League baseball game ever played outside the United States. The Expos beat the Cardinals, 8-7.

April 17, 1969 - It takes the Montreal Expos only ten days in baseball to have one of their pitchers fashion a no-hitter as Bill Stoneman completes the gem in a 7-0 win over Philadelphia.

May 13, 1969 - Mr. Cub, Ernie Banks, drives in seven runs in leading Chicago to a 19-0 drubbing of San Diego.

June 14, 1969 - As the A's demolish the Red Sox, 21-7, at Fenway, Reggie Jackson hits two homers and drives in ten "ribbies."

June 28, 1969 - Don Drysdale was sharp, but he didn't have to be.

He shut out San Diego, and his Dodger teammates backed him with ten runs in the first to cruise to a 19-0 shellacking of the Padres. This is the second time San Diego has been bombed 19-0 in six weeks.

July 20, 1969 - The day Neil Armstrong and Edwin "Buzz" Aldrin became the first men to walk on the moon, Gaylord Perry hits his first Major League homer. In 1962, when Perry came up with the Giants, his manager, Alvin Dark, looked at Perry's anemic swing and remarked, "We'll put a man on the moon before Perry will ever hit a homer." Moments after the first lunar walk, Perry connects. Perry finished his career with six homers . . . the same number of America's manned lunar landings.

August 5, 1969 - In a game at Dodger Stadium between the Dodgers and the Pittsburgh Pirates, Willie Stargell, Buc first baseman, becomes the only player ever to hit a homer completely out of that ballpark. His blast off Alan Foster to right field goes 506-and-a-half feet as the Pirates best the Dodgers, 11-3. Stargell performed the feat again, when his shot to right field cleared the stadium off Andy Messersmith with a 470-footer, May 8, 1973.

August 16, 1968 - While hundreds of thousands of young Americans congregate in upstate New York for three days of music and history at Woodstock, Boog Powell thunders across Seattle's Sick's Stadium for an inside-the-park homer in Baltimore's 15-3 pounding of the Pilots. And in Atlanta, St. Louis Cardinals ace right-hander Bob Gibson reaches the two hundred-strikeout level for an NL-record seventh time, as the Cards whip the Braves, 8-1.

August 19, 1969 - Who needs a strikeout pitch? Ken Holtzman doesn't, as he no-hits Atlanta, 3-0, for the Cubs on a three-run homer by Ron Santo.

August 28, 1969 - Tiger slugger Jim Northrup goes 6-for-6 as Detroit beats Oakland, 5-3.

September 15, 1969 - What good is a strikeout pitch? Cardinal ace lefty Steve Carlton whiffs nineteen Mets, but loses, 4-3, when Ron Swoboda connects for two two-run homers.

September 22, 1969 - Willie Mays becomes the second player to reach six hundred homers as he belts one off San Diego's Mike Corkins. Mays pinch hit for rookie George Foster to face Corkins.

October 16, 1969 - The Miracle Mets win their fourth straight game from the Baltimore Orioles, this one, 5-3, to take the Series in five games.

The Chronicles

Bill Rigney
New York Giants, second base
1946-1953

Bill Rigney, the rail-thin 6'1", 175-pound infielder for the New York Giants is perhaps better known for his eighteen years as a manager for the Giants (both in New York and San Francisco), for the Angels (both in Los Angeles and Anaheim), and the Twins.

A generally light-hitting, fair-fielding player, Rig hit seventeen homers in 1947, following a stance change designed to take the inside pitches the opposite way. He played in 654 games and managed 2,561 games.

The Alameda, California, native was especially happy to move with the New York team to the Bay area, near his home, but his unceremonious dumping in 1960 can only be attributed to high expectations.

Rigney recalls the canning.

June 18, 1960

Rig says, "I took over from Leo Durocher in 1956, and I learned a lot about the game and life from Leo. He taught me about the hit-and-run, pitching changes, playing it like poker with bluffs and strength and going against percentages sometimes. You can't play it the same all the time.

"In 1960, we had a good ball club. Not great, but good. The only problem was, the press had reported all spring that it was a great ball club and should win the league by twenty games.

"Remember, we had finished third last year (1959) and were essentially the same ball club. My lineup card was filled with the names: (Willie) Mays, (Willie) McCovey, (Orlando) Cepeda, (Willie) Kirkland; and we had a pitching staff of (Mike) McCormick, (Johnny) Antonelli, (Sad Sam) Jones and (Jack) Sanford. A very good club, but we were in a tough league and nothing was for certain when the Pirates had Roberto Clemente, Dick Groat, Bill Mazeroski, Dick Stuart, Bob Skinner, Bob Friend and Vern Law. The Braves had Hank Aaron, Eddie Mathews, Joe Adcock, Del Crandall, Warren Spahn, Lew Burdette and Bob Buhl. The Cardinals had Stan Musial, Bill White, Ken Boyer, Ernie Broglio and Larry Jackson, and the Dodgers had Duke Snider, Gil Hodges, Wally Moon, Frank Howard,

Maury Wills, Sandy Koufax, Don Drysdale and Johnny Podres. Any team could win it; Pittsburgh did.

"Well, Horace Stoneham, the owner, believed what he read, that we were the greatest thing since sliced bread. So we started off 33-25, a good start, a .569 percentage — that figures out to eighty-eight or ninety wins (projected over a full season) — and we were in second place, only two games out of first . . . and I got fired.

"Fired, while eight games over .500. I don't know of any other manager besides Billy Martin to get a hook like that. (**Author's Note:** Billy Martin was ten games over .500 with a 52-42 mark in 1978 when he was in fourth place, fourteen games behind Boston when he was replaced by Bob Lemon, who rallied the Yanks to a pennant.)

"So my replacement, Tom Sheehan, who was sixty-six years old at the time, took over and the team didn't play .500 ball the rest of the way (46-50) to finish in fifth place, sixteen games out.

"Even the next year, when the team added Juan Marichal, Matty Alou and Harvey Kuenn, the team still finished in third with only eighty-five wins (under Al Dark).

"That was one time the owner should have been fired, not the manager."

April, 1961

As skipper of the newly franchised Los Angeles Angels the following year, Rig recalls an early season game against the feared 1961 New York Yankees.

"We were playing the Yankees and were going over the Yankee lineup in a pitcher's meeting before the game. Eli Grba had played with the Yanks the year before, so we were letting him give us the 'book' on how to pitch to the hitters.

"We come to Mickey Mantle and Grba says, 'When he hits left-handed pitch him high, and when he hits right-handed pitch him low.'

"So our pitchers do that and he hits a homer lefty on a high pitch and hits one righty on a low pitch and I'm seething and look over at Grba, who says, 'Or is it the other way around?' "

Tony Kubek
New York Yankees, shortstop
1957-1965

Tony Kubek, the American League Rookie of the Year in 1957, was a 6'3", 190-pound shortstop from Milwaukee, Wisconsin, who

Tony Kubek, shortstop, 1960s
Courtesy: New York Yankees

stepped into the shortstop role for the dynasty Yankees after Phil Rizzuto departed (filled briefly by Billy Hunter and Gil McDougald in the interim). Kubek played 882 games as the Yankee shortstop and also filled in in various roles when the Pinstripers needed him to: fourteen games in the outfield; fifty-five at third base; forty-five as a pinch hitter, and a few each at first and second. Kubek was a steady hitter, a steadier fielder, and a three-time all-star.

Kubek, along with second baseman Bobby Richardson, formed what may have been baseball's best keystone combo for an eight-year span from the late-fifties to the mid-sixties—Kubek turned 583 double plays. Kubek and Richardson were the clean-living antithesis to the hard-partying, drinking, brawling Yankees of that era who included Mickey Mantle, Billy Martin, Hank Bauer and Bill Skowron. The fact that Kubek and Richardson were called "the milk shake twins" irks Kubek, who says, "I never drank a milk shake in all the days I played in New York."

He was the victim of one of baseball's most notorious bad hops—in the 1960 World Series—that ultimately became pivotal in the scenario that saw Bill Mazeroski beat the Yanks with a ninth-inning, game-seven homer.

Kubek's uniform number was retired by the Yankees, but as Kubek readily volunteers, "The number was Phil's (Rizzuto); I only borrowed it until they could retire it."

The enormously popular, yet outspoken, Kubek went on to a successful broadcasting career following his days on the diamond. He also waged a two-decade campaign to get the "asterisk" removed from Roger Maris's home run record. On Maris, Kubek says, "Hitting sixty-one home runs was the best thing ever to happen to Roger Maris's career . . . and the worst, because people then thought all he could do was hit home runs when, in fact, he could throw, field, run aggressively and smartly, hit in the clutch . . . and he knew more about the game than anyone in the game. When he was traded to the Cards (in 1967), St. Louis stars Bill White, Dick Groat and Mike Shannon—who was a good right fielder and had to move to third when Roger was acquired—were biased against him when he got there, but they soon learned to love Roger as a great all-around player."

It is not surprising that Kubek chose to offer a Maris tale for this book.

May, 1961

Kubek recalls, "Roger came to New York in 1960 and he always hit third, behind me. Ralph Houk, who took over in 1961 after Casey (Stengel) left, always went with a set lineup: (Bobby) Richardson, Kubek, (Roger) Maris, (Mickey) Mantle, Ellie (Elston Howard), Yogi (Berra), Moose (Bill Skowron), Clete (Boyer) and the pitcher. And Roger, who had hit thirty-nine homers and was the MVP in 1960, always stood in my holes. I'd get to the plate, dig in and make holes for my front foot and back foot. Roger would hit next and put his feet in my "dig-in holes." My stance was his stance and I wasn't about to change it if Roger didn't want me to. I mean, in 1960-61, he hit (cumulatively) .275 with 100 homers and 254 RBIs and I hit (cumulatively) .275 with 22 homers and 108 RBIs, so whatever he wanted was OK with me.

"Roger began 1961 in a slump (he didn't hit his first homer until April 26) and Mick was red hot. The Yankees made Roger get his eyes checked to see if he needed glasses and that really hurt him — he hated that and the doctor's exam.

"Well, in those days, we took trains quite often and it was a great chance to talk baseball — today's players really don't know what they're missing. It was a thirty-six-hour train trip from New York to Kansas City, for example. Well, on this trip, we were headed for Washington and Roger had just spent an hour of the ride talking with batting instructor Wally Moses, who tried to build Roger's confidence. Then Roger spoke with Mickey for a long while, and Mickey — who was great friends with Roger, not like what you may have read in the papers — tried to build Roger's confidence.

"Then Roger sat down and saw me. 'Tony?' he asked, staring at me and picturing how I looked at the plate. 'Are you still standing in the same place? I'm not comfortable at the plate.'

"When we got to Washington, I re-measured my stance and I really couldn't tell any difference at all. I adjusted it slightly and said to Roger, 'Yeah, you're right. I was four to five inches off. What an eye. I'll go back to the old spot.'

"The rest is baseball history. He got red hot and hit sixty-one homers. It's ironic that he used me as a gauge; he hit more homers in 1961 than I hit in my entire career (fifty-seven). And I certainly wouldn't imply that I had anything to do with his breaking Babe Ruth's record. Maybe it was a combination of Mick and Moses and me, and above all, Roger's sweet swing, but I'll always believe those train rides helped us all. We'd talk baseball . . . we were family and we'd improve and study and learn. You can't do that on airplanes, and players and the game have lost something we had."

Mickey Mantle
New York Yankees, outfield
1951-1968

Mickey Mantle, the fleet, powerful, six-foot, 200-pound blond bomber switch-hitter for the Yankee dynasty, was arguably the greatest switch-hitter the game has ever seen. He was undoubtedly the most popular player of his era, depicted in Horatio Algeresque terms as the country boy from the zinc-mining town of Commerce, Okla-

Mickey Mantle, outfield, 1960s
Courtesy: New York Yankees

homa, who found success and the bright lights of Broadway (or at least the scoreboard lights in the Bronx). Injury-plagued and debilitated by osteomilitis, Mantle brought playing with pain to a new art form and was appreciated by teammates and foes alike for his courage.

Cheered in every ballpark in which he played during his later years, "The Mick" placed high on the all-time baseball lists with 536 homers and 1,509 RBIs. The perennial all-star (sixteen all-star selections) won a Triple Crown in 1956, four home run crowns,

191

three MVP's and belted eighteen World Series homers, a Major League record. He is also the World Series career leader in runs scored, RBIs, walks and strikeouts by a hitter. And his hitting of switch-hit homers in ten different games is an all-time mark (since tied by Eddie Murray). Mantle made a run, with teammate and friend Roger Maris, at Babe Ruth's single-season home run record of sixty, only to fall to injury—and to Maris's sixty-one—in 1961. For Mantle, a Hall of Famer who accomplished so much, it was also a case of "what if," as he played in pain for eighteen seasons, missing more than four hundred games due to injury during his career. He had his number retired and a plaque dedicated in his honor by the Yankees. He was elected to the Hall of Fame in 1974, along with his buddy, Whitey Ford.

Mantle's favorite story? Where would a legend begin? He certainly could've reminisced about his debut, April 18, 1951; his record 565-foot blast off Washington's Chuck Stobbs on April 17, 1953, or any one of his treasure trove of exploits. But Mantle was, and still is, a shy man, and his self-deprecating story typifies the man, if not his career.

June, 1961

During the storied 1961 season, Mickey Mantle was tearing the cover off the ball as he was headed toward fifty-four home runs, an assault on Babe Ruth's "unbeatable" record of sixty homers, and was assuming the role of team leader of what is often regarded as one of the two or three greatest teams in baseball history, the 1961 Yankees.

Mantle remembers: "I was hitting everything pretty well but went through a couple of games in which I was trying too hard for homers, was getting fooled on pitches and was struggling. During one game I struck out three times, went hitless, and we lost a close game I could have helped us win if I had come through in front of the hometown fans I felt I had let down.

"I was drained, and I sat in front of my locker at Yankee Stadium with my face buried in my hands. Yogi Berra had brought his kids to the game and his little son Timmy came over and tapped me on the shoulder. I looked up and smiled at the kid, figuring he was gonna tell me, 'Hey Mick, that's OK, hang in there.' "

"I looked up to hear his words of encouragement and Timmy said, 'Hey Mantle, you stink.'

"It snapped me out of my depression and I think I laughed for a solid hour."

Joey Schaffernoth, pitcher, 1960s
Courtesy: National Baseball Library Hall of Fame, Cooperstown, New York

Joey Schaffernoth
Cleveland Indians, pitcher
1959-1961

As an example that typifies what it meant to be a baseball hero from a small town, consider Joey Schaffernoth, a 6'4", 195-pound right-hander from Springfield, New Jersey. Springfield Township is a warm, cozy, friendly farm town with a colonial history — George Washington fought for independence there — and a championship golf course — Baltusrol, site of several U.S. Opens. During the 1950s, every young boy in town (the author included), seemed to have three sports heroes: One was a switch-hitting outfielder named Mickey Mantle (every kid in town was a switch-hitter as homage to the Mick); one was a fleet, switch-hitting teenage outfielder for Johnathon Dayton Regional High School named Larry "Butch" Bellon (who did have several pro tryouts); and the third was a pitcher for the Cubs and Indians named Joey Schaffernoth, who lived on a farm that abutted Route 22 and dead-ended on postage-stamp-sized Becker Road. To all those in this close-knit community of the late fifties and early sixties, Joey was a favorite son. Schaffernoth's career was full of promise, and a blistering fastball, until an arm injury and a misunderstanding cut his playing days short.

It didn't matter that Joey only lasted three years and went 3-8 over his career. To the boys of Springfield, Joey was a bona fide hero, and it was much the same with other young athletes and their followers in countless other American hamlets.

Schaffernoth remembered his first win against Philadelphia in 1959, his first base hit (off Gene Conley) in 1960, and his striking out pinch hitter Stan Musial on three pitches in the eleventh inning at 12:55 A.M. one night in 1961. But the story he chose to share of the pre-Curt Flood, pre-free agency, reserve-clause-slave-contract days of baseball shows how far the game has come regarding players' rights, and makes Schaffernoth an integral part of baseball's intricate history.

July 7, 1961

This story begins on July 7, but it took eight years to end. Schaffernoth tells the story: "I was sold from the Chicago Cubs to the Cleveland Indians in July and was just learning how to improve my mediocre curve, which didn't complement my good fastball. I didn't hit it off with Gabe Paul, the Indians GM, and he was down on me from the All-Star break on, and saw to it that manager Jimmy Dykes only used me in mop-up situations. And, to be honest, I didn't deserve much better, as I was not throwing well.

"With ten days left in the minor league season, Paul called me into his office and told me I was being shipped to Salt Lake City, the Triple-A farm club. According to contractual rules, I had three days to report to Salt Lake City, but Paul insisted that I fly out immediately and pitch that night, as they wanted to make me a starter. I mentioned to him that I had my wife and child with me in Cleveland and that I couldn't just leave them there, so I'll drive to

New Jersey and catch the first plane out, and still arrive within the three days I was allowed. He got angry and yelled at me, and soon I was gone.

"Paul sold me and fellow hurler Dave Tyriver, conditionally, to Washington on October 14, and though I never got back to the Majors, I wasn't through just yet, nor was Gabe Paul through with me.

"I had a great 1962 in the minors. I won eighteen games for Jacksonville and was the International League MVP. At twenty-five, I thought I could make it back. I was wrong.

"In 1963, my rights reverted back to Gabe Paul and the Indians and I went to Paul to negotiate my contract. They wanted to cut my salary from thirteen thousand dollars to ten thousand dollars and here I was, the International League MVP. I asked if I could have an increase back to thirteen thousand dollars if I made the majors and he said 'No.' I went into his room in Puerto Rico where I was playing Winter League and tried to negotiate a slight increase and Paul said, 'Sign or don't play.' I signed. Unfortunately, I hurt my arm and since the team was out of options, they cut me. I had a shot to play on the West Coast but decided, at age twenty-six, that it was time for me to go on to real life and leave baseball.

"The kicker to this story is that the team, the Indians, still held my rights for six years, even though I hadn't thrown a pitch during all that time. In mid-season 1969, eight years after my final Major League pitch, I got a letter from the Cleveland Indians, informing me that I had been given my release. Man, in those days, they owned you — forever — but I was glad I had the opportunity to play."

Whitey Ford
New York Yankees, pitcher
1950-1967

A class act on the mound, Whitey Ford (see 1950s chapter) certainly had more than enough of his own exploits and his own skill to talk about, but he chose to talk about spitballs. Now, it was widely rumored that Whitey was a doctor . . . a ball doctor. And Whitey readily admits that later in his career, he threw spitters, mudballs, greaseballs, cutballs, sliced-cover balls and sweatballs. His first such event involved Willie Mays.

July 11, 1961

"I always respected Willie Mays, probably because he hit me like he owned me. I think he was 9-for-18 against me. Well, I was tabbed

195

to start the All-Star game in San Francisco against Warren Spahn, and the day before the game, Mickey Mantle and I went to a party with Toots Shore and San Francisco Giants owner Horace Stoneham. Now, Mickey and I owed Stoneham four hundred dollars, and when I went to pay him, he challenged me. He bet me the $400, double-or-nothing, that Willie Mays would get a hit off me in the All-Star game. I took the bet. Mickey knew how well Willie hit me and wanted no part of it, saying, 'Absolutely not; Willie hits you like he owns you.' But I pleaded my case confidently and talked him into going fifty-fifty with me.

"During the game, I got the first two National League stars out and then Roberto Clemente doubled off me and I was face-to-face with Willie. I gave Willie my best curve and he crushed it five hundred feet, foul, down the left field line. I threw a slow, sharp breaking curve and he hit this one even farther, but foul. I turned around and looked at Mickey in the outfield, and he just shook his head and scowled, as if to say, 'There goes eight hundred dollars.' I had Willie 0-2 but wasn't confident, so I tried a spitball. To this point in my career, I had never used one in a game, because during practice, I could never control it, and I never had the guts to use it with a game on the line, but since Willie was killing everything I threw anyway, I figured, 'what the hell?'

"I loaded this one up with saliva from my mouth to my fingers to the ball. I fired. The ball sailed wildly at Willie's shoulder. He jumped back to avoid being hit and the ball dropped, veered at a 45-degree angle to the plate and crossed it. Strike three. Mays is out, the inning is over, the crowd, a pro-Willie Mays crowd, is silent, and Mantle is clapping in center because he knows we won the bet. Willie looks at me kind of annoyed and asks why Mick's clapping. When I told him the story later Willie just laughed and laughed and winked at Mick. And because of that success, I found the confidence to throw it in regular games. That pitch probably prolonged my career for four years."

Marv Throneberry
New York Mets, first base
1955-1963

"Marvelous Marv" Throneberry was a 6'1", 200-pound first baseman from Collierville, Tennessee, who began his career touted as a power hitter with a lefty swing tailored to hit home runs at Yankee Stadium, and he ended his career across town with the New York Mets.

Marv Throneberry, first base, 1960s
Courtesy: New York Yankees

Throneberry played 125 of his 480 games in 1962 with the Mets and Orioles, and hit a career-high sixteen homers; he twice hit eleven dingers.

But with the initials M.E.T. (Marvin Eugene Throneberry), he was the butt of many jokes and grew to epitomize the 1962 Mets.

On June 17, in a game against the Cubs, Throneberry tripled but was called out for failing to touch first base. When Met skipper Casey Stengel came out to argue, he was notified by the umpires that Throneberry had also failed to touch second.

Throneberry wants to set the record straight on a few counts.

May, 9, 1962

Throneberry begins, "I was not an original Met; I was traded from Baltimore for Hobie Landrith on May 9. And though we lost 120 games, we were not a bad team. We had good players, but we had poor pitching and relief help and lost thirty-five one-run games. When I was with the Yankees in 1958 and we came back from a 3-1 deficit to beat Milwaukee in the World Series, it was a big team effort . . . the Yankee way. On the Mets, we had Frank Thomas, Charlie Neal, Jim Hickman and Richie Ashburn—good ballplayers. But they were taught the Dodger way, the Yankee way, the Kansas City way, the Phillies way; they were twenty-five players all taught different ways to play. They didn't mesh and made mistakes.

"But I always looked at it this way: There were eight teams in each league and only four hundred players in the Majors out of millions of athletes in the country who wanted to be. We were all pretty damn good players, among the top four hundred out of millions, but the press talked us down so much, they talked us into losing.

"Now, as to the name 'Marvelous Marv.' Every sportswriter in New York took credit for that, but they didn't do it; Mets owner Joan Payson invented it. I hit a home run to win a game and she said, 'Oh, wasn't that marvelous,' and I was called Marvelous Marv from that point on because of her, not some writer.

"And Casey got credit for a line I made up. It was Casey's birthday, July 30, and we got him a cake and I said to him, 'They were gonna get me a cake too, but they were afraid I'd drop it.' It was reported that Casey said it to me, but the writers got that one wrong, too.

"And one final dig at the writers and official scorers. I wasn't a great fielder, of course, but I wasn't as bad as the writers made out. I got errors in the Polo Grounds in the cab on the way to the ballpark. I got errors on throws by infielders that went over my head and into the stands. True. I got errors as part of my reputation, but I still wouldn't trade one moment of my career for anything else in the world. Like I said, I got to do what only four hundred other guys did each year, and I did it for seven years, playing at the same time as my brother (Faye Throneberry), so both of us, from one family, were luckier than millions of families out there who could only dream. We lived the dream."

Joe Pignatano
New York Mets, catcher
1957-1962

Though he spent most of his career with the Dodgers (one year in Brooklyn and three in Los Angeles), the 5'10", 180-pound backstop from Brooklyn may be best remembered as a member of the 1962 Mets. Obtained in mid-season, 1962, he played twenty-seven games for the Mets and hit .232 for them.

Pignatano played 307 games and connected for sixteen homers. He appeared in the 1959 Series as a defensive replacement.

Pignatano's claim to fame may have been the tomato garden he grew in the Mets bullpen when he returned as a coach for his Dodger and Met teammate Gil Hodges, who had taken over the helm for the Mets, but he thinks he is more famous for hitting two homers in the same at-bat. "In the minors for Shreveport in 1955, I got up, batted out of turn, homered, and Maury Wills was called out for not batting. Then I got up again and homered again."

He gives us couple of Casey Stengel stories from his half-season with the 1962 Mets.

July 13, 1962

"I was traded from the San Francisco Giants to the Mets and drove in from Philly (where the Giants were playing) to the Polo Grounds, got a uniform, and sat on the bench. Casey sat down beside me and chatted with me for an hour. A New York reporter, Jack Lang, asked Casey, 'Who's gonna catch today?' Casey grumbled, 'Pignatano, if he ever gets here.' "

August, 1962

"A month later, pitching coach Red Ruffing had to leave the team on personal business and Casey named me pitching coach for a day. His only instructions were, 'If the phone rings, pick it up . . . it's me.'

"Sure enough, in the fifth inning, the phone rings and Casey says,

'Get up Nelson.' Now I'd only been there for a month but I knew we had no 'Nelson.' So I took a ball and placed it on the practice pitching rubber and said, 'Nelson, get up and throw.' Now we had two pitchers named Bob Miller — Robert Lane Miller, a 6'1", 180-pounder who was a twenty-three-year-old righty, and Robert Gerald Miller, a 6'1", 185-pound, twenty-seven-year-old lefty — and the righty Miller gets up. As he's warming up, I asked him why he was called 'Nelson.' He said, 'Casey got us mixed up, and since he saw Lindsey Nelson (Mets broadcaster) interview us both as the 'Two Millers,' he got us confused with Lindsey Nelson so he calls me Bob Nelson and calls the other Bob Miller, Bob Lindsey.'

"Well, in the eighth inning, things got worse and Casey calls and says, 'Get me Johnny Blanchard. I want him to pinch hit.' Now Johnny Blanchard was on the Yankees, not the Mets, so I said, 'You want me to walk across the river (to Yankee Stadium) or take a cab?' Casey barks, 'I'll make with the jokes.' And I was in Casey's shithouse for a month and never played once and I still have no idea who he wanted to have hit, because no one admitted to being Johnny Blanchard. But Casey didn't forgive me, didn't talk to me, and didn't use me."

(**Author's Note:** According to Johnny Blanchard, Jim Marshall was the man Casey thought was Blanchard. But Marshall only played seventeen games with the 1962 Mets until he was dealt to Pittsburgh on May 7, nine weeks before Casey called Pignatano for "Blanchard." So that means Casey was either calling for Blanchard, Marshall-Blanchard, or a third guy he thought was Marshall [who he thought was Blanchard].)

September 29, 1962

"Bob Miller — 'Nelson' — won only one game, that on the next-to-last day of the season. During the season, Case didn't want him to pitch so he used him as a pinch runner instead. Well, he started Bob — Nelson — and in the fifth inning Casey had used all his available pinch hitters so he goes to Miller and says, 'With all that pinch running you do, you'll be great on the bases and I have a feeling you'll get a hit. Sure enough, Bob singles to center field and when he gets to first, Casey takes him out for a pinch runner."

Pignatano tells the final 1962 Mets tale on himself.

September 30, 1962

"I had a lousy career, so it was fitting that I was on a lousy team to finish it up. It was a long, long two-and-a-half months with the Mets, but it was fun and so was my career, so it was fitting that I ended it in a losing game, our 120th loss of the year—worst in this century—and on the last at-bat of my career, I hit into a triple play. Perfect."

Ed Kranepool
New York Mets, first base
1962-1979

Ed Kranepool was a 6'3", 205-pound first baseman from the Bronx, New York, who got to play his entire career for the Mets. He was signed at seventeen and was up with the club for virtually the entire year (1962), yet he played in only three games. In a numerical oddity, the Mets number "7" played his entire career—eighteen years—in New York, as did the Yankees number "7," Mickey Mantle.

The Krane had some good years but never lived up to his expected stardom. He hit 118 career homers; his career high was sixteen in 1966, and he hit .300 twice (1974 - .300 and 1975 - .323). An excellent fielder, Kranepool finished with a career fielding percentage of .993.

The Krane fondly remembers his first Major League manager, Casey Stengel, who was seventy-two in the story below.

March, 1963

"Casey was a legend prior to taking over the Mets, so whatever he wanted was fine with me. I was a first baseman but the Mets already had Gil Hodges, Ed Bouchee and Marv Throneberry at first, so Casey wanted to turn me into an outfielder.

"We were at Miller Huggins Field in spring training in St. Petersburg and Casey, at seventy-two, would go position by position and work with the players. With me, he went to right field and first we'd talk about what the job was in each situation, then we'd take cutoffs, we took throws, and he'd have a coach hit fly balls. He caught one, reared back to hit the cutoff and threw it . . . right down on his foot. He growled at me, 'That's to teach you to keep the ball low.' He gave me the glove and he was gone, never to teach me outfield again. I loved the old man."

Edwin "Duke" Snider
Brooklyn Dodgers, outfield
1947-1964

Duke Snider, the adopted son of the Brooklyn faithful (see 1950s chapter), left the friendly confines of Ebbets Field for Los Angeles, his real hometown, in 1958, but he never left the Dodger Blue family behind him. Snider was a Dodger through and through, so it is with great remorse that he tells this story about his excommunication from his baseball family.

April 1, 1963

"The saddest day in my baseball life was the day I discovered baseball had lost its loyalty and the Dodgers sold me for cash to the Mets. There was no love, no respect, just money. I had given sixteen years to the organization and I was peddled for some magic beans just like an old cow. And in 1964 (April 14), when the Mets sold me to the Giants, it was just money again. And when I went to the Giants, it was the eeriest feeling I ever had in my life to see the word 'Giants' printed across my chest.

"But baseball has its loyalty, too . . . and kindness. Buzzie Bavasi (a long-time Dodger executive) became the GM in San Diego and he showed me loyalty. He told me if there was anything I wanted, he'd give it to me. I could have been his manager if I had asked, but I asked him if I could be his broadcaster. He didn't act surprised and without hesitation he said, 'You got it.' And he gave me a second career (broadcasting) that lasted longer than my first one. And he just did it to be nice, out of loyalty, and that's what baseball is all about."

Bobby Bragan
Brooklyn Dodgers, shortstop
1940-1944 1947-1948

Bobby Bragan, the 5'10", 175-pounder from Birmingham, Alabama, may be more well-known for his managerial career, or his pranks and umpire baiting in the minors. He has served the game in nearly every capacity — as a player, coach, manager, scout, executive, and president of the Texas League.

Bragan closed out his playing career as a catcher after breaking in as a shortstop. In 597 games, Bragan hit .240 but only struck out 117 times in 1,900 trips to the plate.

As a manager, he was always in the second division, but he usually got the best from his talent-poor ballclubs and always gave the press laughs with his fresh approach to the game.

His story is typical Bragan and tells about his days on the job with the Braves.

Bragan says, "I had taken over the Braves and had had a pretty good spring training. When I got to my office in Milwaukee, I was going through the drawers and came across two envelopes left in the manager's desk by my predecessor, Birdie Tebbets.

"The envelopes came with a warning: 'To be opened only in case of crisis,' and they were labeled 'number one' and 'number two.'

"We had a pretty good year in 1963 and went 84-78, so I didn't open the envelopes. But in 1964, we started off poorly, and all of a sudden, the fans, the media, the players and the front office started screaming for a change . . . of managers. I remembered the envelopes and opened the drawer and got out the envelope marked 'number one.' I opened it up, and it read, 'Blame it on me and the old guys.' It was signed by Birdie Tebbets.

"So I immediately went up to the front office and yelled, 'You've saddled me with an old (Warren) Spahn, (Lew) Burdette, (Frank) Bolling, (Roy) McMillan and (Eddie) Mathews. These guys are Birdie's guys; I can't win with these old guys. I need younger players, a team I can build myself so I can win for you.

"That got the owner off my back and the ream rebounded to go 88-74.

"Everything was OK until 1966 when we were seven games under .500 and fans were carrying signs to the ballpark that read: 'Bragan Must Go.' The media and the Braves brass started clamoring for my firing so I went back to my desk and opened that old second envelope marked 'number two.' In it was a note signed by Birdie Tebbets that read, 'Prepare two more envelopes.' "

Jerry Coleman
New York Yankees, second base
1949-1957

As mentioned in the 1940s chapter, Coleman, the high-flying Marine pilot, who lost several years to military service, was a solid infielder for the Yankees on six AL championship teams before he became better known as a baseball play-by-play man.

The King of the Malaprop as a broadcaster for the San Diego Padres, Coleman got his start in the booth with the New York Yankees. He tells a story about a booth blunder that he and booth-mate Phil Rizzuto made that he hopes Mel Allen (the third man in the booth) will never read. When apprised of this story, Rizzuto groaned, "Don't tell Mel."

May, 1963

"It was my first year as a broadcaster along with Mel Allen, Phil Rizzuto and Red Barber, three real pros, with Mel the consummate professional who couldn't tolerate any error in the booth. He wanted perfection and was always totally prepared. He's the best.

"The Yankees were playing a doubleheader against Cleveland and were scheduled to pitch Jack Kralic, whom they had just acquired in a trade with Minnesota, and Sam McDowell against us. They are both lefties and before the game, I walked up to Cleveland manager Birdie Tebbets and asked, 'Is it Kralic and McDowell or McDowell and Kralic? I thought McDowell was to start the opener. Is it Mc-Dowell and Kralic?' This means we think McDowell will start game one and Kralic will start game two. Tebbets says, 'Yeah, it's McDow-ell and Kralic.'

"So I tell this to Mel and Phil and we're just marveling at the control that this kid McDowell has. In the sixth inning, one of our engineers looks at the screen and says, 'Hey, I saw a game in Minne-sota and this guy is Kralic, not McDowell.' For six innings we've been telling everyone about McDowell, only we've got the wrong pitcher. Phil and I, being ex-ballplayers, cracked up. We couldn't stop laughing. Now someone's got to tell Mel (Allen). Phil won't do it and I certainly wasn't going to do it so we got our stat man, Bill Kane, to tell Mel. We watched as Mel got the news. He was so frustrated and so defeated that a mistake had gone on so long, that he just laid his head down on his desk and said nothing.

"But Mel made us pay for the mistake. He decreed that we had to tell the listeners of our mistake, so after telling the world, for six innings, what wonderful control this kid McDowell had, we had to tell them that Kralic was the control marvel we had seen and that McDowell would pitch—and wildly, it was—game two. Phil and I giggled about it for the rest of the broadcast and neither one of us ever forgot it. Just don't tell Mel about it; he still hates that story."

(**Author's Note:** McDowell was twenty-one, a 6'5", 190-pound flame-thrower who walked a lot of hitters and struck out even more; Kralick was twenty-eight and a 6'2", 180-pounder who threw off-speed stuff and painted the corners with excellent control.)

Jim Bouton
New York Yankees, pitcher
1962-1970 1978

Jim Bouton, the hard-throwing right-hander with the flying cap, was a six-foot, 170-pounder from Newark, New Jersey, who was called

"Bulldog" by his teammates. At least, that was until he wrote his ground-breaking book, *Ball Four*, a baseball tell-all tome. After the work was published in 1970, Bouton was called some things that are unprintable in any form.

As a pitcher, Bouton had some wonderful years: 21-7 in 1963 and 18-13 in 1964, pitching a total of 520 innings and fashioning ten shutouts. He threw his arm out the next year and was never the same. He became a knuckleball pitcher in 1968 but never saw much success. He tried a comeback in 1978 — Atlanta owner Ted Turner saw marquee value in Bouton — but that fizzled out as well.

Bouton is still around baseball . . . sort of. He runs a company that packs shredded bubble gum in pouches to look like chewing tobacco; he calls it "Big League Chew."

October 5, 1963

Bouton says, "Before the third game of the World Series in 1963, I was nervous. We had lost to the Dodgers twice at Yankee Stadium and we went to Los Angeles. Sandy Koufax beat us, 5-2, in the first game and Johnny Podres beat us, 4-1, in the second game, but as a team we were still confident that the bats of (Mickey) Mantle, (Roger) Maris, (Elston) Howard, (Tommy) Tresh, (Joe) Pepitone and (Clete) Boyer would get untracked and we'd still win this thing. In those days, being a Yankee brought immense pride and a feeling of overall success. But that didn't help me. I was scheduled for the third game against Don Drysdale, and I had to win to get us back on track.

"I started over-thinking . . . 'there are fifty thousand fans in the stands, millions of people watching on TV, hundreds of reporters swarming about, countless newspapers and magazines writing reports, and all of my teammates looking to me.' So I sat on the bench, all alone, fixating on the pressure.

"If Maury Wills gets on against me, I thought, he's the guy who broke Ty Cobb's stolen base record and he'll probably steal second, third and home on me and I'll be humiliated on national television before I get the first out or face the third batter.

"I couldn't breathe.

"Ralph Terry, a veteran pitcher, came over and sat down beside me. 'Are you nervous, kid?' he asked.

" 'I can hardly breathe, Ralph,' I said.

"He put his arm around my shoulder, looked me in the eye and said, 'Remember one thing out on the mound today. Whatever happens, there are five hundred million Chinese communists out there who don't give a shit.'

"I laughed so hard I almost choked on my gum and I was still laughing when the umpire said, 'Play ball.'

"I was laughing on the mound when I pitched to Maury Wills, and I got him out to start the game. And even though we lost, 1-0 (**Author's Note:** Bouton walked one, threw a wild pitch, and gave up a single in the first for the only run all day), I gave up four hits and Drysdale shut us out on three hits, and even though we were swept in four straight games, I thought about it after the game that doing as well as I did in defeat, I was lucky to be there, alive on a sunny day, laughing and having a good time. If you want it broken down . . . for me, that's what baseball is all about."

Ron Swoboda
New York Mets, outfield
1965-1973

Ron "Rocky" Swoboda was a 6'2", 200-pound outfielder from Baltimore who was one of the cogs of the 1969 "Miracle Mets."

He burst on to the scene in 1965 when, as a rookie, he blasted nineteen homers (which was to be his career high).

The always comical Swoboda had a good glove, and his diving catch in the 1969 Series against Brooks Robinson plays well on the World Series highlight reels.

Swoboda delights in talking about his first Major League manager, Casey Stengel.

April, 1965

"I loved my rookie season and I loved playing for Casey except that he never knew who I was. He called me 'Sa-do-ba,' which is OK, because he called Chris Cannizzaro 'Can-zin-eri.'

"Casey knew I needed to play, and he kept me in 'the Bigs,' and even though I was as green as you can get, he let me play.

"At the time, the Mets organization was hungry for anything to draw fans; we should have printed a disclaimer that any resemblance between this and Major League ball is purely coincidental. But we did have youth going for us. At one promotion, broadcaster Lindsey Nelson called the game from a gondola in the Astrodome, hanging two hundred feet (208 feet, actually) above second base (April 19, 1965).

"We were a legend in New York, a collection of has-beens and never-wases. But I'm playing right field in St. Louis at the old ball-park, and no one was confusing me with Stan Musial. Larry Bearnarth was pitching for us with the bases loaded and two outs. It's raining on and off. Dal Maxvill hits a dying quail to right field into the sun, which was sitting over third base. I put out my glove and caught it . . . except that the ball didn't go into my glove. It was a three-run error. That ruined the game we had been set to win. So I lead off the top of the tenth and pop out to right. Casey never said a word.

"We made three quick outs and hit the field and I left my bat on the dugout steps. It bridged the steps and when I went back out to the field, I leaped up and jumped on the bat and it snapped. Casey leaped in the air and landed on my foot.

"Casey, who was in his seventies, grabbed me by the shirt neck like I was a little kid half his size, and he growls, 'Goddamnit. When you dropped the fly, I didn't knock you. When you popped out, I didn't say anything, but now you've done it. Don't break the team's equipment.' He threw me out of the game . . . and finally got off my foot.

"It was in 1965 that Casey delivered my favorite Caseyism. We had Ed Kranepool, and Krane was in his third year; he was still only twenty and looked like he could beat the world. And we also had a rookie catcher named Greg Goossen. Goose was a rookie catcher who was also twenty, but who had a bent for martinis . . . lots of them. Casey was talking to the players and he says to Krane, 'You are a good prospect, son. Keep working and in ten years you have a chance to be a superstar.' Goose taps Casey on the shoulder and says, 'What about me?' And Casey sizes him up and says, 'Son, in ten years you got a chance to be thirty.' "

Nelson Briles
St. Louis Cardinals, pitcher
1965-1978

Nellie Briles was a 5'11", 195-pound righty from Dorris, California, who won 129 games and lost 112 in his fourteen-year career.

His best year was 1968, when he went 19-11 for the Cards with a 2.81 ERA.

Briles, who sang the national anthem before game four of the 1973 World Series, was on pennant-winning teams in St. Louis (1967 and 1968) and Pittsburgh (1972).

He recalls two "Welcome to the Big Leagues" stories from his rookie year and a tale about a star they had misjudged.

May, 1965

Briles remembers, "Now, in 1965 I was protected on the roster through the bonus rules of the day and rookies were seen but not heard. I finally got into my first game in May. We were in Chicago getting shellacked by the Cubs, 8-0, and I came in. My heart pounded, the adrenalin flowed and catcher Tim McCarver signaled for a fastball. I fired one at the hitter, Glenn Beckert, who took a wild swing and fell down.

"Now my adrenalin is flowing in rivers. I'm as pumped as I can be and as I catch McCarver's next sign, our first baseman, Bill White, calls time out. I ask him, 'What are you doing? I'm on a roll. Did you see what I made that hitter do?' White slowly says, 'Yeah, you made him look like a fool. We all saw it. What are you gonna do next?' I said, 'Locate him. Fastball down and away, then slider up and in.' White shook his head 'no' and said, 'Now if you don't establish your plate, they'll own you for the rest of your life. Knock him on his ass.' One pitch in 'the Bigs' and he wants me to knock down a vet. He wanted to find out about me, if I was willing to be tough and hard-nosed.

"I flipped a fastball under Beckert's chin and he dove away with his helmet flying. 'That's it, Kid,' White yelled. 'That's Big League baseball.' "

June, 1965

"I learned about pranks on rookies firsthand," says Briles. "I had been married in February, two weeks before spring training and I didn't see my wife again until June. On our first trip to the West Coast, I met her in San Francisco and we came back to St. Louis together on a four-engine prop—a seven-hour flight.

"Well, I'm sitting with her about an hour into the flight when Bob Gibson and Bill White came over. I said, 'Bob, Bill, this is my wife, Ginger.' They said in unison, 'Nellie, that's not the wife you introduced to us in Chicago.' Ginger fumed and would not look at me. I said, 'Guys, she doesn't understand. Tell her you're kidding.' They didn't. This seven-hour flight in silence was interminable. Moments before landing, they told her it was a joke to show a rookie the ropes. Ginger still didn't warm up to me for two weeks."

April, 1967

On December 8, 1966, the Cards traded Charley Smith to the Yankees for Roger Maris. Says Briles, "We all knew Roger had hit sixty-one home runs and we had heard that he didn't run out ground balls and was uncommunicative with the press. We did not fully appreciate his value as an all-around baseball player until we played with him.

"I was pitching in relief against the Pirates and before the game the pitchers and a few fielders, Roger included, went over the opposing hitters.

"In a tight game, 2-1, they had the tying run (Roberto Clemente) at second base and there was Willie Stargell, a lefty pull hitter with power, up. I was pitching in my second inning of relief and I checked the positions of the fielders. Roger was straightaway in right field. I whistled and motioned him to play to pull. He moved three steps. I took the stretch, checked the runner, and Roger had moved back. I backed off the mound and yelled, 'Play him to pull.' Roger moved back.

"I fired and Stargell blasted one to right center field. I started to run home to back up the plate and I heard the crowd roar. Roger made the catch. I was astonished. No way. He saved the game. In the dugout, he grabbed me. He said, 'C'mere. Go ahead and ask me.' I said, 'How the hell did you make that catch after I moved you?' Roger smiled and said, 'Kid, you never have to check 'RM.' As soon as you started your delivery I moved eight steps to right center field. You didn't know how good you were throwing. No one was going to get the bat head out on the ball. No way he was going to pull you. I gambled by analyzing you and the hitter.'

"We all soon learned the depth of his baseball knowledge. He was the consummate pro and teammate."

Don Drysdale
Los Angeles Dodgers, pitcher
1956-1969

Charging out of Van Nuys High School, an athlete's school where he fit in well as a second baseman/pitcher a few years after Bob Waterfield (NFL Hall of Fame), at the same time as Robert Redford (*The Natural*), and a few years before Gary Sanserino (Team USA - Pan American Games), Rob Scribner (L.A. Rams) and the author, the 6'6", 200-pound sidewinder called "Big D" was one of the most intimidating pitchers to ever wheel-and-deal off the mound. Drysdale

Don Drysdale, pitcher, 1960s
Courtesy: Los Angeles Dodgers

often commented that he "owned the inside part of the plate." In duels against National League batsmen, Drysdale's rules included, "If they (opposing pitchers) hit one one of our guys, I'll hit two of theirs." He followed up that credo with 154 hit batsmen (currently number three on the all-time list, behind only Walter Johnson and Nolan Ryan). Mickey Mantle even remarked during the 1963 World Series, "I know he wants to hit me today. He even came up to me at the batting cage and said, 'Where do you want it today, big boy?' " He was, along with other "knock-you-down" pitchers of his era (Bob Gibson, Early Wynn and Jim Bunning for example), the fiercest of competitors.

Drysdale, the Van Nuys, California, hero began his career with the Brooklyn Dodgers and was one of the few transition players, along with Sandy Koufax, to establish his career after the club moved west. He was an iron man, pitching more than three hundred innings for four consecutive years (1962-1965), and won 209 games in his career while capturing three strikeout titles and a Cy Young award.

And Drysdale could hit. He belted twenty-nine homers in his fourteen-year career (second in NL history only to Warren Spahn's thirty-five in twenty-one years); he was often used as a pinch hitter and occasionally was placed higher in the lineup than the traditional ninth spot reserved for pitchers. In 1968, Drysdale used his pinpoint control and blistering fastball to fire six consecutive shutouts while fashioning a Major League-record fifty-eight and two-thirds consecutive shutout innings. Characteristic of his teamwork approach, Big D was cheering his successor, Orel Hershiser, as Hershiser set a new mark of fifty-nine scoreless innings in 1988. Drsydale had his number retired by the Dodgers and was elected to the Hall of Fame in 1984.

Drsydale could have fired us the oft-told tale about his celebrated joint holdout with teammate hurler Sandy Koufax in 1965, when the pair sought to split a three-year, million-dollar deal; or his World Series gem (three-hit shutout) in game three of the 1963 World Series against the Yankees (October 5, 1963); but in typical Drysdale self-deprecating humor, he chose to give us a different World Series vignette.

October 6, 1965

"The World Series opener was set to begin in Minnesota. I was 23-12, but Sandy (Koufax) was 26-8 with a microscopic ERA (2.04). Under normal circumstances, Sandy would have started the opener, and manager Walt Alston, I'm sure, would have preferred it that way. But this year's World Series coincided with a sacred Jewish holiday, Yom Kippur, and Sandy, being Jewish, had to miss the game for religious reasons. So 'Skip' (Alston) named me to start on short rest. I knew all along I was a second choice, and my performance did nothing to alleviate that. I got pasted. I lasted two-and-two-thirds innings and got hammered for seven hits, two home runs (to Don Mincher and Zoilo Versalles) and seven runs, and we lost, 8-2. As Alston came to the mound to take me out and put in a reliever, he took the ball from my hand and I said to him, 'I bet you wish I was the one who was Jewish.' "

Tony Cloninger
Atlanta Braves, pitcher
1961-1972

Tony Cloninger was a Lincoln, North Carolina, farm boy with a big fastball, bouts of wildness and a real knowledge of the game. The six-foot, 215-pound right-hander was, for two years (1964-1965), one of the best pitchers in the game, having won a total of forty-three games and pitching 521 innings. In 1966, he displayed prowess at the plate as well, hitting five home runs while going 14-11 on the hill.

Cloninger gave us two tales of unabashed pride ... one for his own accomplishment and one (see 1990s chapter) for the accomplishment of a young man he watched grow up.

July 3, 1966

It was a day for the record books. Cloninger explains, "We were at Candlestick Park to play the Giants and I hadn't thrown a pitch yet when I went up against Bob Priddy in the first inning with the bases loaded. I swung hard, to try to get in a run or two, and hit the thing out for a grand slam.

"I hit my second grand slam of the day off Ray Sadecki and nearly got a chance at a third grand slam. With two on and two out, there was a 3-1 count on Denis Menke. I was on deck. He swings at a high ball around his eyes, a sure ball four, then went down swinging on the 3-2 pitch. Next time up, I belted one to left field ... it looked like home run number three, but Len Gabrielson Jr. leaped up and robbed me of the homer.

"I wound up with two grand slams and nine RBIs, both records for a pitcher, and threw a complete game, which we won, 17-3.

"But this was really the end of my career, though I hung on for six years. I threw in the opener that year, a real thrill, as it was the first game ever in Atlanta (April 12, 1966). We were playing the Pirates and I had only thrown a quick six innings in spring training until then. I pitched a complete-game thirteen-inning loss (3-2). Bobby Bragan (the manager) kept asking me if I wanted to come out, but a pitcher never wants to come out — something I always think about as a pitching coach — and I went all the way. My arm was never the same after that and the last six years were a real struggle. But this day, I had it all . . . the bat and the arm. Once in a lifetime."

Sam Mele
Boston Red Sox, outfield
1947-1956

Sabath "Sam" Mele, who followed up a ten-year career as a player with a seven-year managerial career, was a 6'1" 185-pounder from Astoria, New York. He led the AL in doubles with thirty-six for the Senators in 1951, and was a solid player for more than a decade, though he is more well-known as the manager of the Minnesota Twins, who he brought to the World Series in 1965.

He might have stayed in Boston for most of his career had it not been for some horseplay with Ted Williams. Mele recalls, "Ted and I boxed on a train trip and I caught him in the side and separated his rib from the cartilage. Paul Schreiber, his roomie, said the next morning, 'He can't get out of bed.' We were tied with Cleveland for the pennant at that time, and we lost it. I was traded the next June."

It is his managerial days he prefers to speak about.

July 12, 1966

Mele sets the scene: "In 1965 we won the pennant, so I was named to manage the All-Star game in St. Louis. Billy Martin was my coach, and he was the greatest goddamn coach in the Majors, so I took him with me to the All-Star game.

"We were going over team selections in Baltimore, a few days before the game, and I had lunch with Billy, who had Mickey Mantle on the phone. We picked Mickey to play and he asked if we minded if we would not pick him because his legs were hurting and he wanted the three days off to heal. So we called Joe Cronin (AL President) and told him we were picking Tommy Agee of Chicago.

"We went to New York to play the Yanks and I got cursed: 'How can they take that damn Agee over Mick?' They shouted at me,

'When you take the field in St. Louis, I'm going to shoot you and Tony Oliva.' So I shouted back, 'Shoot me, not Tony O., he's my best player.'

"I got more death threats and the FBI had to escort me from the lobby of the hotel to the field, then, once on the field, I surrounded myself with talent . . . to keep them between me and the stands.

"In those days there was a lot of talk that Billy wanted to stab me in the back and that he wanted my job, so I said to him, 'You wanted to manage, so here. Wear my uniform and take the lineup to the plate.'

"Actually, those tales about Billy Martin were garbage. He was a true friend, a good coach, and once on a fishing trip, we had a lot of beers in this boat and I cast and fell overboard, up to my neck in muck. Billy pulled me out, but before he did, he grabbed the anchor and said, 'I'll throw you this anchor, then I can have your job.' "

Art Shamsky
Cincinnati Reds, outfield
1965-1972

Art Shamsky was a 6'1", 170-pound outfielder from St. Louis with a sweet swing and a quick bat that saw him connect for twenty-one homers in only 234 at-bats in ninety-six games for the Reds in 1966. A role player, Shamsky hit .300 for the Miracle Mets in 1969, playing in 100 games, and .293 the next year in 122 contests. In post-season plays, he hit .538 and knocked out seven hits in the National League Championship Series (NLCS). A bad back cut short his career after playing in 665 games and rocking out sixty-eight homers.

Shamsky recalls a share of a Major League record he wasn't given a chance to break.

August 12, 1966

Shamsky recalls, "Under rumors the Reds were going to leave Cincinnati, possibly for Kentucky—the team was later sold and signed a forty-year pact with the city—I hit four home runs in a row.

"We were playing the Pirates, and (Reds manager) Dave Bristol didn't start me but pulled a double switch in the eighth inning. I hit homers in the eighth inning off Al McBean, tenth inning off Billy O'Dell and twelfth inning off Elroy Face. Each homer tied the game. There were eleven homers in the game; the Pirates wound up winning, 13-11, in thirteen innings.

"We got rained out the next day, but played Sunday the fourteenth and I wasn't in the starting lineup. I couldn't believe it. I was on a hot roll and I was benched. I got up to pinch hit in the fifth inning and homered again as a pinch hitter off Vernon Law for four in a row, but we lost again to the Pirates, 4-2.

"I got calls and telegrams from all over the country. The Hall of Fame called and asked for my bat and uniform. I offered them my uniform, my cleats, my hat—but not the bat. I still needed that for a shot at number five, which I was sure would come the next game. I was sure I'd be a starter against the Dodgers in Los Angeles.

"I get to batting practice and was told that Claude Osteen would start . . . a lefty. So I sat. And as I sat, the pressure just built. I came up to pinch hit in the fifth inning and faced Bob Miller, a righty, and I lined one hard to right field for a single. I just missed getting it all and as I was at first, I wondered, if I had made it five in a row, would I have started the next game?"

Frank Robinson
Baltimore Orioles, outfield
1956-1976

Frank Robinson, the 6'1", 190-pound slugger from Beaumont, Texas, was an intense, hard-hitting, hard-sliding competitor who burst on the scene in 1956 to set a rookie mark for home runs with thirty-eight.

He was known for giving it all he had every time he stepped on the field and brought that same fire to the bench when he managed.

Robinson won the Triple Crown in 1966 and led the league in slugging four times, runs three times, and was a rookie of the year, MVP in both leagues (1961 for Cincinnati and 1966 for Baltimore), a gold glove winner and an eleven-time all-star. Robinson is fourth on the all-time home run list with 586 and tenth in runs scored with 1,829.

Robinson had his number retired by the Baltimore Orioles and he was enshrined in the Hall of Fame in 1982.

Talking of the Hall and his MVP awards, Robby says, "The Hall of Fame gives me a great deal of pleasure because it shows that people respect my career, but individual accomplishments are always shared with teammates, as are MVP awards. They mean very little because they are shared awards. Without the team around you there are no MVPs.

F Robby could have told us about June 26, 1970, when he hit grand slams in back-to-back innings, or his 541-foot homer off Luis

Tiant that traveled out of Memorial Stadium (May 8, 1966) or his first day as a player/manager (April 8, 1975) when he hit a homer as his own DH to beat New York, 5-3, but he banged a different one out to talk of a disappointment.

June 27, 1967

"I loved the team game," says Robinson, "and I loved my teammates, the friendship, the loyalty and the kidding around. Moe Drabowski used to crack me up. He put goldfish in the watercooler; played around with rubber snakes (and real ones) to scare people; and called the Kansas City bullpen from our bullpen just to tick off (Kansas City manager) Al Dark. But one time I really wanted to win something for myself.

"I had won the Triple Crown in 1966 (.316, 49 homers and 122 RBIs) and was really looking forward to the challenge of following that year up with another Triple Crown. My year was going well until I tried to break up two versus Chicago and crashed into Al Weis at second base. I missed the next twenty-eight games with double vision. That ended my hopes and I was really geared for the challenge. I finished at .311, 30 homers and 94 RBIs in 129 games, and that year Yaz (Carl Yastrzemski did win the Triple Crown with .326, 44 and 121. I was on pace and it really killed me that I couldn't compete."

Nate Colbert
San Diego Padres, first base
1966 1968-1976

A quiet, unassuming man, Nate Colbert was a 6'2", 200-pound slugger from St. Louis, who was "Mr. Padre" during the early years of the expansion club's existence.

The two-time all-star hit as many as thirty-eight homers in a season and over a five-year span (1969-1973) averaged thirty homers a year.

Colbert was involved in a baseball oddity, one which he could certainly have talked about (save for his lack of braggadocio); on May 2, 1954, as an eight-year-old, Colbert was in the stands in St. Louis to watch his favorite player, Stan Musial, connect for a record five home runs in a doubleheader. Then, on August 1, 1972, Colbert tied Musial's mark by becoming only the second player to hit five home runs in a doubleheader—he drove in a record thirteen runs in the split with Atlanta.

But Colbert is a humble man, and perhaps it comes back to this event he enjoys talking about.

July 20, 1969

Colbert says, "We (the San Diego Padres) were playing a game in Atlanta and I homered my previous at-bat. As I prepare to step up to the plate for my next at-bat, I hear this deafening, thunderous, stadium-shaking applause.

"Now I was young, and shaken, and tears welled up in my eyes. I started to cry.

"I walked to Cito Gaston, who was in the on-deck circle and I blubbered, 'Cito, can you believe this? Can you believe how great those fans are, cheering for me like that. I feel so proud.'

"Cito shakes his head and says, 'Look at the scoreboard, man.' I look up and on the scoreboard it says, in five-foot-high letters 'Man has just walked on the moon.' That's what they were cheering about.

"I sheepishly look at Cito who says, 'Man, what an ego. I hope you can hit as big as your head.' "

Frank Howard
Washington Senators, outfield
1958-1973

Frank "Hondo" Howard was a 6'7", 260-pound mountain of a man from Columbus, Ohio, who struck fear into the hearts of most pitchers who faced him. He also struck out a lot (155 times in 1967 and 1,460 times in his career), but he struck pay dirt quite often—382 homers, drove in 1,119 RBIs, and hit as high as .296 three different seasons. Howard won two home run titles; he was a rookie of the year and a four-time all-star.

In May 1968, he went on a tear and blasted ten home runs in twenty at-bats over six consecutive games.

Frank Howard is one of those gentle giants with a great sense of humor and a greater sense of humility. His is a self-deprecating wit and it is well within character for him to share one of his less-than-stellar performances. He could have told us about the June, 1963 game in which fans in the right field bleachers pelted him with peanuts, causing him to miss Bob Lillis's fly ball, but that mishap could have been blamed on external forces. Howard prefers to take the blame like a man ... by himself.

September 18, 1969

In 1969, Howard was in the midst of his four-year reign of terror on AL pitchers — thirty-six homers in 1967, forty-four in 1968, forty-eight in 1969 and forty-four round-trippers in 1970 — for the Senators, for whom he was known as "The Capitol Punisher." Typically, Big Frank stayed away from the power and went with the alternative.

"I was with the Senators and we were playing the Red Sox at Fenway," he began. "Ken Brett was a rookie pitcher for them in the opener of a day-night doubleheader, a baseball device in which the owners get twice the gate and we have just enough time between games to tighten up all our muscles and leave us injury-prone for the second game. This story is a tribute to the legendary Northeast fans' appeciation of a great performance.

"In the first game, I went 0-for-5 with five strikeouts. After my fourth whiff, I told Eddie Brinkman, our slick-fielding, light-hitting shortstop, 'I got that rookie left-hander (Brett) in my sights and I'll put one in the nets (home run territory) next time up.' Brinkman joshed, 'Just feature some contact next time.'

"Well, late in the game Brinkman and Lee Maye stroked singles and I'm up. I knew I had Brett. Sure enough, as soon as I hit the batter's box, they relieved him with a right-handed fastballer (Vicente Romo). I step back into the box and Brinkman yells, 'Five and down, Hondo.' I step in and after fouling off two good fastballs, I get fooled and swing and miss on a curve . . . five whiffs.

"Between games we're chowing down on the Fenway chicken dinner. Brinkman is feeding his boiler and looks up. 'Hey, 0-for-5. You'd better bunt for a hit in game two.' I told him to go choke on a chicken bone.

"Game two was different. First time up, I swing and miss for strike three . . . six straight Ks. Next time up, with one on and one out, I get a fastball and belted . . . a one-hopper to short, for a short-to-second-to-first double play, and those knowledgeable Fenway fans, knowing I had gone seven at-bats and made eight outs, gave me a standing ovation. I'll never forget it. It even made old Ted (Williams, the Washington manager) laugh."

1970s

April 29, 1970 to October 2, 1978

The date, April 29, 1970, shows us an oral history of John Roseboro's admiration for a man who many think knew more about pure hitting than anyone else in the game, Ted Williams (and how Williams might have changed baseball history if he had gotten hold of Roseboro fourteen years sooner). The date does not refer to the news briefs that follow. The final date of October 2, 1978, is a story of the intimidating reliever, Goose Gossage, being scared to death in the Yankee/Red Sox play-off game to end the season.

The 1970s began with the Baltimore Orioles and Pittsburgh Pirates dominating the scene. That domination later moved on to the Big Red Machine in Cincinnati, and closed with a resurgence of the New York Yankees. The decade saw the death of catcher Thurman Munson and the baseball births of pitchers Vida Blue and Nolan Ryan. Reggie hit the floodlights and Tom was Terrific.

The names in the news included Gator Guidry, Papa Stargell, Reggie, Brooks and Frank, Dock, Hammerin' Hank and King Kong Kingman; perhaps the decade of hype was best exemplified by the promotion that went sour, "Disco Demolition Night" at Chicago's Comiskey Park.

Selected decade highlights
(in addition to those told in this chapter)

April 18, 1970 - A sign of the future. Nolan Ryan of the New York Mets gives up a leadoff single to Philadelphia's Denny Doyle, then finishes the game without allowing another hit while fanning fifteen Phils in a 7-0 victory.

April 22, 1970 - Another sign of the future. Tom Seaver of the New York Mets strikes out nineteen San Diego Padres, including the last ten men he faces, to garner a 2-1 win.

June 12, 1970 - Pittsburgh Pirate hurler Dock Ellis throws a no-hitter against San Diego, 2-0. He walked eight and got help from Willie Stargell, who hit two homers. Ellis admitted later that he played the game under the influence of LSD and that the field was "melting around him." He pleaded with manager Chuck Tanner to take him out in the fifth.

June 19, 1970 - Washington slugger Mike Epstein drives in eight runs but Baltimore prevails, 12-10.

June 21, 1970 - Cesar Gutierrez of Detroit goes 7-for-7 in a 9-8 win in twelve innings over the Tribe.

June 24, 1970 - Yankee center fielder Bobby Murcer hits four consecutive homers in a doubleheader sweep versus Cleveland. He hits three in the nightcap, won by New York, 5-4.

July 26, 1970 - A good hitters' night for threes and sevens. Cincinnati catcher Johnny Bench smacks three homers and drives in seven versus the Cards, and Orlando Cepeda hits three homers and drives in seven for the Braves versus the Cubs.

August 1, 1970 - Five times two. Pittsburgh's Willie Stargell smashes three homers and two doubles, scores five runs and drives in six in a 20-10 waltz over the Braves. Teammate Bob Robertson also connects for five hits.

August 22-23, 1970 - Pirate star Roberto Clemente has two straight 5-hit games. On the 22nd, he goes 5-for-7, drives in a run and scores the other in a 2-1 win over the Dodgers in sixteen innings. On the 23rd, in an 11-0 shellacking of the Dodgers, Clemente bangs out five more hits.

August 25, 1970 - The game between the Minnesota Twins and Boston Red Sox at Metropolitan Stadium, home of the Twins until they moved to the Metrodome in 1982, is delayed for forty-four minutes due to a bomb scare. The 17,697 fans in attendance calmly wait out the police dog search in the outfield and parking lot.

September 21, 1970 - In only his second MLB start, Oakland A's rookie Vida Blue no-hits the Twins, 6-0.

October 13, 1970 - It doesn't show up in the line score or box score, but as the Baltimore Orioles bury the Cincinnati Reds, 9-3, en route to a five-game World Series championship, O's third baseman Brooks Robinson takes control of the Fall Classic with two fielding gems that define the word "spectacular." He also contributes a two-run double.

April 21, 1971 - For the second time in eleven days, Pirate slugger Willie Stargell poles three homers in a game. In this one, he leads the Bucs over the Braves, 10-2.

July 11, 1971 - Phillies slugger Deron Johnson, who, when he was in the Yankee organization was the first player called "The next Mickey Mantle," hits three homers in an 11-5 win over the Expos to give him four consecutive blasts in two games.

August 14, 1971 - His best pitching may have been behind him, but thirty-five-year-old Cardinal fireballer Bob Gibson finally notches his first no-hitter, an 11-0 gem over the Pirates. He also drives in three runs for good measure.

September 29, 1971 - Ouch. Expos infielder Ron Hunt is hit by a pitched ball for the fiftieth time this season, a new black-and-blue mark. Cub pitcher Milt Pappas plunks him in Montreal's 6-5 win.

October 13, 1971 - Roberto Clemente bashes out three hits in the first night game in World Series history to lead Pittsburgh to a 4-3 win over visiting Baltimore.

December 10, 1971 - The day that will live in infamy for the New York Mets. The Mets trade pitcher Nolan Ryan, outfielder Leroy Stanton, reliever Don Rose and catcher Francisco Estrada to the California Angels for shortstop Jim Fregosi. Fregosi was gone to Texas by 1973, Stanton hung on for five Angel seasons before finding some big power in Seattle in 1977, and Nolan Ryan pitched his way into the 1990s and to Hall of Fame consideration.

April 15, 1972 - Oakland A's slugger Reggie Jackson takes the field in the season opener and is the first ballplayer in "the Bigs" to wear a mustache since Wally Schang caught for the Philadelphia A's in 1914.

July 31, 1972 - Power and speed. Chicago's Dick Allen (aka Richie Allen), becomes the first player since 1950 to hit two inside-the-park home runs in a game; the ChiSox beat the Twins, 8-1.

September 30, 1972 - Roberto Clemente collects his three thousandth and final hit, a double off New York Mets pitcher Jon Matlack in Pittsburgh's 5-0 victory. Clemente never played baseball again; he lost his life in a plane crash while on a mercy mission for Nicaraguan earthquake victims, December 31.

April 6, 1973 - The experiment. Initiated as an experiment that has lasted for more than two decades, the designated hitter era begins as Yankee DH Ron Blomberg walks with the bases loaded against Luis Tiant. He goes 1-for-3 and the Boston Red Sox beat the Yankees, 15-5.

May 9, 1973 - For the second time in his career, Cincinnati Reds catcher Johnny Bench smacks three homers in a game against Steve Carlton. Reds win this one, 9-7. Bench also victimized Carlton for three dingers, July 26, 1970.

July 3, 1973 - Gaylord Perry of Cleveland faces his brother, Jim Perry of Detroit, as opposing pitchers for the only time in their careers. Gaylord loses, 5-4. And Minnesota's Tony Oliva, a premier hitter for fifteen years, not known for his power despite hitting 220 career homers, connects for three four-baggers in this 7-6 loss to Kansas City.

July 15, 1973 - The Angels' Nolan Ryan fires his second career no-hitter, this one at Detroit, 6-0. Most notable in this one was Ryan's fifteen Ks and the fact that Tiger slugger Norm Cash, who had whiffed three times earlier, came to bat against Ryan in the ninth, using a piano leg for a bat. Umpire Ron Luciano noticed the bogus lumber and forced him back to the bat rack. Using a legal piece of lumber, Cash popped out.

April 8, 1974 - Oh, Henry. After tying Babe Ruth with his 714th career homer April 4 against Cincy's Jack Billingham, Braves slugger Hank Aaron becomes the top home run hitter in baseball history as he nails number 715 against the Dodgers' Al Downing. Braves win, 7-4.

April 14, 1974 - En route to a record eleven home runs in April, New York Yankee third baseman Graig Nettles belts four homers in a doubleheader split with his former team, the Cleveland Indians.

June 10, 1974 - It was only a single, but Phillies third baseman Mike Schmidt hits the public address speaker at the Astrodome, some 117 feet high and 300 feet from home plate.

June 14, 1974 - On a day to remember for Nolan Ryan (and one to forget for Cecil Cooper), "The Express" strikes out nineteen BoSox in thirteen innings as the Angels outlast the Red Sox in fifteen, 4-3. Cooper whiffs six times in a row for the Sox. Ryan also strikes out nineteen on August 20 versus the Tigers.

June 1, 1975 - Nolan Ryan ties Sandy Koufax's mark with his fourth no-hitter, this one a 1-0 win over Baltimore. In Ryan's next start, he takes a no-no into the sixth when the Milwaukee Brewers' newest star, Hank Aaron, breaks it up with a single.

July 2, 1975 - Don Baylor joins the four consecutive home run crowd by belting three for Baltimore in this 13-5 win over Detroit. He hit one in his last game to make it four straight.

July 21, 1975 - When 4-for-4 and 0-for-4 equals 0-for-8. Mets infielder Felix Millan bangs out four straight singles only to be erased when the next hitter, Joe Torre, grounds into four straight double plays in a 6-2 loss to the Astros.

September 16, 1975 - Pirates second-sacker Rennie Stennett ties the MLB mark by going 7-for-7 in a nine-inning game. He scores five runs in a 22-0 rout of the Cubs.

April 17, 1976 - Mike Schmidt hits four consecutive home runs and punches out a single while driving in eight runs in a ten-inning 18-16 win for the Phillies over the Cubs at Wrigley. Schmidt entered the game hitting an anemic .167 and belts two off Rick Reuschel, one off Rick's brother, Paul Reuschel, and one off Darold Knowles.

May 2, 1976 - Jose Cardenal goes 6-for-7 and drives in four "ribbies" for the Cubs, to beat San Francisco, 6-5, in fourteen innings.

June 4, 1976 - New York Mets slugger Dave "Kong" Kingman smashes three homers and drives in eight runs as New York beats Los Angeles, 11-0. This serves as a prelude to a colorful, similar event on May 14, 1978.

June 22, 1976 - San Diego hurler Randy Jones, who hails from Walter Johnson's hometown of Brea, California, doesn't throw "heat" as did "The Big Train," but nibbles the plate with precision. In this game, Jones beats the Giants, 4-2, and ties Christy Mathewson's sixty-three-year-old mark by extending his streak to sixty-eight innings pitched without yielding a walk. Jones walks catcher Marc Hill to lead off the eight, ending the skein.

July 4, 1976 - America's bicentennial celebration apparently causes a loss of concentration. During a doubleheader between Philadelphia (America's one-time capital) and Pittsburgh, Phillie catcher Tim McCarver hits an apparent grand slam, only to be called out for passing a teammate on the bases.

July 11, 1976 - In one of baseball's more bizarre promotions, the Atlanta Braves hold "Headlocks and Wedlocks" night, in which thirty-four couples are married at home plate, followed by championship wrestling, followed by a baseball game. Atlanta hammerlocks the Mets, 9-8.

July 20, 1976 - Milwaukee Brewers' aging superstar Hank Aaron hits his 755th and final home run, this one off California Angel hurler Dick Drago, in a 6-2 Milwaukee win.

September 6, 1976 - While kneeling in the on-deck circle watching

Dodger teammate Bill Russell at the plate, Los Angeles catcher Steve Yeager is impaled in the neck by a shard off the broken bat of Russell following a foul ball. The wooden projectile narrowly misses Yeager's windpipe and artery; Yeag has nine bat splinters removed. He soon had bullpen coach Mark Cresse fashion an extension to the catcher's mask to protect his neck in future games, a device that has become standard in baseball and in hockey.

September 11-12, 1976 - The seemingly ageless Minnie Minoso plays in his fourth decade after a twelve-year retirement. The fifty-three-year-old goes 0-for-3 on the 11th, but comes back the next day to single for the White Sox against California's Sid Monge, making Minoso the oldest Major League player to hit safely.

October 14, 1976 - The Yankees get back into the World Series for the first time since 1964 when Chris Chambliss belts a ninth-inning home run off Kansas City reliever Mark Littell for a 7-6 win. Pandemonium breaks out and fans overrun the Yankee Stadium field. Chambliss needs a police escort to touch home.

July 2, 1977 - After tying the club record for RBIs in a game with eight on May 14, White Sox first baseman Jim Spencer knocks in eight again in this game versus the Twins. His first eight-ball came at the expense of the Indians.

July 3-4, 1977 - Dodger third baseman Ron Cey goes 5-for-5 on the 3rd and follows it up with three straight hits the next day for eight consecutive hits against San Francisco.

August 9, 1977 - The White Sox belt six homers against Seattle to tie the team record. Socking four-baggers at Comiskey Park are Eric Soderholm (with two), Chet Lemon, Oscar Gamble, Jim Essian and Royle Stillman.

August 16, 1977 - On the day Elvis Presley dies, thirty-eight-year-old Vic Davalillo wraps up the Mexican League batting crown with a .384 mark and is purchased by the Los Angeles Dodgers for their pennant run.

September 3, 1977 - Sadaharu Oh of the Yomiuri (Tokyo) Giants of the Japan Central League hits the 756th home run of his career, eclipsing Hank Aaron as the top home-run-hitting professional in baseball history.

October 18, 1977 - Reggie Jackson earns his "Mr. October" nom de guerre as he blasts three home runs on three swings to clinch the Yankees' World Championship over the Dodgers in six games. New York beat Los Angeles in this one, 8-4.

April 7, 1978 - His best days behind him, Detroit's Mark "The Bird" Fidrych reaches back to throw a five-hitter in beating Toronto, 6-2.

April 29, 1978 - Despite the perception of his being a singles hitter, Cincinnati's Pete Rose belts three homers along with two singles to take the Mets, 14-7.

May 14, 1978 - In a game as memorable for what was said following the contest as for what happened during the competition, Dave Kingman, now a Chicago Cub, lights up Dodger pitching at Dodger Stadium for three homers for the second time in his career (the first time was on June 4, 1976). Kingman drives in eight runs again, and his fifteenth-inning, three-run blast sinks Los Angeles, 10-7. After the game, a writer innocently asks Dodger skipper Tommy Lasorda what he thought of Kingman's performance and Lasorda's expletive-laced reply—some dozen vulgarisms in less than thirty seconds—silences the once-buzzing locker room and becomes fodder for hundreds of bootleg tapes of the interview.

June 16, 1978 - After three ninth-inning near-misses, Tom Seaver finally nails down a no-hitter—the only one of his career—as the Cincinnati Reds hurler dominates St. Louis, 4-0.

June 17, 1978 - The epitome of "Louisiana Lightning," as Yankees southpaw Ron Guidry strikes out eighteen California Angels in a 4-0 victory, raising "Gator's" record to 11-0.

July 17, 1978 - On the day Reggie Jackson was fined and suspended by Billy Martin for bunting, against Martin's orders, in the tenth inning of a 5-4 loss to Kansas City, a bigger story unfolds in Baltimore where Texas pitcher George "Doc" Medich, a medical student, saves the life of a sixty-one-year-old fan stricken with a heart attack moments before the game by performing heart massage.

August 1, 1978 - Pete Rose's forty-four-game hitting streak is stopped as the Atlanta Braves pound the Reds, 16-4. Brave hurlers who foiled Rose were Larry McWilliams and Gene Garber. **Note:** Atlanta was last in the league in pitching and Gene Garber holds the all-time record for most career losses in relief with 108.

September 7-10, 1978 - The "Boston Massacre." The Yankees are four games behind Boston when they arrive at Fenway for a four-game series. The Yankees sweep into first place by scores of 15-3, 13-2, 7-0 and 7-4. The New Yorkers outscore the Beantowners, 42-9, outhit them, 67-21, and put an exclamation point on a run that saw them move into the lead after being fourteen games out July 19.

September 15, 1978 - On the day Muhammad Ali wins the heavyweight boxing championship for the third time by outpointing Leon Spinks in fifteen rounds in New Orleans, former Dodger star Jim Gilliam dies, the Dodgers become the first team to go over the three-million fan mark at home, and Pirate Phil Garner blasts his second grand slam in two days in a 6-1 rout of Montreal.

October 2, 1978 - The play-off. The Yanks and BoSox play off for the pennant and the Yanks take it, 5-4, on a dramatic three-run homer by Bucky Dent off Mike Torrez. Ron Guidry wins his twenty-fifth game of the season and Goose Gossage comes in to get Carl Yastrzemski to pop to Graig Nettles to end the game.

October 6, 1978 - George Brett bombs three homers in an American League Championship Series (ALCS) game against New York, but the Yankees prevail on Thurman Munson's eighth-inning homer to win, 6-5, and take a two-games-to-one lead.

October 13, 1978 - In the game that changed fans calling all good third basemen "Brooks," to nicknaming them "Nettles," Yankee third-sacker Graig Nettles put on a display of fielding gems to save five runs in helping Ron Guidry stifle the Dodgers, 5-1, to give New York its first win against two losses in this year's World Series.

March 9, 1979 - In an equal rights edict, Commissioner Bowie Kuhn decrees that all reporters, regardless of gender, will be allowed equal access to locker rooms.

May 17, 1979 - The wind is blowing out at Wrigley in the Phillies' 23-22 win over the Cubs. Mike Schmidt hits two homers, including the tenth-inning game-winner; Bill Buckner hits a grand slam and drives in seven runs and Dave Kingman again hits three homers and drives in six.

May 18, 1979 - This game isn't at Wrigley, but Atlanta's Dale Murphy hits three homers against the Giants just the same. Braves win, 6-4.

July 12, 1979 - It was the day after the U.S. space station Skylab went wrong and crashed to earth in bits of fiery pieces. As if on cue, baseball witnessed the classic case of a fiery promotion gone terribly wrong. The White Sox hold "Disco Demolition Night" at Comiskey Park. After losing the first game of a doubleheader, 4-1, to the Detroit Tigers, disc jockeys blow up disco records on the field as fans are whipped into a frenzy. The sellout crowd swarms onto the field and virtually destroys it as a full-scale riot breaks out. The ChiSox forfeit the second game as the field is unplayable. **Note:** This event occurred four years after a popcorn machine fire—June 4, 1974—broke out in right field, causing a seventy-minute delay of the eighth inning, forcing four thousand fans onto the field. The ChiSox won that one, beating the Red Sox, 8-6.

September 28, 1979 - Cardinal shortstop Garry Templeton shows switch-hitting consistency by becoming the first player to connect for one hundred hits from each side of the plate in a single season. He bangs out three hits against the Mets to hit the one-hundred mark righty . . . and he only hit right-handed in his last nine games to force the record.

September 29, 1979 - Pitching and hitting marks to close the season. As the Astros beat the Dodgers, 3-0, Houston righty J.R. Richard whiffs eleven Dodgers to set the NL mark for Ks in a season by a righty with 313, ten more than his own 1978 record. Richard allows only five hits, one of them, Manny Mota's 146th career pinch hit (to break the record Mota shared with Smoky Burgess).

The Chronicles

John Roseboro
Los Angeles Dodgers, catcher
1957-1970

John Roseboro was the Dodger catcher who took over after Roy Campanella's sudden departure from the game, and for the Dodgers' first decade in Los Angeles, Roseboro was the heart and soul of the team, calling pitches and handling the rotation.

The 5'11", 200-pounder from Ashland, Ohio, was also the center of one of baseball's most violent moments. On August 22, 1965, in a game between the Dodgers and Giants, San Francisco pitcher Juan Marichal, batting against Sandy Koufax, complained that Roseboro's return throws to the mound were too close to Marichal's head. He suddenly turned and attacked Roseboro with his bat, leading into a fourteen-minute bloody brawl.

Roseboro caught two of Koufax's no-hitters and often led the league in total chances and double plays for a catcher.

As a hitter, Roseboro had some pop. He hit .287 in 1964 and blasted eighteen homers in 1961. He finished his career playing in 1,585 games, hit 104 homers and delivered twenty-nine pinch hits, but it is his batting and his last stop, a stint with the Washington Senators under Ted Williams, that Roseboro recalls for these pages.

April 29, 1970

Roseboro says, "I went from Minnesota to the Washington Senators in 1970, after a long career with one of baseball's top organizations, the Dodgers. At least I was always told the Dodgers had the best coaches and teaching techniques. But that was before I got to Washington and got to be managed by Ted Williams.

"Ted Williams taught me more about hitting my last year in Washington than I had picked up my entire career elsewhere.

"After watching me bat in late April, he saw this power swing I had all my career and he asked me, 'How many homers do you have?' I said, 'None, Skip.' He said, 'No kidding. You swing from your ass and don't have a zone. Your pinky is off the end of the bat and you're all arms and no leg thrust.' He gave me a five-minute lecture on how hitters are supposed to hit, something I had never heard in fourteen years.

"He said, 'If there is a fastball in your zone, drive it. If it is else-where, go with the pitch and drive it that way. Look for the fastball when you swing.' Then he proceeded to tell me, a lefty, how to hit against lefties — another thing no one had ever taught me.

"I learned more with him that season than everywhere else. I think what a big waste of my time my career was in L.A. Their hitting instructors were supposed to be the best, but they never taught me to think at the plate. Ted Williams advocates hitters thinking up there and then teaches discipline and pitch selection, saying that the pitcher has to come to you and you are in control, not the pitcher; make him do what you want, not let him make you do what he wants.

"Ted got me in my last year. I was thirty-seven, had spent fourteen years behind the plate and was used up. If he had gotten hold of me in 1957 or 1958, I feel confident that I could have had a more noteworthy career.

"I loved playing ball. I loved my career. My only regret is that I didn't have a chance to play it as well as I could have played it and that I didn't have the opportunity to be taught by Ted Williams fourteen years earlier."

John "Boog" Powell
Baltimore Orioles, first base
1961-1977

John Wesley Powell was a behemoth slugger from Lakeland, Florida, who stood nearly 6'5" and weighed around 240. Powell was built for power and he used it to the tune of 339 homers with 1,187 "ribbies," most of which came for the Orioles' mini-dynasty of the late sixties and early seventies, a club that made it to four World Series in six years, including three in a row.

Powell was a four-time all-star and was American League MVP

in 1970, and his sense of humor is as big as he is. He shared two jocular tales for this work.

October 15, 1970

"It was the last game of the World Series, and we wrapped it up in five games by beating Cincinnati, 9-3. Brooks Robinson and I kid a lot about this Series because he was named MVP.

"In game three (October 13), Brooks made two incredible plays at third to keep us in the game until our bats came around. But, and I joke with him on this, his throws were so lousy that I had to use my soft hands to save the play.

"In game five (October 15), Brooks made another couple of great saves, and I had to save the save by digging or stretching to complete the play.

"When he was named World Series MVP and won a new Corvette, I went up to him and said, 'You know, you only made half those plays, I made the last half. I must have saved you thirty times this year, so you owe me. I want half of that damn car.' That really cracked him up, but the truth of it was, even though I am half responsible for about ten of his fifteen gold gloves, that play he made (in game three) in which he went into left field in foul territory and still made the play, still gives me chills."

August, 1971

Powell recalls, "This is the weirdest thing that ever happened to me on a ball field.

"We were in Chicago and I was taking batting practice before a game and I hit one into the upper deck. The ball was hit high and a man with a bald head jumped up to catch it and—SMACK—it hit him right on his bald head. I felt concerned, but I laughed about it; and in batting practice, the stands aren't full so I had a clear view of what happened. I asked someone to see if he was all right and I got prepared to take my next swing.

"On the next pitch, I hit another upper deck shot and—WHAM—it hit the same guy, on the other side of his head.

"I sent the clubhouse guy to go get him; I had to talk to him.

"He was brought down to me and he had two huge knots on his head; I could see (AL President) Lee MacPhail's signature printed on the left side of his skull. I asked him if he was OK and he said, 'Yeah . . . except that after the balls hit me they bounced away and I lost them both.'

229

Willie Mays, outfield, 1970s
Courtesy: San Francisco Giants

"I got him two baseballs and signed them, 'To Jack, your head is harder than this ball.' I got him two tickets for the next game . . . sitting behind a protective screen."

Willie Mays
San Francisco Giants, outfield
1951-1952 1954-1973

Willie "Say Hey" Mays was one of the most exciting and talented players to ever lace up his cleats. The 5'11", 175-pound center fielder from Westfield, Alabama, was as feared a hitter as the National

League has ever had. Mickey Mantle called him "The best all-around ballplayer I ever saw." And during his years with the New York Giants, he was one of the principals in the "who's better" debate involving the fans of Mickey Mantle, Duke Snider and Mays. Mays could do all the five things Leo Durocher said complete players could do: Hit, hit with power, run, field and throw. Mays was the first player to hit thirty homers and steal thirty bases in the same season on two different occasions. His credentials: 660 homers; 2,062 runs scored; 1,903 RBI and 3,283 hits, all well up on the all-time lists. He won two MVP awards, was Rookie of the Year in 1951, earned a batting title, four home run crowns, and four stolen base trophies. The All-Star game was his private domain, having played in a record twenty-four mid-season classics in a row. He always gave it everything he had, and an enduring memory is Mays running out from under his slightly too-large cap as he raced around the bases or glided in the outfield. Mays had his number retired by the Giants and was elected to the Hall of Fame in 1979.

His twenty-two-year career was overflowing with exploits and great days. He was on second base when Bobby Thomson hit "the shot heard 'round the world" off Ralph Branca to win the NL pennant on October 3, 1951. He was the man who raced back in the Polo Grounds, September 29, 1954, to rob Vic Wertz of an extra-base hit with an over-the-shoulder catch in the World Series opener. His eighth-inning homer off Dick Farrell on September 30, 1962, propelled the Giants into a play-off against the Dodgers, and it seemed that for most of his 2,992 games there was some great story to tell about Willie Mays. But for this work, Willie chose to tell two events from later in his career, days during which he stole the thunder from one of his contemporaries.

April 27, 1971

Mays nodded as he spoke of Hank Aaron: "Whenever Henry had a big day, I always seemed to have an even better day. It was like that ever since I first played against him in the fifties. I guess I was always established and he came along, and as good as he was, I always had to be better, so I always made it my business to steal some of his glory whenever we were both on the field.

"In this game, Henry hit the six hundredth homer of his career. He got it off Gaylord Perry to join me and Babe Ruth with six hundred. But I got the headline because I got the hit that won the game, 6-5, over Atlanta in ten — an RBI-single in the tenth. I already had

633 homers and even though I was forty, I figured I'd stay ahead of Henry, but I always had the needle in for Aaron. Whenever he did anything, I just had to do him one better, so when I had a chance to win the game and got my single, I was happy for the club because we won, but then I looked at Aaron as he came off the field and I flashed him a smile and he knew what it was all about. Here it was, a big day for him because of his six hundredth homer, and yet I got the headlines because my clutch hit won the game."

July 25, 1972

Maysland, the All-Star game. "I had just been traded to the Mets May 11, and was happy to be at the game, my twenty-third in a row. Aaron had passed me in career home runs (June 10) and I was beginning to realize that at forty-one, my career was winding down. But the All-Star game, man, that was mine; it was always mine. It was my chance to show the best just what I could do. Hitting against Whitey Ford, Billy Pierce, Early Wynn, Jim Bunning and Allie Reynolds and playing against Mickey Mantle, Ted Williams, Harmon Killebrew, Larry Doby and Al Kaline and then beating them, showed them. Before I played in the All-Star game, the American League dominated, but in all the games I played, we only lost five times and beat them eighteen (tied one). So I used the game as a stage; we all did. And on the National League team we got to kid with each other as teammates when we were enemies during the season. So to play well with Stan Musial, Henry (Aaron), Eddie Mathews, Gil Hodges and Duke Snider pulling for you, was a real kick for me, and I always tried to have an even better game than they were having. It was fun to play the games and be around the fellas, but I was serious on the field.

"The game was played in Atlanta and even at forty-one, I was an All-Star starter. I was announced before Henry because I hit second and he hit third. I got a thunderous ovation, one of the biggest I ever had in my life. I mean they gave me twenty years of appreciation. So when I was announced and heard this long, loud cheer, I took my position on the field and then they announced Henry and he got a good ovation, but not as loud or as long as mine. I even kidded him that they loved me better than him. And every time I got up, the applause was even louder and I wasn't even their hometown boy. So even though Henry did hit one out that day and I didn't, and Brooks Robinson robbed me of a hit in the first inning, I made two big plays in the outfield—one, on a deep drive by Yastrzemski—and he had no plays in the field. I still got him one better, because the fans showed they appreciated me and my ability, and it wasn't until Henry hit his homer (in the sixth inning) that they gave him the same respect."

Jim "Catfish" Hunter
Oakland A's, pitcher
1965-1979

James Augustus "Catfish" Hunter was a classy, smooth, six-foot, 200-pound right-hander from Hertford, North Carolina, who was given his nickname by A's owner Charlie Finley when he signed the pitcher to a seventy-five-thousand-dollar contract. Finley wanted to capitalize on the "farm boy" routine.

Hunter, the dominant pitcher in the American League in the early seventies, won twenty-one or more games for five straight seasons from 1971-1975. An eight-time all-star, he led the league in wins twice, starts once, ERA once, complete games once and innings pitched once. He finished with a record of 224-166 in five hundred games, allowing only 2,958 hits in 3,448 innings with forty-two shutouts.

Hunter was among the first players to sport a mustache as a member of the A's. "We grew them to take Charlie Finley for three hundred dollars," says Hunter. "He offered us the cash for the hair, but half the guys shaved them off as soon as they'd gotten their money."

Hunter was the first big-name free agent to command a bidding war and mega-contract. He signed a five-year pact with the New York Yankees for $3.5 million, far and away the richest inking of its day.

After helping to take the A's to three World Series and the Yankees to three World Series, he was enshrined in the Hall of Fame in 1987 and he had his number retired by the Oakland A's.

The humble and soft-spoken Hunter preferred to stay away from his exploits and talk instead about a volatile manager and also give us a real-life Yogi-ism.

August, 1971

"I was pitching in Baltimore and Frank Robinson had just ripped me for a double late in a game we were winning. Dick Williams (the A's manager) comes out to the mound and says, 'He just hit your fastball low and away?' I didn't answer. He asks again, 'He just hit your

Jim "Catfish" Hunter, pitcher, 1970s
Courtesy: New York Yankees

fastball low and away, right where you wanted it?' I said, 'No, he hit a slider.'

"Dick throws his hat in the air and says, 'You've been getting this guy out your entire life with your fastball and you throw him a slider? Go take a shower.'

"He took me out. He wouldn't have yanked me if I'd said I'd thrown him a fastball."

August, 1978

"Yogi (Berra) was a coach for us at this time and I used to eat breakfast with him every day. One morning in Detroit we were eating and an old-time ballplayer came in and said 'Hi.' When he passed by, Yogi said, 'Hey, Cat. Was that the guy who was dead? Or alive?' I said, 'Yogi, you just saw the guy. You know he's alive.'

" 'Yeah,' said Yogi, 'but he had a twin brother and one of them just died so I want to know if he's the one who died or the one who's alive.' "

Rollie Fingers
Oakland A's, pitcher
1968-1985

Roland Glen Fingers was a 6'4", 190-pound right-hander from Steubenville, Ohio, who was the first Hall of Famer to be elected based solely on his ability as a relief pitcher. Fingers, who retired as the number one save man of all time (since passed by Jeff Reardon and Lee Smith) with 341, is high on the all-time lists for appearances (944-fourth) and wins in relief (107-fourth). His ERA was a sharp 2.90, and he appeared as a starter only thirty-seven times, none in his last eleven years covering 663 relief stints. Fingers led the league in appearances three times, getting into seventy-eight games with San Diego in 1977 and seventy-six and seventy-five games with Oakland in 1974 and 1975.

Fingers won the Cy Young award and the MVP in 1981 for the Milwaukee Brewers and was a seven-time all-star.

Fingers was named to the Hall of Fame in 1992 and had his number retired by the Milwaukee Brewers.

Fingers certainly could have told us about his combined no-hitter (September 28, 1975) completed with Vida Blue, Glenn Abbott, Paul Lindblad and Fingers in a 5-0 no-no versus the Angels, but he chose a hairier tale.

March, 1972

"You may remember," says Rollie, "that the 1972 Oakland A's were the first team in about sixty years to have facial hair. My trademark handlebar moustache came out of that team. And ever since that team went to the World Series, it paved the way for all other players after us to wear moustaches and beards. And it all came about just to nail a guy we didn't like having his own way.

"It's true Charlie Finley, a skinflint owner, offered us three hundred dollars if we'd grow mustaches and look like an old-time team. He was always doing things he thought would be good for promotion; he reasoned that if he gave us three hundred dollars, we could be marketed as an old-time team and he'd sell many more tickets than his $300 investment per player would cost. He was the guy who came up with 'Catfish' Hunter. Jim Hunter's nickname was manufactured by Finley who wanted us all to have nicknames so he could market that, too.

"Anyway, Reggie Jackson came into spring camp that year and hadn't shaved; he was the only guy in camp who wasn't clean-shaven and he was bragging that he'd play with a beard or mustache, and our manager, Dick Williams, didn't like it but didn't want to single Reggie out or get on his case alone unless there were other cases to get on.

"So 'Catfish' and Darold Knowles and I got together and said we hated Reggie's mustache and his attitude and if we start growing mustaches, Dick (Williams) will be able to tell all of us to shave. We can pretend to be on Reggie's side and snap our fingers and say 'Damn, looks like he made us all shave,' and we'll get Reggie's mustache off without actually doing it ourselves. Pretty sneaky. We loved it.

"So as spring training goes on, our hair is getting longer and we go to Dick and he agrees it's time for us all to shave — Reggie, too. Then Charlie (Finley) comes in to the clubhouse and sees our wispy mustaches and Reggie's and says anybody who grows a mustache will get three hundred dollars. He saw the promotion angle and a way to make money, and we saw it as a way to get three hundred dollars from that old tightwad. Hell, we'd have grown mustaches on our asses to get three hundred dollars from Charlie. So we all grew them, Dick too, and the rest is baseball history. So we only grew them to get Reggie to shave and it backfired, but we got three hundred dollars from Charlie and that was even better.

"After we got to the World Series in 1972, 1973 and 1974, it got to be a superstition and I wouldn't have dreamed of shaving it off. And I negotiated the extra three hundred dollars into my contract every year — I don't think any of the other guys did — and it was all to spite Reggie."

(**Author's Note:** Reggie Jackson's mustache made it to opening day (April 15) and marked the first time since Wally Schang sported whiskers in 1914 that ballplayers wore facial hair.)

Hank Aaron
Atlanta Braves, outfielder
1954-1976

"Hammerin' Hank" Aaron, at six-feet, 180 pounds was not built like a home run hitter but he certainly became one . . . and became number one, breaking one of the sport's most hallowed records, Babe Ruth's career home run mark, exceeding the Babe's 714 homers by forty-one round-trippers. He accomplished this despite being hounded by the press and assaulted with an avalanche of hate mail and hate phone calls because he was a new-era athlete going after an icon's standard, and because he was a black man about to break a white player's record.

Even early in his career, the Mobile, Alabama, native impressed his contemporaries with his bat speed, his powerful wrists and his ability. He was such a feared power hitter that when he tried to pull Dodger third baseman Jackie Robinson in by faking a few bunts during a game in 1954, Robinson didn't bite and held his ground, deep at the hot corner. When Aaron later asked Robinson why he didn't come in to protect against the bunt, Robinson matter-of-factly said, "We'll give you first base anytime you want it." In 1960, at which point Aaron had hit only 209 home runs, Mickey Mantle, who had hit 279, was locked in with Willie Mays (250), Eddie Mathews (298) and Ernie Banks (228) as the premier power hitters in the game. As Ted Williams was nearing retirement and Duke Snider winding down, Mick was asked if he, Mays, Banks or Mathews could approach Babe Ruth's 714 and Mantle didn't skip a beat. He prophetically blurted out, "Hank Aaron. He's built well, not too muscular. He never gets hurt and has a great swing, quick without overswinging, and with his wrists, he can hit homers that stronger guys can't." And Don Drysdale said of Aaron, "Trying to get a fastball past Henry Aaron is like trying to smuggle a sunrise past a rooster."

Aaron's credentials: first all-time in homers (755) and RBIs (2,297), one MVP, two batting crowns, four home run titles, four RBI crowns, and an all-star in each of his twenty-three seasons. He had his number retired by the Braves and Milwaukee Brewers and was elected to the Hall of Fame in 1982.

When asked for a story, Aaron thought for a short time. He began, "I could rehash the disappointments — the losses to the Dodgers in the 1959 play-off or to the Yankees in the 1958 World Series when I felt we had the better team—Warren Spahn, Eddie Mathews and Lew Burdette—but we didn't win collectively and we were outmanaged by Walter Alston and Casey Stengel. In the 1958 Series, (Brave's manager Fred) Haney only managed for four games until we were up three games to one; we needed to win one more but Haney just let us play, whereas Stengel managed the Yankees for all seven games and they beat us.

"I could give you the fun times, like when we played the Yankees in spring training and Whitey Ford would have Mickey Mantle call his pitches to me. Whitey would look out at center field and if Mick was standing, Whitey would throw a fastball and if he was lying down, I'd get a curve. Too bad I didn't know the system until they told me about it later. Whitey laughed when he told me, saying he let Mickey call the pitches because he's the one who has to chase them. Those guys were always competitors but always had a good time; they'd have been great to have as teammates, and I can say that after having to face them for years as opponents.

"I could give you September 23, 1957, one of my favorite homers because it clinched the pennant for us in the eleventh inning against the Cards. It was probably the most important home run I ever hit.

"But I'd rather give you my proudest moment in uniform." As the author figured that proud moment would be home run number 715 (April 8, 1974, off Los Angeles Dodger pitcher Al Downing) because Aaron had stood up to the bigots and the hatred and the pressure associated with chasing Babe Ruth's record, Aaron reflected and said, "No, my proudest moment in uniform was a homer that didn't really matter until what occurred afterward."

July 25, 1972

"When I began my Major League career in Milwaukee, after a couple of seasons playing for the Indianapolis Clowns in the Negro Leagues, I played for the Milwaukee Braves. The fans were OK in Milwaukee, and when we won the World Series in 1957—beating the Yankees after they had us down three games to one—the fans showed respect, but I kind of felt like just a performer, not really a part of the community. We moved to Atlanta in 1966, and I was elated because having been brought up in the South (Alabama), I thought it would be like going home to the family. I was wrong. It was still the same old 'performer' show. It's not that I was black and most of the fans were white; it wasn't a racial thing, it was just that I never felt the community ever showed me it wanted me there. I was paid to play and nothing else, and what I really wanted was to be accepted into the family and the community. I got my wish at the All-Star game, held in Atlanta in 1972.

"I wanted to do well in front of the home fans, and I hadn't had many good All-Star games, but when I was announced as a starter in the game, the 53,107 fans were polite but they really didn't show me any more support than they showed Willie Mays or Bob Gibson or Joe Morgan or Steve Carlton. It was business as usual.

"I hit third in the lineup and I was 0-for-2 against Jim Palmer, who struck me out, and Mickey Lolich. I really needed to have a good day, so when I got up in the sixth against Gaylord Perry, with Cesar Cedeno on base, I really concentrated because we were down, 1-0, and I wanted to get a hit. I had faced Perry before when he was in the National League, but that didn't help if he threw his good slider or spitter. I concentrated and I hit his pitch, I think it was a spitter (but he called it a slider), for a home run to left-center to put us up, 2-1 (we eventually won it in ten innings on Joe Morgan's single, 4-3) and the ovation I got was spectacular, almost deafening. It was long and loud and gave me goose bumps. It was the most heartwarming event I've ever had on a ball field. I felt so much warmth. I had always viewed the fans as family and now I felt that love was being returned. Danny Murtaugh (the NL manager) took me out of the game and the crowd was still cheering for me. I caught a flight to Mobile and that crowd at the airport cheered, and when I got back to Atlanta I was cheered again. And really, the homer meant nothing; it was early in a game which meant nothing and I really felt that the applause was for me and not for the ballplayer or the deed.

"Until that point, I never really felt accepted in Atlanta as a human being. I was just a ballplayer who provided some thrills, but it was a very one-sided relationship. I did my best for them but never felt like I was part of the family.

"The huge show of warmth they gave me—and continued to give me from that point on—showed they respected me and accepted me as a human being. It was the most important day and proudest day of my career."

Graig Nettles
New York Yankees, third base
1967-1988

Graig Nettles, the golden-gloved acrobat for the New York Yankees during their return to glory in the 1970s, was a six-foot, 180-pound slugger from San Diego, California, who changed a generation of baseball fans. Prior to Nettles's wizardry at the hot corner, great defensive plays by infielders from little league to the Majors were usually met with cries of "Way to go, Brooks," in recognition of Brooks Robinson's glovework. After Nettles took charge of the 1978 World Series with his defense, those great baseball plays began to be met with compliments of "Way to go, Nettles."

Nettles was a basketball star at San Diego State University and was on his way to a possible NBA career when he grew too muscular for basketball and filled out in baseball proportions. Beginning his career as an outfielder, he became a full-time third-sacker in his third season, and his glove never left him for the rest of his twenty-two-year career plus two seasons in the Senior League in the early 1990s.

As admired as he was for his glovework, he was feared for his power at the plate, particularly at Yankee Stadium, where the dimensions fit his left-handed swing. Nettles retired as the top home-run-hitting third baseman in AL history and finished his run with 390 homers, one home run crown, 1,314 career RBIs and highlight reels devoted to his defense. He was selected the greatest Yankee third baseman of all time in a fan survey in the early 1980s.

Nettles certainly could have made the play by giving us his October 13, 1978, display when his four spectacular stops prevented seven runs to give the Yankees a 5-1 win over the Dodgers in the World Series, but the man known to teammates as "Puff," and one who had his teammates in stitches with his dry sense of humor, chose a little-known tale about how the Yankees got "stuck" with his services.

November 27, 1972

Nettles reflects, "I was really lucky to be a Yankee. It made my career and playing in Yankee Stadium in pinstripes and winning the World Series is the best thing a player can attain. There's really nothing like it. But if the truth were told at the time, I might never have gotten there.

"I was traded during the winter from Cleveland with Gerry Moses to New York for John Ellis, Jerry Kenney, Rusty Torres and Charlie Spikes. I was told over the phone by a Cleveland sub-executive that I'd been traded and I went to New York three weeks later to see Yankee manager Ralph Houk, the only manager I ever really wanted to play for.

"I dropped in to see Ralph and he asked how I was feeling and I smiled and told him, 'I feel great now that my cast is off my leg.' Houk's mouth dropped open and he stuttered, 'W-what cast?' I told him that I had had my ankle operated on just a few days before the trade and I showed him the fresh scars on my ankle.

"Houk muttered something about 'damaged goods' and he shook his head, dumbfounded and said, 'Tsk, tsk, tsk.' He told me, 'Damn. If I had known that, I never would have traded for you. Gabe Paul (Cleveland's GM) really put one over on me.' I put my leg up on his desk and I promised him I would be 100 percent and that I was OK. I don't think he believed me.

"It was the best break that ever happened to me. I never would have been a Yankee and would have been stuck in Cleveland and would never have been in a World Series if Gabe Paul hadn't pulled a fast one on Ralph Houk. And to be honest, at the time, I really had to agree that the Yankees had been stuck . . . with me."

Jim Wynn
Houston Astros, outfielder
1963-1977

Jimmy Wynn, "The Toy Cannon" was a 5'9", 150-pound bundle of energy and power from Hamilton, Ohio. He was much bigger at the plate than his stature would lead people to believe and he poled 291 home runs in his career, including thirty-seven in 1967 and thirty-three in 1969. Wynn hit only .250, largely due to his all-or-nothing swings that caused him to whiff 1,427 times in 6,653 at-bats.

His anomaly season was 1971, in which he hit only seven dingers, but that was due to his being stabbed in the stomach by his wife during a domestic quarrel. He came back the next year and bombed out twenty-four homers.

His 1974 season may have been his most satisfying as he came to Los Angeles and hit a team-leading thirty-two homers with 108 RBIs as he made it to the World Series for the only time in his career.

Wynn favors us with a nugget from that season.

April 4, 1974

"The 1974 season was my proudest all the way down the line. Although in 1975, I did something I'm equally proud of . . . I hit the one hundredth home run in All-Star history (Babe Ruth hit the first). Milestones like that are always remembered, so I'll be remembered in that way in the same breath as Babe Ruth.

"I was traded to L.A. and that was the big time. I loved Houston

Jimmy Wynn, outfield, 1970s
Courtesy: Houston Astros

but we never went anywhere and that was a big park (the Astrodome). The Dodgers had a history and were first-class all the way,
big time.

"In the season opener versus San Diego, the first three times I
got up in front of the hometown crowd, my knees were shaking so
much I had to step out. I wanted to do so well for this new club and
these great fans who cheered me like I was an old Dodger from years
ago.

"I stepped back in and between shakes, my first time up I singled through third baseman Dave Roberts's legs for a base hit. Next time up I hit a line drive single. Third time up I hit a line drive to third.

"Funny, but after that out, I was fine. I just said to myself, 'Good Lord, Jimmy, relax and enjoy yourself. Just play baseball.'

"I did just that and it set the tone for the entire year. We couldn't do anything wrong as a team and went to the World Series—the high point in my career. And while I'm disappointed that we lost, hey, I played in a World Series. Ernie Banks never did, and my Houston teammates never did, either. I loved that year."

Darold Knowles
Oakland A's, pitcher
1965-1980

Darold Knowles was a reliable relief pitcher from Brunswick, Missouri, who stood six-feet tall and weighed 180.

Knowles appeared in 765 games (all but eight as a relief ace), and saved 143 with an ERA of 3.12. He was a set-up man and closer for the 1972-1974 A's mini-dynasty, averaging fifty appearances a year.

He became a household word in the World Series when he appeared in all seven 1973 Series games for Oakland against the Mets, pitching six-and-a-third shutout innings with two saves.

He recalls the chemistry of the 1974 A's and a fight that got them juiced up.

May, 1974

Knowles says, "We were known for our in-fighting. We fought about everything. We had big egos and we really weren't the best example of teamship.

"We were in Detroit and Billy North and Reggie (Jackson) were fighting. Dick Green, Ken Holtzman and I were playing bridge. Vida Blue comes over and tells us to help him break up the fight because he couldn't do it alone. We didn't care. Vida says, 'Help me somebody?' Holtzman says, 'I can't, I've got a two-club bid.'

"Ray Fosse stepped in between them and ripped them apart but hurt his back in the process and had to undergo surgery. But we didn't step in because Billy was winning and it would have been fine with us if Reggie got whipped. I mean, to tell you how we felt about Reggie, we were glad to have him come to bat with the game on the line, but we certainly didn't care for him. We even grew mustaches just to have Reggie have to shave his off, but the plan backfired; not only did he get to keep his, we had to grow ours. But we got paid $300 by Charlie Finley to grow them, and we liked Charlie even less than we liked Reggie.

"Anyway, this fight woke us up and we really didn't have a tough time winning the pennant that year. Fights made that team a team; nothing else did."

Bob Watson
New York Yankees, first base
1966-1984

Bob "Bull" Watson was a 6'2", 210-pound first baseman/outfielder from Los Angeles, who could hit with consistency. In nineteen years he hit .300 or better seven times and finished at .292. He occasionally showed power (twenty-two homers in 1977) and he twice drove in more than one hundred runs.

Watson was signed as a catcher, but moved to the outfield and first base and was a better-than-average fielder. He is a footnote in history for having scored baseball's one-millionth run, and he remembers the event and how he almost missed out. And he talks of the importance of leading a team in the 1980s chapter, and it is that story that dictates his being listed here as a Yankee.

May 4, 1975

Says Watson, "I was simply in the right place at the right time. At the time, I didn't think the run would happen that day. We were forty runs away when the day began and in the first game of a double-header at Candlestick Park, we lost to the Giants, 8-6. At game time for the nightcap we were down to six. In the first inning, we went down one-two-three to John "The Count" Montefusco. I was batting cleanup, so I led off the second and the scoreboard said '2'.

"Count walked me on four pitches and I still never thought about it. Willie Montanez, the Giants first baseman, said to me, 'If you want to steal second, I'll play behind you.' The count to Jose Cruz went to 2-0 and I stole second—I only had three steals all year—and he walked on five pitches.

"Milt May was now up and the scoreboard changed to '1'. May takes a strike then hits the ball into the right field seats for a home run. Normally, I would trot around the bases, but I had a sense of history so I took off on a dead run. The visiting team bullpen was on the third base line and they were cheering me on. I was on a dead sprint for home.

"I didn't know it at the time, but in Cincinnati, with his score-board also reading '1', Davey Concepcion hit a home run — and he can fly — and he was running top speed around the bases. If I jog, I lose out to him, but I ran hard and beat him by two-and-a-half seconds.

"I'll never forget that moment. I even kept a few mementos — a shoe, my uniform. It meant a lot to me because, prior to 1947, no black had ever played in the Majors and thanks to Jackie Robinson, the first black played in 1947 and then a black man scored the mil-lionth run. To me, that was important."

Jerry Koosman
New York Mets, pitcher
1967-1985

Jerry Koosman was a 6'2", 210-pound lefty from Appleton, Minne-sota, who won 222 games over a nineteen-year career. A control pitcher, he was NL Rookie Pitcher of the Year in 1968 and broke Tom Seaver's team rookie records for wins, shutouts and ERA.

Koos finished his career with 3,839 innings pitched in 612 appear-ances, won twenty games or more twice, lost twenty once, and struck out an even two hundred batters in 1976. He was a two-time all-star.

Koos reveals his favorite clubhouse prank, one in which the victim wanted to punch out the perpetrator except that it was kept a secret for three years . . . time enough for the wound to heal.

August, 1975

Koos admits, "I am a practical joker, plain and simple, and baseball teams and clubhouses are perfect for those pranksters like me.

"I set up a guy and it took a lot of planning; those are the best jokes.

"I sent away for a bugging device — it took a few weeks for me to get it, to show you how far I'd go for a good joke — that could be broadcast over an FM radio. I put the FM radio on top of Tom Seaver's locker.

"Now, you have to understand, Tom Seaver is a heck of a nice guy, with a good sense of humor, and he was a god on that team.

"I talked with Mets PR director Jack Simon, who did a perfect Howard Cosell impression. And we prepared this stunt before the first game of a doubleheader against Cincinnati, when all the players were out on the field taking batting practice.

"Now to set this up, the principals involved are Tom Seaver, the

Jerry Koosman, pitcher, 1970s
Courtesy: New York Mets

Met god, who would finish the year 22-9; long-time first baseman Ed Kranepool, who would go .323 with only four homers; Houston Astros infielder Doug Rader, who we hated — we had just gotten into a brawl with him and he was an ex-boxer and hit some of our guys a bit too hard for a base-brawl — and would hit .223 but got twelve homers; and a young pitcher named Doug Konieczny, who couldn't beat anyone but the Mets — he went 6-13 but beat the Mets four times and we never could understand how because he didn't have shit.

"So I put Jack Simon in the team doctor's office and told him to count down from ten after I gave the signal, then pause for five seconds before he started talking.

"Batting practice was over and the whole team came into the clubhouse. I turned the volume down low and heard Simon's 'five-four-three . . .' at 'zero,' I turned the volume up and I left the area.

"I turned around and saw Seaver talking with the team chairman of the board, Donald Grant; shit, I thought, poor timing, but it may work out.

"Simon, who, as far as everyone was concerned was Cosell, began, 'We have an NBC Sports bulletin. This is Howard Cosell reporting. The New York Mets have announced a major trade. They have sent pitching ace Tom Seaver and first baseman Ed Kranepool to the Houston Astros for infielder Doug Rader and pitcher Doug Konieczny. I repeat, the Mets have traded Tom Seaver. We now return you to your local station.'

"Seaver was dumbfounded. I walked over to him and shook his hand. He was as limp as a dead fish. The entire club heard it and it was eerily silent. They were in shock. Seaver was shocked and silent and near tears.

"Kranepool went berserk, he was cussing out the Mets and baseball and was tearing up everything in sight.

"I went over to the doctor's room and told Jack Simon to get the hell out; the joke was over and he'd better not tell anyone or they'd kill him.

"Grant said he hadn't heard anything and he'd straighten it all out, but I think he thought Seaver had been dealt.

"Now, Seaver was supposed to pitch that game and even though he got assurances that the report wasn't true, it really affected him. Still, he went out and beat the Reds, 5-3, in the opener and I won the nightcap, 5-3.

"Three years later, I was on *Kiner's Korner* and I told Ralph Kiner what I had done and Seaver was surprised; he never thought it was me. Now, with my history as a prankster, I wonder how he could have thought it was anyone else."

Ernie Banks
Chicago Cubs, first base
1953-1971

Ernie Banks is "Mr. Cub." The perennially happy and upbeat ballplayer, who thought every day in baseball was a good day to "play two," came out of Dallas, Texas, as a 6'1", 180-pound shortstop. The first black player on the Cubs, Banks is the quintessential class ballplayer who never got to play in a World Series, primarily because his supporting cast of Cubs teammates were often less than stellar. Banks led the NL in homers twice, RBIs twice, was a two-time MVP, and eleven-time all-star. His career totals of 512 homers and 1,636 RBIs put him high up on the all-time lists. He had his number retired by the Chicago Cubs and was elected to the Hall of Fame in 1977.

Ernie Banks certainly had a career full of days about which he could speak, including his five hundredth career homer off Pat Jarvis, May 12, 1970. He preferred, however, to talk about a teammate's day, a day which occurred after Banks's career as a player had ended and he was an observer as a Cub coach.

April 25, 1976

"A story from America's bicentennial stands out in my mind," Banks began. "It was the most touching and most unusual event, one which had the greatest impact on me in my career.

"The Cubs were playing at Dodger Stadium and I was a coach when I saw something that kept me spellbound as the event I watched was frozen in time.

"Nothing much was going on and we are in the field, so I am watching from the dugout when all of a sudden a guy jumps on the field carrying an American flag. He starts to set it on fire and out of nowhere, Rick Monday, one of our outfielders, scoops it up and keeps the guy from burning it. That moment was the happiest and saddest moment of my life.

"When you play sports, you only know people by their stats and the real person only comes out occasionally. That day I learned about Rick Monday as a man, with his loyalties and patriotism. His selfless act made headlines but he didn't do it for that, and when next year he was traded to the Dodgers and in 1981 hit a home run in the play-offs off Steve Rogers to get them to the World Series, it showed what karma he has. And he gave me a moment that still gives me chills."

Rick Monday
Chicago Cubs, outfield
1966-1984

The logical follow-up to Ernie Banks's view of the flag incident is to hear what Rick Monday remembers. Rick, a 6'3", 200-pound outfielder from Batesville, Arkansas, was the first person ever taken in baseball's first college draft, in June 1965. He had a steady nineteen-year career, even if it failed to live up to unrealistic expectations placed upon him by his lofty draft status. Monday, though unspectacular, was a major cog for five division champions and one world championship team. His accomplishments place him neatly as a typical hardworking ballplayer who is representative of the kind of individual who chooses to make baseball his life.

April 25, 1976

Monday paints the scene. "There were 25,167 fans in attendance and the Dodgers won the game, 5-4, in ten innings that Sunday afternoon, but all that is overshadowed by what occurred outside the game.

"I was in center field and Jose Cardenal was in left when a guy runs from the left field foul pole, with a flag underneath his arm, to shallow left field. He spreads the American flag out on the ground — just as if it were a picnic blanket — and my six years in the U.S. Marine Corps Reserves just rushed to my body without thinking. I saw him take out a can of lighter fluid, strike a match, and it blew out as I was running to him. He struck a second match and tried to touch it to the flag; I scooped it up on the run. I just had to save the flag — no more, no less, but it is the moment I'm proudest of in all my nineteen years in baseball.

"The tag line to this is that Doug Rau was given the flag. I finally was given the flag by Dodger executive Al Campanis, and it's in my home now. And the firebug was fined eighty dollars."

Larry Hisle
Minnesota Twins, outfield
1968-1982

Larry Hisle, the 6'2", 200-pound outfielder from Portsmouth, Ohio, was a feared power hitter in the 1970s, winning an RBI crown in

1977, belting twenty-eight round-trippers in 1977 and thirty-four in 1978. He twice hit better than .300 and was quick enough to steal thirty-one bases in 1976. A good outfielder with a strong arm, Hisle looked menacing enough at the plate, but that belied a soft-spoken, gentle personality that got him widely known around the Majors as one of the "nice guys."

Hisle, an orphan, grew up at the same time and in the same general vicinity as Yankee catcher Thurman Munson, and Hisle's story deals with the fact that friendship often takes precedence in life and can even supersede baseball etiquette.

August 24, 1976

Hisle remembers Munson fondly. "He and I graduated from high school in the same year and we always played on high school all-star teams together. We talked a lot when our teams — his Yankees and my Twins or Brewers — played one another. He may have been gruff to outsiders, but those of us who knew him well knew that he was a caring, friendly and loyal person.

"Now in this game, the Yankees were an all-star team on their way to a big pennant year, running away with their division, and we were stuck in the middle of the pack behind strong Kansas City and Oakland teams.

"The Yankees were performing well and were beating us severely. They were up by eight runs late in the game when Mickey Rivers dragged a bunt to try to get a base hit. In baseball etiquette, that's a no-no when you're up by eight runs; you don't try to embarrass the other team. Rivers's bunt rolled foul and he realized he had messed up and even shook his head as if to admit his mistake. Our pitcher, Vic Albury, a lefthander, knew baseball etiquette and with the next pitch, he hit Rivers in the back — WHAM — with a hard fastball. Rivers showed class and nodded as if to say he knew it was his fault, and he had simply forgotten the score was out of hand.

"I'm in the outfield thinking that if the Yankees know baseball etiquette, they must initiate a payback — they just can't let one of their guys get hit on purpose without retaliating to protect their hitters — and that means hitting the leadoff batter for us the next inning . . . and, OUCH, I'm the leadoff batter next inning.

"Normally I talk with Thurman when I bat. He's the catcher and I'm the hitter and we take the time for pleasantries. But I know that it is the catcher who must give the pitcher the sign and call for the beanball, so I figured I'll make this easy for both of us and say nothing.

And Thurman says nothing. Thurman gives the sign to Dick Tidrow, who throws a mean fastball and I tense up because I know this one is going to hurt. The first pitch comes, and it's a good fastball that catches the outside part of the plate. Strike one. *WHEW.*

"Well, sometimes they do that, I said to myself. They have to hit me and sometimes they like to catch you off guard to relax you, then they drill you. I prepare myself for the pitch, tense up, but it crosses the inner third of the plate. Strike two.

"Now I know I've got to swing at the next pitch. I figure they'll probably hit me with this one but I've got to go down swinging and I watch the pitch come inside and low and I swing meekly at it and ground out to short, run it out to first, and hustle back to the dugout. I was perplexed. I sit down in the dugout and wonder what's going on.

"The next hitter up is Dan Ford, who is calm at the plate. Munson flashes the sign, Tidrow throws and — BAM — Ford gets hit hard in the back.

"After Ford is forced at second on the next play, he comes back to the dugout and sits next to me and asks, 'Why did they hit me? Why not you?' I looked out to Munson, who finally looked over at me, and he winked and grinned. Dan had no idea, but Thurman saved my back.

"This time, unspoken friendship didn't violate baseball's unwritten rule of payback, but it did postpone it. Friendship is just as important as baseball etiquette, and Thurman knew that."

Manny Mota
Los Angeles Dodgers, outfield
1962-1982

Coming out of Santo Domingo, Dominican Republic, the sweetest swing in baseball arrived in the person of Manny Mota, the 5'10", 160-pound pinch-hitting dynamo. Mota was as dependable a hitter as there was in baseball for the decades of the sixties and seventies. If he had been a better fielder and had more power, people would have talked about Mota with the same reverence they held for Roberto Clemente. And had Mota not been injury prone (he played in 1,536 games in twenty years, sitting about half the time), he might have ranked high up on the all-time hit lists.

Manny Mota could hit, and he proved it by being the number one pinch hitter of all time, cracking out 150 pinch hits in 505 at-bats with that compact swing.

And most of all, Manny loved the game. Mota says, "I loved play-ing as a kid when there was no money involved, and I played the same way in the Majors — with pride and intensity, except that if I played poorly as a kid, I wouldn't carry it with me. Playing as a professional carries much more responsibility. As a pro, I never felt 100 percent physically well in twenty years.

"As a pinch hitter, I was always confident. I always felt as if I was the best hitter and that I could get a hit. If you don't (feel that way), you'll fail."

Mota could understandably have talked about September 2, 1979, when he got his 145th pinch hit, to tie Smoky Burgess as the number one pinch hitter of all time, or the day he got number 146, but he chose a moment of national pride he got on a playing field off the beaten MLB path.

March, 1977

Mota says, "We (the Dodgers) were playing an exhibition game in the Dominican Republic against the New York Mets and the game was in my hometown; everybody I knew was there.

"I pinch hit and was facing Tom Seaver with the bases loaded. I hit a grand slam to win the game. It was a big moment for me, because I'm not supposed to hit homers.

"When I touched home plate, people had swarmed around to receive me. It was the first time I had ever played at home in a Major League uniform and all I wanted was a good at-bat. I swung hard at the first pitch and it went. It went farther than any ball I ever hit in twenty-six years of playing ball in the Dominican and it was the biggest surprise of my life.

"After the homer, there was a five-minute standing ovation. It was my only Major League at-bat ever there and it was the biggest pinch hit of my life."

Rod Carew
Minnesota Twins, first base
1967-1985

Rodney Cline Carew was a six-foot, 175-pound sweet-swinging lefty from Gatun, in the Panama Canal zone.

Carew could hit, field and run (353 stolen bases). He began his career as a second baseman and became a good first baseman the second half of his career. He was adept with the bat, hitting the ball where it was pitched and using the entire field. He studied pitchers,

Rod Carew, first base, 1970s
Courtesy: California Angeles

pitches and the entire game. He led the AL in batting six times and in hits three times, was Rookie of the Year, won an MVP award, and was a seventeen-time all-star. He hit better than .300 fifteen consecutive times and finished his career at .328.

Rod Carew has his number retired by the Minnesota Twins and the California Angels and was elected to the Hall of Fame in 1991.

Carew talks about the year he made an assault on .400 and fin-ished at .388. The story, typical of Carew, is short and to the point, one of pride and embarrassed acceptance.

June 26, 1977

Carew says, "I was going after the .400 mark and was trying too hard. I had just struck out five consecutive times and we were at home in Minnesota playing the White Sox. It was Jersey Day and there were fifty thousand people in the stands. (**Author's Note:** Carew entered the game hitting .396.)

"The fans gave me a huge ovation when I first got up, as if they knew how hard I was trying. I went 4-for-5 with six RBIs in the game to raise my average to .403 and each time up the applause got louder and louder. By my final hit, they gave me a prolonged standing ovation, and I must admit I was embarrassed by it. Minnesota always accepted me as a person as well as a ballplayer, but this reaction gave me chills. It still does when I think about it. They were applauding me, not because I had won a game — it was a team victory — or because I set a record — I didn't, and it was still very early in the season. The applause was heartfelt and prolonged just because they were warm. I'll never forget it."

Nolan Ryan
California Angels, pitcher
1966-1993

Nolan Ryan, "The Express," was the flame-throwing "Robo-pitcher" from Alvin, Texas, who dominated the game with his blazing 100 mph fastball for a record twenty-seven years. A sure Hall of Famer, Ryan won more than 320 games, pitched more than 5,400 innings and struck out in excess of 5,700 batters, while throwing better than sixty shutouts and hurling more than 215 games in which he struck out ten or more batters. He authored a record seven no-hitters, demolishing Sandy Koufax's previous record of four. His strikeouts totalled over fifteen hundred more than second-place K-man Steve Carlton. His hits-allowed-per-game (under 6.6 per 9 innings) is the lowest in baseball history and his strikeouts per inning (better than 9.5 per 9 innings) is also the best.

Ryan said the best stuff he ever had on the mound wasn't even a no-hit performance. "I pitched a one-hitter for the Angels (July 9, 1972) against Boston that we won, 3-0. I walked the leadoff man, struck out their number two hitter, Carl Yastrzemski topped a ball that rolled weakly between third and short for a hit, and then I struck out sixteen of the next twenty-six guys I faced and retired all of them."

Ryan could have recapped any of his seven no-nos, his four nine-

Nolan Ryan, pitcher, 1970s
Courtesy: California Angels

teen strikeout games, or any number of events from twenty-seven years in "the Bigs." He chose to throw us a curve and talk about the only time he purposely hit a batter. (**Authors' Note:** Ryan is second on the all-time hit-batsmen list with nearly 160, behind only Walter Johnson.)

August, 1977

Ryan drawled, "There's only one guy I threw at intentionally in all my career. (Ryan claims he did *not* intentionally bean ChiSox third baseman Robin Ventura in 1993.) I was pitching with the Angels in 1977 and we were having a poor season. We were playing the Boston Red Sox and they were riding me the entire game. They were up on the dugout steps just bad-talkin' and hollering. I looked over and saw (outfielder) Rick Miller, hollering at me. I said to myself, that's all right, I'll get him.

"I threw hard at him three straight times, and I missed him on all three pitches. On the fourth pitch, I hit him in the ribs. It wasn't as hard as I could throw, but it had a purpose. When I hit him, I walked up to him to see if he had anything to say. I stared him in the eyes and he said nothing. I said to myself, OK, he took it like a man.

"I didn't see him again that year but the next year he got traded to the Angels and I walked up to him, now that he was a teammate, to explain the pitch of the previous year, and he said, 'That wasn't me yelling. I never bad-talked you.'

"The only guy I ever hit on purpose, and he wasn't even the right guy."

Steve Garvey
Los Angeles Dodgers, first base
1969-1987

The cog of the Los Angeles Dodgers' glory years of the 1970s was Steve Garvey, the 5'10", 195-pound first baseman from Tampa, Florida, who was once a Dodger batboy.

Garvey was Mr. Durable, amassing a consecutive-games-played streak of 1,207 games from 1974-1983. A good fielder with a poor arm, Garv made the move from third to first and anchored the longest consecutive infield in the Majors — the Garvey (first base), Davey Lopes (second base), Bill Russell (shortstop), Ron Cey (third base) infield of 1973-1981.

Garvey led the NL in hits twice and finished with a .294 career average and 272 homers. He was an MVP, a four-time gold glove and a ten-time all-star. He hasn't had his number retired and as yet has not been elected to the Hall of Fame, but he has had a junior high school named after him and had his number retired by the San Diego Padres.

His story just backs up his "Mr. Clean" image.

August 28, 1977

Garvey offers, "I was in a horrible slump. I was 3-for-50, with little hope of breaking out of it. I wasn't striking out a lot, but I was hitting one-hoppers to third, dribblers to the pitcher, and easy pops to left.

"I went to Dodger Stadium for a game against the Cardinals and it was 'Nun's Day' at the ballpark. I thought that since I was Roman Catholic and it was Sunday, maybe today I'd get a hit. Then I had an absolutely lousy batting practice.

"Steve Brener, the Dodgers' publicity and media director, came over to me and pointed out a lovely twelve-year-old girl who was sitting above the Cardinal dugout. He explained to me that she had been a gymnast who had been in an accident and was now a quadriplegic. She was also a big baseball fan.

"I went over to her and she was doing well in her wheelchair but was having trouble talking. When I asked her how she was, she just said, 'Will you get a hit for me?' I promised her that my first hit would be for her. Then I realized we were facing Bob Forsch, who was really throwing well and was on his way to a twenty-win season.

"I walked to the plate for the first time, said a few Hail Marys, and then I got into the batter's box saying, 'Our Father who art in heaven . . .'

"I swung and hit a double down the right field line. As I got to second, I said, 'OK, thanks, Lord.'

"Then I hit a home run to left center field, 'Thanks, again, Lord.'

"Then I hit a double, then a grand slam home run, then a double.

"I was 5-for-5, five extra-base hits, five runs scored, five RBIs. I got three standing ovations and we won the game, 11-0.

"But the best part of this story is Annie Ruth, the girl who became my friend that day. I went over after the game and we kept up a friendship. I watched her grow into a fine young lady and into an adult. I followed her career as a greeting card artist who paints with a brush in her mouth, and she followed what I did on the ball field and after my career was over we remained close. What a wonderful day; I got out of slump, made a friend and began a relationship."

Paul Molitor
Milwaukee Brewers, second base
1978-

Paul Molitor, a six-foot, 185-pound infielder, has been regarded by many as the best full-time DH (for his last three seasons) and as one of the best two or three leadoff hitters who ever played the game. Molitor is second only to Rickey Henderson in home runs hit to lead off a game. He was Rookie of the Year in 1978 and has, at various times, led the AL in at-bats (twice), runs scored (three times), hits, doubles and triples.

The St. Paul, Minnesota, native has played every position except pitcher and catcher and was the team leader (along with Robin Yount) in Milwaukee for fifteen years before moving on to Toronto. He has one word on baseball and health that he wanted included for readers of his story: "I was injured in 1980, and out of boredom, I picked up chewing tobacco. It was the worst mistake of my life. I've been chewing it for thirteen years. I'm addicted to it and it has ruined my health, my teeth, my gums and my breath, and the long-term effect may even ruin my family, if I'm not around to enjoy them. Just a word of advice: Don't ever start chewing or dipping, and if you do, stop as soon as you can."

Molitor could have given us a hit-by-hit replay of the time he hit for the cycle against Kevin Tapani of his hometown Minnesota team, May 15, 1991, but he chose instead to tell about his first trip to Yankee Stadium.

July, 1978

"I was in my rookie season and I was playing my first game in Yankee Stadium versus the two-time defending AL champions and reigning World Champions. To say I was in awe puts it mildly. I hope they never leave that park because it is still the most thrilling place in the world to play.

"I was facing Sparky Lyle, the Cy Young winner and best reliever in the game at that time, when I came up in the tenth inning.

"It was the first time I had ever seen him. He had a half-a-pack of Levi Garrett (chewing tobacco) in his mouth.

"As I stepped up to the plate, Graig Nettles trotted from third base to the mound and whispered something to Sparky. He went back to third base and on the first pitch, Sparky hung me the worst slider he ever threw, and I was fortunate enough to hit it into the left field seats for a home run—I only hit six all year.

"As I scored, I saw Nettles go back and whisper to Lyle again.

"During the next game, Graig doubled and I trotted over to him from my second base position and asked him what he said to Sparky. Graig told me, 'Before the first pitch, I told him to watch out for the bunt, I think he's gonna bunt. After the home run, I told him that was the longest bunt I'd ever seen.' "

Reggie Jackson
New York Yankees, outfield
1967-1987

Reginald Martinez Jackson was "Mr. October." He was the "Straw that Stirs the Drink." He had a candy bar named after him. He was ego-driven, outspoken and controversial, and he was also arguably the best money player, clutch-performer, and most talked-about marquee player in the game for two decades. Signed off the campus of Arizona State, the power hitter spent twenty-one years in "the Show," played on eleven divisional winners, six pennant winners and five world champions as he battled with Billy Martin, Thurman Munson, Graig Nettles (a one-punch fight he lost), Mike Epstein (a one-punch fight he lost), George Steinbrenner, and players on several of his teams as well as with members of the press (verbal fights he usually won through intimidation). He was also a success wherever he went, and he rose to the occasion when the occasion called for Ruthian tasks. Most memorable of these was Jackson's one-man show against the Dodgers in the 1977 World Series (October 18, 1977) as he became "Mr. October" with a three-swing, three-home-run performance to win the Series for the Yankees.

Built for power and speed, the six-foot, 200-pound Wyncote, Pennsylvania, native could win games with his prodigious power or his baserunning (228 steals and 1,551 runs scored), but seldom with his glove (he was considered a defensive liability).

Jackson won one MVP, four home run titles, an RBI crown, and finished his career sixth on the all-time home run list with 563 and tops in strikeouts by a batter with 2,597. He was drama that usually had a happy ending as he came through in the clutch time after time with the big game on the line. He was elected to the Hall of Fame in 1993 and had his number retired by the Yankees.

Jackson certainly could have supplied us with details of his June 14, 1969, show in which he hit two homers, a double and a single and drove in ten RBIs in a 21-7 Oakland win over Boston at Fenway Park; or his home run off Roger Clemens (May 15, 1986) to pass

Mickey Mantle on the all-time home run list with round-tripper number 537; but the normally brash slugger, who backed up most of his boasts with results, chose a surprisingly somber moment from his career, one which he said paved his way to the Hall of Fame.

July 17, 1978

An often-told baseball tale is the one about Mickey Mantle in 1951. With his pride hurt, and his career temporarily derailed due to poor performance, the young Mick called his father, Mutt Mantle to come take him home to Oklahoma. Expecting soothing words and a pat on the back, Mick got harsh words and a kick in the rear instead, as Mutt Mantle packed up Mickey's gear, called him a baby, and told him to come back to start work in the Oklahoma zinc mines because that's where he'd spend the rest of his life. Faced with mining, hard work and no kind conversation, Mantle gutted it up and went back to playing ball—eighteen brilliant years of it—and the rest is Hall of Fame history.

Not widely known is Reggie Jackson's own discussion with his father during the days when Reggie wanted to pack it all in. Without this fatherly advice, the Hall of Fame might have one less hero in its midst.

Jackson recalls: "I was really having trouble with Billy (Martin, Yankee manager). The team was going OK but Billy was really on me. We were playing Kansas City and I was up in the tenth inning and tried to hit a homer to win the game. A year earlier, I tried to bunt against Boston (June 18, 1977) and Billy went nuts on me on national television. So I tried to hit a homer but I didn't get one and we lost and Billy suspends me for ignoring his bunt sign. I was only trying to win, but Billy suspended me for five days. I marched in and told him I'd never play for him again and for the Yankees to trade me.

"I went home and my father, Martinez Jackson, was there. It's not that I had such a close relationship with my father, but he was an authority figure and when he said something important, I always listened to him. I told him I would never play for the Yankees again and I'd just sit home until they traded me.

"My father took me by the arm—hard, just like I was still a little kid—looked me in the eye and said, 'Are you a baby? It's time for you to grow up. You're a man, not a kid anymore. You signed a contract and gave them your word that you'd play for them. You have to honor your contract, you have to keep your word. Just keep your mouth shut and do the best you possibly can. Be a man.'

"I did what he said and finished my contract with the Yankees and played every game with all my might and my ability from that day on. And I think it was the most important conversation I've ever had and certainly the most significant moment of my career. I'd think about what he said, and I honored that commitment the rest of my career and it's what kept me going and what ultimately got me to the Hall of Fame."

Rich "Goose" Gossage
New York Yankees, pitcher
1972-

Perhaps the consummate prototypical relief pitcher of the 1970s and 1980s was Goose Gossage. Big (6'3", 200 pounds), hard-throwing (99 mph fastballs) and menacing (Fu-Manchu mustache and unruly hair), Goose went right at his opponents, power-versus-power, day after day.

The nine-time all-star (a lot for a reliever) from Colorado Springs, Colorado, led the league in saves three times; when he came in for the save the game was usually in the refrigerator. His ERA (ten straight years under 3.00) and hits-to-innings ratio were low and his strikeouts-to-inning ratio often exceed 9.0. He appeared in forty or more games in thirteen years.

He was flawless in three appearances in the 1981 divisional play-off and pitched eleven shutout innings in relief for two Yankee World Series teams (1978 and 1981).

Goose talks about fear.

October 2, 1978

Gossage recalls, "The play-off game against Boston was really something. We were fourteen games out on July 19, in fourth place, and we caught (and passed) Boston and, after 162 games, it all came down to one game.

"It's the first time in my life I ever faced any pressure. To me, all my other games were just for fun and this game stands alone. But at the time it didn't seem fair that we must decide a 162-game season on one game; I think a three-game play-off, like they used to have, is more equitable.

"Ron Guidry went for us against Mike Torrez, and though Torrez was a great pitcher, "Gator" (Guidry) was the absolute best that year. But Boston was really tough. They hit the ball hard all over the park

Rich "Goose" Gossage, pitcher, 1970s
Courtesy: New York Yankees

and were ahead. I was getting nervous because I didn't want us to come this far and lose. Then Bucky Dent hits a three-run homer over the Green Monster and we're up.

"With the score 5-4, I'm shaking. I'm scared for the first time ever. I had the fear of failure. I didn't want to lose it for us, and normally, my attitude was I want to win it for us.

"With two out and two on, I'm facing Yaz (Carl Yastrzemski) and the blood was pumping in my ears and I could barely breathe. I had to back off the mound. I said to myself, this is silly. The worst thing that can happen is that I'll be home in Colorado tomorrow. The weight of the world suddenly was lifted off my shoulders . . . and it should. Realistically, the whole world wasn't watching. Putting it in the proper perspective, there's more going on outside in the world. Still, this was a great rivalry (Yankees/Red Sox) and it did all come down to one game; but it was only one game.

"I regained my composure and got Yaz to pop out to third, and when Graig (Nettles) closed his glove on it, I was ecstatic, knowing we had just beaten a great BoSox team; but I also felt it was a shame they had to lose.

"When it was over, my legs banged together with the loss of adrenalin, and I'll tell you, I couldn't feel any differently if my life was on the line . . . scared and full of adrenalin. But it did put another foot on my fastball and the rush of energy gave the pitch movement so it tailed in on Yaz.

"And what's lost in history's recall, because of my save and Bucky's homer, was a spectacular play by Lou Piniella (in right field) early in the game. There was a fly ball and Lou lost it, battled it, and dove to get it. To me, that play saved the game for us, yet few remember it."

1980s

October 5, 1980 to September 20, 1989

The date, October 5, 1980, is the initial oral history offering for this decade. It recounts the story of Bob Watson, who made his mark as a Yankee, and does not refer to the news briefs that follow. The final date of September 20, 1989, is a story of Tony Gwynn and the little things that make a baseball game.

The 1980s saw the collapse of the Yankees, the dominance of Wade Boggs, the best player in the game being, at any given time, Don Mattingly, Dave Winfield, Dale Murphy, George Brett, Eddie Murray, Tony Armas, Ryne Sandberg, Howard Johnson, Mike Schmidt, Andy Van Slyke, Tim Raines, Rickey Henderson or any of a number of players who put together three or four good seasons. The arms belonged to Nolan, Doc, Rocket Roger, Dave Stewart, Mike Scott and Orel Hershiser.

Money skyrocketed and attendance did as well, and baseball moved closer to expansion.

Selected decade highlights
(in addition to those told in this chapter)

April 25, 1980 - How about some help? Montreal's Larry Parrish hits three homers and drives in all of Montreal's seven runs, but it's not enough as the Braves beat the Expos, 8-7, in eleven innings.

May 4, 1980 - Otto Velez of Toronto ties the AL record by smashing four homers in a doubleheader sweep of the Indians. He drives in ten runs.

June 12, 1980 - Washington state's Mount St. Helens explodes for the third time since May 18, and Pittsburgh's "Hit Man," Mike Easler, hits for the cycle in a 10-6 win over Cincy.

June 20, 1980 - That's one homer for every twenty-one and one-third inches. California Angels shortstop Freddie Patek, at 5'4", becomes the shortest player in history to bomb three homers, in California's 20-3 drubbing of the Red Sox at Fenway.

August 19-20, 1980 - New York Yankees slugger Bob Watson takes aim on the Kingdome speakers in Seattle. On successive days, Watson hits a double off the left center field speaker, and the following day boomed a triple off the center field box.

April 27, 1981 - The term "Fernandomania" becomes a household phrase as rookie Dodger lefty Fernando Valenzuela sells out Dodger Stadium and improves his record to 5-0 with a 0.20 ERA in posting his fourth shutout, a 5-0 win over San Francisco. Fernando can't do anything wrong, as he is even hitting a robust .438.

July 10, 1982 - Texas Ranger Larry Parrish clouts his third grand slam in a week—he hit one July 4 and another July 7—this one off Detroit's Milt Wilcox to help beat the Tigers, 6-5.

July 30, 1982 - The Atlanta Braves hold a ten-and-a-half game lead in the NL West when Braves management decides to evict popular mascot Chief Noc-a-homa from his left field tepee to make room for 235 extra seats. The eviction causes a Brave slump that sees the club lose nineteen of their next twenty-one. Bowing to public outcry, the chief is returned to his post and the Braves win the pennant.

August 6, 1982 - Back-to-back times two. San Francisco sluggers Jack Clark and Reggie Smith hit back-to-back homers twice to lead the Giants to a 7-6 win over Houston.

October 12, 1982 - As the Milwaukee Brewers demolish the St. Louis Cardinals, 11-0, in the World Series opener, Paul Molitor goes 5-for-6 and teammate Robin Yount goes 4-for-6.

April 27, 1983 - Astro hurler Nolan Ryan fans Brad Mills of the Expos to move past all-time strikeout leader Walter Johnson as the king of Ks, with 3,509. And for Ryan's old club, California, Fred Lynn and Darryl Sconiers each hit grand slams to lead the Halos to a 13-3 win over Detroit.

May 6, 1983 - Why go for .400? Angels first baseman Rod Carew goes 3-for-4 in a 4-2 victory over Detroit to raise his average to .500, at 48-for-96. He'll finish the year at a mere .339.

May 20, 1983 - In a short-lived battle for strikeout supremacy, lefty Steve Carlton passes Walter Johnson to move into second behind Nolan Ryan on the all-time K list. On this date, Carlton moved to 3,511, ten behind The Express and three up on The Big Train.

May 25, 1983 - Where's the plate? As the Bucs lose to the Braves, 7-0, Pittsburgh pitchers Jim Bibby and Jim Winn walk seven consecutive hitters in the third inning to tie a seventy-four-year-old mark.

June 26, 1983 - Tying Dave Philley's record of delivering eight consecutive pinch hits, Rusty Staub of the Mets connects for a single in the ninth inning in an 8-4 loss to the Phillies.

July 24, 1983 - The "Pine Tar Game," in which George Brett's two-out, two-run ninth-inning homer against Goose Gossage gives the Royals an apparent 5-4 lead, only to have him declared out for having pine tar too far up the handle of his bat. According to the rules, the Yankees win the game. AL President Lee MacPhail overruled the umpires and let the homer stand (see story in this chapter).

August 18, 1983 - "The Pine Tar Game" of July 24 is completed and Dan Quisenberry comes on in the bottom of the ninth to save the win for Kansas City, 5-4, over the Yankees. To mock the game, fans were let in free and Yankee skipper Billy Martin took control. He had his players appeal all three bases, alleging that neither George Brett nor Royals base runners had touched the bags on the game-winner, and Martin put left-handed Don Mattingly at second base, and pitcher Ron Guidry in center field when play resumed. George Frazier was on the mound to whiff Hal McRae for the final out in the top of the ninth, and the Yankees went quietly to end the game.

May 4, 1984 - Dave Kingman, playing for Oakland against the Twins at the Metrodome, clubs a shot in the top of the fourth that goes through a hole in the canvas roof. Shortstop Houston Jiménez and third baseman John Castino patiently wait for the ball to come down. It doesn't and Kingman is awarded a double.

May 6, 1984 - Shortstop Cal Ripken Jr. of Baltimore hits for the cycle in the O's 6-1 win over Texas.

May 16, 1984 - ChiSox catcher Carlton Fisk hits for the cycle in Chicago's 7-6 loss to Kansas City.

May 24, 1984 - The wire-to-wire Tigers increase their record to 35-5 with a 5-1 win over California. This is Detroit's seventeenth straight road win.

June 26, 1984 - Pirate slugger Jason Thompson hits two homers in each game of this doubleheader split against the Cubs, for four on the day.

June 28, 1984 - Boston's Dwight Evans joins the cycle club by smacking a three-run homer in the eleventh inning of this 9-6 win over Seattle.

August 5, 1984 - Blue Jay Cliff Johnson becomes the all-time pinch hit home run king as he passes Jerry Lynch with his nineteenth career blast when coming off the pine. The homer in the eighth inning leads Toronto to a 4-3 win over Baltimore.

September 12, 1984 - New York Mets rookie fireballer Dwight Gooden breaks Herb Score's mark for most Ks by a rookie when he whiffs sixteen Pirates in a 2-0 win to run his total to 247. Score fanned 245 for Cleveland in 1955.

September 17, 1984 - On the day American League slugger Reggie Jackson slams his five hundredth career homer, this one off Kansas City's Bud Black (seventeen years to the day after Reggie hit his first career tater), Mets rookie pitcher Dwight Gooden ties an MLB record for most strikeouts in two games by fanning sixteen Phillies in a 2-1 loss. Five days earlier, Doc K'd sixteen Pirates, for a two-game total of thirty-two.

September 30, 1984 - On the last day of the season, the Yankees' Don Mattingly wins the batting title over teammate Dave Winfield by going 4-for-5 in this victory over Detroit. Winfield went 1-for-4 to finish at .340 to Donnie Ballgame's .343.

April 11, 1985 - Seattle's Gorman Thomas, who thought his career was over after rotator cuff surgery, comes back to hit three homers in a 14-6 clobbering of Oakland.

April 13, 1985 - Rollie Fingers, who already holds the MLB record for saves with 325, saves his 217th AL game in Milwaukee's 6-5 decision over Texas, to break Sparky Lyle's junior circuit mark.

June 11, 1985 - As the Phils destroy the Mets, 26-7, to score the most runs in the NL since 1944, Von Hayes becomes the first player to hit two homers in the first inning of a game, as he puts the exclamation point on a nine-run explosion in the first with a grand slam.

June 27, 1985 - The legendary road of Americana, Route 66, officially ceases to exist following decertification, and San Francisco's Jeffrey Leonard hits for the cycle, but his Giants lose to the Reds, 7-6.

July 4, 1985 - Will they play until the tricentennial? Thanks to two rain delays and a six-hour, 10-minute nineteen-inning game, the Mets beat the Braves, 16-13, on "Fireworks Night" in Atlanta. The game ends at 3:55 A.M. July 5, and the fireworks display starts at 4:01 with a handful of the crowd still on hand.

August 29, 1985 - Number two all-time ouch. When Angels pitcher Kirk McCaskill hits Yankee DH Don Baylor with a pitch, the HBP is Baylor's 190th of his career, breaking the tie for second he was in with Minnie Minoso (behind Ron Hunt). Yanks win, 4-0.

September 11, 1985 - Cincinnati's Pete Rose becomes baseball's all-time hit leader as his single off San Diego's Eric Show is number 4,192 to break Ty Cobb's mark. Reds win, 2-0.

October 14, 1985 - Ozzie Smith, known more for his magic with his glove than with his bat, hits his first Major League home run left-handed. His ninth-inning homer off Tom Niedenfuer wins the game for St. Louis, 3-2, over the Dodgers in game five of the NLCS.

April 29, 1986 - Red Sox fireballer Roger Clemens strikes out twenty Seattle Mariners in a 3-1 win, to break the nine-inning record of nineteen shared by Nolan Ryan, Tom Seaver and Steve Carlton. Clemens doesn't walk a batter and gives up only three hits.

May 31, 1986 - Red Sox third baseman Wade Boggs goes 5-for-5 to jump his average to .402 as Boston beats the Twins, 7-2. Boggs will finish the year at .357.

June 4, 1986 - Barry Bonds, son of former Major League slugger Bobby Bonds, goes 4-for-5 and hits his first home run, off Craig Mc-Murtry, as his Pirates beat Atlanta, 12-3.

September 29, 1986 - Minnesota pitcher Bert Blyleven sets a record he doesn't want as he gives up three homers to Cleveland. Blyleven gets the win anyway, 8-5, but takes over sole possession of the "most home runs allowed by a pitcher in a season" mark. Robin Roberts gave up forty-six in 1956, and the three round-trippers off Bly give him forty-nine for the season. Number forty-seven was hit by rookie Jay Bell.

October 25, 1986 - In what many remember as the "Bill Buckner error" game, with two out and none on in the bottom of the tenth and a 5-3 lead for the Red Sox (who also lead in games 3-2), the Mets answer with singles by Gary Carter, Kevin Mitchell and Ray Knight. After pitcher Bob Stanley's wild pitch allows the tying run to score, Mookie Wilson's topspin slow bouncer goes through Buckner's legs to score Knight with the winning run. The Mets won the series two days later on Ray Knight's homer. Also during game six, Michael Sergio, a Mets fan, parachutes onto the field during the game and holds up play for fifteen minutes. Sergio was sentenced to one hundred hours of community service and was fined five hundred dollars.

April 13, 1987 - Trailing, 2-0, when they come to bat in the bottom of the first against San Francisco's Roger Mason, the first three San Diego Padres to bat all belt home runs. Marvell Wynne begins it, followed by Tony Gwynn and John Kruk.

May 9, 1987 - Baltimore slugger Eddie Murray becomes the first player to belt switch-hit homers in back-to-back games as the Orioles stomp the ChiSox, 15-6, at Old Comiskey.

May 30, 1987 - Eric Davis sets a National League mark by belting his third grand slam in a month in leading the Reds to a 6-2 win over Pittsburgh.

June 1, 1987 - Cleveland's knuckleballer Phil Niekro leads the Indians to a 9-6 victory over Detroit. The win gives "Knucksie" and his brother Joe 530 career combined brother victories to surpass the Perry brothers (Gaylord and Jim), who totaled 529. Phil finished his career with 318, Joe with 221 for a combined total of 539. The Perrys had Gaylord with 314 wins and Joe 215. For trivia buffs, the Reuschels had 230 (Rick 214 and Paul 16) and the Deans only had 200 (Dizzy 150 and Paul 50).

June 28, 1987 - Homers and another black-and-blue record. The day after he hit three homers to bomb the Indians, Oakland's Mark McGwire belts two more to trip the Tribe. And Don Baylor now owns the Major League HBP record as the Red Sox DH is whomped by the Yankees' Rick Rhoden for number 244 in his career, one more than Ron Hunt.

July 18, 1987 - Yankee first baseman Don Mattingly ties Dale Long's thirty-year-old record for homering in eight consecutive games. The Yanks lose to Texas, 7-2.

August 16, 1987 - Montreal's Tim Raines hits for the cycle and goes 5-for-5 in a 10-7 win over Pirates.

August 29-30, 1987 - In a two-day hit assault, Minnesota's Kirby Puckett smashes ten hits and four homers. On the 29th, he goes 4-for-5 with two homers against Milwaukee, and he follows it up on the 30th in leading the Twins to a 10-6 win over the Brewers by going 6-for-6 with two homers, two doubles, two singles and four RBIs.

July 1-2, 1988 - Andres "The Big Cat" Galarraga bangs out nine hits in two games for Montreal versus Atlanta to come within one of the two-game hit record of ten set by Roberto Clemente on August 22-23, 1970 (also tied by Rennie Stennet, September 15-16, 1975 and by Kirby Puckett in 1987). Galarraga comes up with four hits on July 1, and follows it up with five safeties the next day.

July 27, 1988 - Yankee lefty Tommy John commits three errors on one play but the Yanks still demolish Milwaukee, 16-3.

September 17, 1988 - Twins reliever Jeff Reardon becomes the first pitcher to register forty single-season saves in each league as he notches number forty in shutting down the White Sox, 3-1. Three years earlier, Reardon saved forty-two for the Montreal Expos.

September 23, 1988 - Oakland A's slugger Jose Canseco becomes baseball's first member of the forty-forty club when he steals his forti-eth base to go with his forty-one home runs. He swipes two bases and cracks out homer number forty-one in this 9-8, fourteen-inning win against Milwaukee.

September 28, 1988 - In his final start of the season, Los Angeles Dodger right-hander Orel Hershiser breaks former Dodger Don Drys-dale's record fifty-eight consecutive scoreless inning streak by shut-ting out San Diego for ten innings. The Dodgers win it in sixteen, 2-1.

October 15, 1988 - Sore-legged Kirk Gibson is summoned off the Dodger bench and delivers a two-out, two-run, bottom-of-the-ninth pinch-hit homer off Dennis Eckersley to propel Los Angeles to a game one 5-4 victory over the Oakland A's.

May 13, 1989 - Kirby Puckett ties a Major League record by bang-ing out four doubles at the Dome versus Toronto. Puckett is the thirty-fifth player to accomplish the feat.

June 21, 1989 - Chicago White Sox receiver Carlton Fisk sets the AL mark for career home runs by a catcher by belting number 307 in a 7-3 victory over the Yankees. Fisk breaks former Yankee Yogi Berra's record.

July 19, 1989 - Joe Carter hits them in bunches. For the second time this season (he also did it on June 24), he blasts three homers in a game. In this one, he helps Cleveland beat Minnesota, 10-1. Carter also hit two homers a day earlier.

August 20, 1989 - Mets infielder Howard Johnson hits his thirtieth homer in a 5-4 loss to the Dodgers. Johnson thus joins Barry Bonds and Willie Mays as the only players to twice have thirty homer/thirty stolen base seasons.

August 22, 1989 - Nolan Ryan fans number five thousand; his victim is Rickey Henderson, but Ryan's Rangers lose to Oakland, 2-0.

October 17, 1989 - The third game of the World Series between Bay area rivals Oakland and San Francisco is postponed due to a major 7.1 magnitude earthquake which struck thirty minutes before game time. The Series would remain on hiatus for ten days while damage was cleared and the area was declared safe.

The Chronicles

Bob Watson
New York Yankees, first base
1966-1984

Bob Watson was a tough out. As discussed in the 1970s chapter, he was a consistent hitter with good batting skills. He is the only player to hit for the cycle in both leagues, and though his travels brought him from Houston to Boston to New York to Atlanta, Watson's Yankee days are important to him and serve as the basis for this next story (and for his listing here as a Bronx Bomber).

October 5, 1980

Watson says, "I had better years but I hit .307 in 1980 and we won the pennant—my first trip to the play-offs. When I got a couple of hits in the last game against Detroit, it meant that I had led the Yankees in batting. Me, Bob Watson, I led the Yanks and that puts my name in the Yankee books along with Babe Ruth, Lou Gehrig and Mickey Mantle and now, Bob Watson. I can't tell you how important that is to me.

"Playing ball in New York and getting to the World Series in 1981, man, that's baseball. All my other years I just played the game, but this . . . this was baseball. It was a dream come true. As a young man I dreamed of playing in the Majors, an All-Star game and the World Series and thanks to the Yankees, I wound up doing all three. And the fact that we lost to the Dodgers in 1981 . . . we had the better team, but just weren't meant to win."

Mike Easler
Pittsburgh Pirates, outfield
1973-1987

Mike "The Hit Man" Easler was a six-foot, 190-pound outfielder from Cleveland who toiled for ten years in the minors, shuttling up and down from the Majors to the minors for six years before making it to stay. From then on, he was "The Hit Man," a lefty swinger who hit righties like he owned them. His .293 career average and power numbers (twenty-seven homers in 1984 and twenty-one homers in 1980) made him a feared member of the lineup. Born to play DH (his fielding was never his strong suit), Easler hit .313 in that role for the Red Sox in 1984 and .302 for the Yankees in 1986.

Easler hit for the cycle on June 12, 1980, versus Cincy, and played in one NLCS and a World Series for the Pirates, but he chose to relive the one big game in which he played before the hometown fans.

August 9, 1981

"My biggest game had to be the All-Star game in Cleveland in 1981, the first game back following the players' ten-week strike.

"It was the only time I made the all-stars, and after ten years in the minors it was important for me. I was selected by Dallas Green, who knew my hometown was Cleveland.

"My father and mother were there and Dallas put me in in the sixth inning for Dave Parker. There were 72,086 fans there, the largest All-Star crowd ever.

"I was so nervous. When a fly ball was hit to me, I caught it but threw it back in five feet too high.

"Then I came up to bat. I faced Rollie Fingers and I took a 3-2 slider in the eighth inning, on one knee. Was it a strike? I didn't know. The umpire called it a ball and I walked. Down 4-3, Mike Schmidt followed with a home run and we won the game, 5-4. My heart was pumping so fast, it was more exciting than the World Series. I heard Cleveland fans cheer and I felt it was for me.

"I scored and looked to my parents. It was the nicest thing I ever saw on a ball field when they applauded for me."

Von Hayes
Philadelphia Phillies, outfield
1981-1992

Von Hayes, the 6'5", 185-pound outfielder from Stockton, California, was a strong, quick, thin and rangy outfielder who had decent power (twenty-six homers in 1989 and 282 career doubles), good speed (253 career steals), and was willing to walk for the team (121 walks in 1986 and 101 in 1988). His career can be summed up as good but not good enough for those who expected greatness. He generally played well and was a team leader but his detractors always felt he should do more, particularly after the Cleveland Indians traded him to the Phillies for Julio Franco, Manny Trillo, George Vukovich, Jerry Willard and Jay Baller; five-for-oners are supposed to put up Ruthian numbers, not Hayesian stats.

Hayes, nonetheless, had a good career and remembers how it all started.

August 11, 1981

"The day I got called up to 'the Bigs,'" says Hayes, "I flew from Charleston, West Virginia, to Cleveland to play the Milwaukee Brewers in a doubleheader. I arrived at the park in the fifth inning of the first game, got dressed, and hit the dugout in the seventh inning.

"The score was tied and we had a runner at second base with no outs. Bo Diaz was the hitter and he was given the bunt sign. Our manager, Dave Garcia, who is one of my favorite people, saw me and before he even had a chance to say 'hello,' or 'welcome to the Big Leagues,' walks over, puts his hand on my shoulder and says, 'Tie game. Diaz the hitter. There's a right-hander on the mound. Diaz will attempt to bunt the runner to third. If he doesn't get the bunt down, you're the next hitter.'

"Diaz got the bunt down. I was never so happy to see a successful bunt, and Dave smiled at me. 'Welcome to the big leagues,' he said. 'I really never would have played you in that spot anyway.' Then he laughed this hearty laugh.

"In game two I did play and Brewer pitcher Jim Slaton sawed me off inside and I got a broken-bat single for my first Major League hit. Next inning, teammate Bert Blyleven brought me a baseball; he said it was the ball I got my first hit with. On it, he had written, 'First hit off pussy right-hander Jim Slaton, on a broken-bat quail to center field.'

"Later on, he gave me the real, unmarked ball I got the hit with, and I still have it today."

Buck Rodgers
California Angels, catcher
1961-1969

Bob "Buck" Rodgers was the heart-and-soul catcher for the Los Angeles Angels from their inception until their move to Anaheim to become the California Angels in 1965. He then finished his career in Anaheim after five more seasons. One of owner Gene Autry's favorites, Rodgers was called back to skipper the club in 1991 (see 1990s chapter) after serving successfully at the helm in Milwaukee (two flags) and Montreal. In a dozen years as a manager, Rodgers has picked up more than 750 wins.

The 6'2", 200-pound receiver from Delaware, Ohio, was a solid signal-caller who ran things on the field. Though his power numbers and batting average were down, Rodgers was reliable and set the rookie record for games caught with 155.

One of his favorite recollections deals with his Angel playing days in the sixties. "We had a bunch of real wild guys. Ryne Duren and Art Fowler (two pitchers) were always doing outrageous things. Once in San Antonio, Ryne dared a speeding train to run him over. Another time, from the bullpen phone, he called the Queen of England. Once he got through to the president and once he called France. Fowler, well, he left for spring training in February and didn't get back to see his wife until October. One October he got home, says, 'Honey, I'm home.' She asks him to pick up a couple of quarts of milk and he was gone for three days."

The game he chose to share is "an important game because those are vivid and stay with you longer."

October 11, 1981

Rodgers recalls, "It was the strike year and we (Milwaukee Brewers) were in the mini-series with the Yankees. The Yankees won the first two games pretty easily — the first when Oscar Gamble homered in the fourth and Ron Guidry, Ron Davis and Goose Gossage shut us down; the second when Lou Piniella and Reggie Jackson homered and Dave Righetti, Davis and Gossage overpowered us (fourteen Ks).

"Down two games to none, we went back to Yankee Stadium, but my guys had a lot of heart — Paul Molitor, Robin Yount, Ted Simmons, Cecil Cooper, Sal Bando, Mike Caldwell and the rest — and we came back on the road to win two to tie the series. Simmons and Molitor homered to win the third game for Randy Lerch; and in game four, Pete Vuckovich (Milwaukee pitcher) didn't have shit but he ham-and-egged them for five innings and I used four relievers (Jamie Easterly, Jim Slaton, Bob McClure and Rollie Fingers) to eke out a 2-1 win.

"So it all came down to this game to see who would face Oakland in the ALCS and the Yankees kept pounding away at us. Reggie and Gamble homered, (Rick) Cerone homered and I used seven pitchers just to keep us close. We got close.

"In the ninth, we were down, 7-3, and loaded the bases against Gossage. Don Money was up for us and he blasted a pitch over the wall in right. That ball is a home run except that the Yankee right fielder is 6'6" and an ex-basketball player. Dave Winfield jumped ten feet in the air to take that ball away from us and a moment of joy — we thought we had tied it with the homer — became a draining silent sorrow when it was all over. It's amazing how quickly things can change in this game."

Tommy John
New York Yankees, pitcher
1963-1974 1976-1989

Tommy John was the 6'3", 190-pound pitcher with the bionic arm. T.J. had two careers, before and after the radical surgery. He always

Tommy John, pitcher, 1980s
Photo by: Mike Blake

threw a soft sinkerball, but in 1974, he blew out his elbow and Dr. Frank Jobe put it back together with revolutionary surgery (from which no professional had ever attempted to return). After a year of rehab, John came back better than ever, and he finished with twenty-six years in the books as a Hall of Fame candidate with 288 wins and forty-six shutouts.

He was a four-time all-star and pitched in five League Championship Series and three World Series. He won twenty games or more three times, had a career winning percentage of .555, and had an ERA under 3.00 in ten of his twenty-six years.

The Terre Haute, Indiana, lefty, who was famous for inducing hitters to ground the ball into the turf, was generally a fine fielder, but made the record books by making three errors in one play (July 27, 1988).

While T.J. didn't talk about that, he did talk about a pitching performance that wasn't his best, but a day that absolutely was.

October 9, 1981

Due to a long players' strike, baseball had first-half and second-half winners meet in a divisional play-off for the right to go to the League Championship Series. In the American League East, the Yankees met the Brewers.

John plays it out. "We had just returned from Milwaukee where we won two games to go up 2-0 in the 1981 mini-play-offs versus the Brewers. I was to pitch game three; I was 9-8 that year. Now this was the year my son Travis fell out of a window and was in a coma for quite some time. Travis had recovered somewhat and George Steinbrenner came to me and asked if Travis felt good enough, would he want to throw out the first ball; if it made Travis happy, George would love to honor him that way. My wife, Sally, was eight months pregnant with Taylor and she came out with Travis and me and when Travis threw the ball, I couldn't stop crying.

"My closest friend on the team, Reggie Jackson, consoled me and Travis and walked me back to the bench. I was still crying and was trying to get ready to pitch. Umpire Ken Kaiser asked me if I needed more time to get ready and he started to cry. The fans at Yankee Stadium started yelling 'Tra-vis, Tra-vis, Tra-vis.'

"It took me an inning or so to even know where I was, and even though I didn't give up any runs until the seventh, I gave up eight hits and it was not one of the better games I ever pitched. Still, in terms of what had transpired, from a coma in August to throwing

Wade Boggs, third base, 1980s
Courtesy: Boston Red Sox
Photo by: Jack Maley

out a ball in October, this ranks high on my list of greatest days of my life.

"We lost, 5-3, on a homer by Paul Molitor, but I was as big a winner as I've ever been in my life."

Wade Boggs
Boston Red Sox, third base
1982-

Wade Boggs was arguably and demonstrably the best hitter in baseball for the decade of the 1980s, and one of the best hitters of all time. Using Fenway Park's dimensions as his own playground, often hitting better than .400 for an entire season at home, Boggs won five batting titles in six years (1983-1988), while leading the league in hits once, doubles twice and walks twice. He banged out two hundred or more hits seven consecutive years.

The 6'2", 190-pounder from Tampa, Florida (by way of Omaha, Nebraska), showed year after year that his bat control and batting eye were nonpareil, and though he has been accused of monitoring his stats too closely and of being too superstitious (he eats chicken every day, believing there are hits in chicken; draws the Hebrew symbol for life "*Chai*," in the batter's box before every at-bat; and runs his laps and takes his infield at precise times) few can argue that when he is in the lineup, he comes to play.

A prideful moment, May 17, 1992, came when he got his two thousandth hit, a single off California's Mark Langston. He admitted he hadn't been that nervous since little league, but Boggs chose to share his first taste of Big League pride, one which he shared with his family.

March 30, 1982

"One day stands out in my entire career as my best day in baseball. It was the day I found out I had made the club (Boston Red Sox).

"We were in Tampa to play a spring training game against the Reds and it was the day the Red Sox were finalizing their moves to the twenty-five-man roster to take north for the season. I really didn't know if I had the team made or not, and I was nervous.

"Scout George Digby, who had signed me, was at the game with my parents and my wife, and he let the cat out of the bag—he knew I had made the team and told them, but I still didn't know.

"I was 0-for-3 with three strikeouts and, in the sixth inning, I looked up at my wife and she shouted out, 'Congratulations.'

" 'Why?' I asked. 'I've got three Ks already.' Then it dawned on me. I asked her, 'How do you know?' She answered, 'Digby told me.'

"It was all I had ever dreamed of since little league. I had spent six seasons in the minors and I had wanted it so much; I never knew if I'd ever get the chance. I had tears in my eyes and couldn't see. It was the most gratifying moment of my life."

Jim Kaat
St. Louis Cardinals, pitcher
1959-1983

Probably best known for his years with Washington, Minnesota and Philadelphia, Jim Kaat was a 6'4", 210-pound lefty with marvelous control and a great glove—he won sixteen consecutive gold gloves.

"Kitty," out of Zeeland, Michigan, led the AL in wins in 1966 (with twenty-five) and put together back-to-back twenty-win seasons in 1974-75. His career total of 283 wins would seem to warrant Hall of Fame consideration, considering his longevity—twenty-five years—and the fact that his early years were spent with some really poor Washington teams. A workhorse, Kaat pitched 304 innings in 1966, 303 innings in 1975, and threw more than two hundred innings fourteen times.

His musing after a quarter century on the hill: "Tony Oliva was the best table setter ever. I played with Harmon Killebrew and Rod Carew, and Oliva was the most productive . . . for me. I was always the beneficiary of his success at the plate. He was the best there was for a few years. And I got lucky; I only had to face Ted Williams during the end of his career—he got me twice (two homers), and Darryl Strawberry during the beginning of his career—I got him when he was young and inexperienced."

Kaat's contribution deals with the 1982 season.

September, 1982

During the tail-end of the pennant race, St. Louis (Kaat's club) was battling for first place.

"We were playing the Expos and they were knocking the ball all over the lot. They got twenty hits against us—I had zip that day—but we kept the lead over a long game . . . 2-1, 3-1, 3-2, 5-2, 5-4, and so on.

"We fell behind and then got two in the top of the ninth to lead by one. I was sitting on the bench when Whitey Herzog sent for Bruce Sutter to get the save. As soon as Sutter took the mound, I started shaking everyone's hands; it was automatic. He got two out and I'm starting to hum and the dugout was full of happy sounds.

"Then Frank Taveras got a broken-bat single and Tim Raines hit an 0-2 forkball in the dirt over the right field wall for a two-run homer. In four pitches, the dugout became the quietest one I had seen in twenty-two years (to that point). This points out how Bruce Sutter is a special breed of player. He didn't change his demeanor one iota.

"In the shower after the game, he shoved me and said, 'Hey, old timer, what's there to do in Montreal?' I said, 'We can eat, go to a show or have a beer.' He said, 'Let's have some cold ones. I can't wait until tomorrow when we have a one-run lead and I close the door.'

"The next day Joaquin Andujar pitches us to a 1-0 lead through eight. Whitey brings in Sutter and he gets a ground out, ground out and pop out to win the game. That stands out as a key game in my mind. It helped us win the pennant and showed the value of a Bruce Sutter."

Cal Ripken Jr.
Baltimore Orioles, shortstop
1981-

Cal Ripken Jr., the 6'4", 210-pound shortstop from Baltimore, Maryland, went against the accepted image of successful shortstops. He was big, strong and powerful, whereas shortstops were all made out of the lean and lanky—and somewhat shorter—mold B.C. (Before Cal).

The consummate iron man, Ripken played every inning of every game from July 1, 1982, through September 14, 1987, and hasn't missed a game in more than eleven seasons as he takes dead aim at Lou Gehrig's "unreachable" record of playing in 2,130 consecutive games. Ripken is already second on the list at more than 1,800 games.

Ripken, a future Hall of Famer, has won the Rookie of the Year award and has been named AL MVP twice. He has led the league in doubles, fielding chances, and is an eleven-time all-star. If he had speed, he would have been considered one of the greatest all-around players in baseball history; still, his class, style, grace, power (closing in on three hundred homers) and game streak have him stenciled in as one of the game's immortals.

Ripken chose to dwell on excitement of the game.

October 3, 1982

"I love excitement. In the final game of the 1983 Series (October 16, 1983), we won, 5-0, over the Phillies on Eddie Murray's two homers and behind the great pitching of Scott McGregor. From the seventh inning on, the excitement began to build and my pulse was so high, I could hardly breathe.

"But the absolute most exciting series and game I was ever in occurred a year earlier. It was my first year and we had to fight and scratch to get close to Milwaukee, who was in first place. We were three games out with four to play and were going head-to-head with them. We swept a doubleheader (October 1) to put us a game back. Then we beat them again Saturday (October 2), to put us in a flat-footed tie after 161 games. It all came down to one game for the AL flag, the last day of the season, with two future Hall of Famers going against each other—Jim Palmer versus Don Sutton.

"The first three games of the series already left me drained, but the adrenalin flowed for the final game and every pitch was more exciting than the last.

"Don Sutton pitched well for the Brewers and Robin Yount hit two home runs and a triple and they beat us, 10-2. After the game, I sat at my locker with no strength. I just sat there totally drained. It was, at once, the most exciting weekend and the biggest letdown of my career, but it was a pure baseball rush."

Lance Parrish, catcher, 1980s
Courtesy: California Angels

Lance Parrish
Detroit Tigers, catcher
1977-

Lance Parrish, the Diamond Bar, California, catcher (by way of Clair-
ton, Pennsylvania), was a solid receiver with big power numbers for
the Tigers in the early 1980s. The 6'3", 210-pound former bodyguard
for Tina Turner poled 142 homers in five years (1982-1986) for the
Bengals and led them to a World Series in 1984.

Parrish was a six-time all-star and a three-time gold glove winner
and at one time held the AL record for most homers in a season by
a catcher with thirty-two, to break Yogi Berra's mark of thirty. (Parrish's own mark was subsequently broken by Carlton Fisk, who hit
thirty-seven in 1985.)

Parrish shared a story of statistical oddity and one of power and skill.

June 14, 1983

On the power and skill side, Parrish praises an athlete. "The best athlete I ever played around was Kirk Gibson.

"We were playing Boston and Mike Brown, a big right-hander, was pitching for the Red Sox and Gibby really hit him well.

"The first time up, Gibby belted one over the right field roof at Tiger Stadium—one of the few to ever do that. (**Author's Note:** It has been done twenty-five times to date, since 1938 and Babe Ruth's seven hundredth was hit out when it was called Navin Field, July 13, 1934, before a second deck was added.)

"Gibby's second at-bat occurred with Lou Whitaker on first. Gibby slammed one to the right-center field wall, 440 feet from home. Lou returned to first, thinking it might be caught. It wasn't and they raced around the bases, Lou a few steps in front, and Gibby right on his heels and gaining.

"Tony Armas retrieved the ball and fired to second baseman Jerry Remy, who wheeled and fired home. Rich Gedman was blocking the plate and umpire Larry Barnett was on the third base side, in front of home, to get a good angle on the play.

"The throw came in and Lou slid in and Gedman tagged him out. As Barnett turned to follow through with the 'out' sign, he didn't see Gibby, who barreled and slid into him, knocking him into Gedman, shaking them both up. Kirk was safe on the play and was credited with a triple.

"It was the most exciting play I've ever seen in the Majors."

April 13, 1984

Now on to statistics and superstition. Parrish, no stranger to the number "13"—he wore it for fifteen years—laughs at this Friday the thirteenth tale. "I'm not superstitious," says Parrish, "but if I were, it would be because of the game we played on Friday the thirteenth against the Red Sox at Fenway Park. The number thirteen came up an unbelievable number of times. Now, I've always worn the number thirteen—in little league, high school, pony league—and I tried to get it because I identified with the number. But I might have thrown it away that day, because thirteens were running wild.

"One, we (the Tigers) sent thirteen batters to the plate in the first inning.

"Two, I made all three outs in the inning—I struck out after the first three guys got on, and then as the thirteenth hitter in the inning, I grounded into a doubleplay. And, don't forget, I wear number '13.'

"Three, we scored eight in the top of the inning and Boston came back to score five in the bottom of the inning for a total of thirteen runs.

"Four, we won the game, 13-9.

"Five, wearing number '13,' I scored the thirteenth run.

"Six, the time of the game was 3:11—a stretch, I admit, but close.

"Seven, Boston's starter, Bruce Hurst, walked the first two guys in the lineup, then Barbaro Garbey (thirteen letters in his name) hits one foul but Boston first baseman Dave Stapleton (thirteen letters) drops it and falls.

"Eight, Garbey then hits a double play ball to Glenn E. Hoffman (thirteen letters) who lets it go through his legs.

"Nine, Hurst was relieved after getting only one out—mine—after facing eight hitters and was relieved by Mike Brown, who gave up an RBI double to Tommy Brookens (thirteen letters).

"Ten, next up is Louis Whitaker (thirteen letters), who grounds one to Wade Boggs, who throws to Richard Gedman (thirteen letters) at the plate, who drops the ball.

"Eleven, Mike Brown throws thirteen pitches in the inning, his last one, to me, as I ground into the double play.

"Twelve, my team was the Detroit Tigers (thirteen letters), and

"Thirteen, my name is Lance M. Parrish (thirteen letters) . . . all on Friday the thirteenth."

Jesse Barfield
Toronto Blue Jays, outfield
1981-1992 (1993-Japan League)

Jesse Lee Barfield, the Houston, Texas, outfielder (by way of Joliet, Illinois), with the rifle arm and the powerful swing, led the AL in homers with forty in 1986. The 6'1", 210-pounder also showed some speed, stealing twenty-two bags in 1985.

Barfield, who was judged by many to have the best outfield arm in the Majors, won two gold gloves and was a one-time all-star. His propensity for striking out in pursuit of the homer often cut down his average, but his 241 career homers and 716 RBIs in 1,428 games made him a feared bat in the lineup.

Barfield gives all the credit to his mentor, and he narrowed the advice down to the third year of his career.

July 6, 1983

Barfield says, "My uncle, Albert Overton, a big lefty first baseman/pitcher/outfielder in the Negro Leagues — his picture is in the Hall of Fame as a member of the Cincinnati Clowns — saved my career.

"I was struggling — eleven homers and hitting 'two bucks-three' (.203) — and I asked 'Unc' for help. He'd never seen me play. He lived near Galveston, Texas, one-and-a-half hours from my home in Houston. I flew home for the All-Star break and drove to see him immediately, but I called first.

"Now he had this squeaky, high-pitched voice — like when a guy pretends to be a girl — and he squeaks, 'How do you feel?' 'I'm struggling,' I said. 'What's wrong?' he asked. I told him that Toronto wanted me to pull everything and I'm not a pull hitter and I feel wrong. He said, 'Come see me and bring your bat.'

"I drove ninety minutes, he hugs me, and without a word brings me into his house. He drops a magazine on the floor and that became home plate. He said, 'Take your stance.' I did, and he examined it for a brief moment.

" 'No, no, no,' he said, 'you're too close to the plate. You've got long arms. Got to extend them. Get off the plate like I did. Anything inside you can knock out of the park and anything outside you just go with, and with the extension, you'll still have power. Now go home and practice in front of a mirror.'

"Over the second half of the season I hit .300 with sixteen homers. And I hit the first Major League homer ever to clear the right center field fence in Toronto, the first week after the lesson. I called my teacher and said, 'Unc, it works.' The old man shouted, 'I know what I'm talking about. Send me videotapes of your batting so I can make sure you're OK.'

"From then on, I sent him tapes all season long for the next few years and though he never saw me play in person, he studied those tapes and he'd watch them for hours, then send me an urgent message. 'I need more tapes,' he'd squeak. I kept sending the tapes and when he passed on, I lost my uncle, my friend, and my best batting coach, and every home run I've hit since the All-Star break in 1983 are his home runs."

George Brett
Kansas City Royals, third base
1973-1993

George Brett, the sweet-swinging left-handed hitter for the Royals, is destined for the Hall of Fame. His credentials include more than

George Brett, third base, 1980s
Courtesy: Kansas City Royals

three thousand hits, more than 630 doubles, more than three hundred homers, three batting titles, six trips to the ALCS, and two

World Series appearances. He credits the batting instruction of his mentor, Charlie Lau, who taught him to use his power only on certain pitches but to use the entire field on every type of pitch, with keeping him in the Majors.

Born in Glen Dale, Virginia, and brought up with his ballplaying brother Ken Brett in El Segundo, California, George was a six-foot, 190-pound slugger who is as remembered for two "lighter side of sports" stories (see 1990s chapter) as for his glory. In 1980, he flirted with a .400 season average before dipping to .390 at the end (the highest mark since Ted Williams's 1941 figure of .406).

In addition to a day of glory he talks about in the 1990s chapter, Brett discussed a day of infamy in baseball history, the celebrated "Pine Tar" incident.

July 24, 1983

It is a circumstance Brett avoided talking about for years, but he has mellowed on the subject.

In the middle of the 1983 season, the Kansas City Royals were going nowhere, thanks to a red-hot Chicago White Sox team (their dreaded rivals); the Yankees at mid-season were battling for first place with Detroit, Baltimore and Toronto. In this Yankee Stadium game, New York had taken a 4-3 lead and put in their stopper, Rich "Goose" Gossage to save the game. New York's best versus Kansas City's best, as Gossage faced Brett with two out and one on (U.L. Washington). Brett stepped in, his bat slathered, as usual, with "Noah" brand pine tar, for a better grip. Gossage fired his high hard one and Brett swung smoothly, connected, and sent it deep into the right field stands for an apparent 5-4 victory. Brett picks up the story: "I rounded the bases and out of the corner of my eye I saw Billy Martin come out on the field. I circled third and headed for home and Billy already had the bat in his hand and I was confused but not concerned. I figured they were checking the bat to see if it was corked. I got to the dugout and wondered what they were doing; it never dawned on me that my bat was illegal or that they could possibly take away my homer.

"We sat in our dugout wondering what was up. I stared out at umpire Tim McClelland and crew chief Joe Brinkman, and (teammate) John Wathan said to me, 'They're checking your pine tar. If it covers more than eighteen inches (from the knob of the bat), they're not going to count your home run.'

"After hearing that, I was already angry and just as I was saying to teammates, 'If they call me out, I'll kill them all right now,' Tim (McClelland) looked into our dugout, made eye contact with me, stuck his thumb up in the air and called me out. I was irate, as the pictures always show. I told them, I'm not giving up the bat, and as police walked onto the field, I threw the thing into the dugout. Gaylord Perry (one of our pitchers) picked it up and started walking away with the bat. Umpires and security people called to him to stop, saying they needed the bat as evidence but Gaylord threw it to (pitcher) Steve Renko, who ran with it and then threw it to Hal McRae (DH). They were playing keep-away and brought the bat into the dugout. The umps had to come into the locker room to get it and then they took it away under police guard.

"But in the end, it counted, so while I may have been angry, I can't be known as a cheater because the league made it count. A month later (August 18), we finished the game in a circus-like atmosphere and we won the game, 5-4."

Dave Winfield
New York Yankees, outfield
1973-

Dave Winfield's athletic prowess was legendary. The 6'6", 225-pound St. Paul, Minnesota, native was a standout in baseball, football and basketball as a youth, was drafted in all three sports, and jumped right from the University of Minnesota campus to the Majors. A twelve-time all-star, seven-time gold glove, and twenty-year team leader in the clubhouse, "Winny" is a sure-fire Hall of Famer based on consistency and class on the field. It has been said that no one had swung harder, more often, for such a long time, and it is a testament to his athletic ability that he has kept it going as a model of consistency for twenty years. He was one of the first big-time free-agents to jump to George Steinbrenner's corral, leaving San Diego for the bright lights of Broadway ... or at least, the Bronx. His fielding ability was never questioned, nor was his intensity, but "Boss" George often filled up newspaper interviews with scathing reports about how Winfield's long-term contract "took him to the cleaners." Perhaps the caustic relationship had its effect, because during Winfield's eight-and-a-half Yankee years, turmoil and all, Winfield managed to reach the leaders in such all-time Yankee categories as home runs (seventh with 205), RBIs (twelfth with 818), doubles (eighteenth with 236) and runs scored (twentieth with 722). His glove and arm were judged best in the game for the 1980s.

Dave Winfield, outfield, 1980s
Courtesy: New York Yankees

Winfield's only regret was that he couldn't bring more champion-ships to the Yankees, but he cited "interference from above" as a contributing factor.

He chose to give his side of a baseball tale of a "fowl" ball that put him behind bars.

August 4, 1983

Winfield laughs, "The sea gull story. I was warming up in the fifth inning of a game in Toronto at Exhibition Stadium. Every time I'd throw the ball to Don Baylor or to a ball boy, the swarms of sea gulls would just dive-bomb the balls. They were attacking the throws. This one big sea gull was hanging around all game and Baylor and I are laughing, trying to throw close to it to scare it away. We laughed that we bet we could ruffle their feathers. It was on the ground and I figured I'd bounce one in front of it to scare it off. I fired—it was stupid of me—and I short-hopped him and he got it in the head or neck and, unfortunately, I killed it. It never moved as I thought it would. If it had, this never would have been a story.

"Well, the ballboy covered it with a towel, picked it up, and its feet stuck straight up in the air like a cartoon. It was unreal.

"Boos filled the stadium. All of a sudden garbage starts cascading down on me and beer cans and the boos start building to a crescendo from the stands. I responded to all the commotion with a homer and a double and was one of the heroes of the game.

"After the game, (Yankee manager) Billy Martin came up to me and said, 'The police are waiting for you.' I thought he was kidding but before I knew it, the Royal Canadian Mounted Police, in full red-and-black Mountie uniforms, arrested me. They took me in with exhibit 'A', the dead sea gull, his feet sticking straight up in the air. They booked me on a charge of cruelty to animals. I was only detained about an hour-and-a-half but I felt like Dillinger; I looked out the jailhouse bars and there was a crowd looking at me like I was a murderer. Actually, I felt like a white-collar criminal because I was holding a briefcase up to my face to keep from being photographed.

"The charges were eventually dropped—the police didn't want to press charges but some animal rights groups pressed the matter— but it really made me sit up and take notice on how things get blown out of proportion and how important all life is and how animals should be protected.

"Next to my signing with the Yankees, this is the biggest story ever written about me, but the whole thing was silly and an unfortunate accident.

"And the neatest thing was the support I got from all over the world. I got letters from Australia, Europe, Asia, Canada and all over America voicing their comments, pro and con on the event. It was more mail than I've ever gotten for any game, home run, catch, throw, strikeout or error I've ever been involved in on the field. But the outpouring of letters that supported me was gratifying. It really made me feel good, especially at a time when I was trying to play baseball, wondering if I was going to have a record . . . not a baseball record, but a criminal record."

Bruce Benedict
Atlanta Braves, catcher
1978-1989

Bruce Benedict, the 6'1", 175-pounder from Birmingham, Alabama, is the catcher who alphabetically is directly behind Johnny Bench; that's where the similarity ends. He was a two-time all-star and an excellent defensive catcher, leading the league in fielding in 1982, but his hitting resembled that of bench warmers rather than Johnny Bench. He managed a .298 mark in 1983, but was usually around his career mark of .242 — seven times under .230. Benedict did hit eighteen homers in his career of 982 games, but his contribution usually came behind the plate, where he played well and handled pitchers well.

Benedict, who had a gift of gab behind the plate, likes to tell stories on himself, and recalls two from the mid-eighties dealing with a legend and a knife-versus-gun confrontation.

August, 1984

"We were playing the Houston Astros on a very hot, humid night in Atlanta and Nolan Ryan was really intimidating our hitters by throwing heat inside. It was late in the game and Ryan went up to bunt. I was catching Donnie Moore, and Donnie didn't like Nolan and didn't like opposing pitchers who wanted to bunt, so he fired a fastball at Ryan's head. Nollie hit the dirt, dusted himself off and looked at me and said, 'Bruce, Donnie did that on purpose. Do me a favor and let your hitters know that I know that.' I said to Nolan, 'Can you do me a favor and not take it out on me?' Two of our hitters were dusted inside the next inning, but not me. Nice guy, Ryan."

August, 1985

"Pascual Perez was really something for us, a lot of talent but in his own world. He had been suspended the year before (by Commissioner Bowie Kuhn) for an off-season drug arrest in the Dominican Republic, but still won fourteen games after missing a month-and-a-half, but this year he was terrible (1-13). Anyway, he used to come to the ballpark dressed in all-white: white suits, white shoes, white socks, white shirts and a white hat. He also carried a huge knife and would scream in the clubhouse, 'I'll come at ya.' This day he came at Bruce Sutter with his knife and Sutter told him not to do that. Perez waved the knife and Sutter lipped off to him and Perez charged him. Sutter, obviously prepared for this, whipped out a starter's pistol—it looked like a regular gun—and fired two rounds at Perez. Pascual ran out of the clubhouse and never showed that knife around again; he went out and pitched that day, too, and gave up two home runs early. He really didn't have it on the mound that day. I wonder why?"

Gary Carter
New York Mets, catcher
1974-1992

Gary Carter, "The Kid," from Culver City, California, was a 6'2", 205-pound catcher, arguably the best catcher in the National League from the late 1970s to the late 1980s. A clutch hitter, Carter drove in more than a hundred runs four times (leading the league with 106 in 1984) and blasted 324 homers in a career that saw him crouch behind the plate in 2,024 of his 2,296 games.

Carter was a better handler of pitchers than he was a handler of his teammates, many of whom got upset with his ability to attract the press. Feared as a hitter, he was praised for his defensive ability that made him an eleven-time all-star and three-time gold glove.

After toiling in small-market Montreal for his first eleven seasons, Carter went on to the big city, in a trade with the Mets. His first four seasons in The Big Apple went well, but he wore out his welcome in 1989. He prefers to talk about his happy days ... in fact, his first day as a Met.

April 9, 1985

Carter relives the glory: "Opening day. My first day at home in a New York Mets uniform, and we were playing the Cardinals. I was filled with energy and adrenalin. I was juiced. It was a cold afternoon. I just knew sooner or later I'd have something to say about the outcome and it ended in storybook fashion for me.

"We were tied at 5-5 when I came to bat in the bottom of the tenth. The fans gave me a huge applause, like they knew something was going to happen. The press kept saying in the papers that I was the last piece of the puzzle that would bring the championship back to New York. From little fan support in Montreal, here I was in New York with fabulous fans.

"I got ready. Neil Allen delivered a curve that I couldn't get. Then he threw a second curve and I hit it, pulled it deep for a home run. You can't believe the energy in that place (Shea Stadium).

"The fans were shouting 'Ga-ry ... Ga-ry ... Ga-ry.' I got goose bumps. The players mobbed me as if it were the World Series. Even with one World Series in Montreal and two more with the Mets, this one day was the most joyous, most exciting day of my career, and I have to say I'm proud to share it with the fans and my teammates."

Phil Niekro
Atlanta Braves, pitcher
1964-1987

Phil Niekro was a 6'1", 190-pound pitcher who mastered the knuck-leball for twenty-four years on his way to 318 wins, 5,403 innings pitched and 3,342 strikeouts.

Born in Blaine, Ohio, "Knucksie" pitched in the Majors until he was forty-eight; at ages forty-five and forty-six, he won sixteen games each year for the Yankees, who were involved in pennant races. Yankee teammate Don Mattingly said of the forty-six-year-old knuckleballer, "Everyone on this team knows he can still pitch. I wouldn't be surprised if he won twenty ... he's still that good." Along with his younger brother (and best friend), Joe, the Niekros set a record for most wins by a brother act—539. A stable figure in the clubhouse, on the mound and in the community, Niekro won the Lou Gehrig award for exemplary character in 1979.

Phil Niekro had his number retired by the Atlanta Braves, and his induction into the Hall of Fame is forthcoming.

After nearly a quarter-century in the game, Niekro certainly had his pick of memories, not the least of which could have been his August 5, 1973, no-hitter against the San Diego Padres, but that wouldn't be Niekro. He prefers to tell a tale of baseball and family and an act of kindness from an unexpected source. Knucksie also fires a butterfly in the 1990s chapter.

October 6, 1985

"The day I won my three hundredth game was what baseball is all about to me," says Niekro.

"My father was in the hospital on his deathbed, semicomatose, and Joe and I went to see him. I had made four tries for my three hundredth and couldn't get it, and now the season was ending and I promised Dad I'd get it for him. I needed to win it for him while he was alive and I didn't think he'd last until next season.

"The odyssey began when I was getting ready for my start against Toronto—my first try for three hundred—and my Mom called and said I'd better get home (to West Virginia) because the priest is giving Dad his last rites.

"We were in the thick of the pennant race, but the Yankees said I could do anything I wanted—pitch or stay with my Dad—and I called them and told them I'd still make the game; so Joe (who was also on the Yankees) and I told them we'd take a flight out at one-thirty. At eleven o'clock we still didn't know if we should stay or go. I said to my Dad (still in a coma), 'Pap, can you hear me? What should Joe and I do?' He was filled with tubes and his eyes were glazed and I didn't know what the hell to do.

"I was afraid to leave; his lips didn't move, there was no sound. I put my ears to his lips and then Joe saw Dad's fingers move. Joe said Pap wanted to write something. We hunted around for paper and a pen and we put the pen in his hands and held up the paper for about two minutes. Then Dad dropped his hands and Joe saw the paper. Dad had written 'WIN.'

"So we left and arrived at the ballpark at 5:20 and the game was to start at 7:30. The nurse had scheduled Dad to rest and sleep and be rubbed down. We got beat, 5-4. And then we went back to the hospital, and then I'd go back and pitch and lose, and so on. Every time I got through pitching, I'd fly back to Dad and then fly back and lose . . . five times.

"Now it's the last game of the season (October 6), and Dad had gotten last rites again and was slipping away. He may not last the night. I told Joe, 'I'm going to win it for him tonight and I want you (Joe) to pitch the ninth inning so we can share in this; we'll go in together.'

"Then I go out and pitch a shutout and when I told Joe to pitch the ninth, he said, 'No. If I come in, you don't get the shutout and I want you to get this (the oldest pitcher, at forty-six, to throw a shutout).'

"Now unbeknownst to me, because West Virginia doesn't get Yankee games and because there was no radio broadcasts to the hospital, George Steinbrenner had a phone put in my Dad's room and he had Phil Rizzuto and Bill White (Yankee broadcasters) give Dad a play-by-play of the game.

"In the seventh inning, with us up, 8-0, my dad was fully alert and they took him out of intensive care—just by listening to the game.

"I got the win, my three hundredth, and the shutout, and brought my Dad the game ball and a Yankee cap. His lips opened, he smiled, and he squeezed my hand. He was out of danger; all because he loved baseball and lived it through Joe and me.

"He lived until Joe and I became the top winning brothers, passing the Perry brothers (Gaylord and Jim Perry) in wins. Then Joe retired and two months later, in 1988, Dad died. He had nothing else to live for."

Sparky Anderson
Detroit Tigers, manager
1972-

George "Sparky" Anderson was a 5'9", 170-pound second baseman for the Philadelphia Phillies, playing 152 games in 1959, hitting .218, no homers, thirty-four RBIs and six stolen bases; then he was farmed out and never returned . . . as a player.

As a manager, however, Sparky ranks with the all-time greats. From 1970-1978 he skippered Cincinnati's "Big Red Machine" to five pennants, two World Championships and 863 wins — five consecutive seasons over ninety wins and three one-hundred-win seasons during his Cincy tenure.

From there he went on to Detroit where he has been a Motown demigod over fourteen years, accumulating two pennants and a World Championship while bringing his win total to more than two thousand, ranking him as one of the all-time winningest managers (fifth on the list), some four hundred wins over .500.

Known as "Captain Hook" for his strategy of yanking a pitcher before he can get himself in too much trouble, Sparky is known for his penchant of talking "up" a player's skills and being eternally optimistic.

The white-haired managerial patriarch shared the one game that affects his managing skills every time he sits in the dugout, the game that made Sparky "snakebit."

August 29, 1986

"We were playing the California Angels in Anaheim and this game will never leave me because it is a perfect example of what this game is built on; nothing is for sure.

"We had this game in hand. We were up, 12-5, in the bottom of the ninth and the Angels were up with one out and runners at first and second. There was a ground ball hit to Alan Trammel at short who flipped to Lou Whitaker at second for one and on to Darrell (Evans) at first for the game-ending double play. Except that the runner at first was called safe in a close play that is usually 'automatic' at that point in a game. So now there were runners at first and third with two outs and we had the game in our hands . . . except that we never got another out.

"A hit here, a walk there, a weak hit, a bad-hop hit, another walk on a 3-2 pitch that looked like it painted the corner, and that brought up Dick Schofield with two outs and the bases loaded; and we were ahead, 12-9.

"Willie Hernandez was my pitcher, my closer (twenty-four saves that year). His screwball gave Schofield fits and the count was 0-2 when Hernandez threw a high screwball that I thought would be the last pitch of the game. I was right, but not the way I thought. Schofield hit it into the seats for a grand slam, and the Angels won, 13-12. I was numb.

"To this day, whenever we're ahead in the ninth, I am still not comfortable. And when we're ahead in a game, I stay with my regulars probably longer than any other manager because I learned that after twenty years as a manager, there is no security and I don't want to blow another one like that."

Tony Gwynn
San Diego, outfield
1982-

While others around him came and left through the revolving door of personnel in San Diego, Tony Gwynn carved out a long and successful career there. A native of Los Angeles, the 5'11", 200-pound outfielder was often derided for his "baby fat" look. It was often said if he trimmed down he'd be a better ballplayer, but he hit (.327 and four batting titles, four hit leaderships and 275 doubles in eleven years), ran well (led the league in runs scored in 1986 and stole more than 250 bases), knew the strike zone (506 walks and only 291 strikeouts in more than 5,700 at-bats) and fielded brilliantly (only nineteen errors in eleven seasons and four gold gloves).

Still, Gwynn endured the slings and arrows and remained one of the real stars of the game in the decades of the 1980s and 1990s, so it is consistent that Gwynn chose to talk about "the little things" that make a ballplayer.

September 20, 1989

"All through the years," says Gwynn, "the reason I made the ballclub was that I tried to do the little subtle things to help us win. My former manager, Dick Williams, who was the best baseball manager I've ever had, used to talk baseball to me, talk about fundamentals, and he drilled it into me. One day in 1982 he even said to the team, 'Just because Tony G. is there backing you up, doesn't mean you don't have to make the play.' That he appreciated me doing the little things just kept me working even harder to be there whenever I had to.

"Now there's not many ways a right fielder can really save a run, but I did that once and I'm proud of it.

"It was the ninth inning with runners at first and third with two out and we were beating the Dodgers in Los Angeles, 5-3. Alfredo Griffin was up, a righty, and Mark Davis was on in relief for us. I knew from watching Davis that he was wild when he threw to first base and he could just throw the ball away if he fielded a batted ball. Davis pitched it and Griffin swung and hit a big breaking squib between first and the mound. Davis charged off the mound, picked it up, and side-armed the throw wild and down the right field line. I could feel this was going to happen so I was there to back it up; I backed up that kind of play in high school and college and I was always ready to do it in the Majors.

"Griffin didn't see me there and he headed for second without looking. I threw him out at second by a bunch, and we won the game 5-4. For me, being there is the greatest thing, and thanks to Dick Williams drilling it into me, I was there for that play and we won."

1990s

April 9, 1990 to October 24, 1992

The date, April 9, 1990, brings us the first oral history of our final chapter. We are brought into the nineties with Hubie Brooks fulfilling a childhood dream. The final date of October 24, 1992, is Dave Winfield's story of long-awaited glory in baseball's greatest stage, the World Series.

So far, the 1990s have seen expansion (probably not the last of the decade), an expanded play-off format (probably not the last format change in this decade), and the discussion of inter-league play (probably to be experimented with in this decade). The nineties have seen aging heroes perform honorably: Nolan Ryan, Dave Winfield, Carlton Fisk, George Brett, Robin Yount, Paul Molitor, Charlie Hough, Bert Blyleven, Frank Tanana and Dale Murphy.

The decade also has seen the young stars rise: Barry Bonds, Ken Griffey Jr., Juan Gonzalez, Barry Larkin, John Olerud, Tom Glavine, Steve Avery, David Justice, Chad Curtis, Mo Vaughn, Jack McDowell, Frank Thomas, Albert Belle, Randy Johnson, Roberto Alomar, John Kruk and Robin Ventura.

And the established stars continue their magic: Ozzie Smith, Tony Gwynn, Kirby Puckett, Andy Van Slyke, Roger Clemens, Ryne Sandberg, Joe Carter, Fred McGriff, Mark McGwire, Cecil Fielder, Will Clark, Matt Williams, Rickey Henderson and Lee Smith.

Others have found that their best years may be behind them: Don Mattingly, Eric Davis, Wade Boggs, Darryl Strawberry, Jack Morris,

Dave Stewart, Dwight Gooden, Bob Welch, Jose Canseco, Rick Sutcliffe, Steve Sax, Bo Jackson, Tim Raines and Alan Trammell.

Will tomorrow's stars be: Mike Piazza, Bernard Gilkey, Brien Taylor, David Nied, Jeff Conine, Jeff Bagwell, Carlos Baerga, Kenny Lofton, Tim Salmon, J.T. Snow, Dann Howitt, Shawn Boskie, Dean Palmer, Mickey Morandini, Marquis Grissom, Wes Chamberlain, Eric Anthony, Mike Kelly, Ryan Klesko, Bret Boone, Domingo Martinez, Chipper Jones, Javier Lopez, or someone who hasn't even reached high school yet?

Will the Yankees begin a new dynasty? Or will it be Atlanta? Or Toronto? Will the Cubs finally win a World Series? Or the Red Sox or the Angels? Or will upstart Florida or newly arrived Colorado beat them to it? That speculation is what makes tomorrow fun. This chapter of the nineties is being written as you read this, and baseball's history is being added to in the process. And true to the theme of this tome, the best stories will probably be performed, and later told, by those baseball Everymen, the utility players, the gutsy hard-working sub-stars, and the boys of summer who don't get all the product endorsements but who make each day on the diamond as exciting as the previous one.

Selected decade highlights
(in addition to those told in this chapter)

February 4, 1990 - The first Senior Professional Baseball Association season concludes with the West Palm Beach Tropics suffering a 12-4 shellacking at the hands of the Senior champion St. Petersburg Pelicans in the final game of the championship series. The 'Cans get home runs from Steve Kemp and Lamar Johnson in the rout. Such recent Big League heroes as Graig Nettles, Mickey Rivers, Luis Tiant and Dave Kingman play in the Florida-based winter spectacle.

May 24, 1990 - Chicago slugger Andre Dawson is issued five intentional walks by the Cincinnati Reds, to break the record of four in a game held by Roger Maris and Garry Templeton.

May 29, 1990 - Rickey Henderson, back with Oakland, breaks Ty Cobb's sixty-two-year-old career stolen base mark, swiping his 893rd base in a 2-1 loss to Toronto.

June 1, 1990 - The San Francisco Giants are 19-29 and in fifth place, fourteen games behind Cincinnati, when manager Roger Craig receives an unsolicited good-luck charm in the mail—a fan sent Craig a vial of dirt taken from the Iowa cornfield/ball field on which *Field of Dreams* was filmed. The charm works and the Giants respond by winning seven straight; they follow it up with a nine-game winning streak for sixteen wins in seventeen games to run their record to 35-30 and second place, seven games out. After losing the night before to Houston, they begin the dirty hot streak by defeating the 'Stros, 6-5, in eleven innings at Candlestick Park, with Steve Bedrosian beating Jim Clancy.

June 2, 1990 - Six-foot, ten-inch lefty Randy Johnson becomes the tallest MLB no-hit pitcher and the first Seattle Mariners no-no man when he fires a 2-0 no-hitter against the Tigers. Johnson walks six and whiffs eight at the Kingdome.

June 11, 1990 - The ageless wonder known as Nolan Ryan notches an unprecedented sixth no-hitter as his Texas Rangers beat Oakland, 5-0. The Express fans fourteen and walks two.

June 29, 1990 - It is no-hit day in the Majors. In the American League, Oakland's Dave Stewart shuts down the Toronto Blue Jays, 5-0, at the Sky Dome, and a few hours later in the National League, the Dodgers' Fernando Valenzuela stops the St. Louis Cards, 6-0. This is the first double-league double no-no in MLB history.

July 15, 1990 - Two-sport star Bo Jackson belts three consecutive homers, including his one-hundredth career blast, against the Yankees. Jackson then separates his shoulder in the sixth inning diving for an eventual inside-the-park homer off the bat of another two-sport star, Deion Sanders.

July 16, 1990 - Chicago White Sox utility man Steve "Psycho" Lyons suffers an embarrassing moment when after diving into first base to beat out a hit against Detroit, he unbuckles his pants, drops them, and shakes the dirt out of his uniform, forgetting that he is standing in front of 14,770 fans at Tiger Stadium. Tigers win, 5-4. This date in baseball history is also the 124th anniversary of the day (July 16, 1866) Lipman Pike, the first professional ballplayer to hit a home run (in 1871 for the National Association of Professional Baseball Players) and the first ballplayer to be paid for his services, hit five consecutive home runs, and six in the game, as his Philadelphia Athletics beat the Philadelphia Alert Club, 67-25, in a pre-Major-League game.

August 31, 1990 - The first father-son act to play together in "the Bigs," forty-year-old Ken Griffey Sr. and twenty-year-old Ken Griffey Jr. lead the Seattle Mariners to a 5-2 victory over Kansas City. Each Griffey went 1-for-4.

September 10, 1990 - Abbott and Castillo of the Twins were beaten by Abbott of the Angels. Jim Abbott of California throws a gem against Minnesota and its pitcher Paul Abbott in a 3-1 Halo victory that also had Twin pinch hitter Carmen Castillo falling victim to Abbott.

October 3, 1990 - A day for batting championships, and both are won in the American League. George Brett becomes the first player to win batting titles in three different decades. He goes 1-for-1 in a 5-2 loss to Cleveland to finish at .329, just ahead of Oakland's Rickey Henderson at .325. Brett also won American League crowns in 1976 and 1980. The National title is won by Willie McGee, at .335, though McGee was traded by St. Louis to Oakland, August 28. The Dodgers' Eddie Murray finishes second at .330. And Cecil Fielder of Detroit becomes the first American League player since the Roger Maris/ Mickey Mantle home run barrage of 1961 to hit fifty homers when he bombs his fiftieth and fifty-first of the year, in a game against the Yankees won by the Tigers, 10-3.

December 26, 1990 - In the middle of its second season, the Senior Professional Baseball Association folds for financial reasons.

May 1, 1991 - On Arlington Appreciation Night in Texas, Nolan Ryan rears back and fires a record-setting seventh no-hitter (Sandy Koufax is second with four) in a 3-0 win over Toronto. Ryan walks two and Ks sixteen as the oldest pitcher to fire a no-no at age forty-four years, three months, one day.

May 4, 1991 - Cleveland's Chris James sets a club record for RBIs in a game with nine as he smacks two homers and two singles to lead the Indians past the A's, 20-6.

May 20, 1991 - Boston reliever Jeff Reardon records his three hundredth career save to lead the BoSox to a 3-0 win over Milwaukee.

May 23, 1991 - In only his fifteenth start in the Majors, Philadelphia's Tommy Greene no-hits the Montreal Expos as the Phillies win, 2-0.

June 16, 1991 - Otis Nixon of the Atlanta Braves swipes six bases in a game against Montreal to set a modern NL mark and tie the Major League record held by Eddie Collins of the Philadelphia A's set September 7, 1912 (and tied by Collins fifteen days later against the Browns).

June 16, 1991 - Philadelphia rookie Andy Ashby strikes out the side in the fourth inning on only nine pitches, the twelfth time in NL history the performance has been accomplished. Nolan Ryan accomplished the feat twice, once in each league, for the Mets April 19, 1968, and for the Angels July 9, 1972.

June 24, 1991 - Dave Winfield of the California Angels smacks out five hits at Kansas City against the Royals, making Winnie the oldest—at age thirty-nine years, eight months, twenty-three days—to accomplish the feat.

October 5, 1991 - Jim Abbott raises his season record to 18-11 and lowers his ERA to 2.89 with a standing-ovation-inspired 5-1 win over the Kansas City Royals at Anaheim Stadium. What makes the victory, or at least the total, remarkable is that on April 28, Abbott was 0-4 with a 6.00 ERA, making it a memorable season turn-around. Abbott began his ascent with a start during which time his teammate, Luis Polonia, slipped a good-luck doll named "Joe Vu" into the pitcher's locker.

October 17, 1991 - The Atlanta Braves win their first NL pennant since moving from Milwaukee in 1966 behind the six-hit pitching of John Smoltz, as the Braves defeat the Pirates, 4-0, in game seven of the NLCS.

October 27, 1991 - In one of the most dramatic World Series competitions in history, the Minnesota Twins defeat the Atlanta Braves in game seven of the Fall Classic, 1-0, in ten innings behind the seven-hit performance of Jack Morris. Tied, 0-0, in the bottom of the tenth, Dan Gladden leads off with a double, and following a sacrifice and two intentional walks, pinch hitter Gene Larkin lifts a soft deep fly over the drawn-in outfield for the game-winning single.

May 30, 1992 - Baltimore Orioles shortstop Cal Ripken makes it ten full years without missing a game, running his consecutive games-played streak to 1,620 games. He last missed a game May 30, 1982.

May 30, 1992 - New York Yankee hurler Scott Sanderson becomes the ninth pitcher in MLB history to defeat all twenty-six teams as the Yanks bomb the Milwaukee Brewers, 8-1. Sanderson is put on the "Beat Everyone" list with Doyle Alexander, Rich Gossage, Tommy John, Gaylord Perry, Nolan Ryan, Don Sutton, Mike Torrez and Rick Wise, who also conquered all twenty-six existing franchises.

June 6, 1992 - New York Mets first baseman Eddie Murray drives in two runs at Pittsburgh to overtake Mickey Mantle as the all-time leader for RBIs by a switch-hitter. Mantle finished his career with 1,509 "ribbies."

June 20, 1992 - Filling in for public address announcer and former Major League pitcher (Brooklyn Dodgers) Rex Barney at Baltimore's Oriole Park at Camden Yards, Kelly Saunders becomes only the second female in baseball history to serve as a public address announcer. Rick Sutcliffe is outpitched by Scott Sanderson as the Yankees beat the host O's, 9-5, before 45,719 fans. The loss knocks the Birds out of first place and they were never able to move back into the top spot.

September 4, 1992 - Slightly more than three-and-a-half years after undergoing brain surgery, John Olerud of the Toronto Blue Jays, in his fourth season in "the Bigs," has his first four-hit game, smacking out two doubles and two singles versus the Minnesota Twins.

September 8, 1992 - Following a visit to the Smithsonian Institution in Washington, DC, to "get some history," New York Yankee outfielder Danny Tartabull makes some history himself with a 5-for-5 game versus Baltimore. Tartabull drives in nine runs, second in Yankee history only to Tony Lazzeri's eleven-RBI performance May 24, 1936, versus the Athletics. Bull hits two homers and a double and finishes with twelve total bases.

October 4, 1992 - Cecil Fielder finishes the season in a 7-4 loss to Toronto by compiling some historically impressive numbers. His 124 RBIs lead the majors, making him only the second player to lead the majors in "ribbies" three years in a row—Babe Ruth was the other (1919-20-21)—and he became the first Tiger to record thirty-five homers and 120 ribbies three years in a row.

The Chronicles

Hubie Brooks
Los Angeles Dodgers, outfield
1980-

Hubie Brooks, the six-foot, 185-pound infielder/outfielder from Los Angeles, began his career with the New York Mets for whom he played third, shortstop and the outfield. He hit .300 twice in limited appearances and, as a full-timer, got up to sixteen homers and seventy-three "ribbies" but proved a convenient target for Shea Stadium fans who disapproved of his fielding flaws.

He was traded to Montreal in 1985 as part of the deal that brought Gary Carter to New York, and in Canada he became the first NL shortstop since Ernie Banks (in 1960) to drive in a hundred runs.

He hit .340 in eighty games in 1986 before a thumb injury sidelined him.

The two-time all-star bombed twenty homers in his homecoming in Los Angeles in 1990, and it is that return home that gives him the most pride.

April 9, 1990

Brooks recalls, "To play in Los Angeles was a dream come true. You see, my father and I used to sit in the pavilion seats at Dodger Stadium when I was a kid. He'd have a beer, I'd have a hot dog and a chocolate malt. We'd make a day of it, leaving home early, taking the freeway and stopping for breakfast.

"Every day in the pavilion seats I'd dream about playing for the Dodgers and hitting one right to these seats where my Dad could catch it.

"So I finally got to play in a Dodger uniform and I didn't think about my home-run-in-the-pavilion-dream until about the seventh inning of the season opener.

"I thought, 'what if I could hit a home run and win opening day, my first game as a Dodger. What a great way to come back here.'

"In the eighth inning, San Diego was beating us, 2-1, behind Bruce Hurst, a very tough pitcher. I got up in the eighth with a man on and I tried not to think about it, but it kept flooding back. Then Hurst delivered and I hit a two-run homer right into the pavilion seats in left center field—I swear right where my dad and I used to sit—to win the game. (**Author's Note:** The Dodgers eventually added another run to win, 4-2.)

"I felt so proud, prouder than I had ever been on a ball field. My father and a whole bunch of my neighborhood friends were there to see it.

"I drove back home through Elysian Park (where Dodger Stadium is located) and remembered seeing my Dad play ball there. I could have cried. There wasn't a better way to come back home and do it for family, friends and myself and the team. That will always be the greatest moment ever for me in baseball."

Phil Niekro
Atlanta Braves, pitcher
1964-1987

As discussed in the 1980s chapter, "Knucksie" is a sure-fire Hall of Famer, thanks to his dancing knuckleball winning him 318 in twenty-four seasons. The first twenty of those years were spent with the Braves, so when the ball club asked him to throw out the first ball in the World Series, it was only right, as he never had a chance to throw in the Series as a member of the club. Phil tells of his preparation and execution of the moment.

October 19, 1991

Niekro says, "I was asked to throw out the first ball in the World Series opener for the Braves, and I was struck with the irony; the Atlanta Braves never came close to the Series (during my career) and it was always my dream to pitch a Series game for them.

"My brother Joe (Niekro) came up from Lakeland, Florida, for the Series and stayed with me. So we analyzed it, as two pitchers who threw for twenty years.

"So many opening-pitch throwers throw terrible pitches and I wanted to throw a strike. We decided that you can't have a good pitching motion wearing a sports coat, so I'll take mine off, and so many throw it stone cold, so I warmed up with Joe for half-an-hour before the game and I was loose enough to have pitched the game.

"I was wearing Levi's and a sweatshirt and had good mobility. My only decision was whether to throw a fastball or a knuckleball for the strike.

"I get to the mound and the whole crowd is giving me the tomahawk chop. I get on the rubber and all fifty-two thousand fans, circling the whole stadium, are cheering and chopping. I was so geared up and so excited I forgot to take off my sports coat. I wound up — I was going to throw a fastball and I wanted to make the catcher's glove pop. I fired — low and outside and in the dirt. I felt doubly bad because I blew the pitch and because it dawned on me that a hundred million people (around the country) probably wanted to see my knuckler.

"Harry Wendelstedt was the umpire and I asked, 'Harry, was it a ball or a strike?' He said, 'I think the ballboy swung and missed; I'll call it a strike.'"

Tony Cloninger
Atlanta Braves, pitcher
1961-1972

Tony Cloninger, the hard-throwing right-hander out of North Carolina (see 1960s chapter) has a story for this decade, years after throwing his last ball. He has hooked on with the New York Yankees as the pitching coach for the Bronx Bombers under Buck Showalter.

Cloninger tells us of the pride one can only have for a family member or close friend who is special.

May 6, 1992

Cloninger smiles as he says, "This story is about Bryan Harvey (relief pitcher for the California Angels). He was an excellent pitcher at UNC-Charlotte, and I saw him pitch there, but I saw him pitch for years before that. He grew up as my neighbor and I saw him and his Dad (Stan) every day. He was like a son to me.

"When he got out of college, I called the Braves, Reds and Cards; no one wanted him. I pleaded with the Braves to give him a tryout and the report on him was: 'Hard thrower, straight fastball—no movement. Don't sign him.'

"So I played softball with his dad and Bryan (for the professional softball team, Howard's Furniture), and lamented that a kid with his talent didn't get a shot.

"When the Angels finally signed him it made me really proud, but last night (May 6, 1992), *wow.*

"We (the Yankees) were playing the Angels and he came in to protect a 3-2 lead against us. That was the first time that I was in a clubhouse with him pitching against us. He got Kevin Maas and Don Mattingly to ground out, gave up a single to Roberto Kelly—he was hitting .339—and got Mel Hall on a foul to third to save it for Mark Langston.

"I got cold chills. Here's my 'son,' a superstar, getting a save against us. I was so torn. I had tears that he had done so well, but such an empty feeling that he did it to beat us. I was proud and sad at the same time."

Tony Gwynn
San Diego Padres, outfield
1982-

Tony Gwynn has established himself as one of the premier hitters of all time, with a .327 lifetime average through 1992 and four batting titles. As discussed in the 1980s chapter, he has always tried to be an all-around player, but he takes pride in his batting. When a freak injury deprived him of a possible batting title in 1992, he thought it was important enough to talk about.

May 19, 1992

"I was really hot at the plate. I had eleven RBIs in my last nine games and was hitting .369, just a few ticks out of the league lead. We had a night game at home in San Diego against the Mets and I was looking forward to hitting off David Cone because, as good as he is, I was hot and thought it would be a great matchup. I never got the chance.

"I had some errands to run just before my drive to Jack Murphy Stadium, and on my last stop, the bank, I slammed the door of my Porsche on the middle finger of my right hand, breaking the finger. The finger was bleeding, so I grabbed a shirt to use as a bandage. I went into the bank, then went home and wrapped my hand in ice, but I had to go to the hospital and found out it was broken. I missed the game, which we lost, 8-0, and missed more than a month of the season all together. I finished the year at only .317, and while my teammate Gary Sheffield hit .330 to win the title, I feel certain that I could have had a very big year—maybe over .350—if I hadn't been hurt.

"All I can say is, I really feel stupid. Here's a guy making millions for his athletic skill and he slams a car door on his finger . . . stupid."

Buck Rodgers
California Angels, catcher
1961-1969

Bob "Buck" Rodgers was the prodigal son returning when he came back after nine years as a player for the Angels and returned following a decade as manager for other ball clubs (see 1980s chapter).

He tells about an incident that caused him to rethink his priorities.

May 21, 1992

On this day, Rodgers' life, and his team, literally crashed around him.

"We were going from New York to Baltimore on the team bus following a Yankee Series and heading for a Series at Camden Yards. We were all on two buses. I was up front near the driver and some guys were talking, some playing cards. It was quiet; we had just gotten swept by the Yankees and we weren't in great moods, but we were looking forward to playing in that new ballpark (Baltimore). At about two A.M., we were on the New Jersey Turnpike in South Jersey when the bus veered sharply to the right, scratched along the guard rail (for 175 feet), came off the rail and, in what seemed to last forever, we flew through the air and bumped down some 250 feet away into some trees and I was thrown and got injured. (**Author's Note:** Rodgers broke his right elbow, his right rib and his left knee. Eleven hours of surgery later, he had metal screws, metal plates and wires inserted in his joints for stabilization. He was in a wheelchair until July and didn't return to manage until August 28.)

"What really struck me was to see all the players scurrying around to help the injured players (Bobby Rose, infielder, suffered ankle damage; Alvin Davis, back injury; and three team officials and broadcaster Al Conin suffered assorted cuts, gashes, internal bruises and cracked ribs) and we all came together to pull players out of the wreckage. These guys became a family that day and it put several things in perspective.

"Life is short, too short, and I'll manage now like everything isn't the end of the world. Life is to be enjoyed; and baseball is a wonderful way in which people from many walks of life can become a family and help each other out, not only on the field and in the clubhouse, but in life — or death — too."

Ozzie Smith
St. Louis Cardinals, shortstop
1978-

Ozzie Smith is a bona fide Hall of Famer to be. Seldom in baseball history has a fielder so dominated his position in the field in Brooks Robinsonesque fashion. Known as the "Wizard of Oz" for his magic in the hole between second and third, Smith has received accolades for simply being the best shortstop who ever played the game. His mixture of athleticism, gymnastics, acrobatics and baseball put defense into the same arena as offensive displays for those loyal fans who call the Smith-for-Garry Templeton, shortstop-for-shortstop trade between the San Diego Padres and the St. Louis Cardinals, February 11, 1982, the most one-sided trade in infield history . . . in St. Louis's favor. Thirteen gold gloves and a dozen All-Star games later, Smith has also developed into a top all-around player as a hitter (.303 in 1987 and .295 in 1992), base runner (more than 550 stolen bases), contact hitter (949 walks and 524 Ks in 8,087 at-bats through 1992) and team leader.

The 5'11", 150-pound glove god from Mobile, Alabama, backhanded one story from the hole to show he had done his job as a hitter, preferring to let his glove deeds speak for themselves.

May 26, 1992

Before a hometown crowd of 22,494 in St. Louis, in a game between the Cardinals and the Dodgers, Ozzie Smith received a measure of respect for his bat.

"We were batting against Bobby Ojeda and he was blowing us down; by the time I came to bat for the second time, it was the fourth inning and we were down, 5-0. I was thirty-seven years old and was feeling that this was my last season in St. Louis, a place I really love, and I wanted to do something special for the fans and the town. Ojeda threw a curveball and I hit a slicing fly that got past right fielder Todd Benzinger. I ran as hard as I could and when it

Ozzie Smith, shortstop, 1990s
Courtesy: St. Louis Cardinals

was over, I was at third base and had just gotten my two thousandth career hit.

"The fans in Busch Stadium sounded like they were fifty thousand strong and the standing ovation they gave me brought tears to my eyes. The applause told me two things; first, that the fans do care about me as much as I care about them, and second, that maybe now I won't be thought of as a one-dimensional player."

Jeff Reardon
Boston Red Sox, pitcher
1979-

Baseball's all-time leading saves man at one point (before he was overtaken by Lee Smith), Jeff Reardon is on a Hall of Fame course. The six-foot, 190-pound bearded intimidator from Pittsfield, Massachusetts, had registered 357 saves through 1992, with eleven straight twenty-save-or-more seasons. He made his mark for the Montreal Expos but made stops in Minnesota and New York (Mets) before hooking on in Boston.

His blazing fastball made him a two-time all-star, and elevated him to this moment of glory.

June 15, 1992

This record-setting night moved Reardon ahead of Rollie Fingers as the all-time saves leader.

"We were leading the Yankees, 1-0, at Fenway and John Dopson was doing well," said Reardon. "I knew what tonight was all about; still, I was a little surprised that Butch (Hobson, Boston manager) gave me the call because Dobbie hadn't thrown many pitches (93).

"My heart was really pumping from the fourth inning on, and when Phil (Plantier) homered in the fifth, I knew I had a chance. I came in in the ninth and got Mel Hall on a grounder and Roberto Kelly on a fly out. Then Don Mattingly, who's always tough, got a base hit and I was thinking, 'I've got to bear down and get this guy. I can't blow this.' I concentrated and struck out Kevin Maas.

"I really believe this was an important night because Rollie Fingers was probably one of the best pitchers ever — possibly the best reliever ever — and it's very gratifying to be up there with him."

George Brett
Kansas City Royals, third base
1973-1993

As discussed in the 1980s chapter, George Brett was a hard-nosed ballplayer with a competitive nature who had a powerful swing and a talent for hitting. His fielding was largely overshadowed by his bat, as was his baserunning, but Brett was an all-around player who was "The Franchise" for the Royals for three decades.

Brett certainly had some great days and could have given us October 10, 1980, when his upper deck homer off Goose Gossage gave the Royals a three-game sweep over the Yankees and a trip to their first World Series, but he pounded out a hit with his three thousandth safety instead.

September 30, 1992

Brett summed up his crusade for hit number three thousand, saying, "I'm so happy I got my three thousandth hit because now maybe I'll be remembered for something else. I'm not the guy who hit .390 in 1980, I'm always the guy who used a dirty bat (the pine tar incident in 1984) or the guy who got hemorrhoids (1980)."

Brett became the eighteenth member of the three thousand-hit club before a crowd of 17,336 at Anaheim Stadium. "I needed four hits to reach three thousand and I figured it would take a few games and I could do it at home for the Kansas City fans. In the first inning, I doubled off (Angel starter) Julio Valera. In the third, I topped a slow roller that somehow got past second baseman Ken Oberkfell for another hit. In the fifth, I hit a 1-0 forkball by Valera for a crisp single to center — my best hit of the night.

"In the seventh, of course, I knew I needed one hit but I just tried not to overswing. Angel reliever Tim Fortugno threw me a fastball and I hit it well. Then I saw Oberkfell and I thought, 'he's going to catch it,' but it took a bad hop, almost took his head off, and I got the hit.

"I was mobbed by my teammates and I saw my family cheering in the stands. I was in 'Never-Never Land.' I waved my helmet and stood off first base and was talking to first baseman Gary Gaetti. He asked me if my wife was here and as I was answering him, Fortugno fired to Gaetti and before I knew it I was picked off first.

"Here it is, the biggest moment in my career and I get picked off. If I get to the Hall of Fame, I'll probably get a parking ticket."

Lonnie Smith
Atlanta Braves, outfielder
1978-

Lonnie Smith, a 5'9", 175-pound Chicago native, made the Majors with his quick bat and quicker feet. In fifteen years in the game, Smith wasn't on any of the top all-time lists but after nearly fifteen hundred games and almost five thousand at-bats, he proved how valuable an everyday player and platoon man he can be. He was often a first-pitch hitter and adept at the hit-and-run, and if he had been a better fielder, he may have been listed with his contemporaries as one of the great heroes of the game.

One thing a long career can do is erase bad memories and Lonnie Smith was able to do that as he recalled wearing the goat's horns and the kong's crown, both in post-season play.

October 22, 1992

To many Atlanta fans, Lonnie Smith will always be the guy who stopped running in the 1991 Series. Just as Mickey Owen will be remembered for his third-strike passed ball (October 5, 1941) in the World Series, and Johnny Pesky will be chastised for his "hesitation"—see 1940s chapter for his side of the story—(October 15, 1946) in the Fall Classic, and Bill Buckner will be crucified for the bouncer through his legs (October 25, 1986) in baseball's championship, so will Lonnie Smith wear the horns for his October 27, 1991, baserunning blunder.

Says Smith, "I was wrongly blamed for our loss in 1991. There was no one out and Terry (Pendleton) hit his double to left-center in the eighth. If I score, we win, and I didn't and we lost the game and the Series. I stopped at third, didn't score and that was that, but when you lose sight of the ball and the coaches don't pick you up, you have to play it safe, especially since we had no outs and the third-, fourth- and fifth-place hitters coming up. We still should have scored.

"I was really glad to get the chance (the next year) to make things right."

Batting as a designated hitter, Smith faced Toronto's Jack Morris in game five of the Series with the score at 3-2 and the Braves trailing in games, 3-1. Morris had just walked David Justice intentionally to load the bases so he could pitch to Smith.

"The count was 1-and-2 and I was really just trying to get on. It wasn't my best-hitting Series and Morris usually pitches me tough and I was 0-for-2 against him in this game. The fastball was up and away and I went with it the opposite way and hit it over the right field fence for a grand slam.

"I didn't think about last year's play when I came up, but now I can breathe a sigh of relief and maybe they'll stop talking about 1991 and remember me for 1992."

Dave Winfield
New York Yankees, outfield
1973-

As written in the 1980s chapter, Dave Winfield is Hall of Fame material—his 450-plus homers and three thousand hits should get him there without debate. His twenty years in the game serve as a model of consistency and brilliance. After seven hundred-RBI seasons and eleven twenty-home-run years, the perennial all-star right fielder underwent back surgery in 1989 and it was assumed he would never play again. But Dave Winfield is no ordinary person; he is a bona fide baseball legend, and after a year off, he took his big swing back to the diamond, where he had a chance to show what he could do in baseball's biggest showcase, the World Series.

Winfield had gotten to the Fall Classic only once before, the 1981 rendition as a member of the Yankees (with Yankee owner George Steinbrenner constantly on his back). Winfield says: "The man was obsessed in tearing the entire team down as a psychology ploy, so that if we got hot he could take credit for it. He also should have taken credit for every error we made, every strikeout we got, and every game we lost, because he was far more responsible for those than he was for our wins. I really think if he had left us alone we would have gotten to more than just one World Series."

Still, according to the figures, Winfield, who had hit .295 in his first year in Yankee pinstripes, had a miserable October, going 7-for-20 in the divisional play-off (.350); 2-for-13 in the ALCS (.231), and 1-for-22 (.045) in the Series, all without a homer. That prompted George Steinbrenner to remark that instead of having Reggie Jackson, the renowned "Mr. October," the Yankees had Winfield, "Mr. May." Winfield privately seethed and longed for the day he could make up for that performance with a typical Winfieldian one.

Similar to Lonnie Smith's goat-to-hero story above is the day Dave Winfield got his "Mr. May" tag off his back. He finally had a chance to redeem himself for a poor World Series showing in 1981; "Winny" had to wait eleven years for his next shot and he made it a winning one.

October 24, 1992

The Braves had closed the Toronto lead to three-games-to-two and the Series moved back to Atlanta. Dave Winfield had already done his job this year for the Blue Jays—a .290 average, 26 homers and 108 RBIs, not bad for a forty-year-old. But the Series was slipping away. He was hitting only .190 and was hitless in his last four at-bats when he came to bat with the score tied, 2-2, in the top of the eleventh. With two outs and Charlie Leibrandt on the mound, Devon White led off second and Roberto Alomar off first when big Dave walked up to the plate.

Winfield tells the story. "Cito (Gaston, the manager) asked me a few innings before if I felt OK and if my legs were OK. He might have wanted to take me out for defensive purposes, but I told him I wanted to stay in. I was particularly proud of a diving catch I made on Ron Gant in the eighth, and if that was my only contribution to the team's victory, I would have been happy with it.

"I expected to see Jeff Reardon pitch but I didn't care if I was facing Leibrandt. I worked the count full (3-and-2) and was looking for his fastball, which he threw. It jammed me a little. I swung hard— I always swing hard—and lined it inside the third base line and into the left field corner for a double to score both runners." Winfield now had his World Series ring.

"I was the oldest guy in the Series and I was able to help the team by doing something at the right time. I wanted the chance to do better than I did in 1981 but I really never dwelled on it. I've had a good career and always did my best. I was just very happy to be able to put that 'Mr. May' trash to rest so people will remember that if given the chance, I always did my best and usually came through. And this time I came through for the first Canadian team to win the Series . . . in the city in which I was arrested. I love baseball."

Epilogue

Thanks, gentlemen. You've given us thrills for more than a century. We've watched you grow, along with this great nation, into a major part of our lives. While we yearn for the age of innocence and pristine desire to simply play the game, the game in some ways is better than ever.

Have we seen it all?

Has the game's life story been written?

Not by any means. As long as there are eighteen players eager to get out on the field and play a game with a bat, ball and four bases, and as long as there is an American child who delights in what is going on on that field and who dreams about someday taking his position out there, this game has only just begun, and the memories and stories will continue to be woven.

So what lies beyond?

The future, of course, is uncharted, but if the past is any indication of what has yet to be played out, then baseball's future should be glorious.

Baseball is our never-ending story and we've just started the season.

Bibliography

The fact-checking and research phases of this book could not have been completed without the information contained, in whole or in part, in the following newspapers, magazines, newsletters, articles and media guides. Some information has been paraphrased; some statistical reports and historical matter may have been used in or out of context or used verbatim.

Baseball America, *Baseball America's 1992 Almanac*. Durham, NC: American Sports Publishing Inc., 1992.

Baseball America, *Baseball America's 1992 Directory*. Durham, NC: American Sports Publishing Inc., 1992.

Baseball Weekly. Arlington, VA: USA Today, April 22-28, 1992.

Blake, Mike. *The Incomplete Book of Baseball Superstitions, Rituals and Oddities*. Tarrytown, NY: Wynwood Press, 1991.

Blake, Mike. *The Minor Leagues: A Celebration of the Little Show*. Tarrytown, NY: Wynwood Press, 1991.

The Boston Globe. Boston, MA: September 2, 1919.

Charlton, James. *The Baseball Chronology*. New York, NY: Macmillan Publishing Co., 1991.

The Chicago Bulletin. Chicago, IL: September 3, 1919.

The Cleveland Plain Dealer, many clips and news bites from various editions. Cleveland, OH: 1919.

Detroit Free Press. Detroit, MI: April 14, 1984.

Goldberg, Philip. *This Is Next Year*. New York, NY: Ballantine Books, 1991.

The Los Angeles Times, Orange County Edition, many clips and news bites from various editions. Los Angeles and Costa Mesa, CA: 1992-93.

Lowry, Philip J. *Green Cathedrals* (First edition), Manhattan, KS: SABR (Society for American Baseball Research), Ag Press, 1986.

The North American. Philadelphia, PA: September 4, 1919.

The Orange County Register, many clips and news bites from various editions. Santa Ana, CA: 1992-93.

The Philadelphia Press. Philadelphia, PA: September 4, 1919.

SABR (Society for American Baseball Research). *The SABR Bulletin, Newsletter for the Society of American Baseball Research*, many information bites from various editions. Cleveland, OH: 1992-93.

SABR (Society for American Baseball Research). *The Baseball Research Journal No. 19.* Birmingham, AL: EBSCO Media, 1992.

SABR (Society for American Baseball Research). *The Baseball Research Journal No. 20.* Birmingham, AL: EBSCO Media, 1992.

SABR (Society for American Baseball Research). *The Baseball Research Journal No. 21.* Birmingham, AL: EBSCO Media, 1992.

SABR (Society for American Baseball Research). *The National Pastime. A Review of Baseball History, No. 10.* Birmingham, AL: EBSCO Media, 1992.

SABR (Society for American Baseball Research). *The National Pastime. A Review of Baseball History, No. 11.* Birmingham, AL: EBSCO Media, 1992.

SABR (Society for American Baseball Research). *The National Pastime. A Review of Baseball History, No. 12.* Birmingham, AL: EBSCO Media, 1992.

Wolff, Rick, Editorial Director. *The Baseball Encyclopedia* (Ninth edition). New York, NY: Macmillan Publishing Co., 1993.

I acknowledge also the media guides (1992 and 1993), team magazines, press releases and historical information supplied by the following organizations:

Major League Baseball: The *1992 Major League Baseball Media
Information Guide*. The Commissioner's Office, 1992.

Major League Baseball: *The 1993 Major League Baseball Media
Information Guide*. The Commissioner's Office, 1993.

American League:
American League Red Book; Baltimore Orioles; Boston Red Sox;
California Angels; Chicago White Sox; Cleveland Indians; Detroit
Tigers; Milwaukee Brewers; Minnesota Twins; New York Yankees;
Oakland A's; Seattle Mariners; Texas Rangers; Toronto Blue Jays.

National League:
National League Green Book; Atlanta Braves; Chicago Cubs;
Cincinnati Reds; Colorado Rockies; Florida Marlins; Houston
Astros; Los Angeles Dodgers; Montreal Expos; New York Mets;
Philadelphia Phillies; Pittsburgh Pirates; St. Louis Cardinals; San
Diego Padres; San Francisco Giants.

Index